STUDIES IN ROMANCE LANGUAGES: 10

Editor

JOHN E. KELLER

Associate Editor for French

VIRGINIA A. LA CHARITÉ

Editorial Board

French

WILLIAM C. CALIN
ROBERT CHAMPIGNY
LESTER G. CROCKER
J. H. MATTHEWS
MICHAEL RIFFATERRE

Italian

GLAUCO CAMBON
WILLIAM DESUA

Portuguese

EDWARD GLASER
GERALD MOSER

Spanish

JOSE J. ARROM
JUAN BAUTISTA AVALLE-ARCE
OTIS H. GREEN
JOHN W. KRONIK
KARL-LUDWIG SELIG

JEAN-JACQUES ROUSSEAU
ON THE INDIVIDUAL AND SOCIETY

JEAN-JACQUES ROUSSEAU
ON THE INDIVIDUAL AND SOCIETY

BY

MERLE L. PERKINS

THE UNIVERSITY PRESS OF KENTUCKY

LEXINGTON, 1974

I.S.B.N. 978-0-8131-5397-1
LIBRARY OF CONGRESS CATALOG CARD NUMBER 72-81316

A statewide cooperative publishing agency serving Berea College, Centre College of Kentucky, Eastern Kentucky University, Georgetown College, Kentucky Historical Society, Kentucky State University, Morehead State University, Murray State University, Northern Kentucky State College, Transylvania University, University of Kentucky, University of Louisville, and Western Kentucky University

EDITORIAL AND SALES OFFICES: LEXINGTON, KENTUCKY 40506

DEPÓSITO LEGAL: V. 1.696 - 1974

ARTES GRÁFICAS SOLER, S. A. — JÁVEA, 28 — VALENCIA (8) — 1974

To Barbara, Elizabeth, and Janet

CONTENTS

	Page
ACKNOWLEDGMENTS	11
INTRODUCTION	13
CHAPTER ONE. THE SOURCE OF VISION *Confessions*	19
CHAPTER TWO. VIRTUE AS SCIENCE AND ART *Discours sur les sciences et les arts*	49
CHAPTER THREE. NATURE AND NECESSITY *Discours sur l'inégalité*	73
CHAPTER FOUR. THE ENLIGHTENED PRINCE *Discours sur l'économie politique*	115
CHAPTER FIVE. A NATION'S CHARACTER: THE MECHANICS OF DESTRUCTION *Lettre à d'Alembert*	148
CHAPTER SIX. THE EVOLVING FAMILY *La Nouvelle Héloïse*	168
CHAPTER SEVEN. EDUCATION: MATRIX FOR UNIQUENESS AND LEGITIMACY *Emile*	205
CHAPTER EIGHT. SUSTAINING THE INDIVIDUAL WILLS *Du Contrat social*	239
CHAPTER NINE. HISTORY AND INTERNATIONAL RELATIONS. *Du Contrat social; Lettres écrites de la montagne; Projet de constitution pour la Corse; Considérations sur le gouvernement de Pologne*	271
CHAPTER TEN. LEGITIMACY AND NATIONAL POWER *Du Contrat social; Extrait du projet de paix perpétuelle; Etat de guerre*	303
CHAPTER ELEVEN. UNIQUELY EVOLVING SELF	318
SELECTED BIBLIOGRAPHY	330

ACKNOWLEDGMENTS

My indebtedness to the many scholars who have analyzed and discussed Rousseau's moral and political theories is very great and prevents adequate description here. I should like to express my thanks to the Institut et Musée Voltaire *for permission to use in substantially revised form the materials of two of my own articles in the new context provided by chapters one and nine. I am grateful to the United States Fulbright Commission, the American Philosophical Society, the University of California, and the Graduate School of the University of Wisconsin for the financial assistance which permitted me to continue and complete this project. My deepest thanks goes to my wife Barbara who has offered many valuable suggestions.*

INTRODUCTION

My initial approach to Rousseau's moral and political philosophy was in large parth through a study of his views on international politics. I believed this perspective, when it could be justified, would yield new insights into his thought and into the interpretations of it already made by others. Previous studies had dealt almost exclusively with Rousseau's ideas in the context of the state seen as an isolated unit rather than in the context of influences exerted by other nations.

The two early twentieth-century writers who examined Rousseau's views about the international scene did so in a limited way. In his *La République confédérative des petits états*, J. L. Windenberger [1] emphasizes that for Rousseau the principal sources of war were the monarchical form of government and the giant dimensions of many of the states of Europe. Rousseau perhaps considered and discarded the goal of dividing large nations, lost much of his initial interest in the laws of war because of their apparent futility in the face of aggressive practices, and then turned to the union of small states as the best means for their survival. Starting from very scant suggestions offered by Rousseau, Windenberger studies in some detail the kind of association a nation might enter without violating the principle of *volonté générale*. A simple alliance would lack cohesive force and leave its members basically unprotected. The federal principle, providing for direct communication between the central authority and the citizens of each of the associates, might eventually dissolve national ties and form additional large states. The solution

---

[1] (Paris: Picard, 1900).

most clearly implied by Rousseau's system is, Windenberger believes, a form of confederation. Each state would under ordinary conditions retain full authority over its citizens and independence in its foreign policy. In time of war, however, member states would respond, through their governments, as a united nation and would adhere to an emergency code of conduct previously established by agreement.

The other writer who had treated Rousseau's ideas about international affairs was Georges Lassûdrie-Duchêne. In his *Jean-Jacques Rousseau et le droit des gens*, [2] he turns from a general summary of the theory of natural and international law in the seventeenth and eighteenth centuries to a discussion of Rousseau's contribution to both the *droit des gens* and the theory of international organization. He finds wanting Rousseau's emphasis on will in explaining the origin of the state and on the anarchy which appears to prevail in dealings between nations. For Lassûdrie-Duchêne, the findings of modern sociology prove that human societies constitute a natural fact in which art and will intervene only insignificantly. Societies develop and disappear like other natural phenomena according to general laws. They are not the result of choice but are obligations imposed on men. This frame of reference, if it has the disadvantage of needlessly putting large sections of Rousseau's doctrine on the defensive, does not prevent the author from giving for the most part unbiased analyses of Rousseau's attitudes concerning the Abbé de Saint-Pierre, the laws of war, and the concept of confederation.

Both Windenberger and Lassûdrie-Duchêne attempt to treat Rousseau's thinking on international problems as a simple addition, an adjunct essentially unattached to the main body of his political theory. In pursuing a somewhat related approach, I became convinced that this division was a serious mistake. Even to stress Rousseau's international concerns too much could lead to distortion. What was needed and what the present book tries to offer is a full reevaluation of the great themes of Rousseau's social and political thought, of which international relations form no more than a part, albeit an essential part. Rousseau's principles of individual liberty and political power within the nation are closely,

---

[2] (Paris: Henri Jouve, 1906).

even inseparably tied to his ideas about the bonds and frictions existing between nations. Influences move back and forth between these two levels of his thought. The two levels have an organic relationship and structure and must be treated as a unit.

In accomplishing the task of integration, I have come to grips with Rousseau's thought in a step-by-step analysis of most of his major texts. It seemed wise to return first to the autobiographical writings, particularly the *Confessions,* in order to understand better Rousseau's personal attitude toward what he calls fate, destiny, or necessity, toward the liberating power of art, and toward uniqueness of personality, that is, the problem of distinguishing the conduct of the individual from the behavior of the members of a small community, of a nation, and of the species. These conflicting pairs — necessity against art, identification in contrast with idiosyncrasy — recur constantly in the moral and political writings and tie to the conflict which exists between his view of society's cultural evolution on the one hand and on the other his very personal inner vision, his aspirations for expansiveness, virtue, citizenship, and independence.

In the second and most extensive part of this study, I have reexamined each of the major moral, social, or political works in order to find in them Rousseau's response to conditions imposed by necessity, by the exigencies of national and international life. In this context the *Discours sur les sciences et les arts,* far from being destructive of art and science, opens the way to their rehabilitation, implies their controlled use in an ambitiously constructive way intended at least in theory to overcome the perpetual rise and fall of states described in that discourse. To find the scale of values Rousseau establishes in the *Discours sur l'inégalité,* it was essential to examine again his concept of perfectibility and the "progress" toward precivil, international, and civil states of war which that faculty engenders, and to relate this seemingly inevitable course of events to *bonté naturelle,* freedom of will, precivil liberty of the individual, and legitimacy. Such an examination was necessary to determine the relative importance of each of these four notions in Rousseau's presentation of the history first of natural and then of civil society.

The *Lettre à d'Alembert,* so often attacked as an example of bad literary criticism, can more usefully be seen, I believe, in terms of the mechanics of change, designed to explain the transformation under external pressures of a relatively simple people into a sophisticated nation. In *Emile*, three aspects of the education proposed are of vital importance: first, the positive outlets given to individuality; second, the devices introduced to safeguard independence of choice and resist the encroachments of conformism; and, finally, Rousseau's effort to place Emile by his outlook above the nation and in a position to compare and judge all peoples and governments. The *Nouvelle Héloïse* relates to my approach through the implications for the nation of the several variants of community life at Vevey and Clarens, their inducements to responsibility, the kind of shelter they provide, the investigation Rousseau makes of the family's structure, and the contribution the family must make to the nation. With the *Contrat social*, clarified by the *Discours sur l'économie politique*, the *Jugement sur la paix perpétuelle*, the *Constitution pour la Corse*, and the *Considérations sur le gouvernement de Pologne*, the passage is made from individual and community conscience and behavior to the cold realities of statecraft, to the awesome task of preserving the individual's integrity within the framework of the ever-increasing national cohesiveness and international cooperation required of the small state in an attritional world controlled by great powers.

My third step was to recreate from an abundance of allusions Rousseau's understanding of the conditions existing between states. I have stressed particularly his attitudes with respect to the weaknesses or strengths of each nation and his attitudes concerning ecclesiastical law, natural law, international law, and balance of power. Without this background, the sense he gives to sovereignty, contract, government, and foreign policy cannot be fully appreciated. Within each of these concepts, too, the tension between necessity and art, evident in Rousseau's own life, reappears with great force, since the aspirations of the individual, if already limited by the demands of national life, can be even more transformed by the pressure of foreign military might and by the weight of opinion of other nations.

Because of my effort to adhere to an outlook justified by Rousseau's sentimental life, by the full range of his political vision, and by his century's mentality, the twentieth-century criteria used repeatedly and somewhat gratuitously for judging Rousseau as totalitarian or liberal may seem out of place and have been greatly diminished. As a result, Rousseau's motivation can perhaps be seen more clearly and some insight gained into his desire to retain by science and art, whether in the form of education, community planning, or statecraft, the kind of freedom for the individual consistent with the natural incapacity of the species for society.

If my analysis helps to define Rousseau's notion of liberty, my main concern nevertheless is with the implications of the nature he assigns man, the kinds of pressures he introduces into his system, the care with which he describes them, and his justification for having them weigh more or less heavily in the provisions he makes for human rights. From these considerations it is possible to measure the validity of the freedom he has retained for the individual and of the controls he has assigned the state, and to judge them for consistency within the framework of his entire thought. Since the similarities between the political world Rousseau knew and our own are still substantial, this new perspective and point of departure should uncover aspects of Rousseau's doctrine which bear on modern problems.

CHAPTER I

THE SOURCE OF VISION

THE STUDENT OF ROUSSEAU, whether considering his ideas on education, his novel, or some aspect o his moral, political, and economic theory, soon feels the need to return to the *Confessions* for more intimate knowledge of the man, his thought processes, his values, his strengths and weaknesses. The work is made up of two sections. The First Part, in six books, tells of the happy years of his youth and early manhood (1712-1741) spent near Lake Geneva or wandering in Switzerland, France, and Italy. Written while he was still on friendly terms with Hume at Wootton, Staffordshire, in 1765 and later with the Prince of Conti at Trye-le-Château near Gisors in 1767, his memories are for him an escape and reveal also, he claims, the important experiences which helped determine his character. In the Second Part, Books VII to XII, he shows a very different side of his life, the increasing torment from 1741 to 1765 arising from the fears, doubts, and obsessions associated with his literary successes and his falling out with Grimm and Diderot. The period of composition (1769-1770) was one of isolation and terror for Rousseau, and these emotions control the focus of his memory. In an effort to communicate his views, Rousseau read passages of his manuscript in the *salons* which would receive him, but this outlet was soon closed by persons fearful that their reputations might suffer from such an unprecedented disclosure of his and their personal lives. The first part of the *Confessions* appeared in 1782, the second in 1789.

The body of criticism dealing with the *Confessions* has passed through several stages. In the nineteenth and the early twentieth century, a polemic flared over whether Rousseau was a good or a bad man.[1] Later, more attention was given to his accuracy. Critics sought to discredit his story or at least began to look at his statements with "the eye of the examining magistrate."[2] More recently, the art of the *Confessions* has been made the issue, particularly with respect to verisimilitude. Underlying many of the studies in all three categories is the common-sense notion that Rousseau's main object was to make the disclosures about his life convincing. He therefore aimed to communicate with the reader through a wealth of experiences everyone has shared.[3] To be sure, evidence can be found to support this view. The scenes Rousseau gives of his early youth, of his efforts to find himself as a young man, of his loves, his friendships, and the conspiracy against him relate certainly in part to elements in every man's life. Some of his temporal dimensions correspond to our own awareness of objective or psychological time. Devices he uses to uphold his veracity fit well within the verisimilar framework. He often seeks to increase his authority by the utility motive: "The great value of the lesson to be derived from so common and unfortunate an example as my own has made me decide to write it down" (1: 14). He moves toward the reader by supplying information about family background, environment, the quality of his character and emotions. He associates himself with behavior and values usually considered desirable — warmth of attitude toward father, aunt, friends, a sense of shame or pride because of certain acts, love of

---

[1] See Albert Schinz, *La pensée de Jean-Jacques Rousseau* (Northampton, Mass.: Smith College, 1929), for a summary of attitudes expressed in the controversy.

[2] *Œuvres complètes*, ed. Bernard Gagnebin et al. (Paris: Gallimard, 1959-), 1: xxxviii. Cited hereafter as Pléiade. All citations for the works of Rousseau, unless otherwise indicated, are from this edition.

[3] In a very useful article, "Art and Love in the *Confessions* of Jean-Jacques Rousseau," *PMLA* 73 (June 1958): 215-20, Mark Temmer reflects this point of view when he refers to Rousseau's efforts to make "credible and convincing the story of his life" or speaks of his method as "an orderly succession of images drawn from a fund of experiences shared by all." For other studies which stress the literary and artistic side of the *Confessions*, see Richard A. Brooks, *A Critical Bibliography of French Literature*, 4 (*Supplement*): 154-56.

truth, hatred of injustice, of slander, of lying, of inhumanity of any sort. Rousseau is definitely by his intentions a member of the world of integrity and good faith that men usually claim to favor.

But to insist too much on the "shared experience" aspect of the *Confessions* means ignoring Rousseau's own words. He makes it clear that the subject matter is his uniqueness, that any resemblance between his life and the reader's exists at a superficial level only. From the first page on, the reader is bombarded by statements announcing and recalling that Rousseau is "autre," different from other men: "I am not made like any of those I have seen" (1: 5). In the last book he is proud in his belief that the reader has been forced to see "throughout the course of my life thousands of inner emotions completely unlike their own" (1: 645). To make the point so persistently and then to offer the reader experiences known by all, to embrace the reader's world, could have but one effect, a reaction of boredom and disappointment. The fact is that Rousseau's claim to being different seems justified. He has opened up hidden channels of personality. The purpose of his repeated allusions to uniqueness has been no doubt to move the reader closer to the author, to make him ready for the new, the incredible: "Here is still another of these confessions which I am sure in advance will meet with the disbelief of those readers who are always determined to judge me by their own set of values" (1: 644). This anticipation can still be seen as part of the verisimilar technique, although it departs from the concept of universally known experience expressed in the definition already given. By announcing the improbable, then living up to expectations, the author has forestalled objections arising from the limitations of insight any reader must inevitably have with respect to the intimate experiences of an exceptional person.

But to insist too much on this diminished form of verisimilitude raises in turn serious difficulties. Knowledge that the author has been objective enough to recognize dissimilarity between himself and the reader can build very little confidence if objectivity in describing Rousseau's uniqueness is itself open to question. The reader has been forewarned of surprise, his expectation has been satisfied, but then he is left wondering if the episode he has witnessed has not been interwoven with fictional threads. Many readers of Rousseau take this path, rather indefensibly if they are bothered by minor errors in fact, more excusably if they are reacting to his subjective control of the evidence. It is clearly part of Rousseau's technique that he spurns any pretext of being impartial, of putting distance between himself as hero and himself as author. His motive for veracity, that his name will live in history, that he therefore wants a real being to exist with his name, is substantial but hardly reduces his involvement, for he is writing for posterity under pressure and with the aim of setting the record straight, of revealing himself "as he actually was and not as his unjust enemies strive without respite to paint him" (1: 277, 400).

If he points out that truthfulness has psychological rewards, is good therapy, that unburdening his conscience "to some extent has greatly contributed to my resolution to write my confessions" (1: 86), this kind of guarantee has more often than not been taken to indicate a mood of self-justification, of excusing guilt in the name of intention or the pressures of the moment. The presence of the author in all of the confession scenes — explaining, controlling the effect of a deed by self-accusation, regret, or mitigating humor — prevents for the most part the reader's belief in Rousseau's objectivity in matters which seriously involve the emotions. The entire weight of Rousseau's argument is in fact in support of his need to be one with the hero. His memoirs deal mainly not with exterior facts but with an interior world of feeling which only he can know: "I cannot be mistaken about what I have felt, or about what my feelings have made me do; and that is principally the subject of my story" (1: 278). As he writes, his style must vibrate sympathetically with his emotional state at the time of the deed and at the time of its rediscovery: "My uneven and natural style, sometimes swift, sometimes wordy, now discreet, now mad, sometimes serious, sometimes cheerful, will itself become part of my story" (1: 1154, "Ebauches des *Confessions*"). Rather than remain aloof, the author is to immerse himself totally in the hero's personal sentiments.

Rousseau is not for the most part using the framework of verisimilitude. He is never trying to make his world convincing at the expense of either uniqueness or subjectivity. His aim, on the contrary, is to identify intimate feelings in spite of society's standardizing effect: "It is impossible for a man who is constantly abroad in society and continually putting on a front for others not to be taken in somewhat by his own acting, and if he had the time to study himself, it would be almost impossible for him truly to know himself" (1: 1121, "Mon portrait"). His purpose is to free himself from typical attitudes and sentiments. When he says the reader will find certain behavior incredible, he can because of his frankness mean it literally. His betrayal of Marion, his abandonment of Lemaitre, his fascination into impotence by Julietta's deformed breast, his desire to be imprisoned on the Isle de Saint-Pierre are all beyond his own comprehension. The conspiracy against him, the "storm" which has engulfed him, is a mystery: "I do not know if this mystery, which remains one to me, will be cleared up later in my readers' eyes" (1: 406). He wants the reader to take his side, not Grimm's, but he cannot be sure of this result. He is filled with self-doubt, used to having listeners greet the reading of his memoirs with silence: "Madame d'Egmont was the only person who seemed moved. She trembled visibly, but quickly recovered, and remained silent, as did the rest of the company" (1: 656). Except for moments of happiness found in reveries, he is obsessed by the darkness which has enveloped his existence, by the need to prove to himself that his personality can survive the barrier of hostility and indifference which seems to deny the validity of his being.

To remedy these two circumstances — the author's lack of objectivity and his inability to penetrate the significance of his uniqueness — the reader, according to Rousseau, must supply objectivity and establish meaning. The author is to tell everything and avoid the superficial consistency that characterizes the lives of great men, of portraits which impose so-called likenesses of the originals: "One grasps the outstanding features of a person, joins them by imagined insights, and provided the whole represents a face, what difference does it make if the face is a true likeness?" (1: 1149, "Ebauches"). He supplies information about the adverse opinion which upsets him, the relief he gains from confession, the importance of feeling in his scale of values. In the course of the book he also reveals frankly the limits of his memory, the gaps in his documentation, his ability to recall happy memories, his trouble in dredging up unhappy associations, and the laborious nature and method of his composition. He tells where and in what kind of mood he was while writing the first part and contrasts this setting and state with the less fortunate circumstances influencing his composition of the second part. With a kind of perverse pride in being a hostile witness to himself, he uses a revealing vocabulary to describe his most intimate deeds and thoughts: "this strange taste which persisted to the point of depravity and madness" (1: 16); "an absurd combination of boldness and stupidity" (1: 38); "the most extravagant behavior... the absurd pleasure I got from displaying myself" (1: 89); "my stupid blindness... the degree of my madness" (1: 100); his plans "the wildest, the most childish, the most foolish" (1: 101); "my head, tuned to the pitch of a strange instrument, was out of its proper key" (1: 129); "my awkward manner and clumsy phrases" (1: 519); "my imagination... busy creating phantoms" (1: 566).

In part these are self-excusing comments, but through them the reader gets closer to Rousseau's mind, experiences him directly shuddering over the recall of certain events, senses the extent of his pain and joy. Intentionally, Rousseau has made himself the patient, the informant, and has made the reader the doctor, the judge: "I am an observer and not a moralist. I am the botanist describing a plant. It is up to the doctor to determine the use to be made of it" (1: 1121, "Mon portrait"). The reader is to listen to the data Rousseau offers, listen to the tale of an emotionally involved person, and then himself decide what the meaning is. Rousseau's outburst at the close of Book XII that he has told the truth, that anyone who still believes him "a dishonorable man" is himself "a man deserving to be stifled," only strengthens the impression given by earlier statements that the validity of the account lies less in the author's control of the material in order to give a convincing explanation than in an outpouring of authentic detail which the reader must interpret: "If I made myself responsible for the result and said to him, 'Such is my character,' he might think, if not that I am deceiving him, at least that I am deceiving myself."

Rousseau's fear must be, not "that I may say too much or tell untruths, but that I may not tell everything and may leave the truth unsaid" (1: 175). He is well enough known so that the exterior facts can be verified, and "my book stands as witness against me if I lie" (1: 1121, "Mon portrait"). The author is to do no more than literally turn himself into a document for study, to become the "first basis for comparison in the study of men" (1: 3, 1120). The reader must judge the importance of the facts ("I must tell them all, and leave the matter of selection to him" [1: 175]). But the important facts, it must be remembered, are the nonverifiable sentiments which only Rousseau can know, the "succession of impressions and ideas" (1: 174). The reader, as cocreator, finds their sense: "It is up to him to assemble these elements and decide what being they form; the result must be his own work, and if he makes a mistake, the fault will be his own doing" (1: 175). The logic of Rousseau's concept of the subservient author leads to this conclusion.

Rousseau's approach to the reader is not one of verisimilitude in any of the usual senses. He expects his audience to judge him independently of any conventional code of what is probable or proper. The idea of experiences which everyone has shared is similarly not to the point. Recognizable descriptions of places or certain apt simulations of time may excite the audience's desire for identification, but images are mainly important for Rousseau to the extent that they carry his personal feelings. The reader must be observant for what is new. If he is stirred by the belief that he has shared an experience, he may be reacting to a nonessential element outside Rousseau's uniqueness. The reader may also be misled by a logic that the author may seem to have deliberately given to the sequence of his feelings. Again he is in error, for the significance of personal feelings is beyond the grasp of the individual having them. Rousseau writing about himself has purposely avoided attributing to his feelings any meaning in terms of a whole: "When I write, I do not think of that whole, I concentrate only on saying what I know, and it is from this method that the whole is produced and its likeness to the original" (1: 1122, "Mon portrait").

Since Rousseau's representation of life is no more than unique feelings uncurbed by adherence to a code, by the need to find shared impressions, or by a logical meaning he has imposed, it follows that he alone decides when expression is in accord with inner feeling: "I make up my mind about style as about things.... I shall always have the one that comes naturally to me" (1: 1154,

"Ebauches"). It seems certain, then, that verisimilitude in its first legitimate sense is style, the word itself, emanating from the writer's dedication to his feelings, to capturing them accurately through his art, to finding the accent of truth, of sincerity, which may then sound in his words: "If the truth does not make itself evident by itself, it is necessary to conclude that it is not present" (1: 1123, "Mon portrait"). To these data the reader must make a contribution, his own analysis of Rousseau's emotional state, then a synthesis which recreates the man of whom the author himself is unaware. The artist's task is not to convince the reader of meaning. The reader is to convince himself by fashioning Rousseau's feelings into significance. Verisimilitude, then, in addition to truthful style, has a second legitimate meaning, the author relinquishing to the reader all evaluation leading to definition of the author's uniqueness.

If this doctrine seems mainly negative, it is far from empty. It gives appropriate emphasis to differences within individuals, the basic source for any investigation of human nature: "His inner mode of being... is known only to himself" (1: 1149, "Ebauches"). This priority given to the concept of uniqueness underlies also his notion that there was in his day no known human nature in any positive sense, only in the negative sense of the *Second discours*, man as amoral, innocent, free of pressures, his potential for character not defined: "Up until now no mortal has known anyone but himself, if indeed someone has really known himself, and that is not enough for judging his species or the place in it one holds from the point of view of morality" (1: 1158). Consistent with this turning to the unique and this awareness of man's current opacity to man is the imposition of total responsibility on each individual reader. The reader, unique himself, must on his own find in Rousseau a sense meaningful in terms of his own interior vision: "I want to try to make it so... that each person can know himself and one other person and that other will be I" (1: 1158). The object of art is no longer the known and a convincing restatement of its significance in terms of resemblances between author and reader. On the contrary, differences are underlined. Through differences between informant and reader, the latter moves toward the unknown, possibly a new vision of mankind.

Rousseau's uniqueness can perhaps best be introduced in terms of conflict at three different levels: within himself, between self and environment, and between destiny and art. Internal conflict appears in the areas of the affections and of conscience. His expansive emotionality is intense, but so curbed by self-inhibiting timidity that he is filled with the absurdity of his amorous ambitions. As a result, the air of comedy or of the grotesque attaches to the role of fool or victim that his hero in love must usually play: "that ridiculous and pleasurable state" in which on his knees he remains for precious moments before Mme Basile (1: 76); his waiting eight days for what are to become in his mind the incestuous favors of Mme de Warens, "dreading what I desired, to the point of sometimes seriously searching my brain for some honorable way of avoiding this promised happiness" (1: 194); in his passion for Mme d'Houdetot "the absurdity, finally, of being consumed at my age by the most extravagant of passions" (1: 441).

There is extreme inner discord, too, in his moral activities. His conscience, lucid in seeing right, makes him aspire to right, yet is housed in a machine so pitifully weak that he is repeatedly subjected to humiliating defeats. The lie against Marion, the abandonment of Lemaitre, of his children, near disloyalty to Saint-Lambert are only a few instances of his submission to pressures which thwart his intentions and scar the soul. If weakness for Rousseau is a means of self-justification, as so many have said, it brings little relief from guilt: "This cruel memory... so disturbs me that in my sleepless nights this poor girl comes to reproach me for my crime, as if it had been committed only yesterday" (1: 85-86). What is inconceivable, monstrous almost for him, is the incongruity of his purity of intention, his utter helplessness in carrying out certain acts, and the torment that pursues him in spite of his apparent freedom from responsibility.

Two other areas, one related to the nation, the other to personal philosophy, set him against himself and also against his times. In an age of civic callousness, he yearns to be part of a *patrie*, or at least of a *pays*, but he has a concept of the citizen so totally uncompromising in its defense of individual right that he renounces his own citizenship and is cast out by the two governments he had counted on most for shelter. After decrees by Paris and Geneva, his writings for no cause apparent to him seem to have turned his fellow intellectuals into madmen: "Seeking in vain for the cause of this unanimous hostility, I was ready to believe that the whole world had gone mad" (1: 590-91).

As for his personal philosophy, almost overnight because of a new vision received in middle age, he has renounced forever a life of calm to attach himself with total dedication to a controversial concept of truth. The transformation in his character is in itself beyond comprehension: "If you should seek out the way of life most opposed to my true nature, you would find this one" (1: 417). The results — conspiracy, odium, censure, defamation — represent a second revolution, "a terrible and fatal epoch of a destiny which has no parallel among human kind" (1: 418).

In his presentation of affection, conscience, the concepts of citizenship and of truth, Rousseau's uniqueness first means the appearance within himself of deep forces which set him at odds with himself and the world around him. He seems a person with too many senses, with insights which humiliate him in his own eyes and alienate him from other men. This theme of his originality as division and rupture has a definite evolution in the *Confessions*. Internal dissension — expansiveness with timidity, and sane conscience with great weakness — gradually finds its resolution in a certain self-mastery, but at the same time there is aggravation of the more external dispute — liberty and truth opposed to conventional citizenship and opinion. Jean-Jacques, timid yet desiring to expand into a world of adventure and hope at the beginning of Book II, pure in intention yet weak in deed at the end of that book, has become by Book XII, because of strong personal conviction and gradually mounting social pressure, Rousseau beset and depressed by mystery and darkness.

The shift in emphasis from inward to outward struggle has been prepared for by a more fundamental context, antagonism between destiny and art, introduced at the close of the first book in the contrasting views of the hero in youth, led by fate, blinded by his desires and fears, leaving the Geneva of Bossey and Ducommun, and of the hero in old age who sees in art's perspective the Geneva of his youth as paradise lost: "I should have passed... a peaceful and calm life.... Instead of that... what picture am I going to paint?" (1: 43-44).

A climate of helplessness and suffering is attached to Rousseau's conflicts, the apparent side of his uniqueness, by regular and frequent use of the words destiny, fate, fatality, which represent all the influences that have led him from the course hindsight tells him he should have taken, into the life that had to be. These forces recur in three different forms. The first is the accidents of nature, the physical circumstances which have controlled him: the temperaments of father and mother, his physique at birth, early conditionings of many kinds, the impact on his emotions of a cruel master, the spell cast by the first glimpse of Mme de Warens, the chance arrival of Bacle, the intervention of other agents — Vitali, Mme de Larnage, Vintzenried, Grimm. His style often creates for such events a mood of foreboding. In describing the raising of the bridge, which announces his departure from Geneva, he says, "I trembled as I saw those dreadful horns in the air, sinister and fatal augury of the inevitable fate which that moment set into motion for me" (1: 42). By fatality he is to his later sorrow "thrown back without thinking about it into literature, which I thought I had abandoned forever" (1: 416). The unexpected interest taken in him by the *maréchal* de Luxembourg fatefully turns him from his intention to retire: "Heaven, which had prepared for me a different fate, threw me into another whirlpool" (1: 517). The sense of the pressure of events, of his being submerged by powers beyond his control, is expressed even more strongly in the first page of Book XII. Since he is unable to see the hand which guides the plot against him, his misfortunes appear to originate spontaneously: "Disgrace and misfortune fall upon me as if by themselves" (1: 589).

A second element of the destiny submerging Rousseau is social in nature. In spite of his distrust of the behavior and ethics of his day, he shows at times a strong inclination to bow to them. In Paris, he adopts the attitudes of the "very pleasant and basically very decent people" who frequent the establishment of Mme Selle: "I fashioned my way of thinking upon the one I saw prevalent" (1: 344). He is excessively affected by the presence of other people, by the signs and symbols of society, money, status, judgments about his abilities, intrigue, all of them for him forms of intimidation. Invited to appear before the Consistory, he forgets the speech he has been preparing for three weeks: "I played at that interview the role of the stupidest of schoolboys" (1: 393).

The third kind of force binding his will operates through the automatic reactions within him: passions, delirium, revery, presentiment. Under the influence of passion he knows no restraint, no shame, responds to no threat of danger, knows no sense of respect, of *biénseance*. His passions are "very strong, and while they move me nothing can match my impetuosity." But this may last only a minute, and then he falls back into an equally uncontrollable state, "all indolence and timidity: everything alarms me, discourages me, a buzzing fly frightens me" (1: 36).

Revery of the kind which permits foresight, for example, of his happiness with *Maman* is brought on by external conditions. Mme de Warens is absent at vespers. His heart is filled with her. The sound of bells, the chirping of birds, the beauty and calm of the day induce in him a trancelike state (1: 107-08). Revery can also be the recreation of idealized images of his past life, like the dream states into which he escapes on the Isle de Saint-Pierre when he is influenced by the appearance of the lake water (1: 642).

Another form of reflexlike response to external stimuli is presentiment: "For some time vague and sad presentiments had troubled me without my knowing their meaning" (1: 564). Finally, delirium, triggered automatically as are the other states, is best defined as an emotional condition which allows Rousseau to see himself momentarily, his situation, the world around him, in a completely new context. As he leaves Geneva, delirium promises a new life in which he will be free: "Free and my own master.... I entered confidently into the world's wide spaces. Soon my worth would fill them" (1: 45). Later, delirium provides for him the vision of a new social order, first described in the *Premier discours*: "I was in a state of agitation which bordered on delirium" (1: 351-52).

Physical circumstance, social pressure, and his own automatic reactions seem to push Rousseau further and further toward a destiny he does not want, toward a certain fame, toward isolation. No damaging event can be explained for him except "by the blind fatality which was dragging me to my downfall" (1: 525). In the last book he finds that "fate, which has always at the same time placed me too high and too low, continued to toss me from one extreme to the other" (1: 629).

Although this sense of submergence is strong, it is not total. Against destiny's mystifying weight, which he repeatedly admits, he is in fact by his attitudes constantly in revolt. Weakness under pressure can be a justification for the shameful deeds he must confess. He reacts, however, with feelings of guilt, insists in other words on acting as if free. A philosophy of necessity would permit him to discard unpopular views of liberty and truth, to seek success, to make his fortune. He makes adherence to his own views a question of choice: "I could have thrown myself entirely into the more lucrative side.... But I felt that writing for a living would soon have stifled my genius and killed my talent, which was less in my pen than in my heart" (1: 402). Illogical guilt and dedication to truth may also no doubt be seen as compulsions, part of his submergence, but the tacit belief in free choice on which they rest indicates the will to be free. Revery, whether its content is future or past happiness, his states of delirium with visions of a new world, and his presentiments of disaster are further indications of his desire to escape from necessity.

Strict verisimilitude or what convinces the ordinary man did not suit Rousseau. By this frame of reference, his person and works had already been condemned. He required a reader who would think objectively and creatively, who would follow him into his unconvincing world of conflict, contradiction, incongruity, and strange behavior, and who would not judge him by conformist codes which seemed also to be a facet of destiny. In part, his memoirs are the story of his submergence by forces greater than he, forces which in his opinion drove most of the men of his day. But, more important, his originality is to admit and at the same time deny this fatalistic creator, a denial which amounts to the will to use his faculties in order to liberate himself and his possible meaning from destiny's course.

Accidents of nature, heredity, environment, people exerting influence, social institutions, laws, codes of taste and behavior, emotional urges, automatic reactions — the effects of all these are observable phenomena in the exterior world. One may have the sense of controlling them or of being controlled by them in greater or lesser degree. Rousseau is their pathetic victim, and this he feels deeply. But memory holds other feelings reducing the importance of destiny, many of them opposed to submergence. To the prosaic observer, Rousseau unable to take the initiative with Mme Basile is just a victim of the conditionings of his youth, hopelessly submerged. And Rousseau conveys this sentiment. Yet in terms of feeling the scene has also for him another dimension, for in his suspended desire he finds an eternity of emotion, a satisfying experience transcending ordinary opinion's reality and permitting him to be completely himself. The entire range of sentiment, his feelings of emergence as well as of submergence, are Rousseau's reality. An essential theme of the *Confessions* is Rousseau's struggle to put his destiny into perspective, through his art to complete the world of daily action, success, and failure by this interior life of sentiment, by his own temporality.

For Rousseau, the basic validity of feeling as a medium in artistic communication can be understood by what happens in music. When the musician recreates in sound alone what he may have received through many senses, he is dealing ultimately in sentiment: "Even if all of nature is asleep, the person who observes it does not sleep; and the art of the musician consists in substituting for the unfeeling image of the object the image of the impressions which its presence arouses in the mind of the observer; he does not represent the thing directly, but awakens in our soul the same feeling experienced upon seeing it." [4] If feeling is the substance of art, it follows that the strength of impression in the artist's rendering through one sense what he has known through others suggests a gradation among the arts. The force needed for this transference depends on "this sequence of ideas and impressions which warms up the soul by degrees." Painting by this standard is inferior in its imitation, "always cold," since it lacks the succession needed to build the emotionality of the observer, since unlike music it says everything "at first glance." The characteristics of music, the primacy of its appeal to sentiment, and its reliance on the principle of succession, apply directly with some variance to Rousseau's art in the *Confessions*.

---

[4] *Œuvres complètes*, ed. Musset-Pathay (Paris: Dupont, 1823-1826), 13: 50-51, *Essai sur l'origine des langues*.

The autobiographer is to deal primarily in feeling, but through his words he is to reproduce sentiments not inspired by any universally observable event or object in nature. He is to "reveal exactly my inner being" (1: 278), to present his soul as object to be known by the reader for the first time, an object hidden or incomplete in real life, visible only through art, but capable of arousing in the reader new emotions like those raised by a natural object seen for the first time. Love, for example, must not be defined in traditional terms but by Rousseau's very personal experience of it, the effects it produced in him, a completely new phenomenon. Certain feelings which have no names must be imparted to the reader, sentiments somewhat beyond the grasp of the one who has experienced them, which can only be suggested, as for example, a feeling, not love as Rousseau knows it, but "another feeling, less impetuous perhaps, but a thousand times more pleasant," though not friendship either, "more delightful and tender" than that, which cannot be clearly defined, which can be painted only in terms of its effects: "Feelings can only be described through their effects" (1: 104). Everyone has no doubt known a countryside similar to that of Les Charmettes, but Rousseau is concerned not at all with the generalities of experience. He must record his very personal involvement with the setting: "But how can I say what was neither said, nor done, nor even thought, but only enjoyed, only felt" (1: 225). To succeed in the task of communication, style must in theory trace feeling directly without outside influence: "I shall say each thing as I feel it, see it, without study, without constraint, not worrying about the mixture of elements" (1: 1154, "Ebauches").

As for force through a moving succession of ideas and impressions, natural endowment permits Rousseau to give his memoirs this attribute. Basic to his theory of art is the conviction that he is memory-oriented more than action-oriented: "Objects produce less of an impression on me than the memory of them" (1: 174-75). His point is that for an action-guided person each subsequent involvement with an event or object partially erases the memory of a previous involvement. In spite of the passage of time, enrichment of the inner being is prevented. Recounting his life at an advanced age, a man of this type would have few sentimental roots extending to the near past and even fewer to the remote past. For the memory-oriented person, like Rousseau, the situation is very different. After a first involvement has occurred and passed into memory, that memory is more vivid than any subsequent action, so that memory of the subsequent action must always combine with memories already formed: "The first elements... have remained... those which have been imprinted there subsequently have combined with these rather than erased them." Since he is also image-oriented ("All my ideas are in images") recalling in detail rather than abstractly, he has the concreteness of expression needed to reproduce feeling effectively.

The task of the artist, then, of Rousseau in his effort to put his destiny into more valid perspective, is to sort and sift his memories of feeling in order to find the most basic combinations, to trace the deepening of these by subsequent layers, and to offer the entire evolution of his affective life in a valid hierarchy and sequence (1: 174-75). His soul may thus be made transparent by "the chain of feelings which have marked the development of my being" (1: 278). Since for Rousseau the feelings of operational life are identical to the feelings that memory carries, they can be the same as art's recreation of them, the same as the feelings the reader may experience vicariously if he can be induced to relive Rousseau creatively. Only in this sense is communication significant. Life and history, without an art of sentiment to interpret them, are truly the tale of an idiot, the deeds of men who have submitted blindly to events, who do not truly know themselves or their neighbors: "The majority of characters and portraits found in the writings of historians are only fantasies which an author of talent can easily give the appearance of probability" (1: 1121, "Mon portrait").

If feeling is reality, time is largely psychological, dependent on the priority Rousseau gives some events over others as he brings to the surface the sentiments constituting his soul. Two main temporal elements control the materials. The first, basic to his theory and practice of art in the *Confessions,* is the unit of all feeling sequences, the ineffaceable moment, which endures, he believes, without loss and can thus be reproduced through art. An example is the injustice done him by the Lamberciers because of the broken comb: "Writing this I feel my pulse beat faster once again: I shall always remember those moments if I live to be a hundred thousand" (1: 20). Although such identical recall of feeling is no doubt scientifically invalid, repeated allusion to the phenomenon imparts a quality of permanence to Rousseau's kind of reality and counteracts the traditional view of the fleeting, unstable nature of sentiment.

The complementing aspect of time is perspective, Rousseau's personal ordering, spacing, and accentuation of sentimental moments. An illustration is his summary of the Mlle Vulson affair in several lines (1: 29-30). In his account he describes a series of separated moments, each indelibly imprinted in memory, but each replaced by a subsequent state: his immediate emptiness because of her departure; the tone of his letters a little later, which reveal "a pathos strong enough to melt a stone"; his naive exaltation because of her return to Geneva, ostensibly to see him ("She could stand it no longer"); his depression when she leaves again ("For a long time I rent the air with my cries"); his rage upon learning of her marriage, her trip to Geneva having been for a wedding gown; his self-possession twenty years later when he sees her in the distance on the lake ("I gave a start at that almost forgotten name") but has the boatmen alter course in his resolve not to renew "a twenty-year-old quarrel with a woman of forty"; finally, the feeling of humor which envelops the entire summary and indicates the author's emergence from necessity into time as perspective. Time in this sense, given in epitome in the Vulson episode, controls in the *Confessions* all of Rousseau's ineffaceable moments, except that Rousseau is not always so clearly emergent. His perspective often indicates, as in Book XII, an inability to rise decisively above his materials. The struggle between feelings of emergence and those of submergence is then in close balance. Only his will to tell his story, to defeat his enemies with the truth, furnishes a limited sense of perspective, keeps him emergent.

Contributing to time as perspective are other emphases. The sense of time as the present moment is often strong, without relief except in imagination, because past time is only regret and longing — youth in Geneva, Les Charmettes, to whose conditions there is no real return. And future time is rarely hope, is usually fear, the present continued, particularly in Part II — fear of conspiracy, his enemies. The present itself is oppressive — Rousseau trapped at San Spirito, obsessed with the enemies persecuting him after Book VIII.

Attrition in time or time as change appears in the wear and tear of sentiments — Rousseau's feelings toward *Maman* during his first meeting when she is youthful, his despair at her later indifference, his regret at having neglected her, his sorrow upon receiving news of her death. Like present time, attritional time gives perspective an accent of submergence.

Recurrence or perseveration in time appears in the operational continuance of sentiments from early to late in life — his devotion to *Maman*, his dedication to liberty. Suspended time characterizes his periods of complete freedom from pressure, episodes which have a timeless quality — life at Bossey, the day at Thone spent with Mlle Graffenried and Mlle Galley, his moments of revery with escape to the past on the Isle Saint-Pierre. Both time as recurrence and suspended time express emergence.

Objective, measured time is not completely ignored. The memoirs run from his birth in 1712 to the year 1765. When Rousseau mentions departures from this chronological order, the effect is to call attention to chronology even more. But the time grid serves principally to remind the reader that the events did have time and place coordinates. Subjective time in fact reigns within this apparent framework of objectivity. Rousseau influences the order of his feelings by omission or inclusion, which means that different books have different tempos. For example, all books of Part I are of roughly equal length in pages, but Book I covers sixteen years, Book II nine months, Books III and IV eighteen months each, Books V and VI roughly twelve years together. Parts of books receive emphasis by their slow tempo. The first book has a relatively fast tempo, but there are two slow parts, one highlighting the gentle life with the Lamberciers, the other the tormented life with Ducommun.

Perspective, assisted by pseudochronology, tempo, oppressive present, attrition, recurrence, and time as suspension, imposes on the ineffaceable moments of Rousseau's life an intimate psychological time.

The themes which are given sharp focus by Rousseau's use of sentiment and time in the *Confessions* can be divided into four major categories: affections, character or virtue, the citizen theme, and the career or artist theme. These areas have already been briefly mentioned in relation to the conflicts representing Rousseau's uniqueness. The theme of affection includes expansiveness, the enemy, sexuality, friendship, and love.

Expansiveness is originally the individual's need to uncover his heart, to reveal his most secret thoughts: "My heart loved to be expansive in its affection, provided it felt another heart would respond" (1: 81-82). This feeling permeates the *Confessions*, the history in one sense of Rousseau's successes and failures in removing barriers of constraint between himself and others.

The enemy for Rousseau means the inhibitory forces curbing expansiveness — natural shyness and even more the behavioral patterns of other people. It includes insensitivity in Rousseau's father at times, in the Lamberciers, and Diderot's responding coldly to Rousseau's embrace. Some of Rousseau's most intimate friends and loves fail him momentarily and become the enemy — *Maman*, M. de Luxembourg, and others. The trait has completely pervaded character and established a fixed robotlike behavior in Ducommun, Vintzenried, M. de Montagu, the mob that stones him. In its most nocuous form, the enemy is treachery — Vitaly, Montmollin, especially Grimm raising "an edifice of darkness around me which it was impossible for me to penetrate" (1: 492-93).

Sexuality, too, usually appears as a curb to expansiveness. From childhood Rousseau has regarded such union as "odious and disgusting," associates it with "prostitutes" and "debauchery," with the holes near "petit Sacconex" in which he had been told "those people did their fornication" (1: 16). His experience with the so-called Moor at the hospice of Turin causes him to view all male sexual behavior as loathesome and to believe women must have "their eyes indeed fascinated not to find us repulsive" (1: 67). Sex with *Maman* is incestuous, with Mme de Larnage uninhibited pleasure but a purely physical attachment which he soon renounces. Vintzenried's excesses revolt him (1: 265). His visit to the Padoana brings fear and disgust (1: 317). The experience with Kupfel's "poor creature" shames him (1: 355). With Thérèse sex is without love and a burden to health (1: 414, 595). It is hideous in Gauffecour, aged, gouty, and impotent, making lewd advances (1: 390). Rousseau tries not to dishonor the divine image of Mme d'Houdetot with any thought of conquest (1: 444). He is offended by the sordid indiscretions of Sauttershaim (1: 618). Onanism accompanied by fancy is apparently his most lasting adjustment, permits him to find a perverted kind of expansiveness, in imagination to "dispose so to speak of the whole female sex" (1: 109, 166, 316, 595, 1569).

The enemy compromises Rousseau's friendships. Sexuality is a threat or at least an obstacle to his loves. Yet the inclination to expansiveness is not thwarted. Four great friendships enhance his life, then end abruptly: the relationships with cousin Bernard in early youth, closing with the departure from Geneva (Book I); with Altuna in Italy and in Paris, ended by Altuna's marriage, then death (Book VII); with M. de Luxembourg at the Hermitage (Book X), broken by conspiracy, flight, then death; and with Milord Keith before the period of violence and persecution at Neuchâtel (Book XII), closing with the departure of Keith and Rousseau's belief that traitors had taken advantage of their separation to "misrepresent me in his eyes" (1: 596). Other associations respond to a need of the moment, show Rousseau reaching out to an individual who seems to personify one of his own aspirations or urges — the Abbé Gaime, Bacle, Venture, Simon, the archimandrite, Klupfel, Diderot, Sauttershaim.

The most important of the subthemes of affection, Rousseau in love, is too broad a subject to be treated in detail here. It is sufficient to recall briefly the wealth of feelings involved: a child's love for his aunt; love as subservience and sexual excitement during the chastisement afflicted by Mlle Lambercier; vanity in his rivalry for the favors of Mlle Vulson; passion teased and tormented with Mlle Goton; suspended desire with Mme Basile; longing for the proud, disdainful, noble mistress he might worship in Mlle de Breil; the triangular balancing of desires which characterizes the day at Thone; the mother-son-lover union provided by Mme de Warens, which yields at Les Charmettes the rare relationship he calls more delicious than love; the physically satiating experience offered by Mme de Larnage; his impotence in the presence of the demanding beauty of Julietta, who requires a conqueror; the sheltering affection he offers Thérèse; and his genuine love relationship with Mme d'Houdetot, an idealization combining and fulfilling aspirations potential in his other partial loves and responding to Book IX's desperate plaint that he has not found the perfect companion: "Devoured by a need to love that I had never been able to satisfy, I saw myself approaching the gates of old age, and dying without having lived" (1: 426).

Rousseau's presentation of his afective life is carefully controled by temporal devices. Tempo is slowed during the descriptions of his great friendships. Episodes during which time seems suspended are associated regularly with the love theme from Book I through the Mme d'Houdetot affair of Book IX. The enemy motif, becoming stronger in Book VII, increases steadily to peaks at the ends of Books IX and XI and becomes the mystery of Book XII, "the work of darkness in which I have been shrouded for eight years" (1: 589). During these periods time is very otfen involvement in the present. During the night and day of crisis over *Emile,* just before the flight to Geneva, tempo is slowed to an almost hour-by-hour description of events. The relief from this movement offered by the Luxembourg circle is weakened by Rousseau's feeling that the relationship has contributed to his downfall. The Keith friendship is insufficient to lighten the mood of Book XII. The climactic close of the affection theme as something positive, as expansiveness, occurs in fact in Book IX with the Mme d'Houdetot episode, during which a turning away from life to art appears. Rousseau's desire to find a love object is transformed into revery, then into artistic efforts, the preliminary setting forth of the characters of the *Nouvelle Héloïse.* Gradually, Mme d'Houdetot comes to represent Julie: "It was only after her departure that, trying to think of Julie, I was surprised to find I could no longer think of anyone but Mme d'Houdetot." Art has assumed living form, but this form, Mme d'Houdetot, is also more essentially art's form, for she has been first remodeled by art: "Soon I saw only Mme d'Houdetot, but endowed with all of the perfections with which I had just adorned the idol of my heart" (1: 440). Expansiveness in the *Confessions* has thus come to mean basically discontent, the rejection of existing affection in search of an inner ideal, out of reach of sexuality, of the enemy in any form. In spite of the periods of suspended time, of time as recurrence in the persisting search for a higher expression of friendship and love, the perspective is one of emergence through truth only rather than through emotional happiness. And truth is basically the turning from life to art and the destruction of even art's ideal by opinion, slander, and the enemy.

The second category of sentiments, those related to character in its moral aspects, has a series of internally contrasting sub-themes: guilt and innocence, weakness and strength, virtue and vice.

Guilt is present in all of the confessions no matter how insignificant: the early readings with the father, precocious sexual feelings, compulsive stealing. The Marion episode represents a climax and is underlined by time as submergence in the present, indicated by pressure from superiors, from the other servants, by being in the spotlight. Confession continues with exhibitionism, ingratitude toward the Gouvons, abandonment of Lemaitre, his trying to pass for a music master in Lausanne, then incest with *Maman*, another moment stressed by the use of time as entrapment in the present and by reduced tempo. Other high points of guilt are the abandonment of his children and the affair with Mme d'Houdetot. These negative feelings alternate regularly with aspirations toward timeless innocence: Bossey, protection by *Maman*, the day with Mlle Galley and Mlle Graffenried, vagabonding through the countryside, references to the sensuality of certain religious people enjoying flowers and animals, life at Les Charmettes, calm moments spent with Thérèse, his days on the Isle Saint-Pierre. Innocence is not just a part of happiness. Happiness, on the contrary, is much restricted and is always defined for this theme of morality within the limits of innocence, with the result that the tension between guilt and innocence is never obscured. The movement of the books is toward ascendency through personal innocence. His control in the Houdetot affair, which leaves him innocent in fact in spite of guilty passion and gossip, his regaining of equilibrium at Montlouis (Book X), and his departure for Switzerland with calm heart in spite of the hate surrounding him (end of Book XI) are steps in his self-redemption.

This personal mastery is tied closely to the weakness-strength theme, which brings increasing intellectual awareness of the problem of character: first, in terms of the maxim that situations should be avoided which place self-interest and duty in opposition

(1: 56); second, in terms of the forces operating within and upon man: "Climates, seasons, sounds... all act on our machines... all offer us a thousand opportunities... for controlling those feelings... at their source" (1: 409). According to this framework, strength of character or virtue is knowledge of right and of its means and the will to practice right. Weakness is knowledge of right and will to do right, but ignorance of the means, therefore failure in practice, followed by feelings of guilt. Vicious character is knowledge of right and of the means but the will to do wrong. Rousseau, weak at the beginning, attains strength. Grimm is vicious.

The third subtheme, virtue and vice, is the struggle between Rousseau and the enemy, not in terms of the affections, expansiveness opposed to simple hate, but in moral terms — virtue opposed to an enemy aware of right and of the means to control hate but choosing vice. Personal innocence is not enough. Strength implies the ability to conquer vice in others. This is the goal of Rousseau's reform after the first discourse, to challenge vice and its mass voice, opinion (1: 416-17). A climax is reached in Book IX after the Houdetot affair in the confrontation of Rousseau and Grimm. The supremacy of vice is evident in this moment: "I went to Grimm like another George Dandin to offer him my apologies for the wrongs he had done me.... how often boldness and pride become attributes of the guilty, whereas shame and embarrassment are the lot of the innocent.... So I made up my mind to endure everything and say no more" (1: 472-73).

Across the books the movement is from guilt to personal innocence, from weakness to personal strength, but also from personal conviction to a kind of defeat because of withdrawal from the field of battle. From life as relationship of man and neighbor, in which vice and opinion are in ascendency, Rousseau retreats to the world of art, in which virtue in isolation may find adequate expression. He says that in the *Lettre à d'Alembert* (Book X), in the "singular tone which prevails in this work," its gentleness, he expressed, while death seemed to approach, his regret at leaving his fellow men "without their having felt my true worth" (1: 496). After the catastrophe over *Emile* and during the flight to Switzerland (end of Book XI), the emphasis is again on resignation, on innocence isolated and at bay. His enemies should remember that his inclination in the midst of these disasters was to write *Le Lévite d'Ephraïm*, evidence of a "heart without malice which... finds consolation within itself" (1: 586-87). The perspective is in part one of moral emergence through his persisting goals of innocence, strength, and conviction, the equivalent of time as recurrence, and through the calm at Montlouis and during the flight to Geneva, periods of suspended time. But this ascent is always within a broader framework of submergence by the present in the form of pressure from false opinion and vice, and submergence by the attrition felt in the ever-narrowing circle of his person-to-person contacts and of his everyday moral influence on other men.

The third group of themes represents Rousseau's efforts to become a useful member of the community, ultimately the good citizen. His recurring pursuit of this goal occurs within a framework of time as attrition, since subthemes — shelter, exposure, and flight — follow one another with continual variation and degeneration in relation to his civic purpose. Shelter is either a rustic or a highly sophisticated setting, provided there is innocence, equilibrium, absence of pressure, and time as suspension among the members of the group involved. Exposure is either of these settings accompanied by disruptive friction, time as submergence in the present. In spite of incest, Les Charmettes is for the most part shelter, until exposure begins with the death of Anet and is completed by *Maman*'s infatuation with Vintzenried. Flight is the ending of one existence, whether exposure or shelter, and the search for new shelter, which may prove to be exposure, as for example flight from Les Charmettes to Paris.

The alternation of shelter, exposure, and flight persists through the books: the paradise of Bossey, the exposure to Ducommun, departure from Geneva, *Maman*'s fleeting guidance in Book II, the exposure of San Spirito, the warmth of Mme Basile, the shelter of the Roque household (which because of Marion becomes in turn exposure), flight with Bacle from the sheltering promise of a career with the Gouvons, return to *Maman*, and so on. More serious efforts to be useful within a community begin in Book VII's Venice episode, relative shelter ending in exposure. Shelter or success among the *philosophes* comes to mean loss of friends, envy, the hate of rivals, the watchful eye of the French and

Genevan governments. An incompatibility of image steadily develops between on the one hand the citizen as part of the status quo — befriending the poor in the neighborhood of Montmorency, doing simple chores, guarding Mme d'Epinay's fruit trees, copying music, supporting Thérèse and her mother, later becoming the friend of the Luxembourgs, the star of their literary circle — and on the other hand the citizen as scrupulous defender of liberty — the lawgiver of the *Contrat social*, who in the eyes of the powerful (Choiseul, *parlement*, Mme de Pompadour), spurred on according to the *Confessions* possibly by Grimm and Alembert (1: 586), changes from simple subject to dangerous critic, a revolutionary in conflict with the status quo and with a prime minister antagonized, Rousseau believes, by his very efforts at praise (1: 554-57). Flight to Switzerland and renunciation of citizenship are the result, and threats, in spite of Keith's sheltering protection, are made by the government of Geneva and the people of Neuchâtel. After the lapidation, in order to return to shelter within the status quo, Rousseau wants to renounce his role of defender of liberty, to seek imprisonment on the Isle Saint-Pierre, to try to pass again as an ordinary citizen: "I remember that a M. Kirkebergher from Berne, having come to see me, found me perched in a large tree, a sack tied to my waist... filled with apples. I was not sorry that he and others found me similarly occupied" (1: 644). His stay under any condition is denied by the authorities of Berne.

Continuing his flight, he takes up again the burden of his role as lawgiver. Under pressure from governments of his day, especially Choiseul's (1: 653), he comes to believe that his destiny is associated with that of an entire people, the Corsicans, whom the same minister has crushed: "It is time to tell of the fatal incident which came as a crowning disaster and which dragged along with me into ruin an unfortunate people, whose budding virtues already gave promise of one day rivaling those of Sparta and Rome" (1: 648). Rather than finding the life of an ordinary citizen sheltered within an existing nation (time as suspension), he has almost unwittingly lived the future envisioned by his art, with liberty the criterion (time as recurrence), with constant exposure and flight the rewards (time as present and as attrition). The outcome reechoes the moods created by the affection and virtue themes. The impression the reader has of Rousseau's perspective or emotional state is partial emergence through his civic purpose, but in the shadow of a broader framework of submergence by benighted political regimes.

It has been Rousseau's destiny to test by his uniqueness the existing state of affections, morality, and politics. The final theme, which relates to Rousseau's career as writer, traces the formation and tests the validity of art's response to the challenge offered Rousseau by destiny. The question is whether or not he can believe in his power to create an art truly independent of opinion and capable of carrying the uniqueness of his struggle, whether its emergent truth can be communicated to a reader, made as real as or more real than the life, the destiny almost universally accepted by his fellow men.

The first phase of the career theme, predominant in Books I through VI, includes all of the allusions to his psychological and emotional roots, to the environmental factors conditioning his attitudes, to the probings by others — the Gouvons, numerous priests — who intend to help him find a trade or profession. The second, culminating in Book VIII, shows Rousseau groping toward an artistic career: his reading on his own, his study under numerous masters, and his association with men who helped form his literary judgment. There are allusions to his literary preferences, to events affecting his attitudes toward liberty, justice, and religion.

In a third stage, Rousseau has become the artist. He is aware of his own powers and limitations with reference to memory, imagination, and composition. During the performance of the *Devin du village*, he experiences through art a sentimental involvement with the audience: "Sexual passion entered into this more than the vanity of an author ... devoured, as I continuously was, by the desire to gather with my lips the delicious tears I had evoked" (1: 379). From Book VIII on, liberation of self is linked to the origin, writing, and fate of his literary works. The *Premier discours* means a new vision: "I beheld another universe." As a result, "all of my little passions were stifled," his character is transformed. "This excitement was sustained in my heart for more than four or five years" (1: 351). With the *Second discours* he has discovered a standard with which to free himself and mankind, "comparing man as he has made himself with natural man.... My soul... moved upward near to the Divinity" (1: 388). With the *Lettre à d'Alembert*, Rousseau transforms real places and persons by art's perspective. Grimm, Paris, the theater are vice. Rousseau, Geneva, the people of that country are virtue. With the first two discourses the revolutionary person expressed new insights. The *Lettre* provides a new emergence, the understanding that he is alone even among friends who are supposed to know and share his vision. His heart has been "deceived by those it had believed to be of its own character... forced to retire within itself" (1: 495).

From indignant protest against man's servitude, discovery of a standard, experience of his utter isolation, Rousseau passes to the final stage of artistic liberation. He becomes the creator offering a life which tarnsforms the old order: for the affections the *Nouvelle Héloïse* ("People were far from understanding how enraptured, inflamed I could become over creatures of the imagination" [1: 548]); in the domain of character and virtue the image of Emile, the model of strength, living among friends and loved ones who respect his worth; [5] for polity the *Contrat social*, destined to "form the most virtuous, the most enlightened, the wisest, indeed the best nation, taking this word *best* in its highest sense" (1: 405); for the artistic temperament the *Confessions*, the attempt to reveal the uniqueness of Rousseau's inner self.

Belief in the power of art is expressed by the time techniques. Attrition characterizes the early abortive parts of the career theme, but after Book VIII recurrence appears in the will to express the sentiments of freedom, justice, and truth engendered by his opposition to existing institutions. Suspended time emphasizes important moments in his career, for example, his mention of the trancelike states relating to his production of the first and second discourses and of the *Nouvelle Héloïse*. The tempo is slowed during the description of his studies at Les Charmettes (Book VI); his moment of glory as the composer of the *Devin du village* (Book VIII); the description of his literary projects in Books IX,

---

[5] *Emile: ou, de l'éducation*, ed. François and Pierre Richard (Paris: Garnier, 1964), p. 606.

X, and XI; his persecution during much of Book XII, the artist alone and abused yet not wavering in his will to make known his truth. The perspective, determination yet doubt of his power to communicate, is expressed in the words of defiance beginning "I have told the truth," which bring the *Confessions* to a close (1: 656).

In describing Rousseau's art of autobiography, it is necessary to point out four principal stages through which the reader must pass. The first removes him from the traditional verisimilar framework. He next enters a domain of rather mystifying idiosyncrasy and faces the challenge of understanding and explaining conflict rather than standing in judgment of it. He then follows the author's sentiments across a pattern of themes controlled by temporal devices and style. During and after this initiation, he is asked as a final step to find significance objectively himself. Sympathy or dislike would distort his vision, obscure the goal — Rousseau as he was. Art has presented no clear meaning known to the author. It gives no more than subjectively authentic clues to the content and fabric of his being. In view of the emotional nature of the materials, the author's demands on the reader are at an almost unattainable level, since identification between author and reader, if detection of uniqueness is to occur, must rest on a common search for meaning and for one's place, implicit in every human life: "Unravel in one's own heart what belongs to the species and what belongs to the individual" (1: 1158, "Ebauches").

Three principal themes run simultaneously through the *Confessions*. First, uniqueness is defined in terms of conflict, enigma, mystery. Second, destiny, representing all of necessity's forces, restates uniqueness deterministically. At the most definitive level, expressing the data of sentiment and time, is the theme of art with its complementing theme, the objective, creative reader, and its illustrating themes: affection, climaxing in Book IX (the Houdetot affair); character, with peaks in Books X (*Lettre à d'Alembert*) and XI (*Lévite d'Ephraïm*); the citizen, climaxing in Book XII with the lapidation; and the artist, exposing his being from preface to final page. Rousseau's awareness of conflict — expansiveness with timidity, knowledge of right yet devastating weakness, love of country and liberty met by persecution, love of truth met by disbelief and rejection — confirms a taste for solitude which in the opinion of his enemies, he complains, has passed for viciousness. Feelings of submergence by forces greater than his will, such as heredity, environment, his own automatic reactions, cause him repeatedly to interpret this movement of his life toward isolation as fatality. Destiny has created, moulded, and led him. Yet within him, too, there is rebellion in the form of feelings of guilt, efforts to escape through memory and imagination into timeless revery, and a turning to art in his affective, moral, and civic life. Destiny is submergence by necessity, but the possibility remains of emergence through art based on inner sentiment and temporality. His memoirs are the test of this new reality, of his power to transmit it.

Rousseau's isolation is less basically in space (Montlouis, the Isle Saint-Pierre), the thesis of those who stress his clear intellectual ties with the *philosophes,* less in history (longing for Sparta and Rome), the emphasis of those who underline his role as reformer, than in his artistic vision, his awareness of a nonverisimilar yet authentic inner self. Art in the service of the unique personality, in theory at least, means art's flexibility, the uninhibited use of theme, time, and style in order to express the feelings of innovating genius. Under the demands of this task, art has become a very subtle device for exploring, identifying, and communicating the part of personality which in all men resists incorporation into society, the essentially artistic side. If the reader applies the judgments of Rousseau's day, finds him merely "a dishonorable man," then destiny with its connotations of insensitivity, corrupt opinion, and oppressive status quo has won, self-liberation has been thwarted.

In the *Confessions,* liberty is ultimately art. Tension is less between unsophisticated nature and culture than between nature as destiny or necessity on the one hand and the individual as artist on the other. Before the *Confessions,* the self for the most part had been defined negatively. Nature, presocial man's freedom from pressure, was the standard utilized to measure society and its history. In his memoirs Rousseau moves inside the self, defines it in terms of private values, idiosyncrasy. The overwhelming reality and obsession are necessity — the inevitable flow of events forming, controlling, and destroying society, its institutions, and peoples, compromising and crushing personality. Resisting necessity, but constantly threatened by reabsorption into it, is Rousseau's feeling of emergence through an inner, almost uncommunicable self, the matrix for new concepts of nature, society, and the individual. The intuition, not given explicitly but arising from the developing themes, is that his concepts of free primitive nature, of just contractual society, and of his own uniqueness may exist only within the artist, may have no substance without his will, may vanish back into necessity if his art, failing to involve the reader creatively in their formulation, does not attract him to the problems and the values of uniqueness.

Chapter II

VIRTUE AS SCIENCE AND ART

IN BOOK VIII OF THE *Confessions* Rousseau dramatizes his decision to question the most basic values of civilization. Diderot, imprisoned at Vincennes, was now permitted to receive visitors, and Rousseau on a hot autumn day of 1749 set out from Paris to visit him. Walking at a slow pace, he skimmed through the October issue of the literary journal the *Mercure de France* and found news of the essay contest to be sponsored by the Academy of Dijon for the year 1750. The topic, there could be no doubt, was open to daring interpretation, for it asked the participants if the rebirth of the sciences and arts during the Renaissance had contributed to purifying manners and morals. Experiencing by his own account a state of agitation close to delirium, Rousseau says he beheld the vision of another universe. Perhaps influenced in part by discussions with Diderot, he later decided to uphold the most exciting side of the debate and warn his audience that the sciences and arts had corrupted mankind. To his surprise, his essay won the prize. Rousseau published his *Discours sur les sciences et les arts*[1] in the fall of 1750, won an unwanted celebrity as a result, and received along with success the severe criticisms of the defenders of progress.

Between June 1751 and April 1752, in his replies to Raynal, Stanislas, Gautier, Bordes, and Lecat, and in the *Préface de Nar-*

---

[1] Hereafter referred to as *Premier discours*. All citations for this work, unless otherwise indicated, are from the Pléiade edition of the *Œuvres complètes*, vol. 3.

cisse, December 1752, Rousseau rejected any simple answers to the problems he had raised. He insisted that his attack on the sciences and arts did not carry with it any argument for a return to primitivism. Nor were other clear solutions in evidence. Perhaps the virtuous can be helped to retain their integrity and the process of decline somewhat slowed in those only partially corrupted (2: 972, *Préface de Narcisse*). Certainly, Rousseau sees that man's complacent faith in learning and in the uplift of all levels of the population through programs for compiling, popularizing, and disseminating knowledge can and must be shaken. But the direction of history has been set. Continued "progress" in science is a part of the established moral and political order. That Rousseau's attitude has this kind and degree of pessimism is an outlook so prevalent it hardly needs further documentation here.

Yet in my view there is serious doubt that negativism toward science and art is total and unqualified in the *Premier discours*. Two beliefs lead me to another point of view. First, implicit in Rousseau's argument is the premise that more science and art, not less, is needed if man's predicament is to be understood. Second, genuinely positive elements counterbalance the destructive side of Rousseau's assault. With these two ideas in mind, I believe it essential to study again passages less emphasized in the discourse and in Rousseau's reactions to his opponents. Such a review can give new insights into the nature of the destructive current and the elements of the positive movement of his thought. Included in the latter are constructive synthesis, standards of value, the use of international rivalry as a measure of superiority, and new concepts of statecraft and of virtue. These facets of Rousseau's position must be examined if the *Premier discours* is to be understood in sufficient depth to explain the relationship of all its parts.

Since thorough-going skepticism about learning was not a usual pattern of thought during the Enlightenment, the seriousness of Rousseau's purpose in the *Premier discours* was not always clearly understood. It seemed unbelievable that destruction could be his sole end. Many of his contemporaries in fact believed at times that he was reasoning thus mainly in a spirit of challenge and held that he should complete his *tour de force* by next answering the question in the affirmative. In one sense, I believe, he already had in fact made this upward swing. His aim was to destroy only a certain view of science and art in order to prepare the way for a new conception. The positive theorizing of the *Contrat social* does not relate simply to the idea of the *Préface de Narcisse* that "All of these vices do not belong so much to man, as to man when he is badly governed." [2] It relates more substantially to a positive view of history, society, science, and art already well developed in the *Premier discours*. A Cartesian-like structure, I am convinced, is present in this early work. The approach, to be sure, is less by way of a careful inductive analysis than by a somewhat comparable resolutive descent based on eloquence, enthusiasm, and an emotionally based logic designed to put the sciences and arts in the worst possible perspective. Destructive doubt, however, ends in the discovery of a first principle, which allows a compositive ascent to a new synthesis of knowledge. The result is that reflection becomes the ally rather than the curse of man.

After the darkness of the Middle Ages, its pseudoscientific jargon worse than ignorance, man returned to common sense. This apparent progress, nevertheless, is not real for Rousseau and is soon made the first step of subsidence into the period of degradation called the Renaissance. The event came about, not by free choice, he tells us, but by a sort of blind chance or fatality, since the stupid Turk, the least likely agent, the scourge of philosophy, brought about this revolution through the capture of Constantinople.

The second step in the descent may be named pride. Men went too far in the pursuit of perfection, constantly strove to be more sociable, to win admiration and approval, to display talent rather than simply to meet the demands of security and well-being. Corruption, according to this link in Rousseau's chain of reasoning, means partly enslavement to needs arising from the body, but more important, enslavement to other needs continually invented by the mind: "The mind has its needs, as does the body. Needs of the body are the foundations of society, those of the intellect

---

[2] Robert Derathé holds that the turning point between the destructive *Second discours* and the more positive *Contrat social* is this formula of the *Préface de Narcisse* (Pléiade, 3: xciv-xcv).

make society pleasant" (3: 6). The yoke is attractive. Liberty is lost to refined tastes in dress, food, and drink, to uninterrupted pleasures and amusements.

By a third step in his argument, Rousseau notes that men through pride do not simply yield to self-indulgence, becoming soft and effeminate, but follow in their dissoluteness definite rules, a code of conduct which breeds uniformity. The individual thus disappears. Rarely does a man escape the behavior of "this herd called society" (3: 8). Words and action flow no longer from the inner man but from the common notion of what his image should be. Faces become masks inhibiting and concealing suspicion, fear, hate, and love. Every response is calculated. Man hides behind his wit, satire, and irony. There can be no true reliance on one another. Skepticism and doubt prevail. Princes, unaware of the disadvantages of having slaves for subjects, encourage this degeneration. They are surrounded by courtiers, and this by-product of the rebirth of art and science is basically impotent, no more than "a man of wealth," "a man of taste" (3: 7-8).

The loss of integrity produces a fourth stage in Rousseau's argument and in man's ruin, the complete deflation of human goals. Shunned are all of the great aspirations of human existence — love, friendship, virtue, citizenship, truth. Men are preoccupied with useless and inferior aims: "It is not possible for minds degraded by a multitude of futile cares to rise to anything great; and if they should have the strength, courage would be lacking" (3: 20). Since immature interests are prevalent, frivolous youths and women set the fashions, and artists must debase their talents to receive the praise they desire (3: 21-22). Genius is the captive of taste, which in turn is determined by dissolute morals. The lowering of human aspirations is universal, affects every area, including religious belief. Gods which used to dwell in men's hearts and in their homes are relegated to the tops of columns and valued no longer for their meaning but rather for their beauty. These changes reflect the hollowness of an effete and sterile people (3: 22).

The final link in the chain shows the homeland defenseless in the presence of its enemies. Learning, idle debate, and vain pursuits seem more important than virtue, the life-blood of the country. In both the First and the Second Part of his study Rousseau shows how nations, the members of which have become insincere, conformist, and shallow, fall victim in ignominious defeat to less sophisticated peoples.

The message is clear. The arts and sciences can lead to total decadence of the individual, the local community, and the nation (topics to be treated respectively in *Emile,* the *Nouvelle Héloïse,* and the *Contrat social*). But the descent closes with a clear intuition: virtue is power. It is my conviction that Rousseau's exploration of this principle represents a substantial part of the significance of the *Premier discours* and that this positive thrust, which calls for a reorganization of the sciences and arts, has been undervalued in the past because of the inclination to accept heavily negative interpretations based on obvious rather than reliable clues to his reasoning. The illogical but dramatic basis of this first major work lies, it would seem, in an explicitly negative but latently and potentially constructive movement. The attack on the sciences and arts conceals a deeper, more comprehensive plea for their regeneration, a strand of his thesis which comes very clearly to the surface in the closing pages of the discourse.

Side by side with the resolutive descent and supporting the principle of virtue as power is a compositive ascent to a new synthesis, less emotional than the descent, therefore overshadowed by it, but more clearly established in the attitudes of Rousseau's own century. First, his appeal for a new learning is in the name of basic truths. His investigation must be concerned with the down-to-earth matters that affect the "happiness of all mankind" rather than with those "metaphysical subtleties" present in all branches of knowledge: "Here is one of the greatest and noblest questions ever to be debated." He must free himself from the dictates of fashion and from what pleases "the witty, the men who play the roles of free thinker and philosopher." Rousseau plans to cut deeper than appearance, to write for an audience in advance of his century, not for the fashionable: "One must not write for such readers if one wants to live beyond one's century" (3: 3). For opening up this new path, he expects to receive the rewards of conscience, found "at the bottom of my heart" (3: 5). Exulting in the sublimity and loneliness of his task, Rousseau deliberately associates himself with the truly learned, "a few wise men," certainly the members of the Dijon Academy, and through his epigraph with the poet Ovid, whose words he cites from the *Tristia:* "Here I am the barbarian, because no one understands me" (3: 2, 3). At the head of the introduction to the First Part, in which he refers to his own heart as criterion of right, he places lines from Horace's *De Arte Poetica:* "We are deceived by the appearance of right" (3: 5). The implication seems clear. If learning has often in the past dealt in error and falsehood, another possibility exists at the same time. Science and art can be truth-seeking in the highest sense.

Second, in the opening paragraph of the First Part, Rousseau speaks in lyrical if ironic terms of scientific and artistic inquiry: "It is a lofty and beautiful sight to see man emerge somehow from obscurity by his own efforts." He envisions man dissipating through his reason the darkness in which nature has enclosed him. He may rise above himself, soar by means of intelligence toward "celestial regions, traverse with giant steps, like the sun, the vast reaches of the universe." But, and this is "still greater and more difficult," man must study himself, "know his nature, his duties, and his end" (3: 6). This addition helps define for Rousseau complete science and art. Curiosity and ambition must always be accompanied and controlled by values derived from knowledge of the goals of man. In the destructive descent which follows this passage and is made more devastating by the contrast between what is supposed to be and what actually is, the emphasis is exactly on man's blindness and default with respect to duty and ends, and the task of making them a part of everyday life, "If our maxims served as our rules; if true philosophy were inseparable from the title of philosopher!" (3: 7).

Rousseau has associated truth and right with Ovid and Horace, with the truly learned of the past, of his own day, and of the future. He has opposed ordinary erudition to complete science and art. The third step in the ascent is to relate this perspective to a natural standard which is viable, which reappears historically in diverse forms regardless of the degree of depravation man may reach. As pristine model of value, still largely undefined in the *Premier discours* but always present there and in the depth of Rousseau's emotional being, is his insight about the earliest times, when men were innocent and in unknowing harmony with environment: "It is a lovely shore, adorned by the hands of nature alone, toward which one ceaselessly turns one's eyes, and from which regretfully one feels oneself moving away" (3: 22). If men later become generally wicked, at least elements of partial integrity still remain, so that a man knowing art and science may still have virtue.

Rousseau's second model is the farmer, a man applying accumulated knowledge and skills, yet without vanity and show. Powerful and energetic of body, having "strength and vigor" of soul, he is perhaps the only true citizen in an age of physicists, chemists, astronomers, poets, musicians, and painters, specialists who for Rousseau often know their subject only academically (3: 8). Abandoned in the countryside, indigent, despised, the peasant nevertheless gives the populace bread and provides "milk for our children" (3: 26). Rousseau's style mounts in intensity as he speaks of the dearth of such men and the abundance of charlatans who substitute lies for truth (3: 27). Utility must replace dilettantism and incompetence.

The next model is the true philosopher. Honesty, perspective, moderation, and brilliance survive in some men and make more evident the feigned politeness and affability, the hypocritical shield under which the successful hide. To Socrates, Rousseau attributes the capacity to examine and judge the poets, the artists, the orators, and the sophists. Unlike the presumptuous scholars who surrounded him, Socrates was convinced that "I am ignorant of what I do not know." He rejected the illusion that materialistic progress is the highest end. False savants, because they excel "in their speciality," may conclude that they are wise (3: 13). In contrast, after rising above the arts and sciences and seeing their proper place, Socrates refused to permit the dimensions of man to be diminished by any particular philosophy. He did not, therefore, leave books to posterity, but rather "the example and memory of his virtue. It is thus that it is noble to teach men" (3: 14). The opposite of learning for Rousseau is not ignorance but the ability to discern the limits of human understanding.

Another thoughtful man, wise enough to take the measure of knowledge and to raise above it a higher standard, was Cato the Elder. Socrates exercised a healthy skepticism, was superior through humility, through his awareness of man's inability to penetrate certain mysteries. Cato, according to Rousseau, enriched the meaning of virtue by associating the notion of good with a particular object of study, the nation. His oratory described a Rome grown callous to liberty, altruism, and obedience to law. The science and practice of such values had been replaced by words, by the discussion of the futile doctrines of Epicurus, Zeno, Arcesilas.

The final model, complementing nature, the hard-working farmer, the wisdom of Socrates, and the austerity of Cato, is Fabricius — statesman, general, hero, leader famed for his integrity, peacemaking, and devotion to the laws. He parallels nature by his purity of conscience, has the force and vigor of the peasant, the overview of the philosopher, the demanding temperament of the censor. In addition, he knows and uses the theoretic and practical science and art of the statesman and military man. Through him Rousseau makes clear the kind of behavior required of the citizen. He is to serve with unassuming dignity and valor, to prize liberty as the participation of the individual in government, and to have pride in the capacity of his homeland to govern other peoples justly. If this may be called Fabricius/Rousseau virtue, a somewhat aggressive imperialism (François Bouchardy, Pléiade, 3: 1247), it should be noted that in the context the emphasis is on the validity of the source of Rome's authority and power, on the collectivity, an enduring "assembly of two hundred virtuous men, worthy of commanding Rome and of governing the earth" (3: 15). [3]

The steps of the descent showed the seeming inevitability of culture, man's enslavement to needs, his code of conformity, the deflation of human goals, and the destruction of the nation. The descent concluded with the principle that the science and art of virtue, rather than learning for its own sake, are the source of strength. The ascent includes an appeal to this basic truth, concern with the formation of men as well as study of the physical universe. It presents models taken from history, yet compatible

---

[3] For the relative merit of Sparta and Rome, the two republics which are represented most prominently in the *Premier discours,* see Rousseau's later study, *Parallèle entre les deux républiques de Sparte et de Rome* (Pléiade, 3: 538-44).

with nature, until with Fabricius a new synthesis is reached which orders the data of social life into a virtuous collectivity, a source of tremendous power. This resolution and composition attribute to learning two meanings. Rousseau inveighs continually against the single-mindedness with which man tears from nature its riches and secrets. Rivalry over possessions turns each person into an enemy, causes neighbors to become opaque to one another. The signs of culture are opulence, the wanton art forms wealth can afford, and the ability to discuss certain popularized topics. The more each man tries to raise himself through culture's treadmill, the more true individuality is buried under the avalanche of approbation for what is called progress, enlightenment, in fact knowledge reduced to the level required by mediocre minds preoccupied essentially with self-indulgence and profit.

In opposition to this extreme is the learning favored by men of intellectual and moral soundness. Although involved certainly in the conquest of physical environment, they are drawn primarily to the even more baffling problems of human nature, of how to move each man from the "shore" prepared by the hands of nature alone to self-realization within a community, of how to make the association of men in a nation durable and productive.

The usual interpretation of the *Premier discours* — in terms of the conflict between nature, ignorance, and virtue on the one hand and society and its culture on the other — appears therefore to be on unstable ground. Rousseau does at times seem to oppose nature to all culture, for example, by speaking of the scientifically advanced Chinese who were unable to protect their nation "from the yoke of the ignorant and coarse Tartar" (3: 11). It was this oversimplified opposition that Rousseau's refuters erroneously attacked. They argued that power does not naturally accompany ignorance, and of course Rousseau readily agreed with them. That was not his point. In the first place, virtue did not mean for him ignorance and innocence or mere animal brutishness. Virtue in the immediate context of Sparta, Rome, and the other countries he mentions meant love of homeland, vigor in the defense of liberty, and strength of soul and body in this cause.[4] These

---

[4] For the meaning of virtue in the *Premier discours*, see also the discussion of views held by Albert Schinz and M. G. Pire (Pléiade, 3: 1241).

qualities, moreover, were the outgrowth of an informed kind of planning, the capacity to calculate the effects of various types of activity on the nation and its members. Against nations grown soft on learning for its own sake — China, Rome at the time of the late Empire — Rousseau deliberately sets nations which emphasized the art and science of ethics and politics, which had great lawgivers of vision who made virtue the guide of their cultures. They deliberately avoided "this contamination of vain knowledge," thus made "their own happiness" and became "the example of other nations." He glorifies the Persians, the Scythians, the Germans, and the Swiss for their ability to conquer, resist, and survive. Among the Persians, "one learned virtue as we learn science." Virtue in other words had itself become a science, highly developed and exploited by the lawgiver. This nation, as a result, "conquered Asia with so much ease" (3: 11). The early Romans, even in poverty, triumphed during the early years of their republic. The Germans were a contrast to the opulent and voluptuous peoples they conquered. The Swiss by their courage resisted all kinds of adversity.

It cannot be argued that these countries were preserved by chance, that is, by their blindness. Rousseau offers the opposite viewpoint. The peoples who have pursued science only for prestige or curiosity, in an effort to penetrate the secrets of the universe, have in their pride become oblivious to the true values of man, have submitted unwillingly to necessity rather than risen above it. The morally sound nations, on the other hand, have carried science to an even higher level, the formation of men. They purposely resisted materialistic learning by an act of intelligence and will: "It is not out of stupidity that the latter preferred other exercises to those of the mind. They were not unaware that in other regions idle men spent their lives debating about the sovereign good, about vice and virtue.... but they considered their morals and learned to scorn their doctrine" (3: 12). It was by the "wisdom of its laws," by the statecraft of Lycurgus, that Sparta arose in the very heart of corrupt Greece, deliberately preferred virtue to learning for its own sake, drove from its walls "the arts and artists, the sciences and scientists" (3: 12). The debate, in spite of the rhetorical opposition of the words ignorance and culture, is clearly in substance between two kinds of science and art, both advanced, one led by virtue, the other by passion or necessity.

This error, the emphasis on a superficial, merely verbal tension between culture and ignorance in the *Premier discours*, should not be passed over lightly, for it persists even among writers who agree that Rousseau is not preaching a return to primitivism. Rousseau directly or by implication is repeatedly made to champion the scientifically backward nation, the poor nation. He is sometimes, for example, accused of unfairly loading his argument in favor of ignorance by including nations which were rich and highly developed on his list of states which defeated more sophisticated foes. Alexander the Great, if Rousseau describes him as "poorer than the least significant satrap" of Persia, was in fact master of all Greece when he conquered the Persians (3: 20). After swallowing up "the wealth of the universe," Rome fell to Germanic tribes which "did not even know what wealth was." But certainly this contrast is not intended to imply that the Goths were undisciplined hordes without political and military science and art. If the Franks conquered the Gauls and the Saxons England, it is not Rousseau's message that the battle was won by ignorance but rather by the courage of leadership and the solidarity that went with having little and aspiring to much. Spain, with "all the treasures of the Indies," was brought down by the Dutch, a "handful of herring-fishers" (3: 20), yet the Dutch were masters of shipping and trade when they confronted Spain.

Rousseau's argument in this context cannot be that benighted nations have history on their side. He is saying, first, that the function of the nation is to maintain itself in international rivalry rather than to win acclaim for the advance it has given to the human spirit through its arts and sciences. Second, he is insisting that in this rivalry among nations the education and laws that form true citizens are more potent sources of power than the pursuit of beauty, learning, and wealth for their own sake. In any competition between states, no matter what general level of civilization they all may have reached, the nation which has neglected most the science of man, the development of civic virtue, will eventually lose. The point is less to be ignorant, devoid of learning, than to have taught and encouraged virtue, to have created through moral and political science and art a cohesive national group. Rousseau's examples can support no more than this thesis, and he specifically denies the thesis that raw ignorance is virtue and power. The winning states have in their soul a belief in citizenship which carries rich connotations — a sense of common cause, community spirit and purpose, the force and vigor of each individual.

The illustrations of great national defeats which Rousseau draws from history are intended to highlight the perils of the headlong rush toward passion-led science. Emotion rises in his throat as he offers the appropriate image to describe the danger: "Peoples, know once and for all times that nature wanted to keep you from being harmed by knowledge, as a mother wrests a dangerous weapon from the hands of her child" (3: 15). But there is no way of refusing history. Man is deep within its compelling flow. Rousseau's ending to the First Part of the discourse is not so much a refusal or distrust of history, the contention which has been advanced in the past (3: 1247), as a facing up to the problem of meeting fire with fire, science with science. The true adversaries throughout his argument are history as necessity-directed science in opposition to history as the science of lawgiving, with virtue in command of all art and science.

Rousseau's approach, limitedly optimistic, thus has a conditional kind of faith in progress and presents a discriminating view of science, lost sight of by his readers because of his own rhetoric and the broadsides fired by his opponents. At the end of the First Part, he calls for a lucid examination of the human condition. In the Second Part, he advocates using observation and reflection to solve man's problems. These aims and his words have the confident ring of the science of his day: "Let us no longer hesitate to agree about all points on which our reasoning will be found to be in agreement with historical inductions" (3: 16). His attitude is negative only toward the predominant current in history, blind acceptance of necessity. The intent is to look constructively upon virtue-led culture, to find its antecedents, and to measure, as he does in his investigation, the aberrant general course of history, the tale of declining empires, by the neglected but no less real story of the continuing ascendency of other nations formed by statecraft, the science and art of the duties and ends of man.

Nature is not incompatible with history as agriculture or as the learning of philosophers or statesmen such as Socrates, Cato, Lycurgus, Fabricius. But the standard of nature-led culture cannot be found solely in the past. Virtue as innocence or rusticity, Socratic wisdom, the vision of the ancient lawgiver, the patriotism and integrity of the Spartan or Roman hero — these are no more than artifacts. Of Sparta's inhabitants "nothing remains to us except the memory of their heroic actions" (3: 13). The great ideals of early days, although they give clues to the direction history may take, cannot be restored. New models, compatible with existing society and its problems, must be found for the future by bold thinkers: "I did not intend to throw present-day society into confusion.... I saw the evil and tried to find its causes; other more bold or more mad people will be able to search for the remedy" (3: 95, *Réponse à* [Charles] *Bordes*, 1752). The fact is that already in the *Premier discours* Rousseau provides the characteristics of a new standard. To see them, we need only continue to follow the threads of his reasoning.

The direction of history is clear. Passion has given science materialistic goals, necessity reigns, and the result is that virtue must struggle against serious odds. If at times the order seems reversed and true citizenship has prevailed in some states, the decline to inferior ends and means has never for long been delayed. The only solution may be deliberate and knowing use of science and art to establish a new standard compatible with nature and with the somewhat haphazard, relatively ephemeral efforts at statecraft made in the past. If the First Part of the *Discours* raises the problem of uncontrolled science in a constructive way by showing the alternative, a higher standard, the Second Part deals with the psychological and economic roots of decay and asks for more rather than less science and art. These will have different goals, but still science will use observation and reflection, and art will devise practical measures and remedies for regenerating the individual and the nation.

Rousseau's first step in seeking the shape of this new learning is to penetrate beneath hypocrisy, conformism in taste, and the reign of talent, already described in an external way, and to reach down into the root causes which divide a people. Materialistic science does not arise from attributes inherent in man. If the pursuit of knowledge aggravates distrust, tends to make man accept partial goals, learning itself is not the source of this evil. On the contrary, the blame lies in imposed traits, the warps in man created by two kinds of pressure, physical environment and the presence of other men. Curiosity, relative to problems which had to be solved, produced physics and was increased by the study of physics. Eloquence arose from rivalry with other men, therefore from hate, flattery, and falsehood, and soon gave to those urges darker shades. Ethics, born of pride, in turn accelerated its spread (3: 17). To become constructive, science must be freed from these passions in all areas of inquiry. Man is not his curiosity, his ambition, his hate, his pride. It is by necessity's imposition of these passions that he is left unfulfilled, that civic and personal meaning are thwarted by egotistical striving. The cohesive force of the state is then no longer a reality. Each man is emotionally and intellectually locked in negative endeavors — the philosopher preoccupied with errors he takes for truths, the jurist with the injustices created by jurisprudence, most subjects with the pursuit of privilege. Soft, idle, and skeptical, man is incapable of sustained and coordinated action in support or defense of the state (3: 18, 19).

Rousseau's second step in seeking the new learning is to examine in more detail what modern theorists have done to cure this moral and political decay. The discussion is in terms of statecraft, specifically, its provisions in the areas of economics, military science, and education. The state, history has proved, can be powerful only if the individual is morally sound. Rousseau asks if one dares deny "that good morals are essential to the vitality of empires" (3: 19). Yet he has to conclude that modern political thinkers have neglected the science of citizenship. They repeal sumptuary laws. They prate that luxury increases wealth. They think only of business and money, even talk of the varying price of man, which they can calculate to a hair in Algiers or elsewhere. For them, the individual no longer has in his own right moral and political ends; he is no more than a beast of burden. Rousseau questions, then, the value of the largely quantitative approach to the wealth of a nation employed by Petty and Melon.[5] He ridicules, too, their practice of measuring man in terms of his domestic consumption. By this arithmetic one Sybarite would be worth at least thirty Spartans, yet Sybaris was subjugated by a handful of peasants, whereas Sparta made all Asia tremble.

The rivalry and survival of states, the supreme tests, prove the modern theorists wrong. With their attention to money and wealth, they have everything "except morals and citizens" (3: 19-20). Even their nation's so-called brilliance is of no more than ephemeral value. Since the very soul of the people is dying through neglect, artists can reflect only its senile taste: "inimitable Pigalle, your hand will be reduced to sculpting the belly of an ape, or it will have to stay idle" (3: 22). If statecraft were successful and taste emanated from sound manners and customs, artists would portray, not the aberrations of the heart, but the defenders of the country and the great leaders who have enriched it by their deeds (3: 25).

After this assault on the economics of his day, Rousseau moves to another concern of statecraft, the military arm of the nation. Modern soldiers are "cleverly disciplined" and inspired to deeds of valor and bravery. Yet physically they are less than men, lack stamina, cannot endure the rigor of the seasons and of bad weather. Sun, snow, "loss of a few superfluities" can destroy the best of European armies (3: 23).

As for education, modern pedagogs neglect the inner fiber of man. In Sparta, children were trained to recognize and practice prudence, justice, and bravery. The ancient Persians made their sons vigorous and healthy, taught them to ride and hunt, gave them lessons in religion and truthfulness (3: 24-25). Modern education, with a completely different emphasis, leans to futile subjects — foreign languages, the writing of verse, the composition of specious arguments.

Rousseau is not condemning all science and art in the *Premier discours*. He compares one kind of knowledge and training with another. He would abandon any economics based exclusively on the calculation of wealth, goods, property, and money, any system which reduces man to a mere financial asset or liability, which

---

[5] See particularly Sir William Petty, *Political Arithmetick* (London, 1691), and J. F. Melon, *Essai politique sur le commerce* (Paris, 1736).

offers the ostentation, bad taste, and false brilliance of a few as substitute for the citizenship, the military, moral, and intellectual formation of all.

In opposition to such a wasteful approach, Rousseau proposes a more demanding program. Citizens, rather than being treated as mere pawns, must be carefully molded, lifted to the understanding that they form a *patrie*. Art, if the stage of culture permits, must not be a slave to fashion but should express lasting beauty: "Tell us, famed Arouet, how many vigorous and strong beauties you have sacrificed to our false delicacy." Artists should develop themes related to the best in man — his courage, his magnanimity, the awe inspired by God (3: 21). Education must be redefined in order to produce sound minds, good nerves, muscles of steel, an awareness of duty, justice, and virtue. The object of men is no longer the sterile pursuit of goods but the creation of citizens in the very midst of corrupt forces. This challenging goal presupposes a new and modern science and art more complex than any regime which had yet appeared in philosophy or history.

It is in this context that the closing pages of the *Discours* require reconsideration. To be sure, Rousseau may be flattering the judges of the Academy of Dijon by his many references to the merit of true scientists and the need for a new breed of scientist-statesmen. But it should be noted that these concluding remarks complement both the destructive and the positive currents which appear from the beginning to the end of the treatise: the devastation accompanying the rise of materialistic science and art which requires a new solution; his apparent enthusiasm for a science which explores the universe but returns to the duties of man; the standard for a new learning evoked through related models which range from nature to farmer, philosopher, and statesman; in the rivalry of states, the victory of virtue-controlled over necessity-controlled cultures; the attack on existing economics by means of the criteria Rousseau sets for his new science and art. The idea already present in these criticisms and proposals — that a science to combat science is required — is again directly expressed in Rousseau's closing words of praise for academies. They may be compared to healthful herbs found beside harmful plants. Such institutions are to be made responsible for the dangerous trust of guarding human knowledge and morals. They can assure that their members are irreproachable in behavior. The competitions they propose and sponsor may encourage "not only pleasant enlightenment, but also salutary teachings" (3: 27).

But the problem of a cure is complex and requires a more fundamental solution than any existing institution can offer. The drawback is that the best of academies may increase the disease, for even good science and art contribute to "guiding minds toward their cultivation" (3: 27). Besides, printing and publication spread dangerous teachings. Compilers have made many erroneous concepts available to the general public and whetted its thirst for pseudolearning, which turns many men from the practical trades in which they might excel. The answer to these problems may be in prayer to almighty God expressing regret for the past, for one's ignorance and innocence (3: 28), but retrogression is no more than a wish, since science and art cannot be eliminated. Modern problems are too complex to permit of any answer without learning. This element of apparent illogic in the discourse explains the partially justified objections of Stanislas, Bordes, Lecat, and others. But Rousseau, contrary to their accusations, had envisioned, in order to replace the alternative between a rejected status quo and impossible retrogression, a third choice, a new science designing a new order for the future.

In the closing paragraphs, Rousseau resolves the problems raised in the first pages, namely, how to reconcile man's giant strides in conquest of the universe with a return to knowledge of man himself (3: 6). The Bacons, the Descartes, the Newtons, needing no teachers and taking as guide only their vast and original vision, uncorrupted by past and present, must assume an active role in the theory and practice of government (see also 3: 102, *Lettre à Lecat*). They alone can go beyond existing science, provided they are properly stimulated, offered the great task of molding men's souls. This theme of the worthy goal is a major one. It has been repeatedly related to the notion of man as an undeveloped resource, a new domain for science and a challenge to a new type of scientist. In the first pages of the discourse Rousseau calls attention to the importance of his subject (3: 3). The inquiry into the meaning of integrity is even dearer to "good men than erudition to the scholarly" (3: 5). The study of man is a greater object and more difficult than the conquest of nature (3: 6). The noblest of tasks is to teach men virtue (3: 14). Minds preoccupied with trivial matters do not have the courage to rise to anything really great, but must follow the spirit of the times (3: 21).

This idea of the great task, the most important field of study, reaches its highest expression in Rousseau's conclusion. If their love of such glory is encouraged, if they are allowed to escape from their academic realm into the real world of statecraft, great men of natural genius can build monuments to the human intellect and advance the sciences and arts in a saner direction. The examples Rousseau cites are Cicero, prince of eloquence, yet also consul of Rome, and Francis Bacon, who became chancellor of England. Learned men of the highest abilities must fulfill the only mission worthy of them, the creation through art and science of citizens and of a nation: "Only then will one see what virtue, science, and authority can do if, animated by a noble emulation, they work together for the felicity of the human race" (3: 29-30). Rousseau, far from reducing the role of the sciences and arts, implies in the *Premier discours* the need for a new hierarchy in learning, a different Baconian tree of knowledge which would place moral and political philosophy at the summit and by its guidance permit within the existing framework of civilization the use of the other sciences for the benefit rather than destruction of mankind. His innovation is less to have refused history than to have reordered its priorities. By his marshalling of facts and his reasoning, he has tried, in the face of the prevailing natural sciences, to find the bases of a liberating science — statecraft — which holds the key to individual vitality, hence to national power.

This prospect of a new, strictly guided, humanistic reorientation of the sciences and arts is perhaps more disconcerting than either primitivism or materialistic self-interest. Learning is no longer to be independent, if one interprets Rousseau rigidly, but made the servant of the lawgiver. Certain passages of the discourse suggest the degree of control which may be involved. Aennius and Terence, Ovid, Catullus, Martial, and other obscene writers could be in danger of censure and interdiction (3: 10). The speeches and writings of orators and poets would be examined with a severe eye (3: 13). The marbles and canvases of Athens would be suspect (3: 12). Epicurus, Zeno, Arcesilas might not be heard (3: 14). Scientific works of such great men as Bacon, Descartes, Malebranche, Fontenelle, Réaumur, Newton, and Leibnitz would be examined, evaluated for their utility, and perhaps banned (3: 18-19). Circulation of the writings of Hobbes, Spinoza, Mandeville, Berkeley, D'Holbach, and LaMettrie might be severely restricted (3: 27-28). Only an elite cadre of truly gifted men would be expected to read comparable works in the future. No effort would be made to simplify knowledge to the level needed for consumption by the average man. Theoretically, no limitations would be imposed on the fields of investigation open to the natural genius, since his omniscience is an essential safeguard against the future pitfalls into which mankind may blunder. The scientist-statesman would be a man apart, responsible for setting standards, for assessing the degree of corruption of a people, prescribing for its ills, and molding character by the kind of knowledge and training he makes available to the general public (3: 30).

Obviously I have tried to overstate the reasons for alarm. If it seems improper that the majority of a nation's people should live in partial ignorance while a few natural geniuses exercise a higher science and art, a sort of planning for the rest, it must be objected that Rousseau is not blocking the intellectual growth of any man who has the ability to learn on his own. He is simply recognizing the natural limitations of most men and maintaining that popularized information cannot uplift the entire race. If our present-day gap between the specialist and the layman would appear to bear Rousseau out, if the mysteries of science are farther and farther removed from the average man, Rousseau's point would seem to be, for his times and ours, that this widening difference is not fatal to a people. It is prostitution of the meaning of learning which can weaken the efficacy of the nation. Citizenship is not each person struggling to live science and art and implementing the thesis that knowledge is power, but rather the finding of virtue, that is, what each man can best contribute to his community and nation. Some men will be clockmakers, others farmers, some writers. All callings must be respected. The task of the statesman of genius is to create a climate encouraging each man to excel according to his own individual capacities. The object, first clearly sketched in the *Premier discours,* is to counterbalance by the legislator's science and art the spell of fashion, prestige, and possession which aborts the potential of the inner man.

It can be argued that Rousseau did not take seriously this image of the towering presence of the true savant. His words, after the description of the influence the Bacons of this world should have, may indicate irony, for he chooses to rank himself with common men: "As for us, common men, whom heaven has not endowed with such great talents and whom it does not destine for so much glory, let us remain in our obscurity" (3: 30). But if some reservation accompanies his thought in describing the scholar-statesman, at least two facts speak against any significant reduction in the concept. The genius of vision described in this first important work maintains his role, corresponds closely to the prince of the *Discours sur l'économie politique* and the lawgiver of the *Contrat social*. Moreover, Rousseau even in the *Premier discours* has in fact cast himself in the part of the learned man with an overview of all events and situations, thus enabled to judge the course of history and to evaluate the effects on the individual of all aspects of society. The questioning protest addressed to Virtue, "Are so many troubles and so much display needed to know you?" (3: 30), since her principles are engraved in all hearts, can have but one answer in the context of the view of history the discourse has already presented. Man must be trained to virtue through science, art, more control, if he is to hear the voice of his conscience "in the silence of the passions" (3: 30).

In this interpretation of the *Premier discours,* my main concern has been to highlight the constructive current. Past emphasis on Rousseau's negativism toward all learning does not fit well, it is clear, with his thoroughgoing reliance on science and art in other works, particularly in the *Discours sur l'inégalité,* with its use of the data of observation as support for conjectural truth, in *Emile,* which offers pedagogic theory and techniques to form an individual, or in the *Contrat social,* which would transform the national structure by principles derived from a highly developed moral and political philosophy. There is, to be sure, a destructive current, but somewhat Cartesian in nature, a clearing away of earlier belief by systematic doubt, a resolutive descent to the principle that materialistic learning is weakness, that only the science and art of virtue are power. Beginning with the positive notion that the science of virtue must guide all learning, a new synthesis is prepared in terms of virtue. This standard, still incompletely defined in the *Premier discours*, is related to nature, prehistoric, vague, but with recognizable, imperfect variants or models in history. If good can be found along with the prevalent evil in history, certain views have to follow: first, that a neglected area of science needs development, statecraft in a new sense; second, that a new kind of scientist is needed to explore this field, the scholar statesman, a natural genius; and finally, since there can be no return to the past, that a new morality, assuming new characteristics and dimensions, must be discovered for the future.

These three goals — a new statecraft, the scientist-statesman, a new morality — are major innovations in the *Premier discours* and later become basic concepts of Rousseau's thought. In this first work they are already the instruments designed to free individuality from conformity. It may be objected that each of these ideas is hardly original with Rousseau. The aim of uniting king and philosopher to produce a new order certainly is at least as old as Plato, and Fénelon had renewed the idea in *Télémaque*. But there is a difference which has not been pointed out in the past. The basis for guidance of the ruler, according to Rousseau, is no longer revelation, higher reason, or maxims drawn from debate about the ultimate good. His model for the new science is the scientist in the modern tradition, a man like Bacon, Descartes, or Newton, who in his method makes fact the constant companion of reasoning. His political scientist, given this orientation, would examine the pressures on man, the impacts of culture and physical environment, and would reach by this approach plans for education and law capable of releasing the good in man. Virtue in the *Premier discours* is only in apparent semantic opposition with science, for virtue is to become science and art itself, a new learning which is to have "all the scope of a true but disturbing system, of which the question treated in this discourse is no more than a corollary." Supporting the *Discours sur les sciences et les arts* was "the trunk" of a new philosophical structure, "of which I showed them only the branches" (3: 106, *Lettre à Bordes*). If Rousseau has in appearance renounced curiosity's task of understanding the entire universe and has concentrated instead on the duties of man, his very thought, by the scope of its task, which places ordinary science in a subservient position, has implied an even more complicated awareness of man's entire predicament, his relationship to his world. This understanding must necessarily be fed by knowledge from all of the sciences, by the methods of ordinary science, by intellects capable of unveiling through observation and reflection the mysteries of the universe: "a few sublime men of genius who know how to penetrate the veils with which truth is covered" (2: 970, *Préface de Narcisse*).

If it is admitted that Rousseau from the moment of the *Premier discours* is asking for more science, it must be immediately added that a qualitative as well as a quantitative difference is involved. The natural genius is not to be just a man of superior intelligence but through his transcendent understanding a man capable of elevating himself morally. Since Rousseau, more than many of his contemporaries, after seeing the glory of science and art saw also their false, inhuman side and came to regard learning as an enemy, he had to assure for his new science a pure source. His natural geniuses are to be freed from limited, corrupted masters: "Ordinary teachers could only have restricted their understanding by confining it within the narrow capacity of their own" (3: 29). Rather than perpetuate old doctrines, his new statesmen will guarantee the constant renewal of the sciences and arts, will "go beyond them" in the direction of wisdom, will "contribute by their worth to the happiness of the peoples to whom they will have taught wisdom" (3: 29-30). Such leaders will be capable of resisting "the stupidity of vanity, low jealousy, and other passions produced by the taste for letters." The small number of men who "are fortunate enough to join these qualities" hold "the enlightenment and happiness of mankind, and it is appropriate only for them to devote themselves to study for the good of all" (2: 970, *Préface de Narcisse*). Rousseau, in opposing the spread of scientific inquiry to incompetent minds, proposes at the same time to sharpen and intensify its focus among the elite. As background for the *Inégalité*, the *Économie politique*, *Emile*, and the *Contrat social,* there appears always this image, first expressed in the *Premier discours,* of the genius who has emerged from existing cultures, their hates and fanaticisms, and is therefore free to originate truth.

This truth or new morality, the product of statecraft and genius, is for good reason the direct antithesis of any program to popularize knowledge in the manner prescribed by Fontenelle and Diderot. Such dissemination of learning standardizes men, gives them the same goals and interests, makes them uniformly hypocritical, levels their native capacities. The task of the educator and legislator is to overcome these obstacles to each man's expression of the inner self. Although the term *bonté naturelle* is not used, the absence of the words does not mean, as has been held in the past, the absence of the notion. It is certain that already in the *Premier discours* Rousseau implies such innocence, since the self can be a sound source of action, since man must be freed to "listen to the voice of his conscience" (3: 30). It must be added, too, that in this work, contrary to the views of Schinz and Pire, the catalysts for self-discovery are not Plutarchian fortitude or Christian renunciation (3: 1241-42). These are models to be admired in the past, but it would be an anachronism and impossibility to return to them. The value of these models is that they point the way by opposing selfless action to calculation. They suggest the self-mastery and personal quietude which must precede any full return to an inner being. But the future calls for new criteria appropriate to new times and places.

The new morality to be fostered by the scientist-statesman and his statecraft makes the liberation of self the ultimate goal. The uniqueness of each individual being, its enslavement, the salvation of man through its release — these attitudes underlie Rousseau's violent condemnation of conformity: "All minds seem to have been cast in the same mold: constantly politeness requires, propriety commands; constantly usage is followed, never one's own bent. One no longer dares appear as he is" (3: 8). Standards of the past are to be transcended. The moral and political message announced in the *Premier discours,* far from being negative to all learning, is that only through a new science and art — moral and political philosophy discovered by the truly natural genius — can the original self be allowed to appear and be accepted. Only through the self can valid meanings of citizen and nation be rediscovered. Science and art, if this is to happen, must hold in check the conditions fostered by "the politics of our century," must neutralize the tragic rivalry among men described in the *Discours sur les sciences et les arts* and the *Préface de Narcisse:* "the impossibility of living together without taking precautions against one another, without supplanting, deceiving, betraying, destroying one another mutually" (2: 968).

Chapter III

NATURE AND NECESSITY

In 1753 the Academy of Dijon proposed another important subject for discussion, the origin of inequality among men. The topic encouraged Rousseau to develop further the premises of the *Premier discours*. Leaving Paris in November of that year and settling comfortably for a few days with Thérèse in the forest of Saint-Germain-en-Laye, he found the isolation and serenity needed for deep meditation. Reproducing in his imagination the story of mankind's most primitive existence, he sought and found to his own satisfaction the basic secrets of human nature, traced the steps of man's advance into civilization, and tried to explain how intellectual, social, economic, and political progress became the source of injustice, enslavement, and unhappiness. In this contest, his essay did not win the prize, and his views intensified his image as a man apart, a stranger to his own generation, a destroyer more than a builder. At the same time, this work, published in 1755 as the *Discours sur l'origine et les fondements de l'inégalité parmi les hommes*,[1] established Rousseau's intellectual reputation more firmly than before and made him the potential rival of the more conservative Voltaire.

Three approaches to the *Second discours* have proved to be productive. Some scholars concentrate on that aspect of human nature which they believe is for Rousseau the wellspring of

---

[1] Hereafter referred to as *Second discours*. All citations for this work, unless otherwise indicated, are from the Pléiade edition of the *Œuvres complètes*, vol. 3.

activity: *bonté naturelle,* freedom of will, happiness, self-preservation, or Hobbesian fear and hate. Others, while admitting the secular nature of Rousseau's argument, continually return nevertheless to the religious structure of his thought: the paradisiacal initial state, the Fall from grace, the notion of a Babel-like confusion which may be read into his treatment of the problem of language. A final group emphasize the tension in this work between nature and society. For them, nature serves as a standard by which to measure the extent of man's social aberration as he passes through the spans of prehistory and history. Salvation in this last context may come to mankind through chance, another more propitious run through history's deterministic cycle, or may come to only the lucid few who withdraw and watch in sadness society's processes of decay. My purpose is first to uncover Rousseau's own position with regard to these three points of view, as he reacts to his precursors in the field of moral and political philosophy. Then, following the implications of his statements of principle more than the onrush of his polemic, I intend whenever necessary to break away from these earlier interpretations and to find other perhaps more basic and complete patterns of thought underlying Rousseau's concept of statecraft.

Before Rousseau, the portrayal of man's predicament and the presentation of solutions for it had been made traditionally in terms of inherent principles of human behavior operative by nature in support usually of the status quo. The authority of Plato and Aristotle upheld the doctrine of man's reasonableness and sociability. Human reason was supposed to reflect a standard superior to man — natural law, the unchanging rules of justice which are clearly visible only to the philosopher-prince. A gradation of men in intelligence was held to justify the entire social hierarchy, to explain the various levels of privilege, prestige, and debasement among the ranks, professions, and conditions of men from ruler to slave. Wisdom was the true sanction of authority. The king was sovereign by natural endowment, his higher reason. Thomas Aquinas added to this sanction the weight of God's omniscience and omnipotence. Bossuet, in his *Politique tirée de l'Ecriture Sainte,* reinforced this doctrine of duty, of the rightness of a posture of obedience in subjects, by developing with great detail and rhetorical force the doctrine of the divine right of the monarch.

Rousseau makes it very clear that this framework, evolving from Plato to Bossuet, is not his in any substantial way. In the "Dédicace" he states his preference for a nation in which people and sovereign are "the same person," in which all men, including the members of government, are "subject to the laws," in which government and sovereign are distinct notions (3: 112, 114). He denies in the "Préface" that reasonableness is natural and states his intention to develop his principles "without the need of introducing that of sociability." If man has obligations, "it is less because he is a reasonable being than because he is a sensitive being" (3: 126). As for the gradation in native endowment, which does indeed exist among men, nothing assures that such superior capacity will naturally become associated with kingly authority, with power and wealth: "For that would be asking, in other terms, if those who command are necessarily worth more than those who obey, and if strength of body or mind, if wisdom or virtue, are always found in the same individuals in proportion to power or wealth: a question perhaps good for slaves to discuss in the hearing of their masters, but not fit for reasonable and free men who seek the truth" (3: 131-32).

Rousseau is no less negative toward the attempts of other writers to explain man's behavior and the source of society and authority. He specifically calls attention to the inadequacies of Grotius and Pufendorf, the seventeenth-century theorists who best continued the secular thesis of man's sociableness (3: 132). The first, according to Rousseau, made the mistake of attributing to natural man the notion of justice, and the second assumed that the meaning of ownership was known in that primitive period. Hobbes was at fault, too, when he so exclusively concentrated on another kind of conduct supposed natural, a thirst for boundless dominion which resulted in a state of war among men, caused them to fear for loss of life and limb, for violent death, then drove them into civil society by means of an agreement or contract upholding the ruler. Rousseau denies Hobbes's claim "that man is naturally intrepid and seeks only to attack and fight" (3: 136).

It is not my aim to show the inadequacies of these criticisms by Rousseau of several of the great ancient and modern theorists on natural law and right. I want only to stress that his attack on them is made more significant by the absence in his own moral and political philosophy of equally simplistic patterns of behavior. Those scholars who insist heavily on the importance of *bonté naturelle* (as in the passage, "Because man is naturally good, the entire edifice of law can be built on human will alone" [3: lxvii]) may have overstated the case. In Rousseau's own analysis of history, *bonté* or goodness, the balancing of *amour de soi* (love of self) and *pitié* (compassion), was in fact stilled in man before the establishment of civil society and unfortunately replaced by other principles found by reason: "It is from the relationship and combination which our mind can make of these two principles [love of self and compassion] ...that all the rules of natural right appear to me to flow; rules which reason is later forced to reestablish on other foundations when, by its successive developments, it has succeeded in stifling nature" (3: 126). If the quality of the contracting human will is not its mere *bonté*, that principle certainly plays an important role, but much of the strength of Rousseau's argument in the *Second discours* would seem to lie in his realistic inclination to think in terms of many evolving states of equilibrium, each constituted of a number of habits, feelings, or instincts. These include *bonté naturelle*, largely inoperative in history as means, but also other more operational forces — liberty, perfectibility, happiness, power, prudence, right of the strongest, lucidity, responsibility. Each of these "autres fondements" is of concern here, too, for they bear either a causal or a formative relationship to the collective will as legitimacy.

Rousseau wants also apparently to dissociate his thought from theological and religious conceptions, whether reasoning about the supernatural or about revelation through the Scriptures: "Religion commands us to believe... but it does not forbid us to form conjectures drawn solely from the nature of man and the beings surrounding him" (3: 133). He intends to start with a creature deprived of "all the supernatural gifts he may have received" (3: 134). As for the metaphysics of freedom of will, if Rousseau at first uses such freedom to distinguish man from other animals, ("it is above all in the consciousness of this liberty that the spirituality of his soul appears" [3: 142]), he immediately mentions "the difficulties" surrounding freedom of will and spirituality and the disputes which arise over them. He decides therefore to make his identification of strictly human activity on the basis not of freedom of will but of another faculty, one "about which there can be no dispute" — the problem-solving ability, man's observable, uncontested power of self-perfection (3: 142).

These remarks, which exclude from the *Second discours* any planned use of the tenets of religion, are accompanied by a controlled effort to adopt a thoroughly secular method of argumentation. Nevertheless, many writers still see the imprint of religion on Rousseau's thought: "Christian theology, having been abolished, its forms nevertheless constitute the structural models by which Rousseau's thought is organized" (3: liii). Such writers, in addition to finding a state of nature comparable to paradise, describe the beginning of human reflection as a *chute* or Fall and attribute to primitive man the freedom of will Rousseau has carefully, if reluctantly, removed from his argument: "There is nothing necessary in Rousseau's eyes in the passage from perfectibility to perfection, man is free to will it or to reject it" (3: lviii, lxviii). In contrast, I believe that Rousseau did more than declare his freedom from the theological and religious track. The influence of its structures on his description of man's move toward society is incompatible with the attention he gives to comparative anatomy, to unselfconscious animality, and to environment.

The third approach scholars have used — setting nature against society, making nature the standard for measuring man's cultures — rests on grounds which seem convincing. History may not indeed be able itself to offer a standard, and Rousseau seems at times convinced that history offers no norm. For him civilization is determined in large part by circumstances beyond human control. Perfectibility is an adaptive mechanism, not an initiating faculty; it is always led by events and operates "with the aid of circumstances" (3: 142). The determining factors are exterior to man, who remains within his existing framework of activities "until new circumstances cause new developments" in his soul (3: 143). The history of man, Rousseau makes it clear, has been predominantly a gradual change from solitary to social existence under the guidance of chains of physical force. Thus man has been the instrument of change more than its cause: "After having shown that *perfectibility*, social virtues, and the other faculties which natural man had received in potentiality could never develop by themselves, that they needed for that to happen the chance combination of several foreign causes which might never have arisen and without which he would have remained eternally in his primitive condition, it remains for me to consider and bring together the different accidents which could perfect human reason" (3: 162).

If the rationality of traditional philosophy and Hobbesian urges are no longer meaningful, if theology and religion are to be bypassed, if history as real events, not a moralist's account of it, is a story of chance without higher purpose, then two possibilities remain. The standard may be the state of nature itself, its totality rather than any one aspect of human conduct, or it may be man's entire evolution, all of the stages of the *Second discours* taken as a model illustrating both nature and history. The first view is generally accepted: nature is for Rousseau a "regulative concept" (3: lvii) which permits us to determine the degree of subsequent social decay. Yet this carefully documented explanation has serious elements of illogic. The infant cannot be the measure of the grown man. To say that the discourse's purpose is to "show how man excluded himself from natural harmony" (3: lix) is to sacrifice too much man's evolution to his beginnings, which in no way have the value of a comprehensive absolute. Innocence is blind; it depends by its definition on the conscious acceptance of the present as corruption, on the psychological fact that the quest for nature by peeling away social layers was motivated by the feeling that history is unclean. It follows that the end as primeval origins is a standard which at inception has already been subordinated to and negated by fact, bypassed by historicity or actual occurrence. The nature sought is not a fixed, unchanging concept of justice in the Platonic sense. It is revery, escape, the product of Rousseau's impotent flight from society, whereas the soiled and unpleasant circumstances are the real. The latter are in no way a mere reflection of a higher life but the only existence that counts if man is to meet man. Rousseau's standard is not helpless nature alone but the full hypothetical cycle representing on the one hand conjectural nature and on the other conjectural history with its tribal society, civil society, science, and art.

Rousseau's own statements justify serious skepticism about any submission of his thought to even the structural influence of religion. Any simplistic behavioral interpretation would be similarly open to question. His very reasoning processes suggest, too, that for him logically there can be no more than polemical opposition between nature and history. It follows that a correct approach should bring to the fore his allusions to scientific method, to environment, to gradual evolution, rather than impose on his ideas, unless there is good cause, the veil of religious connotation. While insisting less on the identification and isolation of principles or on the tensions between them, it is essential also to go beyond the analytic side of his reasoning, to follow the cumulative build-up of his value system, to find the transcending syntheses which permit additional insights into his intention and meaning. With this preliminary orientation, I shall turn first to Rousseau's statements about method and then to the substantive side of his argument.

Rousseau's basic methodological procedure consists of the traditional analytic resolution to principle, followed by hypothetical synthesis, but with a new insistence that subjective value — his belief in feeling as ultimate reality — control and color the external data of experience. He is not a mechanic tinkering with the parts of a machine to make it start functioning again according to its former rhythm. Neither is he a mere doctor seeking a cure for disease, the evil in history which must be eradicated before human nature can go its happy way. Mechanic and doctor are trying to maintain the status quo, whereas Rousseau is searching for the bases of a new dynamic order. His attack on earlier authorities is directed basically against their inclination to leave out some part of human nature because of their supercilious concern with sophistication. The theorists of *droit naturel*, whether their sources are the Bible, Plato, Aristotle, Grotius, Pufendorf, or Hobbes, have never really looked at the problem as it is: "They begin by seeking the rules about which, for the common utility, it would be appropriate for men to agree among themselves; and then they give the name of natural law to the collection of these rules, without other proof than the good which they find would result from their universal practice. That is certainly a very convenient way of composing definitions and explaining the nature of things by almost arbitrary propriety" (3: 125).

The criticism is undoubtedly too general to be just, informative, or accurate, but Rousseau's intent is clear. His method means undercutting any notion of utility based on present existence alone. He is to begin his search within man, before man has been compromised by any agreement for society's sake. He will set aside "all scientific books which teach us only to see men as they have made themselves" (3: 125). Exterior fact, the ethnological information that can be gathered from voyages of discovery, is to be supplemented by imagination. The latter permits Rousseau to push back the chain of cause and effect to new speculative limits, to understand that natural law has as its basis not rationality but "sensitivity," a "quality... common to beast and man" (3: 126). This approach differs from the Biblical tradition, which sets man above the other animals in a providential order, and from the usual secular tradition which makes thinking the essence of his behavior. Rousseau rehabilitates instead man's animal part; he returns to emotion, gut, muscle, nerves, and flesh as the source of order. Intellect can be snared in rationalization, can deceive man. Instinct and feeling, stable and lasting inside each animal, is for Rousseau the most valid aspect of being.

Conjecture as analysis is followed by an ascending synthesis. Reduction to animality is but the first step toward a complete view of man's evolution: "This same study of original man, of his true needs, and of the fundamental principles of his duties, is still the only good means that one can use to remove those crowds of difficulties which appear concerning the origin of moral inequality, the true foundations of the body politic, the reciprocal rights of its members, and concerning a thousand other similar questions as important as they are badly explained" (3: 126). Rousseau's allusions to finding "natural faculties" are always accompanied by references to "their successive developments," to the need to learn how art has transformed God's original man (3: 127). By his "hypothetical and conditional reasonings," Rousseau intends to do for moral, social, and political life what Buffon and other physicists, departing from general facts known through observation, have done in studying the universe. He will find hypothetical origins in order to explain the entire process of coming into being. Rousseau praises this empirical, conjectural method which he hopes to follow: "reasonings ... similar to those our physicists make every day concerning the formation of the world" (3: 133).

"Formation" is an important word here. The scientist looking at the universe around him can be so lost in the multiplicity of phenomena he observes — mountains, plains, volcanoes, rivers, oceans, swamps, rocks of different kinds, layers of sedimented earth — that he never reaches a satisfactory theory to explain the conditions he observes. He may, however, by interpreting the signs at hand, by knowing the effects of gravitation, of heat, rise to a concept of the origins of the earth. He may posit, like Buffon or Maupertuis, a breaking away of materials from the sun under the impact of a comet, may suppose the rotating movement engendered by the shock, may explain from these beginnings the successive transformations the earth must have undergone to come to its present state. In this whole sequence of events can be found three major elements: the concept of origins or the earth in an original state; the notion of subsequent, evolving stages, the middle; and finally, the present, the conditions we know but now seen in dynamic perspective, since we see beneath the surface to the underlying forces which explain and continue to control the shapes and events around us. We have an intellectual grasp of the whole which turns the disorder first observed into an extremely complicated but regular, relentless order. This is not Rousseau's account of events, but this type of explanation must be assumed from his references to Buffon, to the reasoning of the physicists of his time.

In the field of social science, too, the theorist may at first be locked in the present. He may see only the conflict of passions, the subservience and enslavement of men by one another, may learn to see and accept decay and confusion as the usual face of existence. He may, too, by careful observation of his fellowmen and the animals, by introspection and revery, succeed in loosening the hypnotic hold of the present. He may travel backward in time to a concept of origins, a period in which man was alone and essentially an animal. He may envision a transforming middle period which increased man's faculties, complicated his relationship to environment. Then with new insight he may understand better the highly sophisticated present. Again, as in the physical scientist's explanation, it is out of the question to say the origin is more important than the middle or the end. The three stages form an integral whole, interpenetrate one another on the basis of principle and consequence: "I admit that since the events I have to describe could have happened in several ways, I can make a choice only by conjectures. But aside from the fact that these conjectures become reasons when they are the most probable that can be drawn from the nature of things, and the sole means that one can have for discovering the truth, the consequences which I want to deduce from mine will not for that reason be conjectural, because, on the principles I have just established, one could not form any other system that would not provide me with the same results, and from which I could not draw the same conclusions" (3: 162). In both fields the present has been given depth by the past, the becoming and the beginnings. Validity, too, has been withdrawn from the surface, the seeming permanence of the present, and placed in the explanation by origins and by sequence.

Rousseau's allusions to Buffon and the physical scientists must not be discounted. Their view of formation does not allow Rousseau any significant dichotomy between nature and history. Even the atmosphere of polemic Rousseau maintains seems to be directed principally against overemphasis on the present, the surface of history. He wants a new preoccupation with the entire picture — present, past, and beginning. The image offered through the statue of Glaucus has this sense. Its present disfigurement is deceptive. Taken alone it encourages an incomplete view of man: "Like the statue of Glaucus, which time, sea, and storms had so disfigured that it looked less like a God than a wild beast, the human soul altered in the bosom of society by a thousand unceasingly renewed causes, by the acquisition of a multitude of facts and errors, by changes that occurred in the constitution of bodies and through the continual impact of the passions, has, so to speak, changed its appearance to the point of being almost unrecognizable; and, instead of a being acting always by clear and invariable principles, instead of that heavenly and majestic simplicity impressed on it by its author, one no longer finds anything but the misshapen contrast of a passion which tries to reason and of an understanding which is delirious" (3: 122). Penetrating the exterior to the form beneath does not mean refusal of the changes which have occurred in the past or the present. On the contrary, any effort man makes to find the origins of inequality must be by means of "these successive changes in the human constitution" (3: 123). The idea of a formative beginning and middle deemphasizes the present but at the same time includes it.

Yet it is true that Rousseau expresses regret for each stage in man's development — the growth of intellect, the division of labor, the enclosure of land, the rivalry over goods, the establishment of civil society. This style must be seen in relation to Rousseau's method, the nature-history synthesis. With this background, his lament at each turning point in man's career, as with his own fate described in the *Confessions,* means not a rejection of history but rather the request that a clear look be given to each of the critical steps already taken. Man passed through each stage blindly, pressed by events. Only the man who is above history, who has seen the entire cycle, can know the significance of each developmental step. The polemic complements the method, assures that the reader will not remain content and unseeing within his own narrow frame of reference. For example, habitual attitudes of the present make us accept without question the notion of property. The middle period generated its practice and cannot condemn it. The conceptual beginning lacked even the notion of possession; it had no experience of the goodness or evil of ownership. Only the overview of the entire process of man's evolution can show the dangers of property, the need to control its effects. Rousseau's aim is not to reject evolving forces and their existing institutional by-products, but by polemic to make man dig down to the foundations so as to bring order out of apparent disorder: "It is only after removing the dust and sand which surround the edifice that one perceives the unshakeable base on which it is established and that one learns to respect its foundations" (3: 127). Nature is not a mere yardstick but a solid force sustaining the edifice of society itself. The most corrupt nation survives only to the extent that there remains within it the remnants of natural elements.

Rousseau's statements about method stress parallels with the physical sciences, with the complexity of the process by which man evolved, with the inseparable relationships between origins, transformation, and present. It follows that the substantive side of his argument should reveal in history characteristics compatible with nature yet having their own clear, normative meaning within the framework of necessity.

Nature is what the isolated primitive man received "from his own stock," as opposed to what he acquired through resistance to other men and animals (3: 122). He operates by principles discernible, not to him, but only to the conjectural theorist, for he is subject to a natural law which in the absence of reason and knowledge is no more than instinctive behavior. He blindly practices love of self, the urge to survive, and pity, which is largely negative — the lack of any inherent antipathy for life in another person when that life does not stand in the way of his personal survival. If he kills, it is by need, not by any instinctive hate. This is part of a law of *sensibilité* or "sensitivity" shared by all animals, so that in a sense each species, even the most lowly of animals, has its rights, is protected by a law of necessary, automatic behavior. Rousseau intentionally empties pity at this level of all of its higher meaning. Love of self is essentially a hunger. Pity is the avoidance of struggle and emotional contact with others in satisfying this urge.

By nature men are equal, not in fact but in effect. They may have differences in age, health, bodily strength, qualities of mind and soul (3: 130), but these differences are of no consequence. Moral inequality, the superiority one man recognizes in another, is also absent. No sustained relationship exists among men. There are no notions of just and unjust, of possession or property, of authority, avarice, opression, or pride (3: 132). Equality is essentially the absence of other persons. In the prevailing isolation, no one can be regularly compromised by the life and desires of another.

Nature is remote, lost in time, ages distant from any form of collective life and the records of cooperative activity. The traditional theorists make the step from nature to civil society seem short; the social institutions they derive from nature are expressed as family or tribal life, as patriarchal authority. Hobbes no less abruptly insists on the derivation of society, not from nature, which he sees as a state of war, but from art as agreement. In both instances the link between the natural and the civil state is a logical step, either wisdom turning natural obligation into civil obligation or prudence replacing natural disorder by civil order. Obligation and disorder are absolute, well defined points of departure, each the first premise in a line of reasoning, a concept as filled with certitude as the Biblical account of the state of Adam and Eve.

Rousseau's version lacks the certainty of Scriptural, Platonic, or Hobbesian precedents. Skirting supernatural authority (3: 132), he supposes that man reached what has been called nature through an evolutionary process. He admits that the demands of his subject and the gaps in his knowledge have limited his definition: "However important it may be, in order to judge correctly the natural state of man, that one consider him from his origin and examine him, so to speak, in the first embryo of the species, I shall not follow his structure through its successive developments" (3: 134). The statement shows his desire to make known the difficulty of finding the edges of the state he calls nature, edges so illusive that he must drop any pretense at recording the full process. He suggests very gradual development up to the state of nature. Though comparative anatomy is still too new a science to yield firm results, Rousseau uses it to destroy any inclination the reader may have to accept nature in an absolute sense. The reader must be made to understand that Rousseau has arbitrarily focused his vision on only one segment in man's development: "The comparative anatomist has so far made too little progress, the observations of naturalists are still too uncertain for one to be able to establish the basis of solid reasoning upon such foundations; thus, without having recourse to the supernatural knowledge we have on this point, and without regard to changes which must have come about in the internal as well as external conformation of men, as he applied his limbs to new uses and as he nourished himself on new foods, I shall suppose him to have been at all times identical in form to man as I see him today, walking on two feet, using his hands as we do ours, directing his gaze over all nature, and measuring the vast expanse of heaven with his eyes" (3: 134). The concept of man in the state of nature is no more than an abstraction, a methodological choice of one period in the endless chain of events which is the domain of the comparative anatomist. Intentionally, Rousseau has called attention to the relative, only probable validity of man's "beginning," which is overshadowed by a higher idea — what science may be expected to know in the future.

Yet for the audience of Rousseau's day this empirically based language could be considered the best approach, preferable to Platonic reasoning, the Hobbesian emphasis on mathematical logic, and the theological explanation. Clothing his personal feeling and vision with scientific tentativeness, he argues against the natural viciousness of man, the natural superiority of some men over others, the naturalness of society to men. Natural law is innocent, animal instinct. Equality is unawareness of other creatures. Nature is a timeless stage selected by the theorist from an imperceptibly evolving anatomical structure. Hunger, isolation, timelessness represent the existence man shares with other creatures. These characteristics are not, like the principles usually assigned to the natural state, related closely to the sophisticated present. Looking around us, society seems the prime reality. Looking at the beginnings from Rousseau's perspective, animality seems the prime reality. Man has become humanity, which, given his nature, Rousseau insists, he need not have become. The species had no instinctive orientation away from animality. The study of origins has served to open to question the value or approbation customarily allotted to the present.

Opposed to man's animality is his potential for noninstinctive action. Advantageous bodily organization and a mild stimulus from environment permitted this ability to appear harmlessly in the state of nature. Man watched the other animals and borrowed their skills, brought together in his own person many of their ways for acquiring food (3: 135). "Alone, idle, and always near danger" (3: 140), he had to be clever and quick to survive. But this power to improvise always fell within the scope of the instinct for self-preservation and pity; it did not become an end in itself and never meant a willful passion to excess, to unwitting self-destruction: "It is thus that dissolute men give themselves over to excesses which cause them fever and death." Primitive man knew only "the simple impulsion of nature.... His desires do not exceed his physical needs ... food, a female, and repose" (3: 141, 143).

The state of nature is therefore an incomplete standard, incongruous with the full capacity of man because freedom of will and perfectibility, which constitute humanity, have not appeared in any real sense. Unlike the animal, man at full development can transcend instinctive limitations, can go against *amour de soi*: "Nature commands every animal, and the beast obeys. Man feels the same urge, but he realizes he is free to acquiesce or to resist" (3: 142). This freedom to will, since it carries theological connotations, may be better expressed as perfectibility, the will to invent, to improve one's position, to problem-solve, a power "which, bringing to fruition over the centuries his enlightenment and his errors, his vices and his virtues, makes him in the long run the tyrant of himself and of nature" (3: 142).

Perfectibility does not appear in the state of nature for lack of the challenge which produces it. Environment at rest produces no more than animality. Rousseau has arranged his thought experiment to nurture innocent animal hunger or *bonté*, to permit each self in isolation to remain unbound by others, to encourage the eternal repetition of instinctive acts without a sense of chronology, progress, and the attrition they bring. Such natural characteristics fade steadily into the background once humanity starts its rise. The line of dependence is clear. *Bonté* requires the absence of perfectibility, which can dominate it. This absence is permitted only by a sheltering environment, which in turn must come from God, chance, or art. In the context of the *Second discours*, the source is art, the very way in which Rousseau has set up his thought experiment. Rousseau's state of nature is designed to show the conditions needed to produce animality or *bonté*, which is not cause but only effect, its appearance contingent upon environment as absence of pressure, as liberty. The most basic principle of the standard is not animal *bonté*, innocence, but *bonté*'s underlying environmental explanation, the habit and feeling of liberty, lack of psychological inhibition, absence of pressure. Without this absence, this timelessness, animality loses its innocence and turns vicious through perfectibility.

All the aspects of the "natural" environment are dovetailed to provide this habit and feeling of liberty. The forest offers an abundance of foods, makes shared or sustained labor unnecessary, maintains in man sufficient vigor to assure fitness, the survival of only the strong. Submerged in the present, man is without sickness. Death goes unnoticed. The idea of duty and obligation to others is nonexistent. Since pity is not a positive force for altruism, it cannot turn man against himself. Whenever the individual is threatened ego always asserts its right to the degree required for self-preservation. Man's passions are undeveloped and do not victimize him. He is free from the biological drive of ego for power and more power described by Hobbes. Pity balances ego, restrains it to a sane *amour de soi* consistent with animal behavior. No pressure, it is clear, bears upon man. His only curb is the timeless, static order which cradles him, of which he is unconscious, a curb only to his will's potential aspirations. It is pertinent that the closing paragraphs dealing with the state of nature concern less *bonté naturelle* than liberty, man "wandering in the forests, without industry, without speech, without domicile, without war and without liaisons, with no need of his fellowmen, as well as with no device to harm them... subject to few passions and self-sufficient.... Art perished with the inventor" (3: 160). Man is not free simply from physical pressure exerted by environment, by the presence of other men, or by the superiority of others ("I take twenty steps in the forest, my chains are broken" [3: 161]). He is free also from limiting drives within himself which might compromise his basic animal being.

The first of Rousseau's standards for measuring positive law is liberty as the sustaining, controlling, nonpressuring environment required to permit the innocent, isolated self to appear. It is also the basis later for education designed, as for Emile, to retain the unique individual inside the publicly trained citizen. Law must be compatible with feelings, the inner pulsations of each individual life.

Rousseau's description of the departure from the state of nature has been called by some critics a Fall, by others a theodicy. The first term implies a decision, man's willful lapse from the innocence commanded by God, or simply degradation. The second may mean a vindication of the justice of God in the sense that he did not want evil to exist (3: lix). Although these claims are limited usually to structural influence, their effect needs to be discussed. They add to the discourse religious overtones that Rousseau pointedly sought to avoid. But more important, they either attribute to his argument elements of choice and illogic which are not present, or lead to an exaggerated account of Rousseau's polemic purpose. My examination of this stage of his thought, the development of perfectibility in man, follows the secular form of reasoning he seems to have intended.

The state of nature represented environment at rest. Rousseau's polemic glorification of man's origins served to offset the reader's acceptance of agitation and culture as the usual forms of experience. If one asks why a sheltering matrix should be made the environmental control of man's most primitive self, the answer would seem to be that a thought experiment, like any other, must start with the simplest condition, with all of the variables rendered as neutral, as quiescent as possible, so that basic behavior may be observed. For the next part of his experiment Rousseau must set the scene in motion with the possibility of a resulting change in the relationship of the forces operating in and on man. Environment in upheaval is to produce a series of new conceptions of man.

The initial step in this transformation is the appearance of freedom of will or perfectibility. The former faculty becomes the latter for very clear reasons. Man is the one animal not totally repetitive in his acts. He is like other animals in many ways; all have senses, all form ideas; mechanistic explanations can be given for all knowledge. But willing is another matter. Man in this respect, according to Rousseau, differs from the beast, not in degree, but in kind. All other animals follow the narrowly limited behavioral patterns imposed on their particular species. Bees and spiders have their ways. A cat may die of hunger from inability to feed on fruit or grain. Only man can break out of his animal limitations (3: 141-42). His spirituality lies exactly in this transcendence. But Rousseau's definition of freedom of will introduces a substantial change of meaning with respect to its choices and its very quality. Traditionally, the alternatives had been, on the one hand, the path of innocence or of God and, on the other, animality, flesh, and death. For Rousseau, the choice is between innocence, animality, and intellect, progress. This is an important difference. One might argue that even if the standard is no longer a supernatural one, the idea of free choice itself remains unchanged. But this is not true in the context of either the first or the second discourse. The overwhelming evidence is that man has always opted against animality. This is the very reason for Rousseau's attack on civilization. Furthermore, Rousseau decides explicitly to substitute for freedom of will the notion of perfectibility, which by its definition excludes any notion of Fall, any choice between remaining animal or becoming man. Perfectibility is a "faculty which with the aid of circumstances successively develops all the others and resides among us as much in the species as in the individual, whereas an animal is at the end of several months what it will be all of its life, and what its species is at the end of a thousand years" (3: 142). The tone is in no sense theological; it is scientifically descriptive.

Rousseau's presentation of the trial-and-error accumulation of skills and information resulting from the contact of man's senses and awakening intellect with environment can perhaps be seen as a theodicy, but if this is Rousseau's intention, the results are unconvincing for lack of logical tightness. If religious dimensions are to be given to Rousseau's thought experiment (3: lix), it should be pointed out that the sources of evil are already present in God or in his state of nature, since perfectibility is potential in man, since the molding influence of environment is already operative in nature, since movement and the changes which are to come later within an unstable universe can hardly be excluded from God's plan.

But suppose God is not made responsible for nature's evolution. The argument for theodicy still runs into difficulty. Intellect is a pattern imposed in part by outside events, which could have come about in an infinite number of ways (3: 162). Just as the state of nature was selected without full knowledge of the facts of comparative anatomy, so the rise of perfectibility must be couched in terms of greatest probability rather than of certainty. According to Rousseau, man, upon accepting the challenge of knowing his environment, embarks on a sea of events which offer no orientation, only randomness, infinite possibilities for becoming, for being determined. One may even assume that environment could have left man for many more eras in an arrested state of development. Humanity, civilization need not have occurred. The entire Biblical sequence could have been aborted: "Let us therefore begin by setting aside all the facts" (3: 132, 1302). Hypothesis is in order, therefore, rather than scriptural certitude.

If there is to be an effort at theodicy intended to leave man innocent and still to vindicate God, then irony must enter and God must be acknowledged to be without control over the crushing physical forces he has created. He is as helpless as man in the face of necessity's greater power. Theodicy is at the expense of God's perfection, omniscience, and omnipotence. He has been reduced to the level of imperfection and can be more than that only through faith, which is itself outside the conjectural framework of the *Second discours*. Rousseau's vocabulary, in fact, stresses without irony or mystery the complexity of the pressures acting upon man, their chance occurrence, and the duration of time needed to stir man to cultural progress. He speaks of the "chance combination" of causes, "different accidents," "the surprising power of very slight causes." The timelessness of the first period now becomes a slow-motion perspective: "the lapse of time compensates for the slight probability of the events" (3: 162-63) ... "this slow succession of events" (3: 164).... "the events were slow in following one another" (3: 167). If there are religious implications in Rousseau's account of events, his preoccupation with the processes of learning has results more immediately related to his argument. His detailed description of man's first state helps give credence to the hypothesis of a primitive animal self. Careful, repeated use of the themes of time and chance, allusions to and descriptions of the laboriousness of environment's efforts make man's coming into culture a concrete reality.

Environmental pressure is the operational beginning of intellect. Its stimuli do not occur in any providential pattern. At times they may seem to protect man, as in the first state, at times they may seem to expose him. God is blameless but helpless. Environment is blameless but powerful, for it offers exposure and challenge. Given his potential for perfectibility, man is unable to flee, to remain in a state of nature (3: 142). He must himself create the shelter which environment has withdrawn. Environment in motion and man's perfectibility are then a chance but inevitable combination, a fact of history. Man's growing consciousness of environment as something separate and distinct from himself brings a relationship of hammer and anvil, of man as instrument working on environment as instrument to produce or discover objects useful in satisfying need. Trees are climbed for fruit, ferocious animals subdued for clothing and food, fishing line and hooks invented. Meat is cooked when fire is supplied by a volcano. Reflection thus develops not by choice, but by useful adaptation to external causes. Human contacts are made, comparisons are made, rules of conduct are established, ephemeral engagements are entered into — all out of utility. Man cooperates in herds or again seeks his own advantage in isolation.

This stage has an essential characteristic distinguishing it from the first. Man has acquired the most rudimentary attitudes of science: "I cross multitudes of centuries like a flash.... These first advances finally placed man in a position to make more rapid ones" (3: 167). Knowing how has come to the fore, which means that from unconscious absorption with himself man has escaped into his surroundings, which attract and draw him, which he now consciously embraces with his need-oriented curiosity, which in return gives him new identities as he enters environment more deeply by probing its secrets. Man is on the threshold of expanding into the universe, of holding it in his grasp, as the young Rousseau, leaving Geneva at the end of Book I of the *Confessions*, wanted to fill the universe with his being. If the universe in motion is a clinamen (3: lx), any antagonism with environment is in Rousseau's hindsight, not in evolving man himself. The problem is exactly that man, with the development of perfectibility, does not feel antagonistic to environment but is locked in the embrace of its attraction, the fascination of the personal growth and comfort it promises him.

Through the polemic tone which colors the findings of his conjectural investigation Rousseau turns this blind, unplanned union of environment and perfectibility into the innocent source of moral evil, the "source of all man's misfortunes" (3: 142), "to perfect human reason while deteriorating the species" (3: 162). His perspective is that of a narrator who, having already witnessed the whole cycle of human misfortune, anticipates in the seemingly innocent birth of self-improvement and self-creation the corruption of the most sophisticated societies. Yet the effect on the reader is not rejection of progress, clearly an impossibility, but rather, as Rousseau seems to have intended, lucid recognition of the need for a new evaluation of principles. God and nature (animal innocence, or traditional rationality, or fear) are operationally ineffective. True power and also evil lie in perfectibility's blind embrace of environment, in indiscriminate utilitarianism. If in Rousseau's intent this may be a vindication of God and nature, their helplessness places salvation elsewhere, in the manipulation through statecraft of man's relationship to environment and to other men, so that, while using his perfectibility, man may still act in accord with animality, with his instinct of *amour de soi*, with his habit and feeling for liberty.

In his treatment of the period during which perfectibility first came into play, Rousseau in fact describes that faculty from two points of view. He envisions the ravages it is later to produce, but he also positively stresses primitive man's active search for well-being. Liberty is still strongly entrenched in his psyche: "Taught by experience that love of well-being is the sole motive of human actions, he found himself able to distinguish the rare occasions in which common interest should make him count on the assistance of his fellowmen, and those even rarer in which competition should make him distrust them. In the first case he united with them in a herd, or at the very most by some kind of free association that obligated no one and lasted only as long as the passing need that had formed it. In the second case, each man sought to obtain his own advantage, either by naked force, if he believed that possible, or by skill and cunning, if he felt himself to be the weaker.... If it was a matter of catching a deer, everyone felt clearly that he should for that purpose faithfully keep his post; but if a hare happened to pass within reach of one of them, there can be no doubt that he pursued it without scruple, and that having caught his prey, he cared very little about having caused his companions to miss theirs" (3: 166-67). Effortless satisfaction of need was the way of life in the state of nature. Absence of pressure, liberty for the sake of self alone could be made by Rousseau the lesson of that age. In the climate of exposure produced by the second stage of Rousseau's thought experiment, perfectibility — the active search for subsistence and shelter — becomes a valid supplement to the original standard.

Perfectibility, man's problem-solving infatuation with exterior nature, is slowed by his ignorance of any but minimal needs, basic well-being. He is alone except for occasional ventures into useful association. Rousseau next varies his experiment by a third stage, family and community life, his so-called golden age. Happiness, absent in the unaware satiety of the first man and in the struggle of the second, has now become a conscious goal. Man actively seeks conjugal and family love, enjoyment of commodities, public esteem, or, if the latter is denied, revenge. This life represents "a golden mean," "the happiest epoch," "the best state for man," because it is a resting place before subsequent progress, that is, decline, "the perfection of the individual... the decrepitude of the species" (3: 171). Man's first stage, freedom from pressure, was animal feeling, passive acceptance of sheltering environment. The liberty which came with problem-solving was a lean and hungry striving. The golden age represents enjoyment of the first fruits of man's instrumental union with environment. Men still are free and essentially single because they are independent of others as to their own needs and those of their families, but the self has a master other than survival. Man has gone beyond need to seek pleasure.

In spite of his predominant condemnation of progress, Rousseau can see in family and communal life a positive element capable of enhancing both pristine nature and man's later austere pursuit of shelter. Again the tones of the polemic are softened: "As long as men were content with their rustic huts, as long as they limited themselves to sewing their clothing of skin with thorns or fish bones, to adorning themselves with feathers and shells. ... as long as they applied themselves only to tasks which a single person could do and to arts which did not require the cooperation of several hands, they lived free, healthy, good, and happy to the extent that they could be by their nature, and they continued to enjoy among themselves the sweet pleasures of independent intercourse" (3: 171). The family provides the shelter sought by the individual in the second stage, when perfectibility first appeared in the face of environmental resistance and indifference. The family gives to the young the passive satisfaction of the first period and dulls through carefree enjoyment the drive for future evolution. Buffered by the local or tribal community, the family reintroduces into life after the period of active adjustment to environment an atmosphere of timelessness: "The example of savages, almost all of whom have been found at this stage, seems to confirm that the human race was made to remain in it always, that this state is the real youth of the world" (3: 171).

In the fourth stage of his argument Rousseau reveals the conditions which produced in man an even more basic preoccupation with environment. The integrity of the individual self is more seriously threatened by the will to self-destruction, already foreshadowed in the definition of man's spirituality as the power to choose against his real advantage (3: 141). Men before enjoyed in their group activities the sweetness of "an independent intercourse." Now they are dependent on one another, learn to divide and share their labors. The exchange of goods has become necessary. Property has been introduced. Rousseau leaves no doubt that he is describing at this point the disintegration of man's sense of isolation, his animal love of independence. From passive, unaware acceptance of shelter, a condition in which environment served man, he has, by a steadily increasing infatuation with the environment, shelter, family and pleasures, become the slave to materialistic gain and power.

The vast forests which had helped hide and isolate him become "pleasing fields," but with serious effects: "It was necessary to water them with the sweat of men" and in them "slavery and misery were soon seen to germinate and grow with the harvests" (3: 171). Rousesau's description of the discovery of the secrets of metallurgy has the same destructive tone, though not because primitive man is alienated from his environment. That again is the rhetoric of the theorist's hindsight. The problem is precisely that primitive man blindly adjusts himself to necessity's dynamic course, fails to question the value of that course. The polemical side of Rousseau says that it is as if nature had by presenting obstacles taken precautions "to hide from us" this fatal secret of metallurgy (3: 172). But he demonstrates by his description that the slowness of the tempo and the imperceptible refinement of man's discovery processes are the very factors which explain man's inability to resist this insidious involvement. Rousseau, who for the purpose of his experiment has turned timelessness into chronology with past, present, and future, including attrition and perseveration, has found man devoid under these conditions of any moral sense, of any awareness of the value of simple animal existence.

Further problem-solving is therefore inevitable. Metallurgy and its accompanying arts make agriculture necessary. Men who had provided food for themselves individually now think regularly in terms of the common subsistence. Land becomes important, has to be divided, and the first rules of justice result (3: 174), a justice based not on the individual self but on the value of manual labor to society, on "the right of property," which originally meant self-preservation and reserving goods for real needs with as little harm to others as possible. The inequality which follows erodes the independent status of the self: "Working equally, one earned a great deal, whereas another scarcely had enough to live on" (3: 174). Since prestige depends on quantity of goods, since power to benefit or harm depends on intelligence, beauty, strength, and skill, men have to appear often what they are not: "It was necessary to appear to be other than what one in fact was" (3: 174). Not only has man denied his self through preoccupation with objects exterior to him, he has in fact created for himself a new, false image behind which to hide.

Beneath this rivalry for goods carried on by men now unknown to one another, eager to acquire wealth at all costs, the theorist from his elevated viewpoint can see a conflict between principles, the right of the first occupant against the right of the strongest. Mankind has unwittingly created self-destructive chaos, "brought itself to the eve of its ruin" (3: 176). Each will has become dedicated to the penetration and destruction of the masked wills surrounding it. Existence has turned from the will to freedom into the state of war (3: 176), the antithesis of the original state of nature, the effect of which had been the preservation of each individual self.

This chaotic situation has its positive side. The principle which says that each individual will may be quantitative, may rightfully express itself in terms of force and wealth, is tested and found wanting in two senses — the right of the strongest and the right of the first occupant who by industry has numerically expanded his holdings. The state of war of the *Second discours*, viewed by critics in the past only in a negative sense, has a more significant meaning. Usurpations by the strongest are in turn subject to usurpation: "Having been acquired only by force, force could take them away" (3: 176). Wealth gained through labor is also to be rejected: "By virtue of what do you presume to be paid at our expense for work we did not impose on you?" (3: 176). It would be easy to ridicule Rousseau at this point, to say that he has turned his early men into jurists for the human race: "Do you not know that a multitude of your brothers are dying or suffering from their need for what you have in excess, and that you required express and unanimous consent of the human race to appropriate for yourself anything from the common subsistence which exceeded your own?" (3: 177). But highlighted by this polemical interpretation of the mind of the entire human race is his very pertinent, substantive concern, the one positive conclusion to be drawn from his analysis of the state of war. Underlying history's state of war and explaining it is a quality persisting from nature into history, the resistance to quantitative expansion, the refusal to be bound by force or bought by wealth, mere quantitative means, the refusal to accept for the human will other than qualitative arguments, that is, the appeal to each individual will's liberty: "an express and unanimous consent of the human race" (3: 177). The only just principle which may end the war of man on man reduces quantity to the exact magnitude of each individual's need, permits no other quantitative exclusion of other individuals except through the consent of each and every independent will.

In Rousseau's fifth stage, representing civil union, the natural self, which has become greed and resistance to greed, is restrained from further self-destruction by the creation of a new order of being — polity — which means a renunciation of self in areas of community good. No longer natural beings, men are protected from one another within the confines of the state, but are pawns in a new state of war between artificial entities, collective wills, homelands which have raised artificial standards, which have, for example, made the shedding of human blood a virtue. Death more than life is at times the object of these juggernauts: "The most honorable men learned to consider it one of their duties to murder their fellow men; it reached the point where men were seen to massacre one another by the thousands without knowing why" (3: 179).

But Rousseau's polemic against these events should not be stressed at the expense of his lucidity about the place they occupy in his chain of reasoning. The natural individual self has been progressively diminished by exteriorization or preoccupation with problem-solving, with happiness, with war, with survival through creation of a collective will. The value of this passing of the individual into a collective being is measured not so much by the purity of the wills entering into agreement — *bonté naturelle*, natural goodness (3: lxvii) — as by the more comprehensive and operative attribute of the state of nature — the liberty of the individual, his essential separateness and independence, the persistence of that liberty during the subsequent self-destructive stages of man's history under varying forms. There is, in other words, no rejection of fact by right in Rousseau's argument, as has been held in the past (3: lxv). During this passage into civil society, there is rather a testing and supporting of two notions; first, of civil society and, second, of government, both by the facts — what man submerged in nature and history could accept — and by right — what man, having emerged from nature and risen above history to grasp an overall perspective, may deem legitimate. By both standards, Rousseau finds true merit in history's creation of civil society and government. There is dupery in the act, but there is also for him a mitigating pseudolegitimacy which makes the notion of valid contract an integral part of history and not transcendent of it.

Because of the state of war among men, all future promise must be in art, in an instrument of agreement among men. No matter how imperfect this instrument may be, it is established by collective will, not through conquest by the strong nor through conquest by a union of the weak. These two brute-force principles are measured against all of the factual and normative elements to be derived from Rousseau's argument and are found wanting. Man locked in the primitive state of nature had the instinct of *amour de soi*, the habit and feeling of freedom, the habit of carefree expression of self without pressure. This habit was changed; love of self became pride, comparative advantage. But the will to independent action, although it became vicious, never disappeared in any of the subsequent precivil states. To say that society was established by conquest would be contrary to this fact. Men would willfully oppose any yoke. The strongest, once possessions have been acquired, is no longer merely the strongest but also the richest, so that his successes always generate a nucleus of opposition, render him incapable of any preponderance over the others, even make him as his greed increases ever more vulnerable: "easily crushing an individual, but crushed by groups of bandits; alone against all, and unable because of mutual jealousies to unite with his equals against enemies joined by the common hope of plunder" (3: 177). The rich have become "vulnerable in every portion of their goods" (3: 179).

It would be equally false to say that society was established by a union of the weak. They are less the weak than the poor. The poor have no incentive to initiate a union which would make them go counter to their instinct for freedom "to gain nothing in the exchange" (3: 179). They can have no desire simply to perpetuate their poverty. By the standard of right, too, the theory of civil society through conquest is on untenable ground. Societies disappear in the absence of force to maintain them: "Whatever capitulations may have been made, since they have been founded only upon violence... they are null by that very fact" (3: 179).

The solution that Rousseau does accept, contract, although it represents imperfect agreement because it is inspired by the deceit and shrewdness of the rich, can withstand the test of both fact and right. The strong or rich have the motivation to invent the notion of contract and feel most of all "how disadvantageous to them was a perpetual warfare in which they alone paid all the costs, and in which the risk of life was shared by all and the risk of goods by them alone" (3: 176). The rest, the poor, have been taken in by the cold facts of the situation. They are "crude, easy to seduce" (3: 178). Blinded to the dangers of enslavement, they see their security in "a political establishment" (3: 177).

The contract, in spite of the ruse and treachery involved and its tradition of the simple having been beguiled by the clever, does fulfill also the demands of right. Submerged in the flow of history, the participants are not aware of the problem of legitimacy. But a person emergent from history and seeing the full evolution of man notes that the contract is not based on force, that instinctively man exercises his will, that the agreement is entered into voluntarily: "All ran to find their chains thinking they would assure their freedom" (3: 177). There is an initial agreement, voluntarily entered into, and in spite of treachery, perhaps because of it, there is unanimity. The sanction behind the contract is not natural goodness, which has disappeared. The sanction is the liberty of each individual and the willingness of each to give up a part of it: "Even the wise saw that it was necessary to sacrifice a part of their freedom for the preservation of the other" (3: 178). Some blindly surrender a part of their liberty, some do so advisedly, but liberty and the willful giving away of a part of it are in either case the sources of legitimacy. Any authority based on force is out of touch with both fact and right, whereas the agreement of all, even with its imperfections, joins fact with right, reflects all of the earlier periods.

This giving is consistent with liberty, the integrity of self of the first period, since the individual will determines the degree of restriction on self to the best of the individual's insight at the time. The contract reflects, too, man's problem-solving bent in search of shelter. The advantages are consistent with man's desire for happiness. The contract is sufficiently legitimate, in spite of contamination by history, to transcend life as individual self, to replace the state of war by a reign of law. The contract replaces both nature and necessity by art, by a created collective will into which all the individual wills have entered: "Such was, or must have been, the origin of society and laws, which gave new shackles to the weak and new forces to the rich, destroyed for all time natural liberty, established forever the law of property and inequality, turned a shrewd usurpation into an irrevocable right, and for the profit of a few ambitious men, henceforth subjected the entire human race to work, servitude, and misery" (3: 178). Underneath this polemical tone and its protest is the recognition that the agreement has strength precisely because it is not opposed to right, as would be the theory of the right of the strongest. The meaning for Rousseau is that the standard of right, unanimous consent, is not separate and uncontaminated, a mere measure of history, but at this point has been made to serve history's ends, made to add the notion of right, and therefore of continuing obligation, to mere necessity. He is admitting that materialistic science and art, even when judged by hindsight, have introduced elements of legitimacy into the blind flow of history.

This instrument, only to the degree that it is legitimate, serves to tighten the bonds of society, to strengthen the nation. But legitimacy is also an excuse to justify the authority imposed on each individual. Perfectibility, problem-solving science and art, has given only token attention to liberty, has formed a union mainly dedicated to ambition, hate, the desires that take man outside himself. Yet this instrument embodies certain principles never to be abandoned, only to be purified later in the *Contrat social*. The will to agree, to find a union of wills, is potentially destructive of self as personal ambition, constructive in that it creates equal pressures on the individual wills, so that no will is at the discretion of another. Man has found the will to create a collective self but lacks the genius to do that with expertise. The creators have been badly motivated; they think of their private gain rather than the general good. Submerged in history, they lack the moral and intellectual lucidity of Rousseau's perspective. The stage is set for a great legislator to dominate materialistic goals by science and art as virtue. He does not appear. Man continues gropingly: "In spite of all of the labors of the wisest legislators, the political state remained still imperfect, because it was almost the work of chance and because, since it was badly begun, time in discovering faults and suggesting remedies could never repair the vices of constitution; people kept mending endlessly, whereas it would have been necessary to begin by clearing the area and setting aside all the old materials, as did Lycurgus in Sparta, in order to raise afterwards a solid edifice" (3: 180).

In the sixth stage the relationship between collective will and magistracy is established (3: 187). The idea that men chose their chiefs before the confederation, threw themselves into the arms of an absolute master without conditions and for all time is, for Rousseau, contrary to fact and to right. Without positive goodness, warring man's essential characteristic is his freedom, his rejection of any arbitrary, other than self-imposed, pressure: "The worst that can happen to one man is to see himself at the discretion of another.... What equivalent could he [an asbolute master] have offered them for the concession of so fine a right?" (3: 181).

Rousseau's style intensifies as he describes this animal feeling in man: "As an unbroken stallion bristles his mane, strikes the ground with his hoof, breaks away impetuously at the very approach of the bit... barbarous man does not bend his head for the yoke that civilized man bears without a murmur" (3: 181). There is then no basis in natural, psychological fact for the master-slave relationship. Nor is paternity a natural-right basis for government. Will and judgment had in fact to come before the family, given man's sense of liberty, of natural separateness. Collective recognition established the authority of the father: "An individual was not recognized as the father of several individuals until they remained assembled around him" (3: 182). A father, too, has no authority except in terms of his utility to his children. This hold soon passes as they grow strong enough to fend for themselves, to exercise their own liberty of feeling and action.

Before government can be explained, the pseudolegitimate collective will of the fifth stage must be assumed operative, ready through agreement to create an executive force. This kind of a transfer of responsibility can be tested and found valid both by the facts of history and by the standard of right. Man, formerly a private being, has been transformed into a citizen, a part of the collectivity. How, then, do kings or magistrates come into existence? Such a government can not derive simply from natural human will, but must derive artificially from the will of the congregation. Such a willful creation is a hypothetically necessary fact. This most probable sequence of events for Rousseau revolves around the principle of inconvenience. The pledge by all members of the group to observe the agreed-upon general conventions did not work well enough. Lawbreakers easily avoided punishment, so that the newly established law was meaningless: "Inconveniences and disorders had to multiply continually for men to think finally of confiding to individuals the dangerous trust of public authority" (3: 180).

This fact is consistent, too, with right or the insight gained from an overview of all of man's evolution. The sanction again, as in the formation of society, cannot be *bonté naturelle*, as so many scholars have maintained in discussing this aspect of Rousseau's theory. Animal amorality, instinctive behavior, which means freedom from any original flaw, would permit man to be independent of any sanction higher than the product of the human wills in congregation. It follows that the divine sanction or grace which moves from God to ruler, by-passing the people, is no longer justified on the grounds of evil in the individual wills. But all of the wills need not have *bonté* or the equivalence of grace. The operative principle is the collectivity which derived its sanction, not from *bonté*, damaged through intellect, but from the freedom of each individual will, whether good or corrupt.

Unanimity makes the laws valid, including the law to create a government. Law is the correct word here, for although Rousseau uses the term contract — "I limit myself in following common opinion to consider here the establishment of the Body Politic as a true contract between the people and the chiefs it chooses for itself" (3: 184) — this is in no way a contract of submission, as Derathé would have it (3: 1355). The theory of a contract by which one would oblige only one of the parties, a contract of submission "which would only be to the detriment of the one who binds himself," and in favor of an absolute master, is contrary to liberty, "the most noble of man's faculties" (3: 183), liberty of the parties involved and of their descendants. Life and freedom are the "essential gifts of nature" (3: 184). The contract to provide an executive has to subsume the initial social contract and its higher ends, according to the words of the inventor: "In a word, instead of turning our forces against one another, let us gather them into one supreme power which governs us according to wise laws, protects and defends all of the members of the association, repulses common enemies, and maintains us in an eternal concord" (3: 177).

Just as history's social contract has its share of legitimacy which keeps it strong in spite of the element of hoax, which permits it for a time to endure, so this second contract has powerful forces for legitimacy, is in fact a part of the law that all, including the government, agree to obey: "I limit myself... to consider here the establishment of the body politic as a true contract... a contract by which the two parties obligate themselves to observe laws which are stipulated in it and which form the bonds of their union. The people, having on the subject of social relations united all its wills into a single will, all of the articles on which this will is explicit become so many fundamental laws obligating all of the members of the State without exception, and one of these laws provides for the choice and power of the magistrates charged with watching over the execution of the other laws" (3: 185). The government even in this passage is an agent of the will which established the laws in the first place: "This power extends to everything that can maintain the constitution, without going so far as to change it." The prince is obliged to "use the power confided in him only according to the intention of the constituents ... to prefer on all occasions the public utility to his own interest" (3: 185). The people is obliged not to the government but to the laws which the government must enforce, that is, the fundamental laws.

This legitimacy always within the context of history does not mean there are no abuses. Legitimacy in establishing government, as in establishing society itself, means that the institution is created by agreement. The parties may agree to too much or too little or to the wrong things. They may obscure the line between sovereign and executive, so that inequality will appear and grow in direct contradiction to the legitimizing principle of liberty. But by the nature of the act there is a degree of legitimacy which alone permits the nation to continue to survive. Implicitly in every civil society and its government, according to Rousseau, there is an element of legitimacy. Through transformations of liberty as power, as happiness, as pursuit of shelter, there is a link to natural liberty which makes the hold of government more certain, more insidious: "It therefore appears certain to me not only that governments did not begin by arbitrary power, which is only their corruption, their extreme limit which finally returns them to the sole law of the strongest, for which they were originally the remedy, but also that even if they had begun thus, this power, being by its nature illegitimate, could not have served as a foundation for the rights of society, nor consequently for instituted inequality" (3: 184). Society and government both presuppose legitimacy, laws with the principle of unanimity behind them. If arbitrariness or force prevails, there is no lasting civil society and government. The strength of civil society and government is proportionate to the degree of their legitimacy or the involvement of all of the wills.

There is a union of nature and history, of right and fact in Rousseau's effort to show the problem of creating a new artificial standard, legitimacy, the measure of every society and of every government. *Bonté* has been largely inoperative in man, who has passed from amorality to immorality during the course of history. It may be used in the doctrine of the theorist only to negate the doctrine of original sin. On the other hand, the doctrine and habit of liberty, made possible by the notion of original *bonté*, remains active although modified in history, both in fact and in right. Liberty, in other words, is preserved, if unwittingly, within the institutions of history in the form of a partial legitimacy, even if this legitimacy is appreciated at the intellectual level only in Rousseau's hindsight: "He [barbarous man] prefers the most stormy liberty to tranquil subjection" (3: 181).

The point for Rousseau in formulating his civil standard of legitimacy is not to repudiate history but rather to show that civil institutions without a rudimentary basis in right, congruous with both nature and history, could not have been established, could not even for a short time have replaced the right of the strongest or the state of war. Legitimacy is not above necessity and history, is not locked in nature as origin. A degree of legitimacy existed without the true legislator as natural genius and without the developed sense of responsibility of the true citizen. In the *Second discours* legitimacy in both society and government evolves realistically within the context of necessity and explains the power of an imperfect instrument to perpetuate the status of powerful and weak, rich and poor. Legitimacy is inextricably wed to necessity, curbs man's inclination to remain politically unobliged, unbound, and empowers him to have in unequal amounts all of the things beyond the state of nature that he has learned to need. This miring of the natural standard precludes any oversimplified treatment of the problem of society and government by dichotomy — nature versus history. It assumes a standard growing in complexity of meaning and in number of devices as nature adjusts to and is transformed by history. Natural liberty has been reexpressed in new shapes — in the individual pursuit of well-being, the sheltering family within a tribal community, the resistance to quantitative expressions of ego or to force and wealth, and finally in civil society's pseudolegitimacy, which is always overshadowed by an atmosphere of ambition and continuing greed.

Legitimacy as an unplanned part of history lacks permanence, since the political system without true statecraft must continue to evolve according to the dictates of necessity. Following upon pseudolegitimacy is a seventh stage in which the pursuit of happiness, goods, and prestige preoccupy men, distract them, keep them from forming the civic sense needed to preserve their liberty: "The most adroit politician would never succeed in subjecting men who wanted only to be free, but inequality spreads without difficulty among ambitious and cowardly souls, always ready to run the risks of fortune and to dominate or serve almost with indifference, according to whether inequality becomes favorable or adverse to them" (3: 188). Blinded by the goal of status, men are more interested in winning petty victories over one another than in resisting the chains with which the government gradually binds the entire populace (3: 187). The positive principle lacking in this stage is responsibility. Legitimacy implied the active participation of each citizen in the expression of community will, whereas the government knows only policies of oppression: "One would see oppression increase continually without the oppressed ever being able to know what its limit would be, or what legitimate means would be left them to stop it. One would see the rights of citizens and national liberties gradually die, and the demands of the weak treated as seditious murmuring" (3: 190).

The final civil stage, calling to mind the final precivil stage of destruction and war, is a period during which nations designed to protect the individual are destroyed from within and by each other. Differences in wealth, rank, power, and talent increase. Pressures from other states become the excuse for reducing the rights of the citizens. The ruler ceases completely to be a creature of art, dependent on an equally artificial collectivity; he assumes the role of a private person, and in short imposes the right of the strongest on his subjects. Just as before, men, by nature's feeling for liberty and history's continuing pursuit of independence, demanded union and government on a basis of unanimous agreement, an act destructive in intent of the possibility of any natural self holding authority, so now the same feeling and habit destroy an authority posing as collective will and government but which indeed has proved to be, not law, but the will of a private master and his passions. The principles sustaining the reign of justice have vanished: "It is here that everything is brought back to the sole law of the strongest, and as a result to a new state of nature different from the one with which we began, in that the first was the natural state in its purity, and this last one is the fruit of excessive corruption" (3: 191).

With the disappearance of legitimacy, the bonds of society have withered away: "The uprising which finally strangles or dethrones a sultan is as lawful an act as those acts by which he the day before disposed of the lives and goods of his subjects. Force alone maintained him, force alone overthrows him: everything thus happens according to the natural order" (3: 191). There is deep significance in the expression "excès de corruption," excessive corruption, for it means that the societies of history cannot abandon legitimacy completely and continue to survive. History produces nations in varyings degrees of legitimacy. History then is not completely evil; it retains in fact principles which generate opposition to sheer force. Those who make Rousseau condemn or reject history attribute to him too unrealistic a stance. Only if liberty must be destroyed can history be condemned by right, whereas history's revolution proves the indestructibility of liberty, the weakness of illegitimate regimes, the need for legitimate ones

Since this cycle from nature to civil society and revolution has usually been regarded as a negation pronounced upon history, the glimmer of hope offered by Rousseau that man may return to legitimacy (3: 187) appears to negate the negation in either of two senses: as a law of history, a determinism which will offer new and possibly better cycles; or as the reward of virtue, according to a kind of religious pattern, the granting of salvation to those few who have resisted corruption. But the emphasis of scholars has always been on Rousseau's general pessimism concerning man's fate, because essentially for him, according to this interpretation, history is degradation (3: lxviii). These alternatives, however, do not cover all of Rousseau's intent. They are drawn more from the rhetoric of the *Discours* than from its principles.

The chain of Rousesau's substantive reasoning shows that nature and history are not incompatible. If the state of nature is a standard by which to measure history, it is also much more than that. Nature as the habit and love of freedom, as potential perfectibility, has entered into history and been transformed in its temporal course, not inevitably for evil but often for good. This process includes in the narrator's vision the following justifiable steps: 1) a search for well-being; 2) family contentment within the local community; 3) resistance to the right of the strongest; 4) a legitimate social contract and government, in spite of the unwitting gullibility which accompany them; 5) responsible citizenship rather than the pursuit of prestige; and 6) the right to revolution in the name of liberty, of legitimacy, of the more perfect social instrument men may possibly forge. Liberty, the standard of the natural state, has been complemented by the civil standard of legitimacy, which was originated by man's perfectibility within the context of history itself. Salvation need not be gained only through a possibly new deterministic cycle or through withdrawal by the virtuous few to the margins of society, but may come through an approach more consistent with the *Premier discours* and the movement of the *Second*, through the intervention of science and art: "by clearing the area and removing all of the old materials, as Lycurgus did in Sparta, in order to build afterward a good edifice" (3: 180). The will to revolution may be followed by the will to lawgiving, with statecraft heading the tree of science and art.

Revolution and a new order do not necessarily imply freedom of will in the traditional sense of being able to fix on a standard higher than the self, regardless of whether this control is personally and immediately advantageous or harmful. It is essential to return to Rousseau's use of the term freedom of will in the *Second discours*. In the state of nature, freedom of will distinguished man from the instinctive patterns of other animals. He could learn from them, acquire their skills, and unwittingly pursue new needs and desires, often to his own disadvantage. At first, a static environment saved him by limiting the consequences of his choices. Once environment was set in motion, perfectibility was brought into play, and freedom meant no more than the option between different problem-solving means, with the choice usually imposed by necessity. For example, man could remain in the state of war and survive by plunder, or he could invent the contract. Circumstance

— the violent threat to life and goods, the ignorance of some, the greed of others — really decided the issue. But once the cycle is complete and man has full knowledge of his predicament, freedom of will is no longer blind perfectibility. Rather than deciding in ignorance, reacting to necessity's stimuli, he has knowledge.

At the end of the *Second discours,* Rousseau can see, because of his interpretation of history, the solution to "an infinite number of ethical and political problems which the philosophers cannot solve" (3: 192). The *philosophes* have taken civilization for granted, have not questioned its meaning, or have exalted it, whereas Rousseau has shown its gradual transformation of values over long periods of time, has got outside of history, has reduced it through his science and art from the level of epic or tragic glory and patriotism to a conflict of principles. Man has changed morally. There are ages of freedom, but predominantly ages of slavery. A man like Cato may be born too late, be an object of astonishment to his fellowmen, whereas in an earlier age he would have governed them and been truly appreciated (3: 192). But the vision of one man with insights not of his age may be worth more than all contemporary opinion, customs, and policy. Such a man, Rousseau, the reader perhaps, not only can see, as in the *Premier discours,* the need for a better order, but may be able to explain how the wrong order came about. "He will explain" through the model of the *Second* how man passed from nature's man to man's man, but just as important from legitimacy to enslavement (3: 192-93). Freedom of will has become enlightened perfectibility. If man understands the problem of civilization, his faculty for improvement will at some time lead him knowingly to follow the positive but muted, nonrhetorical aims set forth in the discourse; he will direct his strivings toward a citizen-oriented national union and government.

Not until the last pages of the discourse is the deepest meaning of this goal — responsible order — made clear. Liberty is again exalted in the contrast of savage man and falsely civilized man: "The former breathes only repose and freedom.... the citizen, always active, sweats, is agitated, is endlessly tormented" (3: 192). But Rousseau's glorification of liberty now is in a different context. It offers hope, since the faculty of perfectibility has been linked to legitimacy rather than to happiness and power. The problem has become the resolution of this paradox: "What represents the supreme happiness of one [civilized man] would reduce the other to despair" (3: 192). The resolution must come through reconciliation of nature and civilization, for the literal absence of pressure enjoyed by the simple savage can no longer be the sole object. The means for change must be the political rehabilitation of the self: "Such is in fact the true cause of all these differences: the savage lives within himself, sociable man... knows how to live only in the opinion of others" (3: 193). Man must overcome "the spirit of society and the inequality it engenders" and again find his "natural inclinations."

The problem is the inequality that society fosters, not the inequality that is in nature. Writers in the past have insisted only upon inequality in the distribution of goods, and Rousseau indeed gives this serious attention in attacking the situation in which "a handful of men are stuffed with superfluities, while the starving multitude lacks the necessities for existence" (3: 194). But he has something much more basic in mind. He is denying any ready-made justification of the fact of social inequality, any justification based on the assumption that such a result is proof of superiority of intellect in the rich, an invalid principle "that would be like asking... if strength of body or mind, wisdom or virtue, are always found in the same individuals in proportion to power or wealth" (3: 131-32). Rousseau is not, on the other hand, discrediting any theory that bases moral status on true native physical or intellectual ability (3: 1301). He has assumed differences among individuals all the way. Only their isolation makes such variation unimportant in the state of nature. There each man belongs to himself alone.

At the close of the discourse Rousseau defines liberty, which is legitimacy in the civil context, more precisely in terms of preserving natural inequality, "physical inequality," this is a better measure of justice than evenhandedness alone, which would mean partially neglecting nature when creating the new civil instrument. Art must follow closely the pattern set by nature (3: 194). Rousseau has not slipped this principle in "somewhat surreptitiously" at the end (3: lxix). He has contended throughout the discourse that a preponderance of wealth in the hands of some has hidden the natural ability of others, that the quantitative criterion has replaced the qualitative criterion of the isolated individual, his right not only to be and become a citizen through the wisdom of science and art, but to realize fully his personal self within civil society. The situation must not be allowed to exist in which "a child may command an old man," "an imbecile lead a wise man" (3: 194). The real problem of inequality can be solved only by giving to each self protection against the quantitative impact of each other individual self, with the effect that no more than natural inequality can survive: "It follows from this study that inequality, being almost null in the state of nature, gathers its force and growth from the development of our faculties and the progress of the human mind and finally becomes stable and legitimate by the establishment of property and laws. It follows further that moral inequality, authorized by positive right alone, is contrary to natural right whenever it does not corrrespond in the same proportion to physical inequality" (3: 194).

This just proportion has two results. The first is that it prevents the excessive influence of the wealth and power of any one individual or group of individuals on the congregation. The second is that this precisely measured inequality encourages the reappearance of nature. The basic meaning of injustice is that inequality of wealth and power makes men blind to natural capacities. A natural genius, a Descartes, a Newton, a Bacon (*Premier discours*), may not be allowed to express his abilities, his vision, may be bound by an order based on mediocrity. The witty may in such a society outshine the great talent. Love of self, *amour de soi*, the instinct to self-preservation, to be oneself to the fullest capacity and in one's own terms, is lost unless legitimacy provides conditions in which a multiplicity of natural endowments can be expressed and can replace the usual deforming attention to greed, shrewdness, and duplicity in the struggle for wealth and power.

If the state of nature alone is the standard, a state in which no comparison is possible, hence no leveling in native physical or intellectual force is practically recognized, then the need for equating moral force to natural endowment is not visible. This problem appears only when the state of nature is compared to the two principal states of history, natural society and civil society. In the state of nature, native endowment cannot be suppressed nor the danger of its loss anticipated. In isolation, the self is all-important. In natural society, with the rise in wealth of the few, the threat to native capacity is for the first time visible; yet men can flee, avoid those areas controlled by the powerful. It is only in civil society that the influence of the few can become binding on conscience through agreement, then can be turned from such legitimacy to institutional usurpation, so that the individual, regardless of natural endowment, even the fool, may be placed in a position to command. It follows that only the complete nature-history model, the conjectural standard of man's evolution, can show the need for refining legitimacy to include individual gifts. Rousseau's polemic condemns only one part of history, man's progressive exteriorization of the self. The positive effect of his rhetoric is to make man scrutinize his evolution, to make him find, as has Rousseau, the measures which encourage and protect natural capacity, not as a past condition but as a planned future which will guarantee the fulfillment of each individual self.

In its deepest sense, the *Second discours* is a search for the environmental stages which have led man to self-awareness. In the first state of nature man is oblivious to his own individuality, the existence of others, the passage of time, his surroundings. Each self passively fills the universe with its need without any dividing line between the ego and the sheltering environment. The body moves and the senses function, but the mind does not yet draw conscious information from experience. Without knowing it, the individual is absolutely free, uncompromised by pressure from physical events or from other men or by a universal defect inherent in human nature. In a second stage he expresses self in response to upsetting events caused by an environment in motion. Dimensions of time and space slowly enter his consciousness. He embraces his surroundings actively in an elementary problem-solving sense. Exposure makes him distinguish between self and the objects and other men he encounters. A goal narrower than total freedom begins to orient his activity. To find well-being, he engages in random cooperation with other men. This positive benefit develops into the need for family life within a sheltering tribal community. Comfort, security, respect for beauty, strength, and happiness further obsess him with life as knowing, as acquiring, as expansion into the exterior universe, the "hors de soi." Yet the still relatively innocent and free happiness of this third stage, the golden age, holds a threat, the destruction of self, for each man in a group represents pressure on another, competition for nature's riches. In a fourth stage, men are characterized by tooth-and-nail agressiveness, flight from one another, the search for security in the power they can gain by sweat and force. Each self has become its material wealth. Its ambition wants to possess the entire earth. The only positive aspect of this behavior is the successful resistance each man makes to the enslavement of his self by the might of another.

Since raw force, the right of the strongest and the richest, is not an efficient and durable instrument for the protection of life and possessions, the self, now subordinate to the notion of interest, replaces force by right, defined as a common good each man's will can accept and support. In hindsight, this agreement can be seen to be legitimacy, the whole embracing all of the parts, changing itself to accommodate the agreed-upon needs of the parts. The self which was first natural freedom and isolation and second an independently striving instrument wedded to necessity's challenge has now become a mere fragment of will burdened with the responsibility of discovering, understanding, and maintaining the integrity of a collective will, the safeguard of civil freedom. But the meaning and value of this revolutionary move from natural, individual oneness to artificial, legitimate oneness is only imperfectly seen. The shrewd still think in terms of personal gain, still manipulate national power to their own advantage, while the majority seek merely happiness and status within the framework of ambition set by the leaders. Each self has attained the status of an agreeing will, the psychological component essential to legitimacy, but the common interest, the substance of justice, evoked more than known, veils the practice of usurpation. Because civil society is enclosed, both by laws binding conscience and by its geographical frontiers, no man can escape an inevitable division by class, on the one hand masters and on the other slaves.

Since civil society without legitimacy is in effect no more than nature as the right of the strongest, since the natural criterion for manhood is liberty, self has become for the moment exclusively the despot, a ruler above the law who nevertheless uses the law to bind other men and thus places the entire might of the nation behind his private will. In the face of this subversion, each enslaved self again finds natural liberty and regroups into a new collective will — the fury of the mob, "the uprising which ends by strangling or dethroning a sultan" (3: 191). This act, representing not legitimacy but again the right of the strongest, since its aim is not law but the destruction of the master, is "as lawful as those acts by which he [the sultan] disposed the day before of the lives and the possessions of his subjects." Imprudence in having misused and misunderstood the liberating force of collective responsibility is at the basis of these disorders: "Whatever may be the outcome of these short and frequent revolutions, no one can complain of the injustice of another, but only of his own imprudence or of his misfortune" (3: 191).

But suffering and misery are not the final expression of self. The nature-history model created by Rousseau's thought experiment and dedicated to Genevans, to Athenians, to mankind "from whatever country you may come" (3: 133), prepares an emergent self that knows man's predicament and the force of nature, necessity, and art. It offers a new goal which has been implicit at every stage, the implementation through statecraft of a deeper legitimacy than that found in history. Gross inequality in wealth and power, which brings inequality before the law, is to be eliminated. The segment of history's line from civil union to revolution proves this to have been Rousseau's intention. Near equality in wealth, permitting equality before the law, also favors the appearance of natural capacity, of natural inequality, since wealth and its trappings of sophistication no longer take precedence over the self as individual quality. Moral inequality, the greater influence exerted by one person than by another, can be justified only if it is proportionate to natural endowment. The farmer, the merchant, the artisan, the common laborer will find their place. By law a legislator, a prince may be required to be a man of great natural gifts rather than an office-holder by heredity or by venality. In this sense man has moved from a conformist pose exterior to self back to a life seated in the inner resources of his being.

CHAPTER IV

THE ENLIGHTENED PRINCE

LESS KNOWN THAN THE FIRST and second discourses, the *Discours sur l'économie politique* [1] nevertheless represents a vital link in Rousseau's reasoning, for it attempts to define precisely the legitimate role of government in the state. Its first section establishes that administration must be according to law. The second deals with the government's duties with respect to the liberty, security, and education of citizens. In the third and final section Rousseau describes some of his views on public finance. The work was first published as an article of the *Encyclopédie*, volume 5, November 1755, when Rousseau was still in friendly collaboration with Diderot, chief editor of that vast instrument of information and philosophic propaganda.

The *Economie politique* has for a long time stood in uncertain relationship to the *Second discours* and to the *Contrat social*. In the absence of conclusive information, some scholars have placed its period of composition before the *Second discours* (Pléiade, 3: lxxiii). One of their reasons is the *Economie*'s description of society in such lines as these: "The body politic, taken individually may be considered as an organized, living body, similar to that of man" (3: 244). This view, it has been argued, taken literally, is organic and must therefore antedate the more mechanistic attitudes of the *Second discours* about society's evolution. It relates also more closely to the thesis that civil society has clear antecedents in nature. A second and related reason usually offered is

---

[1] All citations for this work, unless otherwise indicated, are from the Pléiade edition of the *Œuvres complètes*, vol. 3.

that the *Economie politique* revives the traditional notion that man is naturally sociable, since, rather than stressing the barriers which nature places between man and society, Rousseau gives an account of sociability in terms of cooperation resulting from mutual needs (3: lxxiv). The majority of scholars, however, place the composition of the *Economie politique* after that of the *Second discours*, and most relate its message more closely to the *Contrat social* than to the *Second discours* on the ground that the latter deals with the state of nature and the "origin of government," whereas the *Economie* stresses the functions of government. According to this view, the *Second discours* "serves as prelude to the *Contrat social*," the *Economie politique* being "an extract from it" (3: lxxiv).

Both those who would make the *Economie* antedate the *Second discours* and those who would link it closely to the *Contrat social* separate the *Economie* in aim and content from the *Discours*. They neglect the complementary goals, the theories and maxims which unite these two works, and which indicate an emphasis different from that of the *Contrat*. For me, the *Economie politique* represents Rousseau's solution to problems raised in the *Second discours* and must be seen as the positive counterargument to the often negative thrust of that study. Its period of conception and composition was probably close to that of the *Second discours*.

Before examining these very basic relationships, it is necessary to take another look at the arguments used to separate the *Second discours* from the *Economie*. The passage of the *Economie* which refers to society as an organism may be seen in its context as a convenient device for showing the subordination of one part of the state to another: "The sovereign power represents the head; the laws and customs are the brain" (3: 244). The statement is hardly an earlier, naive expression of Rousseau's political thought. The point being made is that government is the agent of the general good and the general will. The insistence is not on the idea that the nation is a living organism, but rather for the most part on the artificial, inhuman structure of the state, the objective, passionless nature of its soul.

Similarly, the argument for the influence of traditional themes about the natural origins of society cannot be taken seriously. In both the *Economie* and the *Second discours*, sociability is very definitely derived from mutual needs, but these are acquired rather than natural needs. The difference is that the *Second discours* condemns in polemical tones and by temporal distance the almost inevitable movement toward cooperation, whereas the *Economie* takes for granted man's entrance into society and seeks to make the best of the situation already lamented in the *Second discours*. The *Economie*, furthermore, explicitly rejects organic and naturalistic views. It stresses that the moral whole which is the state ("the body politic is therefore also a moral being which has a will" [3: 245]) has been discovered by intellect and created by art. The state, unlike the family, is not natural: "But how could the government of the state be similar to the family's leadership, the foundation of which is so different? The father being physically stronger than his children, paternal authority, so long as they need his help, may correctly be said to be established by nature." It is in contrast to the natural family that Rousseau describes "political authority purely arbitrary in its institution," founded only "on conventions" (3: 241), with a magistrate who governs only "by virtue of the laws" (3: 242).

The arguments to show that the *Economie* is closer to the *Contrat social* than to the *Second discours* do not hold up well, either. As Robert Derathé has effectively outlined them, their substance is that the *Economie* has two innovations which are not in the *Second discours* but which are in the *Contrat*: "the distinction between sovereignty and government, as well as the concept of the general will, therefore the essential theses of Rousseau's political thought" (3: lxxiv). For me, however, it is very difficult to suppose that the notion of state as convention rather than nature, the distinction between sovereign and government, and the idea of the general will as sovereign had not already, as early as the *Premier discours,* become at least tacit guidelines for Rousseau's thought. The condemnation there of materialistically oriented intellect and science is universal, whether they are put to political or physical science ends, so that the state is certainly seen as a part of science's aberration, as convention, as something acquired, willed, and artificial rather than natural. The concept of a people's solidarity, although the term general will is not used, is contained in Rousseau's contrast between vigorous, conquering nations and effete, declining nations. The notion that government is not to be self-serving but is to express the national good, is present in the description of the great states of antiquity whose legislators succeeded in forming a people dedicated to the community, whose governments served the national collectivity. Sparta over Athens, young Rome over Imperial Rome — their superiority indicated a law-given cohesive force, with each individual turned toward the national center rather than inward toward personal gain alone.

The distinction between sovereign and government, the idea of a general will are much more than implicit in the *Second discours*. The people, Rousseau says, has joined "all of its wills into a single one" in order to establish "fundamental laws which obligate all the members of the state without exception" (3: 185). This legislating will which establishes laws for the whole group is made distinct from the government, which is no more than one of the institutions provided in law by the will of the group: "and one of which [laws] regulates the choice and power of magistrates charged with watching over the execution of the others.... The magistrate... binds himself to use the power confided to him only according to the intention of the constituents" (3: 185).

Additional attitudes, more specific than Rousseau's general views on nature, convention, and sovereignty join the *Economie* to the *Second discours*. These criteria, I hope, will provide new insight into the organizing principles and the meaning of both works.

First, in the context of the *Second discours* the immediate and most general problem is a viable relationship between government and people. Political history, according to Rousseau, has been largely made up of corrupt leaders and dupish followers. The prime movers in establishing civil government are the rich. It is they who feel most strongly the need for laws. Through their shrewdness they make association seem beneficial to all men, rich and poor, so that unanimity, the acceptable basis for union, is attained. It is the rich who as princes or magistrates later promote corruption, and the people are vulnerable to their seduction: "The magistrate could not usurp illegitimate power without creating servile deputies to whom he is forced to yield some part of it." Everyone soon becomes an accomplice of the government in that each because of ambition becomes less concerned about his own dependence than about his desire to make others dependent on himself, all men "looking more below than above themselves" (3: 188). The few who initiated the association thus become despots and later, as the result of their destruction of liberty, must face revolution by the people. The passive, docile, servile citizenry becomes the violent mob which restores the state of war.

In this interplay between government and people, which drives man from the natural state of war to the civil state of war and anarchy, both predominant actors, prince and subject, have been submerged in history. Legitimacy appeared and was lost without man recognizing its value, except in terms of narrow self-interest and greed: "The rich, pressed by necessity, finally conceived the most deliberate project which has ever entered the human mind; it was to use in his favor the very forces of those who attacked him, to turn his adversaries into his defenders" (3: 177). The benefits to be derived by "a few ambitious men" in this way subjected the human race "to work, servitude, and misery" (3: 178). Nevertheless, the first government, it will be remembered, was not arbitrary: "Governments did not begin by arbitrary authority, which is only their corruption, the extreme limit, which finally brings them back to the sole law of the strongest for which they were originally the remedy" (3: 184). The most vexing lesson of the *Second discours* is, therefore, not that those who initiate and benefit most by legitimacy are the same as those who corrupt that principle, but that chains of necessity have made this inevitable, that the vices which made social institutions necessary also make abuse of them part of the flow of history: "Any government which, without being corrupted or changed, moved always exactly according to the goals of its institution, would have been instituted unnecessarily ... a country in which no one eluded the laws and abused the magistracy would need neither magistracy nor laws" (3: 188).

In other words, social institutions in spite of their establishment by art and their original soundness have remained a part of history's grinding necessity. The inventors of the state have treated the nation as if it were their family, subject to their personal authority and ambition: "The ambition of the leading men took advantage of these circumstances to perpetuate governmental posts in their families: the people, already accustomed to dependence, repose, and the comforts of life, and already incapable of breaking its chains, consented to let its servitude increase in order to assure its tranquility" (3: 187). The need for permanence was felt: "How necessary it was to public repose that divine will intervene to give sovereign authority a sacred and inviolable character which would take from the subjects the fatal right to do away with it" (3: 186). But, as these words show, inviolability was to come from outside as *deux ex machina*. It was not understood that the nation held within itself the seeds of permanence. Treated as if it were a natural association, the nation grew and died as if it were a family. The tone of the *Discours* in describing the results of this corruption of political institutions by greed, desire, ambition, and hate indicates that this humanization should if possible have been avoided.

If governments must lead and people must follow, if states are not to be treated as personal possessions, subject to the passions, whether love or lust of their rulers, it follows that the concept of the leader must change. An idea often repeated in the *Second discours* is that government must correct itself, that its real interest is to form its people for liberty, to diminish inequality so that it cannot compromise liberty. By its dedication to the *Souverains Seigneurs* of the Republic of Geneva, the *Discours* is associated with a plea for responsible leadership: "I would have fled, as necessarily ill-governed, a republic in which the people, believing it could do without its magistrates or only leave them a precarious authority, would imprudently have kept for itself the administration of civil affairs and the execution of its own laws" (3: 114). Rousseau stresses in the "Dédicace" the possibility of good government, of the election from year to year of the most capable and most honest citizens to "administer justice and govern the state" (3: 114). The way out of situations of inequality and its evils is expressed in terms of government and its influence over people, not in terms of initiative from a new kind of man (Emile), from a model local community (Clarens in the *Nouvelle Héloïse*), or from the power of the general will itself *(Contrat social)*. This last work usually expresses distrust of government, the need to curb its corporate will. In the *Second discours*, along with necessity's course, which means enslavement will continue "until new revolutions dissolve the government altogether or bring it closer to a legitimate institution" (3: 187), is the alternative that the people could have been molded into free citizens. This civil liberty must come about through the action of government, through its education of the people for citizenship, as occurred in Sparta, an exception to the abuses which usually befall government and people because that nation had leaders who transformed rather than simply restrained men: "except for Sparta alone, in which the law watched principally over the education of children, and in which Lycurgus established mores which almost made it unnecessary to add laws; laws, in general less strong than passions, contain men without changing them" (3: 188). In the atmosphere of flux and decline which pervades the *Second discours,* the allusion to Lycurgus does little more than suggest the new kind of leader needed to give stability to the nation, but it is clear that rather than destroy liberty, the ideal for government would be to create men with Spartanlike integrity: "The cleverest politician would never succeed in subjecting men who wanted only to be free; but inequality spreads without difficulty among cowardly and ambitious souls" (3: 188).

Liberty is legitimacy, subordination of the prince to the laws agreed upon by the people in assembly. The thrust of the argument of the *Second discours* is that rulers prepare their downfall by placing themselves above the law. Historically governments have failed to value the precious instrument at their fingertips, to understand that in legitimacy is their strength: "Such a constitution ... must have appeared all the better, because those who were charged with watching over its preservation were themselves the most interested in it; for the magistracy and its rights, being established only on fundamental laws, as soon as they were destroyed the magistrates would cease to be legitimate, the people would no longer be bound to obey them" (3: 185). But Rousseau's emphasis is on degeneration of the concept, and the conclusion is a warning to government. The prince who first promoted civil association in order to avoid the conditions of the right of the strongest is eventually totally dispossessed because of his illogical persistence in that right for himself alone: "The contract of government is so totally dissolved by despotism, that the despot is master only as long as he is the strongest, and as soon as he can be driven out, he has no basis for protesting against violence" (3: 191). The basic theme is the advantage to government of legitimacy, adherence to the contract between ruler and people, the execution of law always in the spirit of the more fundamental social contract grounded in the national good and will.

The *Second discours*, in short, stresses the domestic problems of the nation, namely, the predominant yet corrupting force of government in national life; the continuing reign of necessity rather than statecraft in political matters; and man's failure to recognize in the nation a completely new order of existence, a legitimate civil order, with the result that princes have regularly subverted that order, have mistaken the nation for their family, have tried to possess the state as if they were at the same time both legalized and natural masters despotically independent of the will of the people.

A final problem to which Rousseau gives less attention in the *Second discours* is international relations. The formation of one nation produces rival nations, each with its own laws, interests, and blindness to the needs of other states. This "division of the human race into different societies" (3: 179) brings "national wars, battles, murders, reprisals, which make nature tremble and shock reason" (3: 178-79). A void exists beyond the frontiers of each nation. The rise of sovereignty and citizenship in history has meant a loss in man's emotional expansiveness: "Natural commiseration which, losing in relationships between societies almost all the force it had between men, no longer dwells in anyone except a few great cosmopolitan souls who surmount the imaginary barriers which separate nations and who, like the sovereign Being who created them, embrace the whole human race in their benevolence" (3: 178).

In the *Economie politique*, though not in the *Contrat social*, the message is equally clear that the way to meet these problems within the state must be through government. The *Economie* reads as if were the answer to the problems raised by the *Second discours*. A point-by-point parallel can be established between the steps to despotism I have derived from the argument of the *Second discours* and the clarifications of them made in the *Economie*, first on the level of principle and then on the level of specific practice.

A central if tacit conflict of the *Second discours* is that between man's intellect and his ignorance. Civil society is a product of art, of instrumental reason, an agreement among wills producing a new collective being. Yet such inventiveness is accompanied by man's unawareness of the significance of this new entity, of the demands it makes on him if revolution is to be avoided and the promise of national life fulfilled. The *Economie* analyzes the problem. Domestic, household economy must not be confused with public economy. The nation is not an analogue of the family (3: 241). Rousseau underlines the fallacies in this belief. No matter how large the family grows, even to the extent of a vast empire, the ruler of such a "family" would still be an ordinary man with "the faculties of the father" (3: 241). A real father has the superiority of his physical force over his children, whereas in the nation men for the most part are physically equal. The ruler, if no more than head of a family, could not consistently maintain his sway. A father has natural love for his children, which makes him want to fulfill his duties toward them. The leaders of the state have no such feeling and serve their function to the extent that the people "have a right to require them to do so" (3: 242). A father is the source of his children's property. They can inherit only through him. In the nation, each member brings his own possessions, by agreement turns possessions into property, and then establishes government only in order to "guarantee private property, which is antecedent" to administration (3: 242). If the members of the family work it is to increase the property of the father in anticipation of a later inheritance. When the members of the state work for the state or contribute to it, the purpose is to create public funds with which to keep all of the citizens in peace and abundance, and thus to advance the collective enterprise.

For Rousseau the sense of all these contrasting characteristics is that natural cycles of birth, maturity, death, renewal, and extinction belong to the family, whereas permanence, endless life should theoretically and practically be the nature of the state. The state created through art can be free of necessity's grasp, can avoid the growth and decadence of family existence and of nations conceived as mere families, can resist the cycle of rise and decline found in the *Second discours*. Life for the state must be mechanistic perfection and equilibrium, involving replacement of parts without alteration of the substance, a state of permament youth, as, for example, maintenance of the Roman Republic in its days of vigor. The goal is complete planning and control, so that the nation may "endure forever in the same condition... do no more than maintain itself... and it can easily be proved that any increase does it more harm than good" (3: 242).

This claim to the transcendence of necessity by statecraft has a corollary. The family has a natural hierarchy. Only one person can efficiently lead such a unit, and that must be the father. The mother by her condition, which includes periods of childbearing, is at times inactive. Her conduct as bearer of children must be subject to censure. It is the father, too, who must provide for his children's wants and for the well-being of his servants. If these arguments seem unconvincing, Rousseau's overall logic is precise, for he means that a family leader has a kind of natural suitableness for his task or is eliminated by the stress of events, replaced by another. The same may not be said of the public leader. He is not removed by any such pressure. A child or an idiot may be in command. He may be motivated by purely selfish interests, may follow during his lifetime the behavior described in the *Second discours*.

But if the nation is a product of art, it follows that the ruler cannot be allowed to be natural, a simple creature of passion. The ruler must be as artificial as the nation of which he is the leader. His profile must be established by law. No family, human, or sentimental consideration must be allowed to obscure the demands upon him: "To do right, the first [the father] has only to consult his heart; the other becomes a traitor the moment he listens to his: even his reason must be suspect to him, and he must follow no other rule than the public good, which is the law" (3: 243). The laws represent the values of the state, established at the nation's institution by agreement. They are not subject to change unless change comes as a result of new agreement. The ruler must be selfless if he is to see the public need, the basic law. He must, in short, be the antitype of the too human prince of the *Second discours*.

According to the *Second discours*, such legitimacy is present at the inception of the nation as the only acceptable basis for union. Its wasting away is synonymous with decline of the state;

its absence brings revolution and a return to the state of war. The *Economie* describes the mechanics of the legitimacy which constitutes the state's permanence and the ruler's selflessness, which provides the state with artificial vitality without resorting to natural modes of life.

Legitimacy is an interrelationship and subordination of parts. If any one of the parts atrophies, the state is diminished to that extent. Perhaps the most critical relationship for government to understand is its subordination to the sovereign, the subservience of the corporate will of the leaders to the general will of the people: "Distinguish also between *public economy*, which I am to talk about and which I call government, and the supreme authority, which I call sovereignty.... The sovereign power represents the head; the laws and customs are the brain, the center for the nerves and seat of the understanding, of the will, and of the senses, for which the judges and magistrates are the organs; commerce, industry, and agriculture are the mouth and the stomach... public finances are the blood... the citizens are the body and the limbs which make the machine move, live, and work" (3: 244).

But this subordination does not mean diminishment, weakening of the governmental function, or its relative unimportance, a common but misleading interpretation of Rousseau's theory of government. Government must know its place in the chain of communication, but its function is as vital as that of the rest: "If this communication ceases, if the formal unity vanishes and the contiguous parts no longer belong to one another except by juxtaposition, the man is dead, or the state is dissolved" (3: 245). Life exists not in the sovereign, the laws, the government, the finances, or any other single part. The life of the nation is the "self common to the whole, the reciprocal sensibility and internal correspondence of all the parts" (3: 245). This complex being has the will to its own preservation and happiness, and in this sense is a moral force with a general will which represents justice: "The body politic is therefore also a moral being which has a will; and this general will, which tends always to the preservation and the well-being of the whole and of each part and is the source of the laws, is for all the members of the state, in their relation to one another and to it, the standard for what is just and unjust" (3: 245). It is therefore to the life of the whole and its will to live, not to the sovereign people alone, that the government is then ultimately dedicated. The government must act in a manner consistent with the life of a national moral being.

The description of the state as an organism must not be read out of context. Rousseau's intention can best be understood by relating the much-discussed passages just cited (3: 244-45) to the themes which have already been found to be central to the *Economie:* public economy is not similar to family economy; the king's position is not analogous to that of the father of a family; the nation is not natural but artificial, an invented thing, an instrument, a machine. These propositions represent Rousseau's controlling and prevailing attitude. But the machine is highly complicated and suggests a parallel with the human organism. The nation has a soul, its own moral life evolving in close relation to the pressures of history and geographic situation. One might call the nation an instrumental or mechanistic organism. But to avoid any suggestion that Rousseau has slipped into a doctrine holding that civil society has a natural basis, I prefer a more accurate definition implicit in his words and reasoning: the nation is a life-like machine.

The prince or government has a dual relationship to this artificial entity. With respect to its good, he is the scientist investigating the nation's existence, assuring that the mechanism is adjusted to constantly changing domestic and foreign goals. In this function he is essentially intelligence, independent and transcendent of the machine, a creative intelligence, not a mere part or cog or organ of the whole. But the prince is also in another capacity the agent of the collective being he has produced. When acting from within the nation, he does not directly obey the general good or justice as viewed from outside, but must operate through the machine's artificial civil head, that is, he must win the consent of the sovereign people, which is part of the process of executing the good. It is therefore not enough that the government have the sanction of a Platonic idea of justice or of God as supreme authority. The understanding of national good discovered scientifically by the government must have the support of the people's will before that good is executed.

The government thus has two masters. The first is the good of the whole which the prince must discover empirically for his nation by research. His action is free and unhampered in this quest except for his conscience, the obligation to prevent interference from any private or corporate interest he may have. In this domain the government has a vision which is superior to the sovereign people and encompasses all parts of the nation in order to know the whole. The second master includes both the will of the sovereign people, whose consent must be won before laws consistent with the good can be legislated, and also the laws already legislated. The latter, if they already express the good, must continue to be executed or, if they are false, may be reformed by the standard of the empirical good newly discovered by government, but they must be reformed, of course, again with the consent of the sovereign people. Execution, therefore, does not mean simply that the government is a servant. It means also that the government transcends the state to understand in the first place what its good is in order to prepare the sovereign power and the rest of the whole to assimilate the good. As the *Economie*'s reasoning continues, the rest of its evidence sustains this interpretation of Rousseau's much debated organic description of the state and the functions of the selfless prince in a context of complex political machines.

A fourth concept of the *Economie*, after national permanence, selflessness of government, and the legitimate relationship of the prince to the whole, is the myopic, local vision of each sovereign people. The closed nature of national justice is one of the reasons the government is intellectually superior to the sovereign people, less blind. Since the sovereign legislates only selfishly, sees and legislates only according to national interest, its laws no matter how perfect from a national viewpoint, are complete only in the sovereign's own terms. Only the great city of the world, which includes all nations, has comprehensive validity (3: 245). Rousseau's emphasis on this may relate, as some scholars maintain, to the cosmopolitanism of the Stoics (3: 1395), but more immediately it responds to the negative description of man's history given in the *Second discours*. The *Economie* stands as philosophic counterweight to the image already cited from the *Second discours*, that of man's degradation through the agency of the few who by instituting society replaced the precivil state of war by international wars (3: 179). Inferior, debased governments, acting in the throes of necessity, as if the nation were theirs, a family to be guided by emotional bonds, by their whim, must be turned about. They must be made to recognize, first, in the context of domestic policy, the complexity of the machine they control, its potential for permanence, and their own place in it. Secondly, in the international context, they must recognize the solipsism of each national unity.

For the people to envision a good higher than the national self-interest is to weaken the national spirit, its cohesiveness. But the government is not so bound. It is part of the national entity, can know its good, must act through the sovereign. Yet the government has also the characteristic of particularity. The ruler executes the law of the nation and applies it to individuals in specific cases. Because of this attribute, too, the government has the task of foreign policy. It enters into treaties with other nations whose effect is to heighten or diminish the state of war existing among all nations. In this way it creates a form of law not general in any context, either national or international. In the *Second discours* chaos and revolution were seen as being triggered in part by the aggressive foreign policies of despotic rulers intent on making men forget their love of liberty: "Men were seen to massacre each other by the thousands without knowing why" (3: 179); "One would see the multitude oppressed within as a result of the very precautions it had taken against what threatened it from without" (3: 190).

In contrast to this tale of disaster, the governmental practice prescribed in the *Economie* is couched within a framework of loftier principles. First, the fallacy of the nation as family warns the prince against seeing change and growth more than preservation and permanence as the pattern of national life. He avoids the dynastic orientation which can lead the nation into a policy of aggrandizement, can make him confuse "the good of the state" with "that of the leaders," can cause him to practice the "maxims ... inscribed at length in the archives of history and in the satires of Machiavelli" (3: 247). Second, the fallacy of leader as father warns him against relying on his own passionate nature as guide. Instead, he must be the incarnation of science and experience in order to know "public reason": "Thus nature has made a multitude of good fathers of families; but it is doubtful if, from the beginning of the world, human wisdom has ever made ten men capable of governing their fellowmen" (3: 244). Third, the fallacy of ruler as sovereign warns the prince against trying to make his wisdom and will the source of authority. The sovereign legislative will of the people is the test of the government's definition of good. Finally, the fallacy that the law of any one nation can be the standard of right warns the ruler that the area of international relations is complex and filled with thorns, and invites him to know a wider vision filling the void between nations described in the *Second discours* (3: 178-79).

Rousseau is realistic. He admits in the *Economie* that "the voice of the people is in fact the voice of God," but he judges that voice: "It is not impossible for a well-governed republic to wage an unjust war" (3: 246). He seeks to enable the prince to see an order of generality higher than national sovereignty:

> It is important to observe that this rule of justice, though certain with respect to all citizens, may be defective with regard to foreigners... the will of the state, though general for all of its members, is no longer general in relation to other states and their members, but becomes for them a private and individual will, which has in matters of justice a higher standard in the law of nature... for then the great city of the world becomes the body politic, for which the law of nature is always the general will, and in relation to which the different states and peoples are no more than individual members.
>
> From these same distinctions, applied to each political society and its members, flow the most universal and certain rules by which one can judge if a government is good or bad and in general evaluate the morality of all human actions. [3: 245]

A paradox is apparent in these principles. The ruler of history presented in the *Second discours* is blinded by passion, yet he is the absolute master of his people, independent of its consent until the final explosion. The ruler of the *Economie*, armed with insight, aware of the principles characterizing the modern state, is intellectually free to find the good of the nation through his science, yet is bound by the consent of the inhabitants of the state whose whole and parts are under investigation. Truth about the artificial moral being, the nation, and its good can be countermanded by the will of the people. The doctor's diagnosis may be rejected by the patient. An ignorant sovereign people, overruling the wise prince, may repeat by its initiative the patterns of the *Second discours*. To say that natural goodness in men or their natural love for liberty would prevent this result, even in a people blinded to its true needs, is untenable for Rousseau. It would mean denying the argument of the *Second discours*. To distinguish between a leader subverting a people and a people subverting itself, to say the despot can bring ruin but the collectivity cannot ruin itself, would mean that a people without truth is in its matter-of-fact existence indestructible, so long as its blind will is given free reign, a *reductio ad absurdum* which would make the *Economie* itself pointless.

Rousseau's position is, on the contrary, that the natural content of the collectivity, man, is no guarantee of permanence. The sovereign people can be wrong. It follows that the collectivity requires shaping from outside by a master craftsman who knows the principles of government. To the question "whether the magistrates belong to the people or the people to the magistrates" Rousseau may at first appear evasive. He says he prefers popular government, defined as unity of the interest and will of leader and people; but this is no evasion, for this unity is made to depend on the rights of mankind (3: 247). It is clear, then, that those "who are in fact the masters," the rulers, are to find the right through science and to assure its acceptance by the people through art. If science is order from on high, Platonic rationality or divine revelation, the ruler is unbound by any earthly will other than his own. The sanction is direct to the ruler, the representative on earth of that kind of intelligence. Rousseau, however, has placed the sanction here on earth in the very palpable, willful approval of the nation's citizenry. The ruler is still intellectual master, but his science and art must no longer be facile. They must include, first, his laborious empirical investigation of the nation's means to survival in terms of its resources and policies, and, second, an equally arduous investigation of national character in order to find the education needed to induce the collectivity to accept the truth or laws or good it requires. These two concerns will be discussed in detail in the pages which follow. But as a guidepost to my interpretation I should stress at this point that deeply embedded in Rousseau's concept of "legitimate or popular government" is an eighteenth-century version of the philosopher king as master; for if policy is dependent on popular will, that will is first formed by the ruler's scientific and artistic genius.

Rhetorically in the *Economie politique,* the sovereign people is master; it "has the right of legislation, and obliges in certain cases the body of the nation itself, whereas the former [the government] has only the right of execution, and can bind only the individuals" (3: 244). The structure of Rousseau's thought, however, would seem to indicate a very different substantive meaning. His principles of *économie* have changed the simple ruler or despotic master of the *Second discours* into an enlightened master. The practical maxims Rousseau derives from his principles bear out this interpretation, make the government itself the ultimate source of sovereign will, open for government new areas of control and manipulation. Rousseau seems to have been forced into this pattern by his consideration of the leverage required to make his location of authority in the people operational.

The first practical rule of legitimate government is that the prince must be a true agent of the legislative will. This follows from the principles of selflessness and subordination. The *Second discours* showed why those principles were usually not implemented in history. Ignorance, passion, and greed kept men from understanding in any deep sense the value of a legitimate association, kept them from seeing that such association alone could replace the reign of force. Kings acted as if they were fathers of families organizing the realm to increase their own wealth and that of their children. They believed national growth was their personal growth in wealth and therefore practiced a policy of war and aggrandizement (3: 187-90).

The *Economie,* answering the *Second discours,* assumes that government can exercise self-discipline and shows the conditions and advantages of popular or legitimate government. Government in the *Second discours* meant essentially the corruption of law and was destined to promote "the change of legitimate power into arbitrary power" (3: 187). Enlightened government has the opposite function, "to watch over the observance of the laws of which he [the prince] is the minister, and on which his entire authority is founded" (3: 249). A prince who places himself above the law makes others reckless and inobservant of the law: "The republic is on the eve of its fall as soon as anyone can think that disobeying the laws is a fine and worthy act" (3: 249). Enforcemente of the law does not necessarily mean severity. If the laws are wise and their justice made clear, administration takes care of itself: "The strength of the laws depends still more on their own wisdom than on severity" (3: 249). Legislation must already have provided for every need relative to climate, custom, national temperament, and national interest. The function of the government under these circumstances is mainly to inspire love of the law; in that task "the talent of ruling" resides (3: 250).

This means directing the wills of the citizens even more than their actions, preventing crimes rather than punishing the citizens (3: 250). If the citizen succeeds in overcoming remorse, punishment will not bind him either. Government must not simply maintain the peace by force. It must make justice a behavioral pattern in the minds of citizens, "make them what one needs them to be; the most absolute authority is that which penetrates into man's innermost being, and concerns itself no less with his will than with his actions" (3: 251). Rousseau asserts clearly the power that the government is to have over the fiber of each individual. Government prepares and forms the will to want to obey the laws, that is, the recorded needs of the general will for any given period: "It is certain that peoples [nations] are in the long run what the government makes them" (3: 251). If a leader is to command men, he must first form men; if he is to command citizens, he must first form them: "If you would have men obey the laws, make them love the laws, and make it so that to do what they should, they need think only that it is their duty" (3: 251-52).

But the government is more than a former of obedient wills, it is also an interpreter of the laws, and even more than that, for at times it supplements the legislator. If the latter has the task of "making the laws conform to the general will," the government must express the general will whenever it has not spoken explicitly, in a sense give unwritten laws: "There still remains an infinity of details of administration and economy which are left to the wisdom of the government" (3: 250). In such cases the ruler is to follow "the spirit of the law, which must serve in deciding cases which the law has not been able to foresee," or if the sense is not clear, he must find the view of the general will. He need not consult the people in this matter; in fact he would preferably rely on his own selflessness: "It [the people] should be assembled all the less, becaues it is by no means certain that its decision would be the expression of the general will; because this means is impracticable in a large nation, and because it is rarely necessary if the government has good intentions, since the rulers know well enough that the general will is always on the side which is most favorable to the public interest, that is, the most equitable choice; so that it is necessary only to be just to be certain of following the general will" (3: 251).

The example that Rousseau cites shows the ultimate weight of the prince in the matter. If in China the government by the action of some petty official is unjust, there is a public outcry. The prince then immediately suspends and blames his officers. Upon review of the case, to the extent that there is sedition in the outcry, the seditious are punished, but the prince "always discovers ... just grievances to redress" (3: 251). The context is in part that of the *Second discours*. The government has wide freedom of decision, has only the spontaneous protest of the people to restrain it, except that in the *Economie* the leader is assumed to be motivated by justice. He is enlightened enough to know that injustice eventually weakens the state and the executive. He follows the law and its spirit, forms the citizen for obedience, and voices the general will through executive decision, thus making his position more solid and reinforcing the foundations of his reign. He bypasses at times the expression of the sovereign will in assembly, but never the good of the organism itself.

Closely related to the first rule — making administration consistent with the laws and the general good — is the second — that all of the particular wills should be taught to relate themselves to the general will, defined as the preservation and well-being of the whole (3: 245). This goes deeper than the first rule's insistence that the wills should be induced to want to obey already established laws. The wills must be taught to desire consistently the general good, to practice a dynamic reaching out for the general good. Again the treatment is more in accord with the *Second discours* than with the *Contrat social*. The latter is concerned with determining procedures for finding the general will, with outlining steps for its expression in law, with weighing the merits of various governments from the point of view of their corruptibility or opposition to the general will. The *Second discours,* on the other hand, takes it for granted that there is a general good for each nation and that the goal of government has been to sacrifice this general good to its own. The *Economie* similarly takes the general good for granted, similarly places the government in the driver's seat, but has government seek not to bypass good by corrupting the citizens but to instill virtue in citizens, that is, to establish "conformity between the private will and the general will" (3: 252). It is not enough that the government be wise. The inner beings of both people and leaders must be virtuous or government soon has no more than the appearance of wisdom. Legality cannot substitute for virtue: "The corruption of the people and of the rulers extends finally to the government, however wise it may be: the worst of all abuses is to obey the laws only in appearance in order in fact to break them in safety" (3: 253).

Since virtue means in part wanting and willing what those you love want and will, it follows that humanity must be circumscribed, given the very narrow limits of a nation (3: 254-55). Patriotism is the key to virtue, then, but what is the key to patriotism. The answer again involves the ruler in the sense assigned to him in the *Second discours,* as the initiator, the real master who controls the people. But now he is the enlightened prince who knows the ages of mankind, who penetrates back through the precivil state of war, man's golden age, his initial subjection to necessity. Thus the prince knows the importance to innermost man of the absolute, isolated, single self expressed by the image of the most primitive state of nature. The integrity and dignity of the individual more than anything else must be guarded by the government if a man is to love his nation: "The public confederation... would by right be dissolved if in the state a single citizen who might have been helped were allowed to perish; if a single one were wrongfully held in prison, and if a single case were to be lost by an obviously unjust judgment" (3: 256). The welfare and liberty of each single citizen are the common cause of the whole state. Only the most illustrious nations provide examples of the protection which "the state owes its members and of the respect it owes their persons" (3: 257). Free nations alone know "the true value of a man." The Romans were distinguished more than any other nation "by the respect of their government for individuals" (3: 257).

But dignity of self demands more than protection of each man's life. It demands protection of the quality of his rights. The law must be evenhanded. The government must see to it that the weak are protected from the powerful, the poor from the rich, so that no individual self is made subservient to another. Rousseau's enlightened prince must fight any source of the inequality condemned in the *Second discours:* unequal distribution of men over the national territory, the development of luxury arts at the expense of useful and laborious trades, the subordination of agriculture to commerce, unjust taxation. Venality, too, damages the individual's integrity, breeds envy, fear, and doubt, explains "mutual hatred among citizens" and their indifference to the common cause (3: 259).

Rousseau's reasoning takes these steps: Virtue comes from patriotism. The key to patriotism is the liberty or dignity afforded the individual by the state. Man's love of liberty derives from nature. A state must guarantee a civil equivalent of natural liberty in order to earn the love of its citizens. But the idea of the state is unnatural, moves counter to man's evolution from *amour de soi* to *amour-propre*, that is, counter to the private interest arising in history. The ruler must therefore eradicate private interest if his art is to prevail. He can do so only by working through the young, by forming them. Education, as the rise of corruption in the *Second discours* showed, must have two objectives. First it makes liberty synonymous with legitimacy. Each citizen must associate regularly his fulfillment, his aspirations with the instrument which holds selfish interest in abeyance. Secondly, education means giving each individual the training and discipline needed to permit the nation to survive. All citizens must be taught to live the nation's life, "to understand, so to speak, their own existence only as a part of its existence ... to identify themselves in some way with this greater whole ... to lift continually their souls to this higher object and thus transform into a sublime virtue this dangerous disposition from which all our vices are born" (3: 259-60).

The goal is certainly close to the *Contrat social*'s more formularized statement: "transform each individual... into part of a greater whole" (3: 381). But the instruction to make each citizen assimilate the soul of the state is a direct response to the dilemma raised in the *Second discours:* "The vices which make social institutions necessary are the very ones which make the abuse of these institutions inevitable" (3: 187). Men following necessity, led by the corrupt, fall into patterns that emphasize greed, mistrust, and vanity (3: 200). Individual ambition as a goal alienates men from the state, since each citizen is in competition as in the state of war. Benighted governments of the *Second discours*, thinking that this kind of conflict hidden under pseudolegitimacy is the way to personal power, destroy the cohesive force of the nation they rule, hence their own power.

The enlightened ruler of the *Economie* uses education to make possible society by consent. In this process the government brings to bear science, will, and action. Sovereignty in the *Second discours* is negatively expressed, consent by unanimity being the only form of union acceptable, given man's nature, and the articles of such agreement being kept to a minimum. The *Economie* introduces the countermovement to the pseudolegitimacy of the *Second discours*. An enlightened prince, "an attentive and well-intentioned government" (3: 262), predisposes the minds of children to virtue through instruction given by the most worthy citizens of the nation, "illustrious warriors," "honest magistrates." This instruction "in common and in the bosom of equality" emphasizes the laws of the state and maxims about the general will, inculcates respect for them, takes possession of the feelings and minds, replaces the "sterile and vain chatter of sophists" by a continual glorification of the nation: "If they are surrounded by examples and objects which constantly remind them of the tender mother [the nation] who nourishes them, of the love she bears them, of the invaluable benefits they receive from her, and of the return they owe her, we cannot doubt that they will thus learn to cherish one another mutually as brothers, never to desire anything but what society wants" (3: 261).

If the government has been successful, it has taught the citizen to love the law that the collectivity has already sanctioned. It has made the citizen see his own interest in the national good, the preservation and well-being of the entire nation, which is synonymous with justice. Public education, as the definition of good determined by the prince, that is, "in regulations prescribed by the government and under magistrates established by the sovereign" (3: 260, 261), has determined the very quality of the individuals or elements which are in assembly to determine the future good to be legislated. Under the dedicated, selfless conscience of the government, educational input must inevitably condition legislative output.

The third task of government, after responsible administration and education for citizenship, is the provision for public need (3: 262). A passage of the *Second discours* deals with the matter but stresses corruption: "One would see politics limit to a mercenary portion of the people the honor of defending the common cause; from that policy one would see the need for taxes arise, see the discouraged farmer abandon his field, even during periods of peace, leave his plough to fasten on his sword" (3: 190). The *Economie*'s principles and maxims are designed to prevent such deterioration. Government holds many functions later assigned to the legislator in the *Contrat social*. The important area of taxation is controlled directly by a government responsible mainly to its own definition of the national good after objective study. The people is asked to sanction a program largely beyond its own intellectual competence.

Rousseau says in the *Economie* that the right of property is "the most sacred of all the rights of citizenship, and more important in some respects than liberty itself" (3: 263). This is evident, he thinks, for a number of reasons. Property is directly tied to the preservation of life. It is easier to usurp and harder to defend than life. It is therefore the clue to the motivation of most citizens and gives the law an emotional hold over their actions. The argument is a reminder of the state of war of the *Second discours*, of its thesis that a right to property on the basis of subsistence need existed before the establishment of civil society; a reminder, too, of the thesis that the shrewd rich first invented the idea of association in order to defend excessive holdings even more than to defend life. Unless Rousseau is to reject history — its golden age of family existence and acquisition, the state of war arising from rivalry over property — he must assume that property is to enter civil society as well as man. In the name of the original state of nature, its isolated self, its completely uncompromised individual, the congregation could agree to abolish property. But history, action, and matter of fact are important to Rousseau. Property owners are the matter of fact. He assumes, therefore, that the government, which must train men's minds to love the law and the general good, will make provision for property. His words express well this superior political vision of the government, limiting any unrealistic option by the sovereign people: "In general, although the institution of the laws which regulate the power of individuals in disposing of their goods belongs to the sovereign, the spirit of these laws, which the government should follow in their application, is that from father to son, from relative to relative, the goods of the family should leave it and be alienated from it as little as possible" (3: 263). In spite of the authority of the sovereign will, there is little suggestion that it will be allowed to dispossess the rich or diminish their holdings. Rather the government is to give the rich a firmer place in society, to convince them that society favors them and that they should therefore give more than the poor to the public treasury. The *Second discours* showed the reasoning of the selfish rich. The *Economie* provides reasoning for a more selfless rich, attempts to reconcile rich and poor.

But Rousseau's explanations are comforting to property owners at any level. Part of the father's property should fall to the children, since their labor has contributed to it. The shifting of rank and fortune would lead to instability because "those who were raised to become one thing, finding themselves destined for another, neither those who climb nor those who fall can acquire the maxims or the perspective suited to their new state" (3: 264). If this is principally a reassurance for the rich, the poor are to be appeased also. In the context of the *Contrat social*, where emphasis is placed on the legislation of taxes under the authority of the people's will, the problem of the initial guidance needed by that will is not stressed. In the *Second discours* the government's role is predominant. This is exactly the problem. The governments of history have usually pushed the assessment of taxes beyond the general will's consent. The *Economie* repeats that problem in summary form: "The people, for its part, more aware of the greed of the rulers and their mad expenditures than of public needs, murmurs at seeing itself stripped of what is necessary in order to supply others with what is superfluous" (3: 264). The problem is for government to walk the tightrope stretching from rich to poor, to determine what each segment of the population can give, and to demonstrate justice or concern for the whole and each of the parts: "If the contributions are voluntary, they produce nothing; if they are forced, they are illegitimate; and it is in this cruel alternative between letting the state perish and attacking the sacred right of property, which is its support, that the crux of the difficulty of just and wise economy lies" (3: 264). The enlightened prince, then, must offer to the general will a kind of ideal picture of what the traffic will bear.

His guidelines are several and of a practical nature. Consistent with the principle that the state, unlike the family, is a permanent, enduring self, is the notion of public resources which yield their own income and lighten the need for taxation of individuals. Such public property should preferably be not in money but in lands: "*domaine public*, if it is in land, and the latter is much to be preferred over the other" (3: 265). Rousseau's reasoning is that income for the nation through its own lands is a financial expression of the general will and creates an atmosphere of trust, respectability. This emphasis is to be seen in the reference to Bodin, "who considers public domain as the most respectable and sure of all the means," and in the reference to Romulus, who in the initial distribution of land provided a third of it for the collectivity, for the Roman Republic itself. Such public holdings must be regarded as sacred once they have been assigned to or accepted by an assembly of people. The check on government to insure against misappropriation or misapplication is not to be books and auditing but virtue, "the integrity of the magistrate" (3: 265).

Another guideline is the maxim that an increase in the need for public revenue indicates a decrease in the moral hold a government has over the people of the nation. The government must therefore restudy its own position at any moment it calls for an increase in public income, must "not neglect to search out the distant cause of this new need" (3: 266). Rather than follow this decline in the moral fiber of the people, made evident in its excessive demands on the public treasury, the government must strive to fortify the people against increasingly sophisticated needs, must practice "the most important maxim in the administration of public finance, which is to work harder to prevent needs than to increase revenues" (3: 266). The ruler must also resist his own corporate interest for increasing revenue, must oppose the history of enslavement outlined in the *Second discours,* whether his extraneous goals are the brilliance of a court or foreign conquests (3: 268-69). The people are unable to resist the appeal to grandeur and the call to arms if that is what the government wants. The concept of the predominant but enlightened ruler is always present in Rousseau's argument. The prince must lead, not follow the general will, must prepare the people for the best fiscal policy, including a relative stability in the holdings of each citizen, emphasis on a productive public domain, minimal public expenditures, and just assessment of individual holdings.

Legitimate assessment needs further definition beyond the leader's talent already mentioned for finding what both rich and poor can accept. The problem relates to the nation as a "moral being." Legitimacy lies in exact apportionment of the tax burden (3: 270-71). A head tax, "at the same time real and personal," should be proportionate to the amount of property each man holds, to the portion of income he can devote to luxury goods, and to the financial advantage each man receives from the political association. If a rich man's possessions are ten times as great as the poor man's and his consumption of luxuries is high, he clearly benefits more than does the poor man from a collective police, in terms of pleasure, privilege, and the protection of goods. He should therefore expect to pay proportionately more in taxes. Rousseau adds that the flow of tax income spent by the state is toward the rich, who are in a position to sell the government goods and services, so that "even in paying their share, they have an evident interest in increasing" their taxes (3: 272). Since the planning involved in establishing economic justice calls for an almost superhuman integrity and vision, the notion of the enlightened ruler is again inescapably present when Rousseau speaks of

THE ENLIGHTENED PRINCE 141

an "operation which the Platos and Montesquieus would not have dared undertake except with fear and while asking Heaven for understanding and integrity" (3: 273).

Taxes on land call particularly for enlightened control. Their effect is to draw money away from the country to the city, to help the artists, artisans, and merchants at the expense of the country dweller. A tax on wheat usually diminishes the amount produced, but the need for this staple by all men prevents any rise in price. As a result, many go hungry and the farmer is impoverished by bearing the burden of the tax (3: 273-74). Abundance of money from the resources of commerce and industry may make a nation relatively stronger than its neighbors, but within the nation the financial weight of the farmer is always less than that of the merchant and industrialist, "so that the farmer finds himself more burdened without having more resources" (3: 275). Any tax policy which saps the farmer consumes also the energy of the state, attacks the nation "in its very source" (3: 275). The countryside becomes depopulated. The nation loses much of its real wealth, "for the worst scarcity for a nation is lack of men" (3: 275).

The government must tax the importation of goods the nation does not need and tax the exportation of goods it does. And the tax on luxuries should be paid by the consumer rather than the provider. The rich then have a choice. They can decide to incur only useful expenses or they can continue to be extravagant and pay heavy taxes. The distinction between luxury goods and necessities leads Rousseau to a further conclusion. Taxes on necessities must be approved by the entire assembly, since such taxes involve each member. To fail to seek such approval can have "dangerous consequences" (3: 277). But the situation is different for luxuries, "goods one is free not to use" (3: 278). Since not all of the members of the congregation are involved, the general will need not be consulted. The contribution of each individual who buys luxuries "may pass for voluntary so that the private consent of each of the contributors takes the place of the general consent of the entire people" (3: 278). Rousseau admits that this idea that the members of the government or the rich may tax themselves to benefit the poor, to "spare others at their own expense," may not be taken seriously by some, may be assigning too much idealism to the wealthy and powerful. But he chooses to assume that the government is not "by its position" the enemy of the people (3: 278). Rousseau closely ties the concept of the national whole to financial matters. The ruler must know the effect on the entire state of the smallest economic measure; he must have a fiscal policy which gives top priority to national health. Mixing mechanistic and organistic images, Rousseau says the national "machine" could not be "injured in any part without the painful impression being carried immediately to the brain, if the animal is in a state of health" (3: 244). This concept of the life-like machine is behind the distinction Rousseau makes between the true statesman who gives attention to the economic whole and the leader interested only in revenue, in money as power. The former, thinking of the nation's "common self," has as his end "the good of the nation rather than the raising of money through taxes" (3: 275).

In the *Economie politique* Rousseau gives a new definition to the enlightened prince. This is not the enlightened despot of Platonic tradition who fulfills the natural intellectual order by using his superior vision of changeless ideas to realize here on earth a perfect state. This is not a ruler by divine right either, the representative of God on earth. Success in understanding the machine of state and in laying for it enduring foundations is the measure of Rousseau's prince. The ruler described in the *Second discours* does not give promise of such creative and legitimate behavior, but his fate is solid argument for the *Economie*'s program. Failure results from introducing into statecraft human passion, family concepts, and therefore ill-conceived domestic and foreign policy. The version of history given in the *Second discours* prepared the way for the *Economie*'s description of a depersonalized, objective political science and art. Science and art here mean a search for *volonté générale*, the general will, in two very distinct senses which past writers on Rousseau's political theories have not separated. The prince must see the nation in terms of a twofold principle, first, *volonté générale* as the nation's will to survive, the general good viewed from outside, and, second, the people's will to consent, its participation in the democratic process. The prince's science finds the first, his art helps form the second. His is no servile role. He may aspire to reach beyond the human, to become the selfless creator of the nation, of its sovereign, of its law.

Although in the *Economie* the government sees the national good and through education forms the sovereign will, the prince is not identical with *volonté générale*. The *Second discours* also makes this clear. But there is another even more striking resemblance between the two works. The prince of the *Economie* embodies the godlike intelligence that the legislator alone represents in the *Contrat social*, where one senses an alliance of legislator and sovereign people against government. In the *Second discours*, when Rousseau speaks of solid institutions, he has in mind those of great lawgivers such as Lycurgus (3: 180), but the notion of government held in check by the legislator's genius is absent: "Nascent government did not have a constant and regular form.... In spite of all the labors of the wisest legislators, the political state still remained imperfect, because it was almost the work of chance" (3: 180).

The same lack of clear opposition between the two concepts, government and legislator, holds in the *Economie*. The notion of government is in fact almost one with the notion of the legislator. Strictly speaking, the legislator's task is to "bring the laws into conformity with the general will" (3: 250), the nation's will for survival. But the government is capable of supplementing that role on its own, of forming a people capable of obeying the law and also of reaching wise decisions by assuming an almost legislative role. The prince of the *Economie* suggests self-discipline and vision, characteristics not assumed for government in the *Contrat social*, but posited as essential by the problems raised in the *Second discours*. Signs of this legislator-government are everywhere present in the *Economie*'s vocabulary and phrasing: "Unity of interest and will between the people and the rulers" is to be the point of view (3: 247). When the leaders command, it must be always with "that celestial voice," "that salutary organ of the will of all" (3: 248). The legislator is to provide for needs of place, climate, soil, and custom, but there still remains an "infinity of details" in administration and economy left to the "wisdom of the government" (3: 250). The government cannot confine itself to mere obedience, but must form citizens, "make them" what it is essential "that they should be" (3: 251). Love of country, too, is to be inspired by governmental wisdom, for government is not the object of suspicion but the protector of the people: "Let the government leave to them enough of a role in administration so that they may feel they are at home" (3: 258). Through education "an attentive and well-intentioned" government provides beforehand against the evils which sooner or later result from the indifference of the citizens to the fate of the nation (3: 262). By his administration of public funds, finally, the prince seeks not just to raise money but to improve the social and moral atmosphere of the entire nation (3: 275-76), to express the general will in economic terms.

This concept of the enlightened prince does not appear to be inspired by abstract idealism, but is grounded in action either observed or proved necessary in the real world. Matter of fact is to some degree a basic consideration in all the works of Rousseau discussed so far. The *Confessions* have as an overpowering motivation the task of awakening a too sophisticated and conformist society by the concrete presentation of sentiment through art, of liberating Rousseau and other men by describing an individual and unique life of feeling in a manner complete enough to make that existence as real as the everyday actuality hitherto known. This obsession about bringing his personal life into the public mind persists in Rousseau's repeated attempts to reveal his innermost psyche to his listeners and readers in the *Dialogues* and the *Rêveries*. In the earlier political works the mood is somewhat different, but the goal is the same — to find support for his views in the real world.

The *Discours sur les sciences et les arts* asks that the ruler reap from the great natural geniuses of his time the fresh vision and moral purity needed to form a free and enduring people. It tries to give credibility to that request operationally by presenting evidence that certain nations of ancient and modern times, which allied government with moral as well as materialistic science, remained for a long period uncorrupted: Sparta and Rome, the relatively vital Holland, England, and Switzerland, as contrasted with Athens, Imperial Rome, Austria, Spain, and France.

The *Second discours* offers an approach to history that is highly descriptive. Each period of man's evolution is presented in detail, documented wherever possible by references to animal life, human behavior, gleanings from the ancient and modern historians and from voyages of discovery. But any such vast synthesis is necessarily incomplete, and Rousseau therefore warns repeatedly that this matter of fact is hypothetical, that different conclusions may later come from additional evidence. When he very clearly uses analysis in studying the course of man's existence, he tests his definitions operationally. He defines natural law, for example, in terms of *amour de soi* and *pitié*. Pity has an ineffective role in history; it does not prevent the natural state of war, and with the establishment of national life it dwells, Rousseau says, only within certain high-minded men of cosmopolitan outlook (3: 178-79).

This impracticable law, as general as the "great city of the world," is used in the *Economie* principally as a standard to suggest the limitations of national law, to open the ruler's mind to a broader context than justice defined by his own nation's sovereign good and will. Love of self, on the other hand, remains operational throughout man's history, although it is transformed into pride and becomes an ingredient in the right of the strongest. At the moment of the establishment of civil society it represents love of independence, which makes only a form of union based on unanimous consent acceptable to the members. This principle of legitimacy, dignity of self, is still operational at the time of revolution.

Liberty as legitimacy, in both the *Second discours* and the *Economie*, moved justice away from *pitié*, a universal natural law, toward national justice, "the division of the human race into different societies" (3: 179, *Second discours*), groupings small enough to permit mutual affection among fellow citizens: "It seems to me that the feeling of humanity evaporates and is weakened by its spread over all the earth .... it is good that humanity, concentrated among citizens, should acquire new force from the habit of seeing one another, and from the common interest which unites them" (3: 254-55, *Economie*). But if legitimacy, the good of the national whole as accepted by all members of the congregation, is in a sense the reduction of justice to the matter of fact, even that principle unassisted, cannot withstand the test of time. The legitimacy of the *Second discours* proved to be a tentative and imperfect instrument subject to decline, revolution, and anarchy. The stumbling block was the faulty organization of the many parts of the political machine, one of which — government — gave selfish orientation to the rest and was despotic master of the rest in fact. It follows that if the machine is to be properly operational for permanence the relationship of its parts must be changed; for example, the sovereign power must truly reside in the head or people rather than in the organs or executive; the concepts controlling the function of the machine must be changed to accord with its artificial, conventional nature. But more important, since in history the people has repeatedly played the role of dupe, the concept of the government, the only possible initiating agent, must be changed from the shrewd and powerful, who cannot have true survival power since they are only human, to the enlightened prince, who will follow the dictates of the nation's artificial "common self," will assure the "reciprocal sensibility" and the "internal correspondence" of its parts, and will thus prepare the nation for survival (3: 245).

The *Second discours* derived a standard — legitimacy — compatible both with nature as isolation or freedom of self and with history or necessity's egotistical striving. It also emphasized the role of government in violating this standard, corrupting the people to the point of enslavement. The positive threads of that discourse are the statesmanship of Lycurgus and the notion that in legitimacy of rule lies the strength of the nation and of the executive will, which is the government. The *Economie politique*, taking up those threads, makes government the agent of transcendence; it incorporates philosopher into prince in a very modern way, since its doctrine is that nations must be legitimate, not for reason of abstract or divine justice, but because of man's demonstrated thirst for liberty and self-fulfillment. The prince and his people, in the long view which has been forced upon them, are in effect not free to be unenlightened. In blindness ruler and nation cannot long endure. Time as the present seems to favor despotism, but time as perspective condemns it. The ideal prince is will and action made selfless by his vision of history's cycle. As a scientist, he must know the situation and needs of his nation. As an artist, he must create through his art the general will required to legislate that national good.

Rousseau's principles for making legitimacy enter history operationally often seem unrealistic in their description of the complex phenomena involved, particularly in their reliance on the prince chastened by his privileged view of the history of mankind and of empire. But his orientation seems to be empirical, to be based on what for him, with his limited psychological, anthropological, and political data, were intended to be reasonable approximations of the matter of fact.

Chapter V

A NATION'S CHARACTER:
THE MECHANICS OF DESTRUCTION

The *Second discours* and the *Economie politique* in describing the civil state made three observations: first, each nation exists under pressure from internal and international conflict; second, the fate of the nation rests in large part on the quality of the relationship between people and government; and third, unless the government actively forms and maintains the character of the people, the latter will become corrupt and degeneration and destruction of both people and government will follow. Underlining these tenets of operational necessity, Rousseau in effect asked that the prince accept the scientific and artistic challenge of creating a people. Government, one part of an immense artificial whole, the nation, is not by its function the enemy of its people but is dependent itself on the welfare of the entire state. If this theory of the *Economie* cannot be implemented, both government and people are helplessly destroyed by necessity — "the state is dissolved" (3: 245). The same viewpoint underlies the *Lettre à d'Alembert*. Basically a political tract, it introduces an important aspect of Rousseau's thought on national power.

The Genevans did not have a theater and Voltaire, living at Les Délices in their midst, was obliged after a time to stop staging even his own private performances. It was partly under his guidance that d'Alembert in the article "Genève" (1757) of the *Encyclopédie* proposed that the civil authorities allow a theater in Geneva. Rousseau could not tolerate the idea. In the *Lettre à*

M. d'Alembert sur les spectacles (1758)[1] he gave his reasons in a calm and measured tone. His resignation, he tells us in Book X of the *Confessions,* was related to his quarrels with Diderot, Grimm, and Mme d'Epinay, his break with Mme d'Houdetot, the belief that he was dying, and his urgent desire to find peace of mind in the pleasant country setting provided for him at Mont-louis. As a result of this affair Rousseau became distrustful of the Genevans, feared they might accept more and more Voltaire's way of life, and came to regard Voltaire as the enemy of Geneva and of Jean-Jacques himself.

It has been easy sport for critics to blame this work for being what Rousseau never intended it to be, literary criticism. The *Lettre* must be removed for the most part from that context, to which it has been repeatedly and superficially assigned with words of scathing criticism. It must instead be placed in its rightful political framework. René Wellek's remarks, which follow, for all of their penetration, illustrate well the inclination to measure the *Lettre* by the standards of literary criticism alone and to omit the broader concern which gives a truer indication of the article's meaning. It does not seem to me certain at all that the ideas of the *Lettre* cannot interest us today, that Rousseau confuses life and art in this study, that he becomes entangled in contradictions because of a moralistic point of view. Wellek says, "The whole argument seems of little relevance or even interest today. The famous criticism of Molière's *Misanthrope,* in which Rousseau takes the side of Alceste, proposes a complete rewriting of the play. Rousseau obviously sees himself as the misanthrope and wants Molière to justify him at every point. It is bad criticism, which confuses life and art, Molière's Alceste with a hypothetical human type. Logically Rousseau's rigid moralism is contradicted by his own frequent recognition that each society has the art it

---

[1] Hereafter referred to as *Lettre.* All citations for this work are from Jean-Jacques Rousseau, *Du Contrat social, Discours, Lettre à M. d'Alembert* (Paris: Garnier, 1962). This edition has been used because of availability. All citations have been checked against the *Lettre à M. d'Alembert sur les spectacles,* ed. Max Fuchs (Geneva: Droz, 1948), which gives the text of the first edition of the *Lettre,* published in 1758.

wants and needs."[2] A very different impression emerges if the text is seen in the larger framework of Rousseau's political thought. The alleged confusion between life and art disappears, as do the contradictions, and the accusation of naive moralizing is greatly opened to question.

D'Alembert in his enthusiasm over the brilliance of the Parisian theaters, their prestige and imitators throughout Europe, had in Rousseau's opinion painted too seductive a picture of the artistic, moral, and intellectual effects to be derived from establishing a theater at Geneva. Morality and virtue were about to be wedded to art and intellect, a simple people uplifted by a superior culture. In the *Lettre*, Rousseau quotes a passage from d'Alembert's article: "In this way Geneva would have plays and manners, and enjoy the advantages of both; the theatrical performances would form the taste of the citizens, and give them a fineness of tact, a delicacy of sentiment which is very difficult to acquire without this aid: literature would profit without the advance of libertinism; and Geneva would join the prudence of Lacedaemon to the refinement of Athens" (p. 124). No one was expected to doubt this result. But in fairness to Rousseau it must be admitted that the claim did raise a serious and most interesting sociological problem, the impact of one civilization on another, a frequent concern of Montesquieu, Voltaire, Diderot, and other *philosophes*, and a particularly appealing lure for Rousseau, since the question paralleled in more specific terms the earlier one answered in the *Discours sur les sciences et les arts*.

D'Alembert's proposal really called not for literary criticism but for a social study. Rousseau was completely justified in answering in that vein, and in adding therefore the possibility that the theater might have an adverse effect. A citizen of Geneva need not hate the theater to doubt that its institution can be harmlessly accomplished overnight. Rousseau would in fact have overlooked the most important issue if he had confined himself to measuring no more than the literary merits of the plays he mentions. His *Lettre* seems to represent an effort to see the prob-

---

[2] René Wellek, *A History of Modern Criticism, 1750-1950*. Vol. 1, *The Later Eighteenth Century* (New Haven, Conn.: Yale University Press 1955), pp. 62-63.

lem clearly in several different perspectives. He considers the motivation of the playwright. He tries to penetrate the psychology of the audience. He determines the kind of influence a play may have on the spectators. These three concerns lead him to an understanding of the value of this impact, permit him a relativistic weighing of the notion of cultural superiority, and, finally, produce his argument in favor of strictly national culture, an argument carefully joined to the evidence he has established and to the rest of his political theory.

Two of the treatise's main observations about the stage are precisely that its apologists naively confuse art and life, and therefore attribute to theatrical production advantages which it does not offer. The theorists, first, believe that the playwright has for one of his principal goals the teaching of a moral lesson. According to Rousseau, neither writers of tragedies nor writers of comedies have this in mind. The author must adapt his plays to the customs, traditions, and taste of any given people. This is the basic rule which transcends all others, the need to please the audience, since taste is relative to time and place: "It is in this way that the diversity of amusements is born according to the different tastes of nations. An intrepid, grave, and cruel people wants deadly and perilous entertainment, in which valor and cool courage shine. A ferocious and intense people wants blood, combats, terrible passions. A voluptuous people requires music and dancing. A gallant people wants love and refinement. A frivolous people wants joking and the ridiculous. *Each is led by his pleasures.* To please them, there must be amusements to favor their inclinations, whereas what is needed is the means to moderate them" (p. 135).

Because authors must cater to varying emotional, moral, and intellectual levels, the term "good" applied to a play means usually, not morally good, but basically either opportune or understandable to as wide an audience as possible. Art may succeed on this basis and not be even artistically good: "It is said a good play never fails, and indeed I can believe that. It is because a good play never shocks the morals and manners of its time" (p. 136). To claim that Molière sought to teach virtue and attack vice, was controlled by moral criteria, would be to call him a fool and to ignore his genius. He did not by error or negligence present the misanthrope as a too serious, too scrupulous, humorless bore. He did this because he knew his business. His goal as a writer of comedy had to be to make people laugh. To do so he had to please contemporary taste: "If these distinctions are correct, Molière misunderstood the misanthrope. Can it be supposed he did so by mistake? No, of course not. But this is exactly how the desire to make people laugh at the expense of the character forced him to degrade it contrary to the character's truth.... The misanthrope and the man in a rage are two very different characters. This was an opportunity to distinguish them. Molière was not unaware of that. But he had to make the audience laugh" (p. 154). If Molière's prime purpose had been to teach, he would have had to change the play, so that Philinte would be ridiculous and Alceste remain sincere but admirable. But Molière was too wise to moralize. The theater is not a school for virtue: "But then the audience could only have laughed at the expense of the man of the world, and the author's intention was to make them laugh at the expense of the misanthrope" (p. 155). Rousseau even says that rewriting the play to transform the character of Alceste would have had disastrous results. Any elevation in tone would have made the play fail: "I see only one inconvenience in this new play, which is that it could not possibly succeed" (p. 155, note). The *Misanthrope* in Rousseau's eyes was a masterpiece perfectly adapted to its audience.

Regnard in the *Légataire Universel* went further, made his audiences applaud the "most criminal acts,... theft, imposture, lying, cruelty" (p. 158). But he is not to be blamed, for the theater is not supposed to instruct. Those who have tried in a moral sense to reform the theater have written unsuccessful plays: "These failings are so inherent to our theater that by trying to remove them, it is disfigured. Our modern authors, guided by the best of intentions, write more refined plays, but what happens as a result? They are no longer truly comic and produce no effects" (p. 159). When writers increased the love element on the French stage, it was not to cure the excesses of that passion, but rather as a clever means of responding to public taste: "No longer being able to maintain the force of comic situations and character, the love interest has been reinforced. The same thing has been done in tragedy to take the place of situations drawn from political interest we no longer have and from simple, natural feelings which no longer move anyone" (p. 159). Men of truly great genius, even Corneille and Racine, strove principally to please rather than to edify: "These productions of intellect, like most others, have for their end only applause. When the author receives it, and the actors share it, too, the play has attained its purpose, and no other benefit is sought" (p. 143). Rousseau repeatedly admits and appreciates the brilliance of the plays of Molière, Racine, and Voltaire. They knew exactly what they were doing. They strove to excite, to move, to stimulate the emotions and intellect. Any other stated goal, especially the moralistic one, is rationalization or a peripheral consideration only, not a part of true playwriting.

The second sense in which Rousseau separates art from life is in his denial that the theater could function in an educational way even if a writer were ill-advised enough to try to teach. The best attempts would be futile. The theorists of tragedy claim that its role is to "purge the passions by exciting them" (p. 137). This, Rousseau says, cannot be proved to happen. The artist must favor the "passions which we like" (p. 138) and cannot, because of the formula — taste determines art — try to moderate or control them. The theater therefore does not produce the "advantageous effects that seem to be expected of it" (p. 138).

Rousseau repeatedly points out that the pity and fear aroused in us by tragedy are remote from real life. The intrigue is never confused with real action. The stage representation is but a fable and cannot stir us to alter the course of our existence: "The theater has its own rules, principles, and morality apart, as well as its particular language and style of dress. We say to ourselves that nothing in all that relates to us, and that we should believe ourselves as ridiculous to adopt the virtue of its heroes as to speak in verse or to put on Roman clothing. That is just about the effect of all these great sentiments and brilliant maxims... to relegate them forever to the stage, and to present virtues to us as a theatrical game" (pp. 141-42).

If Crébillon intended to attack vice and teach virtue, he failed to reach his audiences with his lesson. The events of French tragedy are too unconvincing, "so far from us," the characters "so enormous, so bloated, so chimerical" (p. 148). Rewards and punishments on the stage do not affect manners: "By showing them [the people in the audience] that we want to instruct them, we no longer instruct them" (p. 143). Even if a tragedy has a moral purpose and ending (for example, Voltaire's *Mahomet*) the fury of fanaticism will never be abated by philosophy in plays or books. Men must be ready, Rousseau insists, to "leave philosophy behind, close the books, take the sword, and punish the impostors" (p. 146).

The supposed lessons taught by comedy are equally nebulous. If comedy realistically painted the manners and customs of a given time, people would not understand the message: "an ugly face does not appear ugly to the one who wears it." If it tried to use caricature, men would avoid being ridiculous, but their vices would still prosper. The vicious would even be given an advantage over the virtuous: "Ridicule ... is the favorite arm of vice. With it, the respect we owe to virtue is attacked deep within our hearts" (p. 142). Even the plays of the "moderns" which aim to treat and correct so many prejudices and abuses, plays such as those of Nivelle de la Chaussée and Diderot, resemble sermons more than true comedies and tragedies and are perhaps even less effective: "They are very instructive, if you wish; but they are even more boring" (p. 159). For Rousseau, any project to rewrite the masterpieces of Molière, Corneille, or Racine in order to make their content and message more enlightening would be sheer nonsense.

The principal motivation of the poetic genius, according to Rousseau, is never to teach virtue and correct vice. If it were, he would fail. A creative person would be hampered in his art by moral concerns. The audience, too, would revolt against any such effort at indoctrination. The writer's aim is to please by appealing to the taste of his day, and the audience would react unfavorably to any form of moralism which fell outside of its own conception of taste and manners. Speaking strictly from the artistic point of view, whether from the vantage point of the author or from that of the spectator, it is an error to mistake art for life. Artists and their audiences are clearly not aware of any impact of art on life. Art simply must follow life, that is, taste and *mœurs*, if it is to succeed. There can rarely be a revival, a new implantation of virtue in a corrupt people. This minor theme of the *Discours sur les sciences et les arts* and of the *Second discours* has been given a central position in the *Lettre*. There can be no reform through the theater, no elevation in spirit of an already corrupted audience.

After rejecting moral goals and effects for the theater and expressing sarcasm about efforts to adapt the theater to education, Rousseau discusses another problem, an influence which, with respect to other media such as television, concerns us today: What is the subconscious effect of a play's content on its audience? Approaching the question cautiously, Rousseau indicates that there is need for additional, careful investigation: "Everything is still a problem concerning the real effects of the theater. Since the disputes it causes are only between men of the church and men of the world, each side views the matter only with prejudices. There are, Sir [d'Alembert], studies which would not be unworthy of your pen" (p. 133).

Good, bad, and corrupt do not have in this context the religious meaning Wellek attributes to them when he says, "He [Rousseau] draws on the whole arsenal of the antistage controversy carried on for centuries by Puritans, whether Catholic or Calvinist." [3] Rousseau's meaning is related more to the empirical study of effects than to any absolute standard. An avid theatergoer himself, he finds that audiences become more sympathetic to Phèdre's passion or Medea's crimes through seeing the performance: "I suspect that any man, to whom the crimes of Phèdre or Médée were described beforehand, would hate them more at the beginning of the play than at the end" (p. 139). Incest has become in fact less fearsome, more familiar, an object of compassion. Crébillon similarly accustoms men to scenes of bloodshed and violence; he may even have a warping influence on men's minds and emotions: "The massacres of the gladiators were not so barbarous as these frightful plays. Blood was seen flowing, it is true, but the imagination was not soiled by crimes which make nature shudder" (p. 148).

The constant emphasis in the theater on love as a pleasure of the senses glorifies it, gives "a new energy and coloring to that dangerous passion" (p. 159). This innovation also may tend to reinforce the ascendency of women over men: "A child would

---

[3] Wellek, *History of Modern Criticism*, 1: 62.

not know how to eat his bread if it were not cut by his governess. That is the image of what goes on in the new plays" (p. 161). The claim that a play may help correct the excesses of this passion is belied by Rousseau's observations that "the spectators are always on the side of the weak lover" (p. 164). In Molière's plays there are deceivers and dupes. The dupes are always honest but simple men, usually fathers, mothers, the old. The deceivers who always succeed and win the approval of the audience are the shrewd, the malicious, sometimes wives, children, the young, servants, those who are polite and attractive but insincere. Unconsciously, the audience is led to accept this reversal of the order of any just society: "See how this man Molière... upsets the whole order of society; how scandalously he overturns all the most sacred relations on which it is founded; how he derides the respectable rights of fathers over their children, of husbands over their wives, of masters over their servants" (p. 149). Alceste is clearly a man of virtue. He loves truth, but the truth is made to appear always petty, secondary to *bienséance,* for Molière cleverly exploits what is laughable even in man's search for truth, the absence of a sense of proportion, Alceste's "ridiculous fury about matters which should not move him" (p. 153).

The artist offers no lesson, the audience wants only to be pleased. But unknown to artist and audience, and in spite of the preachments about moral goals by well-meaning theorists, "real effects" are produced in most theatergoers (p. 133). The issue involves the nature of these effects, whether they can be called good or bad. Rousseau's answer even on this point is not rigidly moralistic nor absolute in any sense. Rather he gives what amounts to the mechanics of the effect in terms of the relative sophistication of an audience. For Parisians the impact is far from damaging. The theater can be useful in France. Because art adapts itself to taste and taste reflects morals, if morals are worldly-wise, then taste already includes that kind of wisdom. Art simply makes allowance for the degree of refinement already present in the audience, and no harm is done. This is presented by Rousseau as an interaction of forces without any references to sin and immorality. He merely describes a mechanism which prevents any highly sophisticated culture from becoming either better or worse because of art. Parisians could in fact, Rousseau ironically suggests, do many worse things than frequent their relatively innocent theaters: "Since preventing them from occupying themselves is to prevent them from doing harm, two hours a day stolen from the activity of vice prevents the twelfth part of the crimes that would be committed" (p. 169).

Such an argument does not apply to the Genevans. But even in considering the influence on them, Rousseau does not become moralistic. He adds to his own theatergoing experience the perspective of an outsider, not with wit or philosophy, a Rica or Usbek, not with the deadpan of a Candide, not openly, but by the tacitly assumed viewpoint of a simple Swiss, Jean-Jacques himself, seeing plays performed by a Parisian troupe. He feels no guilt, for this form of entertainment is authorized and generally accepted. He is dazzled if bewildered by the costumes, the setting, the sound of the voices, the great personages he sees, the emotions constantly crossing their faces. His simple mind likes color, novelty, and he watches with fascination. No moral question crosses his mind. He has only admiration for these princes and princesses performing before him. He may fall in love with a beautiful face, be moved with compassion because of his absent-minded inability to distinguish at first between real life and stage life, he may be too naive to react conventionally and instead reacts viscerally, as do even his more sophisticated Parisian counterparts when a discovery scene or a reversal has been particularly well done.

Pleasure soon controls this naive viewer, who is not formally announced by Rousseau but who is essential to his argument. Pleasure also leads the Parisian audience, but there is a difference. The hidden impact on the simple Genevan, as he continues to frequent the theater for the pleasure it offers, gradually affects his taste and ultimately his attitudes in a deep sense, for there is much more to a play than its explicit lessons or the rewards and punishments which come from the cause-and-effect relationships constituting the action. There is the entire ambiance created by the author's presentation of social attitudes and human relationships. Emotional moods and intellectual poses are expressed by the actors. There are, too, the *singeries* required by the Parisians for whom the author wrote the play in the first place. These are the elements which may permeate the naive spectator's psyche without his knowledge. The general effect, for example, of the stage spectacle is to distort, to enlarge our natural inclinations, to give a new vigor to all of the passions (p. 137). The hitherto untroubled person may thus acquire the taste for strongly expressed emotion: "The harm for which the theater is reproached is not precisely that of inspiring criminal passion but of disposing the soul to feelings which are too tender and which are satisfied later at the expense of virtue. The sweet emotions that are felt do not have a definite object in themselves, but they produce the need for one. They do not precisely produce love, but they prepare the way for its being felt" (p. 163).

Contrary to what d'Alembert maintains, there can be no possible benefit for a Genevan in such an influence. Rousseau is arguing relatively, using two sets of people. It would be impossible to teach virtue to the Genevans by using a Parisian play no matter how well intentioned its moral purpose might be. The Genevans are already either virtuous or not within their own frame of values, in the sense of simplicity, rusticity, patriotic fervor. Any new quality imparted to them must be justified by the dubious argument that Genevan virtue with the addition of Parisian virtue is superior to Genevan virtue alone.

At this point it is helpful to raise the question of what constitutes vice for Rousseau. Vice is not natural flaw, nor deviation from an idealistic or divine standard, nor violation of the ten commandments. Neither is it passion. Vice is departure from the behavior required for the well-being and survival of the social whole in which a person finds himself integrated. It would be impossible to teach most Genevans this kind of error in any explicit, obvious way. Taste derived from the *mœurs* required for acceptance into Genevan society would leave a true citizen too naive to understand the message. If he should understand it, he would be inclined to resist the seduction. But his deeper transformation, already set in process by contact with foreigners and with Swiss returning to Geneva, could be accelerated by any authoritative recommendation of the theater as something of absolute value in itself, the thesis of d'Alembert and the *philosophes*. Imperceptibly, a new taste and mores could be introduced. The direction of flow would be the opposite of the movement observed for a sophisticated audience. There, mores determine taste, taste determines art. But with the unsophisticated audience, the artist plays the initiating role, comparable to that of the shrewd rich who introduced men to civil society in the first place.

Only the scope of the deception is different. The brilliance of the esthetic appeal of art, and also art's claim to teach, captivates taste. The process can be described negatively: it begins with the curiosity of the naive, their inability to distinguish the Parisian meaning of value from the Genevan meaning, their emotional attraction to the imposing presence of actors and actresses, their submission to pleasure, and their gradual and unconscious absorption of foreign manners and attitudes. As a result *mœurs* or mores are gradually broadened, attitudes of understanding and tolerance are acquired, and study is encouraged, including study of the theater, of taste, of mores. Thus, the Genevan audience becomes through sophistication the Parisian audience. The normal mechanism for sophisticated society is now again operational: mores determining taste, which in turn determines the art the author must present.

The meaning of this mechanism is that the worldly cannot go back, become less refined, but must continue to advance, although, as with Rousseau, that may mean acquiring the wisdom which describes the sociological dangers of the theater to the unsophisticated. The latter can unwittingly through the theater acquire worldliness, enter the mainstream of European life, sacrifice their national character to it, and in turn become captives of advanced civilization.

Rousseau could be wrong. For d'Alembert, the Genevans had nothing to lose and much to gain. Most *philosophes,* too, whether English, German, Italian, or Russian, believed in the value of French culture, in its goals of understanding, tolerance, cosmopolitanism. They even found that other cultures were inferior to it, imitated it. They spoke of its universality and came to regard it almost as an absolute. Their relativism was often in terms of the degree to which other cultures attained French culture or fell short of it. In contrast, Rousseau's relativism is more thoroughgoing, closer to that of Montesquieu. Each nation is a whole, has its own good strictly in its own terms.

For Geneva, the problem is complex. First, economically the Genevans cannot afford a theater. The people would neglect tasks far more useful to the nation: "The people of Geneva supports itself only by work and has what is necessary only insofar as it denies itself any excess.... Everyone is busy, everyone is active, everyone is hard at work.... Its arms, its use of time, its vigilance, its austere parsimony are the treasures of Geneva" (pp. 197-98).

Second, since through the theater the Genevans would absorb the attitudes of writers representing the French nobility and bourgeoisie, the general will and spirit of the Genevans could be weakened. Through a theater expressing foreign cultural traits, they would learn unconsciously to forsake their dedication to family and neighbors. They would be diverted from the basic sanity of their own national life. From tragedy they would learn to weep over fables, the misfortunes of fictional people. From comedy they would learn to mock rather than to understand their fellow citizens: "People think they are brought together in the theater, and it is there that they are isolated. That is where they go to forget their friends, neighbors, and relatives" (p. 134). French artistic imitation deals with extreme forms of existence, deeds beyond the proportion of man, exaggerated forms of love, subtle, comic relationships which are absent from the real life of a Genevan: "Celebrated actions, great names, great crimes and virtues in tragedy; comic situations and the amusing in comedy; and always love in both. I ask in what way morals can profit from all this" (p. 143). Since the French theater is decadent, "true beauties," now "eclipsed," have been replaced by "insignificant, but pleasant accessories," so that the audience sees "romances under the name of dramatic plays" (p. 159). Patriotic attitudes will be lost to wit, frivolity, feminine taste (p. 206). Genevans will lose the courage, force, and pride which arise from simple man-to-man relationships, emotions experienced daily by the Spartans and Romans: "Whether a monarch governs men or women, that should be rather indifferent to him, provided he is obeyed; but in a republic, men are needed" (p. 204).

This counterfeit life style will be accentuated and symbolized by the "talent of the actor," which is itself the art of "counterfeiting himself, of putting on a character other than his own" (p. 186). Rather than their natural spontaneity over real life tasks, citizens will acquire the sedentary habit of staring at actors who play at life. They will learn to enjoy "exclusive entertainments which sadly shut together a small number of people in a gloomy cavern, which keep them fearful and motionless in silence and inaction" (p. 224).

Finally, this degeneration of *volonté générale* through loss of economic responsibility and a politically cohesive spirit would mean also the loss of artistic integrity. In the realm of culture each nation has its own art relative to the needs of its people, valuable in terms of the taste and mores of that people. This art is not to be regarded as inferior because of the predominance or mere quantitative acceptance of another nation's culture. Universality of art indicates widespread and deep conformity, a leveling and degeneration of national character and taste. The artist's native genius must be diluted, must become more and more general in its appeal in order to win universal acceptance. The nation, isolated Geneva, is a better shelter for nourishing art than is all of Europe if truly individual genius is the source of art.

There is no contradiction in these implications between what Wellek has called Rousseau's "rigid moralism" and "his recognition that each society has the art it wants and needs" (p. 62). Rousseau has analyzed a sociological problem most astutely in terms of the mechanics of influence. A predominant culture, Parisian and European, threatens the national heritage of a small nation. Unless there is active resistance by the leaders of that nation, its people under the imperceptible influence of the theater will absorb all of the attributes of the predominant culture. D'Alembert's defense of this imposition in the name of brilliance and moral benefit shows, in Rousseau's opinion, a total lack of feeling for a higher value — the individual character of the people which is being artistically, intellectually, and morally subjugated. It can be argued further that the very souls of small nations which might produce great artists in the future are thus being destroyed.

All of these results could come from d'Alembert's confusion of French art and life with all art and life, with one absolute life style. This confusion leads him to maintain that a people should allow itself to be elevated by a foreign and superior art if it truly wants to live the good life. Rousseau's counterargument is his own formula for expressing art's relationship to life — that the artist must follow national taste and mores. This is the only normal order. According to him, to speak of substantial change originating in art would have to mean rendering a people less sophisticated, reversing the course of history, which is impossible.

Art is always in the position of deepening but following sophistication. Such progress is not a substantial change. The arts arose when chance and natural man's needs were ready to produce them. Art as beaux-arts is a product of the creation of political art, of mores, of taste, and has to meet the demands of a people, just as unanimity of social contract was the only political instrument that men before collectivity could accept from the hands of the shrewd. Legitimacy was essential but left side-effects which led to slavery, just as the beauty of French theater would be needed to captivate the curiosity of the Genevans but would carry hidden effects which might corrupt them. Ideally, once individual need has been abandoned, collective need is the new master and art is again the servant of need. The beaux-arts with their creations parallel the political world, but they must never be, on the alleged authority of nature or of history's necessity, placed above any collectivity. To say the Genevans need the French theater to improve their national life is to equate the French nation with the Genevan nation in some way, to say that their two wills require the same good. This is to posit the existence of an art above national life, an art responding to all of mankind, to assume that artificial beings like the state can have a shared interest as if they were all one whole, mankind. The contrary is true. Each nation has its own life and its own good, and each needs its own particular theater to respond to that good.

For a time in the *Lettre* Rousseau partly plays d'Alembert's game. He assumes that a theater is necessary but insists that it should be a theater suited and subordinated to national good as expressed in national taste and mores. That his condemnation of the theater is not rigid, that he does not find it inherently sinful, is seen in the admiration he finds for a kind of theater in history which properly subordinated beaux-arts to political art. The theater of the Greeks served to preserve independence of national character rather than to destroy it because it reinforced their patriotism by its content, the great deeds of national heroes, and because its mode of presentation was uplifting, in the open air and among all of the assembled people (pp. 146-47, 185). In this way it became a cohesive force unifying the nation. In theory, Genevan authors might compose plays adapted to the taste of the Genevans (pp. 220-21); they might dramatize their national heroes, put William Tell on the stage, for example. Unfortunately, French taste would make this impossible. Its canons require heroes and heroines of high rank, the predominance of the love element, the portrayal of flaws in human personality, a rigid system of versification. According to Rousseau, there can be only one theater in Europe because French tradition, its prestige, and its rules smother any independent theater; in effect they make the normal priority — subordination of beaux-arts to national political art — impossible in Geneva.

It would be better, then, to do without the theater altogether, not to compete in that category. Since French theater, a national product, now passes as a universal, absolute form, the Genevan government must find art forms more meaningful to the Genevans themselves. It is customary to make fun of Rousseau's ideas about what this national art should be, but his aim, perfectly logical if unrealistic, is to form an ambience of national spirit around the Genevans, thus to illustrate the means of protecting any small collectivity. It is not just a question of denying the theater to Genevans but of taking positive measures to slow or stop the relentless working of the mechanism by which a so-called predominant culture controls the taste, then the *mœurs* of minor cultures. He wants to preserve those stubborn pockets of nonconformism. Classical French theater in its decadence is therefore deliberately made all the more hideous by his measurement of it through the perspective of an unsophisticated culture, a perspective which reveals its affected sentiments, its imitation so different from reality, so preoccupied with love, its appeal to a jaded taste, to passivity.

Rousseau offers by way of contrast the image of a people more fresh, more immediately alive. He would preserve its more spontaneous, individualistic spirit: "Such is the simplicity of true genius... it compares itself to no one; all its resources are within itself.... In a small town, proportionately less activity is no doubt to be found than in a capital... but more original minds, more inventive industry, more really new things are there, because the people are less imitative, because, having few models, each draws more from himself and puts more of his own into everything he does; because the human mind, less spread out, less drowned in vulgar opinions, elaborates on itself and ferments better in tranquil solitude; because in seeing less, more is imagined; finally, because, less pressed for time, a man has more leisure to pursue and direct his ideas" (p. 170). He opposes to French taste or European taste, which the Genevans would receive inappropriately, an originality to be preserved by more direct means than the theater, means which involve the participation of each individual directly in the artistic activity, which do not imitate action but have their own reality through spontaneity — public festivals, dances, games, races. "It is in the open air, under the sky, that you should meet and give yourselves over to the sweet sentiment of your happiness. Let your pleasures not be effeminate or mercenary, let nothing that has the smell of constraint and selfishness poison them, let them be free and generous like you.... one must have been there with the Genevan people to understand with what ardor they enter into... these festivals... they are no longer that steady people... no longer those slow reasoners... they are lively, gay, and tender.... I offered the festivals of Lacedaemon as a model for those I should like to see among us.... everything in them was infused with a secret patriotic charm,... with a certain martial spirit befitting free men" (pp. 224-26, 232). At another level, Rousseau's own experimentation in the *Nouvelle Héloïse* would appear to be in part an effort to satisfy this same need to express the soul of a people.

When writers say that Rousseau in the *Lettre* repeatedly confuses art and life, they seem to mean that he posits a type of person upon whom the playwright should model his characters and a form of justice which his intrigues should be careful to imitate. This means learning to obey one standard and no other, the puritan's moral code. On the contrary, according to all of the evidence, Rousseau admits that the author must do and does in fact the exact opposite. The artist's two concerns are to express his genius as best he can and to communicate the result, his art, to the audience. This last need means that his genius is compromised by whatever taste his audience may have. If he tried to moralize to a sophisticated audience, his plays would not succeed. If he elevated the vocabulary, images, action, and thought of his plays above the taste of his audience, if he failed to praise or disparage the old or new social order when the audience expected it, he would fail.

But there is another important factor in playwriting — art's hidden effect. With reference to a theater operating within its own culture, it is usually inaccurate to speak of any real harm derived from its productions, except to say that a people which, for example, insists on a subject-matter loaded with cruelty, depravity, and violence reinforces its corruption, just as a people which insists on sincerity and patriotism strengthens its patriotism. Between cultures, however, it is clear to Rousseau that nocuous borrowing can occur. For a worldly people to adopt a countrified style of life from a rustic nation is beside the point, of course, since the former cannot escape its refinement. It has done no more than add another kind of sophistication, the affectation of simplicity. But acceptance by a rustic nation of another people's theater involves a leap toward character change. It means in effect a departure from the order appropriate to civil society and a return to the order of historic necessity.

Within any artificially created order, such as the state, it is clear that the people, the collectivity, determines art, for example the quality of its theater. Political art controls fine arts; that is the true order of priorities. Between countries, the order may be reversed, for a state of cultural warfare exists, and the more sophisticated state's art may subjugate the unsophisticated nation's art, then its taste and mores. Political art's shield, *volonté générale*, has been penetrated and its will, its own artistic needs, bypassed. There are from then on two powers within the nation' competing at the same time for the people; for example, the will of Geneva and the will of the French nation as it is felt through its art. Cultural conquest is underway and the eventual destruction of the nation's spirit must follow. That is the essence of the matter. Men like d'Alembert, who preach the value of the French theater, claim that French art has reached such perfection that it requires imitation by all, as if it were an absolute, whereas in fact, given the individuality of each state, its circumstances of time and place, there should be as many national expressions of art as there are states.

For artistic as well as political reasons, according to Rousseau, artists must move down the abstraction scale, must throw off the belief in universal forms of art. They should seek the originality of emotional, moral, and intellectual content that each national character has nourished. Since each national will and art have intrinsic value, life need not be advanced sophistication and art the reflection of it. The *philosophes* see the history of art as an ascending line with French art at the zenith of prestige, closing history. They seem to imply by their reasoning that nature, history, sophistication, universality, and art are all to be conjoined. Rousseau contradicts this view by placing value also in the origins, the state of nature which was without sophistication. Without natural sanction, since nature no longer means the advancement of the intellect, sophistication is no more than a phenomenon of history, an outgrowth of necessity's bringing together of individuals in time and place. In this change from a framework of one person to a framework of more than one, there is something more important than sophistication or intellect guided by vanity. The only substantive value which parallels nature by means of art is civil consensus. Art, to be sure, needs nature, that is, the natural genius of the artist. Art also utilizes sophistication, not as an end in itself, but only as a gauge to know the audience's level. But the real object is to pass beyond both nature (genius) and sophistication (a particular audience) in order to find and express the life of the artificial consensus (the nation). In a sense art should not reflect human life at all. It should not be the self-interested desire of the artist to create or the desire of a group to laugh, to be moved deeply through vicarious fear, pity, or love. Rather it should be a selfless analysis of the nation's spirit. D'Alembert suggested that Geneva should have a national theater. Rousseau replied in terms of what a national theater for the Genevans should be, and found that this art form, because of what it had come to mean, would be incapable of expressing the buoyant, active, youthful personality of the Swiss.

The calm tone of self-righteousness which Rousseau maintains in this work is weighted, however, less against the Parisian theater than against d'Alembert's failure to attach value to the independent *moi commun* or common self of each nation. To the extent that other European nations have allowed French culture to represent them, they are on the way to losing their own national spirit and vitality. The *Lettre* rebukes also the tacit claim that the French theater speaks for its own people. In reality, it represents for Rousseau only a part of the nation, an aristocracy which insists that an artist respond to their too human wants rather than to the life of the entire nation.

In the *Lettre* Rousseau probes the meaning of a project with serious sociological ramifications. Because of this orientation, his sin is not that he confuses art with life, but perhaps that he insists too much on the relationship between esthetics and the political foundations of the nation. The artist's source should be in the nation. There are as many sources as there are nations. There can be no one universal culture for mankind. The artist finds the soul of his nation and directs his art to that end, rather than letting it follow individual genius alone, or autonomous canons of taste, or the will of an elite bent on pleasure. For Rousseau, since the collectivity should be small, like Geneva or Corsica, this is national inspiration in the sense of regionalism more than of statism, although the idea of safeguarding the cohesive spirit of the nation against foreign influence is always the predominant concern.

CHAPTER VI

THE EVOLVING FAMILY

No EXCUSE SEEMS NECESSARY FOR GIVING the *Nouvelle Héloïse* a full chapter in a discussion of Rousseau's ideas on the foundations of national power. The importance of this work's contribution to his system has been frequently recognized (Pléiade, 2: xx, xlii, liv). Some of his main themes — the opposition of provincial life to the decadence of brilliant cities, the glorification of antiquity at the expense of modern nations, the tension between passion and duty, the education of children, the struggle between deism and atheism — appear in his novel, either amplified beyond their expression in the earlier writings, or used to supplement topics explained in *Emile* and the *Contrat social*.

Some readers may question the sequence in which I am discussing this work, after the *Lettre à d'Alembert*, since the inspiration and planning for the *Nouvelle Héloïse* came earlier, its composition was the more sustained effort, and its content was perhaps sentimentally closer to Rousseau. He was already imagining some of the characters for his novel and forming its overall plan by 1756. The *Lettre* spoke to the problem of an immediate threat to the Genevan people, whereas the novel was in part an artistic effort to know and reveal the spirit of a community still relatively free of European sophistication. The order I am following is determined by another more basic consideration, the scope and major emphases of these two studies as they relate to the other works dicussed in this book.

The *Discours sur les sciences et les arts* raised the problem of man's predicament and gave but a glimpse of the solution in a new ordering of knowledge which placed moral and political science and art in control. The *Second discours* found in nature and history the principles to guide statecraft — natural liberty (isolation and independence) and civil liberty (legitimacy). The *Economie politique* argued in a context of matter of fact for the predominance of the enlightened prince in national affairs, for control through his vision and art of the formation of the sovereign people, for the concentration of every kind of power, intellectual, physical, and moral, in the executive's hands. The subject of the *Lettre* was the people itself, here placed in an international context, viewed from outside by Rousseau. Seeing himself in the guise of counselor to its government, he offers warnings about the vulnerability of the Genevans, the threat to their national soul from continued penetration by French/European culture. I have discussed the *Lettre* (1758) before the *Nouvelle Héloïse* (1761), *Emile* (1762), and the *Contrat social* (1762), not because of its earlier publication, since in conception and even in initial plans for composition these other projects were anterior to it, but because this order is most suitable to my examination of Rousseau's thought. The movement is from Rousseau's first view of society, to his standards, to the operational problem of applying these at the level of the prince, of his people, and now at the level of the family.

Rousseau had moved to the Hermitage in 1756. Close to Paris yet free for the most part from its intrusions, he was determined to complete many projects, including the editing of certain manuscripts of the Abbé de Saint-Pierre, the preparation of a treatise of his own on education, and the formulation of principles relative to political institutions. But memories obsessed him as well as the regret that he had reached advanced age without having experienced any deep and lasting sentimental attachment. His imagination began to fill this emotional void with idealized characters for a novel and the visits of Mme d'Houdetot in 1757 soon provided a real and passionate love with which his fictional Julie and Claire could be associated. Finished in the fall of 1758, the work's publication in late 1760 or early 1761 was met with unprecedented success. Rousseau's correspondence for the period January to May 1761, the many letters of praise and admiration he received, bear witness to the immense enthusiasm engendered by the *Nouvelle Héloïse*.

But his pride in this novel was accompanied by serious doubts. His moral aim, he realized, had at times interfered with his esthetic goals. Even more important was his anguish, a sort of moral crisis which arose from the feeling that this kind of artistic effort, a love story, gave the lie to the austere principles he had always expounded. A summary of the epistolary novel's six parts helps explain Rousseau's mixed reactions and prepares the way for my discussion of the text.

In Part I, Saint-Preux, the young tutor of Julie d'Etange, falls in love with his pupil. This modern Abélard is of unknown origins. His Héloïse comes from an aristocratic family. Both Saint-Preux and Julie understand that the Baron d'Etange, often away from Vevey, will on his return oppose their marriage. Because of Julie's fear, Saint-Preux departs for the mountainous Valais region. After this trip, he stays at Meillerie, across the lake from Vevey. Separation is soon unbearable. The couple meet again, and Julie becomes Saint-Preux's mistress. Both Julie and Claire, her cousin and closest friend, are unable to soften her father's attitude. Milord Edouard Bomston, English friend of Saint-Preux, also fails to overcome the Baron's class prejudice. The Baron, moreover, had already promised his daughter to M. de Wolmar. Saint-Preux, overcoming thoughts of suicide, leaves for Paris.

Part II describes the despair of the lovers. When Bomston offers to arrange their elopement to England, Julie refuses to wound her parents. Saint-Preux from Paris describes French society. At the close of this part, Madame d'Etange finds Saint-Preux's love letters to Julie.

In Part III, Julie's position is weakened by the death of her mother, since she now experiences feelings of guilt even more strongly. The Baron can insist on the marriage with Wolmar more effectively, and Saint-Preux, responding to Julie's plea, gives his consent. When Julie falls ill from smallpox, Saint-Preux rushes to her side and himself contracts the disease. Sickness and this new indication of love do not alter the realities. The marriage with Wolmar takes place. Saint-Preux again thinks of suicide, but dissuaded by Bomston, departs for a voyage around the world, concluding Part III. After several years, Saint-Preux returns

(Part IV) and stays at Clarens, home of Wolmar and Julie. The passion of the lovers is far from dead. In the absence of Wolmar, a trip across the lake to revisit Meillerie proves the intensity of their feelings and reveals only a somewhat tentative control of love by the dictates of marriage and motherhood.

Part V describes the charm of life at Clarens, the discussions and silences permitted among friends, the rural economy, the outdoor life, harvests, the community festivals. Julie suggests that Saint-Preux and Claire, now a widow, should marry. Wolmar's atheism and Julie's love for Saint-Preux continue to mar the idealism of the group.

In Part VI, the threat of passion is still a major concern. Saint-Preux and Claire refuse a *mariage de convenance*. Julie turns more and more toward religion. When her son falls into the lake, she saves him, but her own death from the shock, the cold, and perhaps a fatal wish, is imminent. The closing letters describe Julie's last thoughts, feelings, and wishes.

It is hard to pass by the novelistic side of the *Nouvelle Héloïse*, but I am using this work primarily as a document to shed light on Rousseau's political thought. My justification is that earlier treatments of the question of paternal authority in this novel have seen Clarens in static perspective. Although some critics have emphasized the realism in Wolmar's attitudes, or the Machiavelian aspects of a planning dedicated to success through manipulation of the members of the group, it has become traditional to make this Clarens Rousseau's ideal, an ideal which combines elements of realism with reason, morality, and religion in search of a regime perfect within itself for the most part and remote from the wider national world, a self-contained dream world nestled beside its sheltering lake. Realism, it is often held, makes this utopia even more valid. The words of René Pomeau in the introduction to his edition of the novel present this approach very clearly: "Let us however praise Rousseau, who against the custom of most utopian thinkers, has not eliminated from his plans economic constraint.... At Clarens, domestic economy and politics are permeated by ethics; and ethics by religion."[1] Practical economic

---

[1] *Julie ou la Nouvelle Héloïse*, ed. René Pomeau (Paris: Garnier, 1966), p. xxx.

considerations are certainly joined with idealism to form this community, but there are also for Rousseau, as I shall stress, deep flaws in its structure which lead him to transform even Wolmar's regime.

Rousseau viewed the family as a source of strength for Sparta and Rome. In the *Nouvelle Héloïse*, I believe, his concern is precisely with the relationship of the family unit to the problems of national power. The generosity of most of the leading characters, their usually humane motivations, make all the more interesting the causes which in a very complete sense destroy the perfection Wolmar has given Clarens. There is weakness in this community, not so much in the sense of individual vice, as in the inadequate authority and familial relationships established under d'Etange and persisting during subsequent stages of the family until the death of Julie. Wolmar's kind of reason, dedicated to rehabilitation, introduces new and basic defects of which his atheism is only the symptom. Rousseau's merciless exposure of the fallacies underlying the Clarens "ideal" has been overlooked because of the prevalent and traditional belief that Wolmar's Clarens is Rousseau's answer to the family question rather than simply the statement of the problem that he tries to resolve in the last chapter. In seeing this ideal of Clarens as an appendage, the setting for the action and characters of the novel, writers also have failed to recognize that the community is in meaningful evolution, that a testing of varying family structures is underway as the action unfolds. This dynamic element suggests that Rousseau's notion of feasible reform has not moved away from government or people to the level of the family, as many have maintained, but rather that the family is seen as an integral part of his wider system, that different families are being examined in an investigation which is not an end in itself but is rather the means for finding the family organism best suited to a people and government both dedicated to the general good of the nation.

Since I intend to deal principally only with one aspect of the *Nouvelle Héloïse*,[2] the family, I have found it convenient to divide my study into five parts. The first deals with the family

---

[2] All citations for the *Nouvelle Héloïse* are from the Pléiade edition of the *Œuvres complètes*, vol. 2.

in a city environment, the next three with the family in a country situation — at Vevey under the authority of the Baron d'Etange, then at Clarens under Wolmar, and, finally, at Clarens as it is to be in the absence of Julie and with the ascendency of Saint-Preux. My conclusion attempts to find the meaning and place of the family in Rousseau's political thought.

The family in the city appears initially and in greatest detail in Saint-Preux's letters from Paris, particularly in Letter 21 of Part II. In the Parisian mode of marriage, Saint-Preux finds natural sentiment absent (2: 270). Sincere love is denied to girls of marriageable age and allowed only to married women. They alone can follow their heart and its right, which "excludes from their choice no one except their husband." Natural sentiment finds its place mainly through adultery: "A woman who had not feared to soil the conjugal bed a hundred times" would not hesitate to blame innocent young lovers (2: 271). Wedlock is a contract without any sincere meaning, "an arrangement between two free persons who agree to live together, bear the same name, recognize the same children" (2: 271). The relationships between adulterous lovers are scarcely more meaningful, "last hardly more than one visit" (2: 271). This shallowness of marriage and love has a basic cause. Men have ceased to be individual men, women to be individual women: "A man is always a man, all are almost equally good.... at a certain age all men are just about the same man, all women the same woman" (2: 271-72). Men are uniformly effeminate, women uniformly artificial. The latter direct high society and assume an active role in wielding power rather than raising a family: "Olympus, Parnassus, glory and fortune, are both equally under their laws" (2: 276). Women have become "a hundred times more like men of merit than loveable women" (2: 278). Rousseau's criticisms of aristocratic family life in Paris serve to highlight the problem of all family life, man's loss of identity in a society grown too sophisticated, the need for a return to valid conceptions of man and woman and to a belief in the value of the individual.

Against this backdrop of degradation, it is easier to see in correct proportion the family problem at Vevey and Clarens. There the confusion resulting from the negation of manhood, the effeminacy of men, is not a threat, and each man has his distinguishing characteristics, his particular faults and virtues. The problem can therefore be presented in terms of man's evolution into the type needed to sustain a positive family union while still retaining individuality. The tension between discipline or type and independence or the idiosyncratic self must be maintained if the family is to thrive. The meaning of this conflict will become clear as my analysis proceeds. For the present, it is enough to say that this conflict parallels the everyday person that Rousseau was and the Rousseau of sentiment as revealed in the *Confessions*, except that there the emphasis was on revealing through art the depth beneath the surface, whereas here the emphasis is on revealing man's individual sentiment transformed into a higher being, the father as community leader, a concept of citizenship to which Rousseau may have aspired but to which no facet of his own life corresponded unless through the confused image left by his own father.

The Baron d'Etange, although head of a family, represents irresponsibility, selfish concern for his own pleasures, preoccupation with his nobility, and little regard for the well-being of his family. His concept of service to the state is military, and this emergency kind of virtue has taken precedence over his other duties, including the raising of his children. This task he has left to his wife, who has selected a tutor for the children on the basis of his "acceptable talents," which she thought would not be "useless" (2: 31). Her concern is less to discover and form character than "one day to surprise her husband" by Julie's progress in studies which she "hides from him with that in mind" (2: 32). Julie is in fact isolated within her family because of the "inflexible severity" of her father and its results. Her mother is "weak and without authority" (2: 39). Her brother is dead. Claire, the only person on whom she can depend, belongs to another family and is often absent. Both girls have been exposed in their early years to the tales of Claire's governness, not a very desirable informant: "She spoke to us endlessly of the maxims of gallantry, of the adventures of her youth, of the intrigues of lovers" (2: 43). The education supplied by Saint-Preux has been of greater benefit to Claire than to Saint-Preux and Julie: "She is really the only one of the three who retains any part of everything we learned" (2: 57). This is not because his ideas on education are bad but because their souls are troubled (2: 58-61). In the absence of parental guidance and religious influence, their love develops, and they think of elopement in spite of Julie's personal sense of filial duty: "That would have wounded deeply the best of fathers: that would have plunged a dagger into my mother's heart.... I had to destroy my parents, my lover, or myself" (2: 96).

Fear soon becomes the predominant emotion inspired by the Baron: "I know my father too well to doubt that I would not see him immediately pierce your heart by his own hand, if indeed he did not begin with me" (2: 145-46). Throughout her pregnancy Julie expects either to be killed by him or to win his consent to let her marry Saint-Preux, but a miscarriage prevents the latter alternative (2: 345). The Baron has been a father *in absentia*. Without having guided his family, he nevertheless expects it to survive without other support than his reputation and the fear his image commands. For him the family is to be a shelter, a retreat in his old age: "I myself, after having lived almost independently within the bonds of marriage, feel that I need to become again a husband and father, and I am going to retire into the bosom of my family" (2: 492). He is an adult yet still a child who expects to find within his own neglected family the comfort his father may have provided for his own childhood.

The Baron's egotism and negligence are accompanied by blindness to the merits of those around him and an inclination to measure people by their rank, to discount the importance of their feelings. Rather than know persons, the Baron knows their place. The arguments of Lord Bomston, representing integrity and enlightenment, are insufficient to overcome his prejudice against Saint-Preux. The Baron, in the words of Saint-Preux, is not interested in the "greatness in the depth of my soul," but only in the "meanness of my fortune" (2: 89). By intimidation and an appeal to conscience after the death of Madame d'Etange, he overcomes Julie's resistance. His appeal to filial duty wins, too, her consent to the marriage with Wolmar: "Do you want to bring about the death of the entire family?" (2: 348).

The family atmosphere provided by the Baron has been unsteady. Flashes of paternal love and kindness have been regularly stilled by prejudice and tyranny. Warm emotions have come from another source, the triangle represented by Julie, Claire, and Saint-Preux, a triangle also present at the end of the novel. But the themes joined to that final relationship are significant for their fruition, whereas earlier their meaning is in the incipient conflicts they present. These prevailing themes are first, virtue as social acceptance, the Julie theme; second, virtue as *amour de soi*, love of self, and as manhood, natural integrity, the theme of Saint-Preux; and third, passion and death, which relates closely to the first two themes.

Julie's character during the first three parts of the book has been seriously distorted by critics in the past. During the period in which the Baron is in charge of Clarens, from the beginning of the novel to Julie's marriage to Wolmar (Part III, Letter 17), she has always been seen as essentially passionate. Her love and fall seem to be a reaction to the Baron's regime. Wolmar is supposed to teach her control and wisdom, to make her the nucleus of his perfect community. Yet the fact is that her sense of compassion and transcendent altruism, which makes her the center of any group, is already, along with passion, strongly emphasized in Books I and II: "But you are surrounded by people whom you cherish and who adore you... an entire town proud of having seen you born, everything occupies and shares your affection" (2: 73). She spreads her "irresistible charm over everything that surrounded her" (2: 115). In Fanchon Regard's words she is already a protector: "You never tire of consoling the afflicted" (2: 119). Her powers for good ("What a strange authority you have") are for Saint-Preux "more divine than human" (2: 122). In the context, more than just in the language of love, these words indicate his growing awareness of her moral strength. After his departure for Neufchâtel, he feels in fact the "unknown happiness" she had predicted: "I am experiencing already the compensation you promised me, you whom the habit of doing good has taught so well the enjoyment to be found in it" (2: 122). Lord Bomston senses in her immediately "a character still more stamped with perfection" (2: 198). The heart feels this perfection "even independently of love.... there is only one Julie in the world." Claire attributes Julie's power, which can move parents, lover, even Wolmar "at a mature age," "friends, acquaintances, servants, neighbors, and an entire town," not to beauty, wit, or grace, but to "that tender soul and that sweetness of affection which knows no equal... the gift of loving... which makes all hearts fly to meet yours" (2: 203-04).

Because of her natural love of mankind, Julie wields an influence over any group she enters, becomes its center. Yet this perfection has its dangers. Much of the interest Rousseau has given to Julie lies in her potential instability. The reader is often made to feel and anticipate a possible movement from virtue to vice. Bomston, speaking of her moral perfection, raises also the image of her certain degradation if she cannot make her love for Saint-Preux legitimate by marriage: "Young lover, do not be mistaken about it any longer, renounce the confidence which was your undoing: you are lost, if you must still fight love; you will be disgraced and conquered; and the sense of your shame will gradually silence all your virtues" (2: 198). Chaillot had the first insight into this kind of weakness: "The better she thought of your reason, the more she feared for your heart" (2: 45). Julie's own justification to Saint-Preux of her marriage to Wolmar is based on this same idea of an inevitable passage from virtue as expansive social oneness with her surroundings to virtuous love (Saint-Preux), to degenerate love: "Would I have had greater respect for the rights of a past love than I had for the rights of virtue, while they still possessed their full control over me? What certainty could I have had that I would love only you in this world.... the habit of vice would have eliminated my abhorrence for it" (2: 356).

Accompanying Julie's love for Saint-Preux (a danger because under the circumstances it means exclusiveness, separation from the family, perhaps even eventual moral degeneracy since the distinction between an exclusive passion and profligate passion is only a matter of degree) is her radiating warmth, which makes her fit easily into any community. Virtue as expansiveness, solidarity with family, fear of the excesses of her loving nature and the consequent rejection by society — these are basic elements in Julie's character from the beginning. They foreshadow and determine in large part the second Clarens period, the family under the direction of Wolmar, Parts IV through VI.

Wolmar's characteristics need only brief mention here. He is fifty, vigorous, free of emotions, dedicated to order. He is capable of detecting the hidden currents motivating an individual and a community. Rousseau makes it clear through this antithesis with the Baron that the d'Etange regime and the elements coming from it, the love of Julie and Saint-Preux, even the marriage to Wolmar, were products of either necessity or providence, forces beyond human planning. If providence was involved in the form of natural goodness, the forces of necessity were the determining factors. Since the Baron acted for the most part according to his automatic urges, his prejudices and passions, Julie and Saint-Preux, too, were forced to seek their natural right in the midst of society and were inevitably buffeted by convention. Nature, even if providential, has to be assisted by science in order to survive in society, and Wolmar supplies this help. His reason must gauge the force of nature, Julie's love, and the force of society's inflammation of that love. By artificial devices he must cool this exclusive passion, reduce it again to Julie's natural expansiveness for family and community, hold Julie to her intention that Saint-Preux shall be no more than the "lover of my soul" (2: 364). Evil can come from good, from Julie's expansiveness.

Rather than blame Julie for her "weakness" and "fault," as did the destructive Baron, Wolmar's approach is to restore her confidence. He shows her the soundness of her judgment even in its waywardness: "Congratulate yourself, instead, for having been able to choose an honorable man at an age in which it is so easy to be mistaken, and for having taken formerly a lover whom you can have today for a friend before your husband's very eyes" (2: 495). In him Rousseau's notion of the legislator appears again. After studying the elements of a situation, Wolmar reassembles them in a dynamic way, in this instance, not the nation, but the family and its surrounding community, so that, according to Julie, each part thrives, realizes itself to the utmost, yet contributes freely to an uninhibiting whole: "The order he has established in his household is the image of the order which reigns in the depths of his soul, and seems to imitate on a small scale the order established in the government of the world. You see in it neither that inflexible regularity which produces more inconveniences than advantage and is bearable only to the one who imposes it, nor that mistaken confusion which, because of having too much, makes everything useless. The master's hand is seen in everything without being felt; and he has planned the first arrangement so well that everything now goes on by itself, and one enjoys order and liberty at the same time" (2: 371-72).

To be complete, this order must if possible include Saint-Preux, because he is in Julie's heart. Again, the point of departure is the state of the individual's soul. Saint-Preux's coming is made contingent upon his own conscience: "If there is nothing there to frighten you, come without any fear" (2: 416). The psyche must be made to adjust to the matter of fact. Saint-Preux's love is to be broadened beyond Julie to include the existing conditions imposed by necessity — Wolmar, the children, Claire, the opinion of the community, the provincial life itself, the cultivating, planting, and harvesting. In other words, he must place the general good and its will over any private interest.

Julie receives Saint-Preux from her husband within the context of friendship: "It is only as he is honored by your friendship that he will from now on have mine" (2: 421). Openness of feeling is the rule: "The first step towards vice is to make a mystery of innocent actions." Wolmar's frankness ("Live when the two of you are alone as if I were present, or in my presence as if I were not there" [2: 424]) brings to bear the full weight of authority ("M. de Wolmar began to gain such an ascendency over me"), an authority acceptable because it is passionless: "No man hates me; a man without passion cannot inspire aversion in anyone" (2: 429). Saint-Preux later may contribute actively to the general good as tutor: "Perhaps we may one day enjoy with more advantage than you think the fruit of the efforts we are going to make" (2: 428, 437). Wolmar thus arranges the lives of those around him with detachment, but he is not "independent of them." Rousseau's vocabulary stresses science and art. Wolmar must observe men, use their qualities, combine events and human will into a meaningful pattern, "like fine symmetry in a picture, or like a piece well played on the stage" (2: 490-91).

But science and art without God lose their sense of proportion, may carry the legislator's function too far, may try to transcend nature and necessity by perfection rather than by adjustment to the matter of fact. Rousseau parts company with Wolmar, sends Godless talent in spite of its successes to ultimate defeat. His method is to spread irony over Wolmar's atheistic creations by showing their secret reliance on providential notions, by giving them, as he does Wolmar, attributes of divinity, by emphasizing the vulnerability of atheistic confidence.

Any religion, any system is for Wolmar but "one more dream" (2: 592, 621). He believes only in what his senses and intelligence tell him will work under given circumstances after weighing the forces in balance. He knows his operative arrangements will not last forever. What is created by man's artifice is subject to disruption by the unexpected. It is futile to attribute to "human matters a solidity that is not in their nature" (2: 529). Wolmar's only system is a doctrine of calculated control. His pleasure is in the science and art of manipulating physical, intellectual, and emotional forces, in making them bend to his intelligence and will. Yet he lacks the emotional involvement and fixed principles which would destroy the validity of his judgment and his ability to adjust to new facts. Behind his view of order, however, in spite of his professed atheism, there is in fact an absolute principle which explains his reliance on men, which suggests a providential root in his thinking: "All characters are good and sound in themselves, according to M. de Wolmar. There are, he says, no errors in nature. All the vices that are attributed to man's nature are the effect of the bad forms [training] it has received" (2: 563). Rather than rely totally on education and environmental influence, he would therefore listen to each individual's nature, try to adapt education to it (2: 564). Rousseau in a footnote underlines what he finds to be a discrepancy in an atheist, his attention to origins, his attribution of absolute value to the primitive nature of man: "It is a surprise to find M. de Wolmar holding this doctrine, which is so true" (2: 563). Arguing from observation, rejecting and scorning all systems, Wolmar, a declared atheist and an intelligent one, passionless and therefore not suspected of influence by any hidden mysticism, has reached a position implying not just an order created by man, but a higher order, perhaps more Newtonian than Platonic or Christian, but an order ontological, permanent, and transcending man's creation of order. This providential nature may be inoperative without man's education, yet it is present for Wolmar and of absolute value.

The social result of such order is to make the family association of individuals, each member in his proper place, an end in itself, never a means to an end. Progress is to be in the qualitative improvement of the individuals and of their relationship, not in quantitative expansion. Wolmar's watchful eye is always present. He talks with the peasants, "informs himself about their situation; he examines the condition of their land, he assists them if they are in need from his purse and with his advice" (2: 402). He gives attention to wife and children. The calm, the shelter, the isolation of the community, with its protecting water and mountains, remind Saint-Preux of "my delightful Island of Tinian" (2: 441). Deliberately, felicity is made to include all members of the family and community, not just the masters. Emphasis is on abundance, convenience, and utility, not richness and luxury: "this is no longer a house made to be seen, but to be inhabited" (2: 441). The lands of the family are not farmed out for cultivation by others. The members of the family are directly responsible for all work and pride themselves in their skill and industry. The object is to make the fields produce to the maximum "in order to feed more men.... to permit many people to make a living" (2: 442). All of the workers, because of the incentives provided by Wolmar and the affection and attention they receive from Julie, become as if members of the family and receive their formation from it: "They have, so to speak, only changed fathers and mothers, and found more wealthy ones" (2: 445). As a result, Wolmar and Julie produce, along with crops, "good servants for their own personal service, good farmers to till their land, good soldiers for the defense of the homeland, and honest people for any position into which fortune may call them" (2: 455). Since the emphasis is on satisfying the needs of as many men as possible, not on accumulating wealth for its own sake, since they have invested "more safely than profitably," a calculated risk is always present: "A property which does not increase is subject to being diminished by a thousand accidents" (2: 529).

But Wolmar has put his faith in men, not in wealth. He assumes his children will work enough to make the patrimony sufficient: "Should not the industry of each enter into the calculation of his wealth?" (2: 529). By concentrating on the true needs of his family he has avoided the distortion wealth places between man and reality: "Disorder and fancy have no limits and make more men poor than do their true needs" (2: 530). Their work in the fields, in the vineyards is a source of joy and "a continual festival" (2: 603). Gone are waste, misery, exploitation. The fields and their workers have been restored to their rightful purpose: "Time of love and innocence, in which women were tender and modest, men were simple and lived in contentment" (2: 603-04).

Wolmar's order means the restoration of men to their natural place through a higher science, moral and domestic economy. For him this accomplishment is purely secular, but Rousseau again touches Wolmar's creativeness with irony. Just as his philosophy of order is deistic, so now his community is made to carry the glow of religious enthusiasm. To color the atmosphere of Wolmar's Clarens, Saint-Preux is made to use religious and Biblical references: "the gifts of Providence.... times of the Patriarchs.... O Rachel.... O gentle pupil of Naomi." Wolmar's cold, calculating goodness has created amidst poverty and suffering a Biblical, pastoral age of tenderness and love (2: 603, 604).

Wolmar's philosophy of calculated order aims to restore Julie and Saint-Preux to their natural integrity: "He has done enough for us and for himself, if he has allowed us to find ourselves again" (2: 665). He gives a new quality to the lives of country people. His talent is to create order out of chaos. Yet his atheism is to become a source of disorder. There are, too, conflict and inconsistency in his behavior, reasoning, and accomplishments: his atheism is a secret to everyone except his immediate peers; he admits the absolute value of human personality; the results of his domestic economy are a reminder of Biblical felicity. It would be but a step, Rousseau suggests, for Wolmar to find a divine order behind this artificially constructed community, but there are several forces which keep him in the atheist's camp. First, he abhors the fanaticism of the cult with which he was associated as a young man. This, however, can no longer be a reason for him, since he is surrounded by people holding more mature interpretations of Christianity. Second, and more serious, he recognizes the existence of evil on earth, and this evil indicates for him the impotence of any first mover: "From this existence alone he deduced a lack of power, intelligence, or goodness in any first cause" (2: 595). Third, he lacks the depth of sentiment that would allow him to know the presence of an order higher than any he could impose. Saint-Preux expresses the problem:

"We will never win this man back; he is too cold and is not wicked; it is not a matter of moving him; the inner proof of sentiment is missing in him" (2: 594).

This intellectual refusal and emotional inability to accept a first cause are directly related to Clarens and the plans Wolmar has for Saint-Preux and Julie. The creation of well-regulated universes is the "only reward ego receives from my continual studies" (2: 491). Gradually, Wolmar seems to go beyond the simple function of legislator. Like the lawgiver, he has superior insight into individual character, "some supernatural gift for reading our innermost feelings" (2: 496). He encourages men to suspend reason as calculating common sense and to obey only their interior voice, "if your heart could silence your reason" (2: 499). The results of this abandonment to conscience within the atmosphere of control he provides are "a marvel," "a great miracle," according to Wolmar, the paradoxical joining of opposites in Saint-Preux and Julie: "They love each other more ardently than ever" and "nothing remains in their relationship but a virtuous attachment" (2: 508). The evil Wolmar admits in order to refute the existence of God, he plans by science and art to exclude from Clarens. But either such a conquerable kind of evil is no argument against God, or Wolmar has an ego monstrous enough to have replaced God by his own atheistic science, has become Jupiter himself in the absence of belief.

It should be added that two characteristics attached to Wolmar's method, permanence and self-denial, presuppose a belief in order above the human capacity for it. Wolmar expects against his own principles that this cure will be permanent for the individuals involved. It is as if men were to become transcendent beings on earth. The nation, an artificial creation, can in theory attain permanence, can last as long as it has a redefinable general good. But each man and his family are natural; therefore they are subject at any moment to defeat, growth, decline. Only at the level of the nation, as citizens, are men to become selfless whenever matters affecting the general will and its good are at stake. The family is of a completely different, human order in which each person has the right to be full and complete as a human being. Yet Wolmar, in order to accomplish his dream, asks Julie and Saint-Preux to remain devoid of passion under the most trying circumstances. His belief in nature is accompanied by a denial of nature. All men and women are to be as passionless as he. Pride has made him substitute his created world for God's more complex world. He has turned the family into a dehumanized unit. By confidence and conscience he aspires to overcome completely the forces of chance and necessity.

His creatures, Rousseau indicates, have passed the tests imposed on them. Saint-Preux has acted frankly toward the husband, has withheld his trust until he was sure of Wolmar's goodness, a hesitation which won the approval of the older man (2: 428-29). Julie and he have withstood the crisis of Meillerie (2: 517-22). Saint-Preux has forgiven the Baron (2: 605). He has proved himself to Bomston: "No, dear Wolmar, you have not made a mistake; the young man is trustworthy" (2: 649). But Wolmar by the Meillerie test has aspired to a certainty not of this world: "Have I uselessly pleaded your cause against you, and would Madame de Wolmar be satisfied with a virtue which can endure only under certain circumstances? As for myself, I am more demanding; I want to owe my wife's faithfulness to her heart and not to chance; and it is not enough for her to be faithful, I am offended that she should cast any doubt on her fidelity" (2: 497). The order Wolmar hopes to establish is unearthly perfection. Julie makes this order fall within a larger divine creation: "This small room contains everything that is dear to my heart, and perhaps everything that is best on earth; I am surrounded by everything that interests me, the entire universe is for me in this place.... my imagination has no longer anything to do, I having nothing more to desire; to feel and enjoy are the same thing for me; I live at the same time in everything I love, I am filled with happiness and life: come, death, when you will! I no longer fear you, I have lived, I have anticipated you, I have no new sentiments to know, and you have nothing more to hide from me" (2: 689). Such complete enjoyment, she knows however, is not in the nature of man, since it renders hope and imagination superfluous: "One enjoys what is obtained less than what is hoped for, and one is not happy except before being happy. In fact, man, who is greedy and limited, made to want everything and possess little, has received from heaven a consoling force which brings everything he desires close to him, submits it to his imagination...

But all this advantage disappears in the presence of the object itself; there is then no longer anything to embellish this object in the eyes of the possessor... illusion ceases as soon as enjoyment begins. The land of imagination is the only country worth inhabiting in this world, and the nothingness of human things is such that except for the Being who exists by himself, there is nothing beautiful except that which is not" (2: 693). To attain perfection is to end the need for life. Psychologically Julie has found death before the accident.

Her death, opening to question the power Wolmar attaches to intellect, discipline, and humanly created perfection, may permit him to hope, to imagine beyond his own will, to find for the first time religious meaning in the very destruction of his own vision. Clarens as repose, peace, stasis is a place which in the matter of fact does not exist except in the superficial sense of human beings who have for a moment succeeded in generalizing, dehumanizing their naturally private goals. Through irony, by Biblical allusions, by underlining its aspirations to permanence and idealism, Rousseau has converted Wolmar's secular Clarens into not utopia but a mythical paradise created by the Olympian calm of Wolmar and his belief in a meaningful natural order. But Rousseau has not rejected all of Wolmar's community, which has many sound and worthwhile features. Rather he has castigated the man, the father, the community leader who has become no more than intellect, who, with faith only in structure, in the interrelationship of men, neglects the full substance of man, who calculates the behavior of individuals in order to make them part of his machine but cannot know their feelings, their hopes, their limitations. D'Etange's neglect was due to ignorance, passion, pride, and his submersion in necessity. Wolmar represents the *philosophe*'s transcendence of life and history through science and art, which is good, but he represents also the escape into a world so controlled that even the family and the human souls within it are seen as subject to complete analysis and predictability.

Julie's death has meant for critics in the past the probable conversion of Wolmar and also an early expression of Romanticism's later exaltation of the theme of love as desperation, death, and union through death. These two major insights into Part VI, as I have just indicated, fall far short of its meaning. First, Wolmar himself has been effectively condemned by the time of the Chillon episode. His conversion, as important as it may be to Julie's motivation, is philosophically, in the framework of the entire story, still less important than the collapse of his atheistic society, for the ending of the novel holds proposals by Julie for a more positive ordering of family life. Furthermore, death at the close of the work is hardly in the spirit of Romanticism's association of love and death. It is directly related to a new context introduced in the form of a more realistic existence for the people of Clarens.

As background for this interpretation of Part VI, it is essential to review briefly the transformations of the death theme as they occur in the course of the novel. The place of death in Parts I and II has usually been subordinated by critics to an emphasis on life as love and its rights. It is, however, only in these early letters that the relationship of death to love reveals clearly what has been called Romanticism's meaning. Despair, melancholy, suicide are constantly associated with love. References to death show love's force. Death is seen as a means of uniting lovers, as a protest against unhappy love. The natural affinity which exists between Saint-Preux and Julie makes their separation the equivalent of death. The first letter of Part I suggests that "heaven has established a secret conformity between our affections, as well as between our tastes and ages" (2: 32). For Saint-Preux it is a question of "being cured or dying" (2: 33), and the theme of suicide is introduced strongly in Letters 3, 9, 14, 18, and 19. With Saint-Preux's departure for Meillerie, Letter 25, Julie adopts the same language: "A deathly languor has taken possession of my soul" (2: 88). The symbolism of Letter 26, to Julie, is of death: a "place... sad and dreadful... suited to the state of my soul... bleak rocks" (2: 90). Saint-Preux closes with an allusion to the "rock of Leucate, last refuge of so many unfortunate lovers" (2: 93). The thought of suicide, the danger to Julie's own life, drive the lovers back to life, and their love is consummated (2: 95).

The love-death theme returns, but never again so desperately, nor in this exclusively sentimental sense of the spiritual union of lovers. Rather there are inventive plans for meeting: "What is the good of excessive prudence?" (2: 107). For Julie it is not separation of the lovers but any waning within themselves of the intensity of love, an intensity which makes love its own justification, that becomes the dividing line between life and death (2: 209). The emphasis at the same time is on establishing rendezvous in a "remote village" (2: 109, 112), the sacrifice of physical union to good works in behalf of Fanchon and Anet ("this word 'virtue' must... demand sacrifices" [2: 118]), and the joys of union: "Is not so touching and tender a union enough for our happiness?" (2: 141). The theme of death becomes, too, the practical problem of keeping Saint-Preux alive if the Baron learns of their affair (2: 146), if Bomston's honor cannot be satisfied (2: 156). There is also the idea that the actual death of one of them could cause through heartbreak the death of the other (2: 164). Love and death have become very much less elevated in their tone by entering into the everyday stream of community relationships.

In Letter 65, when Claire has served as go-between for Julie and Saint-Preux to convince the latter he must depart, several new variations on the theme of death occur. Fearing that Claire is trying to say that Julie has died (2: 183), he speaks of suicide, believes that separation cannot be long. But reason, not desperation, is the principal tone. His despair is expressed, not in solitude, but in conversation with Claire, M. d'Orbe, Bomston. The separation is made acceptable, and Saint-Preux, rising to greater self-control, does in fact depart with Bomston (2: 178-88).

When in Part II the suicide theme returns, the words about death are the same but the emotional context has changed. The real goal has become life: "O rocks of Meillerie which my wandering eye has measured so many times, why did you not assist my despair! I would have regretted life less if I had not felt the value of it" (2: 191). In Letter 2, Bomston tells us that Saint-Preux "is ashamed of his state" (2: 192). As for Julie, her choice is between Clarens and Saint-Preux, and she places honor, filial duty, and security above union with Saint-Preux in England (2: 202). She seeks in Bomston security for Saint-Preux (2: 209). She repeatedly exhorts Saint-Preux to be a man (2: 213). Because of his resignation and courage, she praises him for his "vigor of feeling" (2: 221). Saint-Preux's visit to Paris, Letters 13-27, shows him for a time reconciled to separation. At Mme d'Etange's request that he remain away from Julie, death is no longer part of his response.

After the death of the mother, he gives his consent to Julie's marriage. His letter to the Baron indicates his pride, control of self, the ability to set the record straight, to stand up for his point of view (2: 326). His visit to Julie during her sickness with smallpox completely reunites them in sentiment. The religious experience of the marriage counters any plan for a lover-mistress relationship. Romantic love has thus been replaced in a gradual evolution toward maturity. For Julie, this means a return to the family to become protector, shelter for others, a stance consistent with her basic altruism and expansiveness. Saint-Preux has a philosophic discussion with Bomston on suicide (2: 377-86), then departs on a sea voyage around the world. His goal, as stated to Claire, self-mastery, is consistent with his pride: "You will see me worthy of appearing before you, or you will never see me again" (2: 376). Self-preservation in the sense of learning to accept life, to endure his feelings, to find himself is now for him the natural goal of man.

As a result of this evolution of their characters, there can never be a serious return to the first desperate suicidal passion. Self-discipline is their intention more than the rights of lovers. Any remnants of Romanticism's kind of love in Parts IV, V, and VI are in fact well within the context of the family's priority. The needs of the community and the problem of each individual's place in the community are the major concerns of Julie's final letter, to be read and passed by Wolmar to Saint-Preux after her death (2: 740-43). The idea of its closing paragraph is that death will reunite them for the first time in virtue, since in the absence of society, natural rights need be the only consideration: "Virtue, which separated us on earth, will join us in eternity. I die in this sweet expectation" (2: 743). But virtue, the sense of what is just under certain conditions, is still the standard, not passion in revolt against social restraint. In the same letter, in fact, much greater attention is given to the on-going family. Insistence on her self-perpetuation through a new order she will establish around Saint-Preux is unmistakably present: "Your duties, your pleasures, your friendships, all will be her work. The bond of your union [with Claire, "another Julie"], formed by her, will make her live again; she will die only when the last among you have died" (2: 741).

This hope is accompanied by the correction of three unstable elements in the old regime: First, atheism: "Be a Christian in order to make him [Wolmar] become one" (2: 742). Second, the unsatisfactory Julie / Saint-Preux / Wolmar triangle, which was to have been renewed by Saint-Preux's return as tutor to the children: "That union was not good.... It is Heaven's blessing to have prevented it" (2: 740). Third, the absence of any truly masculine presence is corrected: there may now be a complete union between lovers ("Claire and Julie will be so joined in your feelings that it will no longer be possible for your heart to separate them... you will have loved with a legitimate passion and enjoyed an innocent happiness" [2: 742]); or, perhaps even more important, Saint-Preux is to become a figure supplying strength for every member of the family, including the children ("I do not know what concern their education will cost you"), Claire, and the former family head, Wolmar, "your liberator," "the most unfortunate of mortals" (2: 742). Most of Julie's final letter, seven paragraphs out of eight, are preoccupied with this reform and renewal of Clarens. The carefully prepared dramatic end is in fact a philosophic beginning prepared with equal care. We must now return to the causes and roots of this new order.

Julie's rejection of Wolmar's atheism is implicit from the beginning of the novel in her expansive kind of love. Her relationship with Wolmar is never in terms of the union of souls that characterized her love for Saint-Preux. Such love, she says, is not necessary to form a happy marriage: "Honor, virtue, a certain compatibility, less of positions and ages than of characters and temperaments, are enough between two partners." These can produce "a very tender attachment," more durable than love and no less sweet (2: 372). Julie and Wolmar complement one another, sensibility and tranquility: "If I were as calm as he, too much coldness would reign between us" (2: 373). He is understanding, she is compassion. Together they form a "single soul." The lack of passionate love is an advantage: "If he had loved me too much, his presence would have troubled me" (2: 373). Unfortunately, there are also differences which inhibit attachment, an atheism which stems from lack of feeling, a religion which rests in large part on sensibility: "In this great harmony of beings, in which everything is the voice of God... he sees only an eternal silence" (2: 591-92). No longer satisfied with a union based on opposites, Julie must transform his soul if her own "communicative soul" is to expand into his, to avoid this basic incompatibility, "so sad a division between those for whom everything should be in common" (2: 592). She abhors, in addition to the barrier atheism presents to her own outflowing love, the offense it represents to God and his providence: "What horror... to imagine the Supreme Being vengeful of its unrecognized divinity, to think that the happiness of the one who is the cause of her happiness must end with his life, to see only a sinner in the father of her children" (2: 592).

Wolmar, another Socrates through his understanding, has in his family avoided all of the pitfalls of materialistic society except one. His science, no matter how moral, has taken for its standard the static perfection of the state of nature, has tried to chain history itself. History is dynamic, changing, striving. Any complete standard must provide for history or temporal existence. Julie knows only too well the forces that threaten the artificial equilibrium of Clarens: "She tries with greater care to gather around him [Wolmar] those transitory comforts to which he limits his happiness. 'Ah!' she says with sadness, 'if the unfortunate man confines his paradise to this world, let us at least make it as sweet as possible'" (2: 594). But transitoriness does not mean just the distinction between Clarens and eternity, between the "living eye" and the "eternal eye," between the *Elysée* created by art and God's eternal design. It means more immediately the difference between the *bosquet* of Clarens and the *Elysée* (2: 472, 485, 496).

Clarens is unstable for Julie partly because its master has no relation with God, but also because its triangle must refuse part of man's nature. The groundswell of feeling present in Parts I through VI menaces the order Wolmar has established. Words and passages of longing continually appear: "What a soul his was!... How he could love!" (expressions of feeling by Julie just before Saint-Preux's return [2: 403]); the "same image still reigns in my heart" (the words of Saint-Preux [2: 415]); Claire's remark to Julie that "another thing very capable of worrying a husband is that something, I don't know what, remains in your language, something moving and affectionate when you speak of the one who was dear to you" (2: 433); Julie's continuing self-doubt: "My heart reassures me when reason should alarm me"

(2: 499); Wolmar's constant testing of Saint-Preux and growing confidence in him, as opposed to his admission of inadequacy in penetrating Julie's heart, "a veil of prudence... so many turns around her heart that it is no longer possible for the human eye to see into it, not even for her own to do so" (2: 509); the Meillerie crisis and her protest after it, "You are playing cruelly with your wife's virtue" (2: 514); the emotionality of both lovers when reminders of the past intervene, making it impossible for "Claire to keep from smiling, Julie from blushing, and I from sighing... an unbearable weight suddenly descends over my heart" (2: 609); the contrast between Saint-Preux's expression of confidence to Wolmar and one letter later his dream of presentiment, his hysteria and need to return to Clarens to see Julie (2: 611-19); Julie's fear that Claire may herself succumb to Saint-Preux's attraction, her wondering "if the confidence which was my undoing is completely without danger for you" (2: 631-31).

The very confidence, in fact, on which Wolmar has built his paradise is gradually made by Julie's remarks the source of its future destruction, so that in Letter 6 of Part VI the problem can be explicitly approached. Julie tries to prevent Saint-Preux's return and with it the danger from chance or circumstance of triggering a fall by associations with the past: "Love is dead; the senses continue to live, and their delirium is all the more to be feared, because the only feeling that limited it, now no longer exists, and everything is the occasion for a fall" (2: 665). Everything around Saint-Preux will excite his passion — Julie, Claire, Fanchon (2: 666) — and Julie foresees the disaster: "It is from him that the disorder in my household comes" (2: 668). Passions must be controlled by avoiding temptation, but Saint-Preux, overconfident under Wolmar's guidance, "does not hesitate to enter into the most foolhardy kind of struggle. Only thirty years old, he is going to shut himself up in isolation with women of his own age" (2: 666).

In addition to the instability inherent in atheism and the persistence of passionate love, Wolmar's regime lacks stability for another reason. Julie, the feminine principle of *pitié*, is the nucleus of this group. In her and in all true women, according to Rousseau, *amour de soi*, the faculty to struggle, survive, and resist, is not dominant. Rather, ego expresses itself in the form of love, an instinct hard to distinguish from the *pitié* which is their essential feminine trait. Saint-Preux stresses this lack of worldly strength in Julie, her passivity, when he describes her role in the Clarens economy: "If, to her misfortune, she had been born among those unhappy people who groan under the weight of oppression and struggle hopelessly and fruitlessly against the misery which consumes them, each lament of the oppressed would have poisoned her life, the common desolation would have overwhelmed her, and her beneficent heart, exhausted by pain and concern, would have made her continually experience the evils she had been unable to relieve. . . . Instead of that, everything here animates and upholds her natural goodness. She does not have to weep over public calamities" (2: 532). Her lack of *amour de soi*, an essentially masculine trait, is not supplied by Wolmar. He is reason. Since rigidity characterizes the moral triangle which has become the condition for the Clarens paradise, Saint-Preux, who does have *amour de soi*, must nevertheless bend to the atmosphere of *pitié*, of expansiveness, or depart. The quiescence of total felicity must therefore drive Julie to new and higher outlets, to the hope for a higher communion, the longing for the divine object which alone can give meaning to a secular perfection devoid of the striving principle of *amour de soi*. Triangular Clarens not only cannot withstand the onslaught of passion, vice, and time as attrition, but means, contrary to Wolmar's expectation, the negation of happiness: "That is what I experience in part since my marriage and your return. . . . My friend, I am too happy; happiness bores me" (2: 694).

The culmination of society at Clarens is not Wolmar's Clarens built around Julie, but Julie's Clarens built around Saint-Preux. Julie has signified emanating love and altruism; more than any of the other characters her nature was from the beginning turned to expansiveness, denial of self, the pursuit of perfection, and absolute perfection is death: "My happiness is fixed, I tear it out of the hands of chance; it no longer has other limits than eternity" (2: 727). More than *pitié* as expansiveness, the other natural instinct, *amour de soi*, masculine courage and vigor, is to be the basis for the new Clarens.

So many critics in the past have emphasized Saint-Preux's weakness, his filial relationship to Julie, parallel with Rousseau's to Madame de Warens, that this new order does not at first seem convincing. Yet Rousseau has definitely prepared this outcome and showed his intention early in the novel. Saint-Preux is a character constantly in growth toward a manhood more complete than Wolmar's. His weaknesses are impatience and imagination, which make him despair in his love or fear the worst for his loved ones. In contrast to the heroic Bomston and the reasonable Wolmar, he seems too sensitive and emotional. Because of emphasis on this side of his character, his most important characteristic has been overlooked.

Unlike the more stereotyped characters (d'Etange, Bomston, and Wolmar) Julie's lover has almost universal potential. His plebian origins have left him less standardized by class. His sensitivity and education assure his ability to meet and mix with people of rank higher than his own without any danger of becoming mercenary or being corrupted by their prejudices. His *amour de soi*, trueness to self and integrity, force him to struggle constantly to defend his own feelings and principles. This involves his program for study: "It is always better to find by oneself the things one would find in books: that is the true secret... for making them part of oneself" (2: 58). This means avoiding standard definitions of the good, the true, and the beautiful: "I do not give you any other definition of virtue than a picture of virtuous men, nor other rules for good writing than books which are well written" (2: 59-60). Thus the individual does not follow the analytic dictates of others. He must "exercise his sight as well as his feeling, judge the beautiful by inspection as he judges the good by feeling" (2: 59).

Saint-Preux feels to his depths and cannot be restrained by the tradition of stoical moderation and silence. Julie's kisses for Saint-Preux, totally surrendering to his sense and feelings, are a torment threatening life itself: "they pierce, they burn... they would drive me insane" (2: 65). This is not intended as hyperbole. Rousseau is describing through Saint-Preux a new experience of love, the reactions of a person like himself whose sensitivity is heightened beyond the normal. Julie notes that no man ever had so loved or could so love again. It is through such depth of feeling that man reaches the sense of reality needed to flaunt convention. This lovers' union is for Saint-Preux sacred without society's contract: "What have you done that divine and human law cannot and should not authorize?" (2: 100). Bomston, in his defense of Saint-Preux, must cut away the usual standards and fathom the potential in the individual: "All the gifts which do not depend on men, he has received from nature, and he has added to them all the talents which depended on him" (2: 168). His nobility is not "written in ink on old parchments, but is engraved in his heart" (2: 168-69). It is hard to define him. Like Julie, he has no particular, distinguishing trait, but if less perfect than she, he is known by his whole being, which is revealed gradually, according to Bomston, is dynamic in the impression it makes on others: "The first time I saw your lover, I was struck by a new feeling which has continued to increase day by day as reason brought its own proof" (2: 197-98).

Saint-Preux's opaqueness is an indication that he distrusts others. He refuses to give himself to others, except gradually and very selectively. *Pitié* is not developed in his being in proportion to *amour de soi*, so that he is incomplete, bound up within himself, and needs very much those individuals with whom he can communicate: "Wandering without family and almost without homeland, I have only you on earth, and love is my only possession" (2: 73). It is therefore difficult for Bomston to see what Saint-Preux "would be without you [Julie]" (2: 198).

Rousseau forms Saint-Preux's manhood as the story unfolds, has him learn to live for others as well as for himself and for Julie, tests his soul by the prejudices which in large part must determine his fate and separate him in life from Julie. This is the meaning of Julie's exhortation in Part II, Letter 7: "Remember then to be resolute, learn to bear misfortune, and be a man. Be again, if I dare say so, the lover Julie chose" (2: 213). Her immediate meaning is that she has troubles enough without his lamentations ("It's for me to be weak and unhappy") but it is she who by marrying Wolmar will take the easy, conventional way rather than the escape Bomston has offered: "You will have to contract an alliance disavowed by your heart. Public approval will be forever contradicted by the cry of your conscience; you will be respected and contemptible: it is better to be forgotten and virtuous" (2: 200). Following her character, divided by her compassion for parents and her love for Saint-Preux, she remains passive in her refusal to go to England, whereas Saint-Preux's reaction is despair over acts he cannot control, an outcry against a society represented by the Baron, which refuses in the name of "barbarous maxims" to respect, not the rights of passion, but human rights: "Whatever the authority you abuse may be, my rights are more sacred than yours; the tie which unites us is the limit of paternal power, even in the judgment of human tribunals; and when you dare appeal to nature, it is you alone who are defying its laws" (2: 326). In the final analysis it is Julie's expansiveness which has frustrated the claims of *amour de soi*. The person endowed heavily with altruism finds in place of her lover a substitute in the community. When this community reaches a point of perfection, her individual self, according to Saint-Preux, loses earthly meaning: "One would say that since nothing on earth can satisfy the need for love with which she is devoured, this excess of sensibility is forced to rise to its source.... hers is a truly inexhaustible heart which neither love nor friendship could consume and which carries its overflowing affections to the only Being worthy of receiving them" (2: 590). The task of man, on the other hand, is to develop natural dispositions by facing the world, its persons, trials, and obstacles, to have the experience of controlling and moving them.

For Saint-Preux, the absence of a loved person means hopelessness and death. For Julie, on the contrary, total felicity means hopelessness and death. Julie's principle, love itself, the gift of loving, loses its meaning with consummation as perfection, and must expand into death. Saint-Preux's principle, *amour de soi*, preservation of self, is deeply disturbed by loss of its immediate purpose, Julie, but death does not logically or psychologically follow, since the sacrifice of self for any object, earthly or divine, other than liberty, is a denial of liberty of self. *Amour de soi* calls, not for eternity of giving, an exhausting of love unto death, but a change of object until an object again compatible with self and life is found. The object, a particular woman, can be exchanged for another, or if love is too deep to permit substitution, *amour de soi* must block love's destructive force by learning to express itself differently. Saint-Preux's despair, Bomston advises him, is inconsistent with manliness, that is, with the active desire to survive as an individual, to impose one's will in the expression of self: "You are not a man; you are nothing; and if I did not look ahead to what you may be, such as you are, I see nothing in the world inferior to you" (2: 387). Saint-Preux and every man must learn this about life, that "it is up to you alone for it to be a good, and if it is an evil to have lived, that is one more reason for continuing to live" (2: 390). He must "acquire again the taste for life," must live instead of reasoning about life: "Reason alone will not restore reason to you." He is to accept life actively: "A multitude of new and striking objects must tear a part of your attention away from the person with whom your heart is exclusively preoccupied ... it is only in the turmoil of an active life that you can again find repose" (2: 394). The voyage of Admiral Anson provides the answer, and the gradual transformation of Saint-Preux in the direction of manly vigor is made evident by his words and actions and the comments of those around him.

On his return, he admits to Claire that he owes everything to her. Rousseau in a note interprets this to mean that her protection of Julie has brought him "the honor, virtue, and peace of the one he loves" (2: 416). Without the test of Julie's refusal, he would not have risen above love to greater thoughts and deeds, to a more selfless love. His ego would have remained turned toward self-destruction instead of developing its full capacity. Julie finds that in contrast to his former timidity, he now has "the confidence of a man forthright and sure of himself" (2: 427). Love of truth has cured him of his fondness for metaphysical systems. His posture expresses his inner strength, "his bearing is more assured ... his gestures, lively and quick when he is animated, are besides more serious and sober." He is a sailor, his attitude "calm and cool, and his speech fiery and impetuous." He has the energy of youth, the majesty of maturity (2: 427). He becomes the friend and admirer of Wolmar because the latter in his way is able to determine life rather than be determined. But Wolmar sees in Saint-Preux even greater capacity: "It is only passionate souls that can fight and conquer. All great efforts, all sublime actions are their doing; cold reason has never accomplished anything illustrious, and we triumph over passions only by opposing one to the other. When the passion for virtue comes into its own, it alone dominates and holds everything in a state of equilibrium" (2: 493). Bomston, too, sees in Saint-Preux the chance for the fullest development of self through experience and discipline. In twelve years, Saint-Preux has known the entire range of feeling, has "acquired, still young, the experience of an old man" (2: 524). But his virtue is still second-hand: "Do you know what has always made you love virtue? It has assumed in your eyes the form of this admirable woman.... You speak with warmth of the manner in which she fulfills her duties as wife and mother; but you, when will you fulfill your duties as man and friend.... your letters still express a tone of softness and languor that displeases me.... If Julie were weak, you would succumb tomorrow and be only a base adulterer" (2: 525).

Now that Saint-Preux has learned to accept life, he must learn not just to admire virtue but to live virtue. Helped by Wolmar, he is able to see Julie within the context of the entire community, that is, to relate his love to time, to distinguish between past and present: "I prefer the sadness of an imaginary regret" (2: 510, 527). But this conquest of self releases another danger, sexual appetite (2: 663-66). Before and after the accident at Chillon, Julie knows the marriage of Saint-Preux to Claire is the way out, the natural way, "for I shall never be satisfied with you and myself until you are in fact what you should be, and until you love the duties you have to fulfill" (2: 670, 742). Her death imminent, her vision clear, she is describing psychological and physical necessity. The ascetic triangle, Wolmar / Saint-Preux / Julie, dedicated to expansiveness and constraint of exclusive passion, is to be replaced by a new, more natural triangle, Julie-Claire, love as altruism / Saint-Preux, *amour de soi*, masculine vigor and striving / Claire, love as sexuality. Claire's and Saint-Preux's protests may prevail, and the close of the novel requires that, but Julie has described the order dictated by virtue, the adjustment of the selves to necessity without guilt: "Your objections against this union are going to become new reasons for forming it. How will you ever be able to speak of me without becoming tender toward one another?... It is in this chaste union that you will be able without distraction and fear to busy yourself with the duties I am leaving you and after which you will no longer be at a loss to say what good you have accomplished on this earth" (2: 742). Saint-Preux has passed from the position of outsider to Clarens, the object of Julie's love and her father's early hate, to the leader of Clarens and complete self-realization. All of Julie's people look to him for support, her "father, her friend, her husband, her children, everyone waits for you, wants you; you are needed by everyone" (2: 740).

The meaning of the word family has changed with the passing leaders. For Rousseau, marriage in the city suffers from the loss of individuality among men. Each has been conditioned to a conformist, effeminate pattern of behavior by the prestige of Parisian women. The relationship between man and wife is not based on the qualities of the partners. There is no personal understanding between them. Everything depends on convenience, social prestige, money, the need for sexual gratification, the game of seduction. By contrast, in the country, variety in the format for family life may be observed. The ties are not all good. Rousseau deliberately tests the structures of three groups, Vevey under d'Etange, Clarens under Wolmar, and, finally, Julie's proposal for future constitution of Clarens under Saint-Preux and Claire.

Pride, cruelty, and neglect predominate in d'Etange's leadership. The members of the family are routinely affectionate, but also strangers to each others' deep emotions and needs. They are supposed to know their place, not to claim rights transcending the father's definition of justice. Paternal authority, the limit of desire and need, is upheld by d'Etange's arrogance, his wife's submission, his choleric temperament, and the power of his arm. Julie's fear that he might in rage take her life or Saint-Preux's is well-grounded. D'Etange's idea of service to the state is military. The task of developing men and citizens of integrity has gone unrecognized, been left to chance. Only because of his advancing years has he become a regular member of his household.

Wolmar's regime goes to the opposite extreme, replacing passion by understanding. Planning characterizes his leadership. Each person's need is recognized within the context of the family's good. Comfort, security, and self-realization are the goals, and provision is made for them. The economy is sound, based on the increased productivity and diversified use of the existing lands rather than on the expansion of holdings. Good sense, skill, industry, solid management, good will, and altruism are everywhere in evidence. The spirit of the community is excellent. The cycle of seasons passes in timeless bliss, enjoyment, beneficence. Yet there is a moral flaw. This is a never-never-land, a machine so perfect it seems at first to require no God but Wolmar. Hope, imagination, and change are no longer needed. The basis of Wolmar's authority is confidence in human integrity. His example is impeccable, effortless, because he is passionless. Less selfless creatures, whether servant or elite, Julie, Saint-Preux, must live in fear of the momentary lapse which may mar this dream. Rousseau's condemnation through irony of this false leadership is twofold. First, he shows that Wolmar's Clarens, in spite of its many good features, particularly its economy, is at its innermost moral core unearthly, inhuman, an atheist's creation. Julie, a person who believes in God, that is, in her own incompleteness, must in this environment of perfection wish herself into death, into heaven, if human hope and imagination are still to find expression. Second, this perfection with its atheistic self-sufficiency is basically false, only surface reality. Underneath are associations from the past, deep emotional ties which can never be eradicated by intellectual means, whether observation, analysis, or intuitive gifts. Julie points out that if this threat could be removed, as Wolmar, Saint-Preux, and Bomston believe, there would then be another more degrading temptation, perhaps held in check formerly by the sincere feeling now eradicated, the temptation to satisfy simple sexual appetite with any partner. Accident is recognized by Wolmar only in the sense of something to be included in his planning, for example, the future adaptability and industry of the children. Accident is unknown in its other sense of the totally unexpected, the incalculable, the utter contingency of the present, the fall of a child into the lake, Julie's plunge and sickness, an accident which in her mind prevented other, future moral crises and falls, therefore a providential "accident" provided by God to destroy the brittle universe created by a good but limited man (2: 740-42).

The final regime, based firmly in Julie's continuing love of Saint-Preux, has more dynamic principles. Rather than having character as intellect alone, Saint-Preux has a many-sided, deeply complex personality. A plebian of intelligence, ability, and training, he can associate with men of all walks of life, whether Parisian fop, English gentleman, the members of a naval expedition, Swiss nobility, or peasant. After suicidal despair, he is molded into a man of action who has known hardship, adventure, and responsibility. Through his travels he has acquired a vision beyond his years, knows problems in philosophic perspective as well as in their detail, has the ability to observe, to reason, and to put his conclusions into action. Almost abnormal sensibility and depth of feeling give permanence to his emotional ties, whether love or friendship. He is a passionate man of strong sexual drives. At the age of thirty, in Julie's opinion, his temperament is not compatible with the asceticism required by Wolmar's Clarens. Unlike Wolmar, a foreigner, he is in his native land, knows the heart of his people. He has their customs and some of their faults. He is a believer. Confidence in him may be built, not on wisdom alone nor on remote superiority, but on more human characteristics, the legend of a past love, of a hero who has returned, of a sensitive, religious, vulnerable man who has found himself, a person whom time, close association, and shared patriotic feeling could show worthy of trust. Clarens may again assume attitudes of life through Saint-Preux's *amour de soi*, may overcome the death now associated with Wolmar's and Julie's perfectionism. At the close, which is heavily veiled in death, the goals of the future family are never lost from view. Saint-Preux is to be the source of new life in Wolmar's, Julie's, and Claire's final letters. Rousseau has given Saint-Preux the characteristics needed to meet the primary goal of the family, a leadership offering cohesiveness and shelter in which the old may be comforted and in which the young may grow and be educated.

Saint-Preux embodies for Rousseau the good traits of all of the earlier regimes. D'Etange's willfulness is in Saint-Preux subordinated to the community's good. The cold, defeated reason of Wolmar, who now senses his inadequacy, now is close to conversion, contrasts sharply with the greater power of souls who participate more fully in life, who strive to follow a design higher than their own. Julie's flight toward death and God is made to appear a part of life, for sentiment establishes a continuity between life and death. The argument leaves no place for atheism except in the troubled, isolated Wolmar. Rousseau uses logic, a most persuasive rhetoric, and the poetic image of a tired old man incapable of understanding his deep grief.

But all other doctrines, not just Wolmar's, fall before Saint-Preux's vitality, his sense of freedom. Perfection had brought fear of a future fall, had made Julie see on all sides "risks to be run." With her own death certain, herself removed from the danger of infidelity, she can accept and see the viability of a Clarens run according to Saint-Preux's way, his belief, expressed in his last letter to her before news of her death reaches him, that man must rely not on society alone, the conventionality of d'Etange, not on sheer rationality, Wolmar's harmony, nor on the quietism of which Saint-Preux accuses Julie ("Are you going to be nothing more than a devout person?"), but on the freedom of man. This, in Saint-Preux's life and words, means striving for the good with the powers God or nature gave man: "Creating man, he endowed him with all the faculties needed to accomplish what he asked of him, and when we ask him for the power to do good, we ask him for nothing he has not already given us. He has given us reason to know what is good, conscience to love the good, and liberty in order to choose it. Divine grace consists of these sublime gifts, and since we have all received them, we are all accountable. I hear a lot of reasoning against man's liberty, and I despise all these sophisms; because no matter how well a reasoner proves to me that I am not free, inner feeling, stronger than all his arguments, repeatedly disproves them, and whatever side I take in whatever discussion may arise, I sense perfectly that it is only up to me if I take the opposing point of view" (2: 683, 685).

Passing the responsibility for goodness to God alone, man forfeits freedom of will as much as he does by atheistic doctrine. Man's fate is essentially his own choice and action. Divine grace is nothing more than our own power to understand good, to feel it, and to will it in our lives with the conviction that God is behind us. With Julie's death, there has been a rejection of perfection and a return to normal life. The family in which an Emile may be formed has appeared. The emphasis has been placed on life's immediate problems, on the struggle required in the midst of emotional crisis: "Think of the problems that await you, of the duties imposed upon you, of the person to whom you have promised them. Her children are in their formative stage and are growing; her father is aging steadily; her husband is uneasy and disturbed" (2: 745).

Writers often seem to assume that Rousseau intended to apply to Clarens the principle of *volonté générale,* to treat the family as if it were a complex machine, artificial like the nation. They imply at times, too, that through disillusionment with governmental action he came to see the family as the solution to the problem of social ills. There may, of course, be elements of truth in such an interpretation, but it is important and is one of the aims of this study to see Rousseau's ideas on the family in more comprehensive perspective. First, it is true that for Rousseau the family within civil society, the context of Clarens, can no longer be simply natural in the sense of being built on uncontrolled human nature as it appears in any of the transformations by necessity in the *Second discours.* The d'Etange regime, based on a father's vanity, is rejected. The description of life in Paris points up the error of marriage based on rampant sophistication. The family, Rousseau makes it clear, must be made subject to science, planning. Wolmar comes close to the correct concept. His paternal benevolence and wisdom produce an ordered economy with emphasis on the qualities and basic needs of the individual. Julie's concern, too, includes a calculation of the pressures on Claire or Saint-Preux, of the needs of the children, her husband, her father, and a consideration of the family's general good. But the direction of Rousseau's investigation leaves no room for supposing that the goal of science relative to the family is the same as that relative to the state. The latter has an artificial common good and an artificial common will; in theory it can have permanence. The family, on the contrary, was already in nature before civil society appeared. It must be built around the natural will of a particular human being, whether d'Etange, Wolmar, or Saint-Preux. Science, which on the national level must dehumanize each member of the congregation in order to let him think and live the artificial good and will at certain levels, must provide at the same time within that wider circle and on the family level an area in which man can think and live in a natural way, which means under the will of a father motivated by the natural instincts of *amour de soi* and *pitié.*

Rousseau destroys Wolmar's regime. It was founded in error, has principles similar to those of the nation, emphasizes equilibrium more than individuality, makes human nature bow to a common good, dehumanizes man. The family is not the nation. The private interest of the members of such a local community are too personal to be curbed. A Julie, except in dream or death, cannot live beside a Saint-Preux without falling. Wolmar has in part misunderstood the function of the family. He has tried to rehabilitate souls already formed, to include in his family elements better left out. In the real object of the family, the raising of children, he shows more insight, indicates to Saint-Preux that the self of each individual must be permitted to expand according to its bent without restriction by the collectivity in any substantial way affecting its inner life. Saint-Preux proposes forming "a perfect model of the reasonable and respectable man, then bringing each child into harmony with the model by force of education" (2: 564). He wants to "correct nature." Wolmar protests against any such curbing of the individual self: "It is not a matter of changing character and bending what is natural, but on the contrary of pushing nature as far as it can go, cultivating it, keeping it from degenerating; because man thus becomes everything he can be, and the work of nature is completed in him by education" (2: 566).

The function of the nation is to establish a condition parallel in effect to the individual who is isolated in the state of nature, that is, to protect each man's independence, but in terms of equity, equal treatment before the law, equal right to participate in the sovereign, equal obligation to think and live the sovereign good and will. Buffering the individual from his national commitment and responsibility is the family unit dedicated to the good in nature's terms. With Julie gone, without the burden of guilt imposed by an impossible triangle as collective good, Saint-Preux may perhaps finds his own happiness with Claire, Julie's intention, and raise the children according to their inner selves: "I sensed that in order to guide man, the way of nature is always best" (2: 579). Science as planning can restore the family to its natural goals.

This science presupposes a civil society already in operation, already providing the shelter which permits the family to turn inward on itself, to create men, to tap the uniqueness of each individual, so that each man when he has received in addition education for citizenship is both unique self and part of the artificial collectivity or sovereign. But in a very deep sense Julie's planning is no more than an improvement on Wolmar's. Marriage is still to be *de convenance* rather than on a basis of affinity, the spiritual, emotional, and physical union of lovers. In the absence of loved ones uniquely destined for one another, reason suggests the most suitable arrangement. This is practical and realistic, for time passes, loved ones die, life must go on, children must be raised, sexuality cannot always be thwarted.

Yet Rousseau does not allow us to conclude that Claire and Saint-Preux will necessarily be joined. Society cannot overcome the feelings of individuals that easily. Each self has its very particular wants, associations, loyalties. No exchange of identities, Claire for Julie, Saint-Preux for M. d'Orbe, is possible if married love is to have meaning, if persons are to be true to themselves. The only genuinely valid family nucleus was Saint-Preux and Julie, victims of circumstance as were Abélard and Héloïse. All other kinds of relationship are variants of the Parisian loss of identity by which truly individual sentiments are sacrificed to happiness in a less personally involved sense. This happiness, certainly not so degrading as the *salon* game of worldliness which Rousseau heavily condemns in this novel, is the less degenerate, more respectable game of duty, respect, dignified stoicism, and denial of affinities and passions which the family in a society free of prejudice would not require. To accept the matter-of-fact, existing society is for Julie to marry Wolmar, for Saint-Preux to marry Claire. Rousseau's idealistic refusal is a protest against compromise, an insistence on what might have been if men were free to follow their inclination. The marriage of reason is not to be totally condemned. It has degrees of sincerity, it is useful. But for Rousseau the marriage of love, satisfying each person's individual, private need, should be the goal and the rule rather than the exception, for it can provide for the nation the soundest, most productive family unit.

CHAPTER VII

EDUCATION: MATRIX FOR UNIQUENESS AND
LEGITIMACY

WRITTEN BETWEEN 1757 and 1760, *Emile* appeared in 1762 and was widely read. Its ideas can be said to have very soon started new trends in educational theory, but the reaction of the authorities to its religious doctrine was disastrous for Rousseau. After his stay at the Hermitage in 1756-1757 and at Montlouis, 1757-1758, he found new shelter in May of 1759 at the Petit Château of Montmorency, where he was the guest of the Duke and Duchess of Luxembourg. Rousseau now enjoyed the hospitality of the highest ranking nobility, of a figure very close to royal power. The publication of *Emile*, its condemnation by *Parlement*, and that body's order for Rousseau's arrest revealed the falseness of his new-found sense of security. An embarrassment to the Duke and Duchess, he departed for Switzerland in haste, June 9, 1762. Until 1770 his existence was to be characterized by wandering, flight, and exposure.

Emile has sometimes been treated from the viewpoint of education alone. More often it is made to relate to Rousseau's political system. The work's bearing on his other writings concerning government, sovereignty, and justice has not, however, been sufficiently explored. In my view and in spite of the usual claim, *Emile* is not separated from the *Discours sur les sciences et les arts*, the *Second discours*, the *Economie*, the *Lettre à d'Alembert*, and the *Nouvelle Héloïse* by a substantially different constructive tone and approach. The goals of *Emile* were prepared by the so-called "negative" works, the two discourses which I have interpreted in a more positive way by emphasizing standards Rousseau derives from both nature and history, namely, freedom and legitimacy. The *Economie,* dealing with enlightened government and its goal of legitimacy, the *Lettre,* with freedom as national character, and the *Nouvelle Héloïse,* with the family framework conducive to private freedom — all form, in conformity with principles of the first two discourses, the backdrop for studying the individual in the contexts of contemporary society's sophistication, history's downward spiral toward tyranny, and the claims on the individual made by government, nation, and family. *Emile* deals with the problem of the inner self, a theme often previously evoked by Rousseau: "Return within oneself.... listen to the voice of one's conscience in the silence of the passions" (Pléiade, 3: 30, *Premier discours*). "Sociable man, always outside of himself, does not know how to live except in the opinion of others" (3: 193, *Second discours*). The *Economie* expresses respect for the dignity of the individual. In the *Lettre* there is admiration for the originality of the individual Swiss. Julie, Wolmar, and Saint-Preux want to discover the individual nature of each child under their supervision.

There must be no misunderstanding about the meaning of the words self, nature, and originality in the allusions just made. By individual self is meant the idiosyncrasy of nonconforming character, which is the goal, as I hope to show, of the education outlined in *Emile. Emile* is not a description of universal man, as so many critics have maintained. This very usual explanation has been well expressed by François and Pierre Richard in their introduction to *Emile.*[1] They say that *Emile* deals with the "natural man." This is not "the primitive man, ridiculed by Voltaire," described by novelists of the time such as Marmontel in *Les Incas,* or presented with facile documentation in the memoirs of voyages of discovery. The natural man of *Emile* is "a civilized man without civilization, a generic being, stripped of everything the race, the epoch, and the place could have brought him that is particular, in short, universal man in his most general

---

[1] *Emile: ou de l'éducation,* ed. François and Pierre Richard (Paris: Garnier, 1964), pp. v-vi. Except where otherwise indicated, references are to this most available of the editions of *Emile.*

and durable characteristics." Thus for François and Pierre Richard *Emile* deals with a type inspired by the classical writers of the seventeenth century and by the great writers of antiquity, such as Seneca, Epictetus, and Marcus-Aurelius. The problem faced by Rousseau, then, according to this evaluation, was one of finding the essence of this universal man: "Let us then extract the essence of this nature.... So much the worse if Emile and his tutor, pure and too perfect creations of the mind, do not live with an individual life."

It seems true that Emile is not an individual with particular, explicitly given traits. But it is equally true that he is not a type in the usual sense any more than the natural man of the *Second discours* is such a type. In both works the definitions of man are in largely negative terms. The liberty of primitive man is absence of pressure. Since the physical environment surrounding him is in perfect equilibrium, each individual can appear in his primordial entirety during that stage of his development. Man is alone. Within the framework of his shared instincts of *amour de soi*, *pitié*, and potential *perfectibilité*, the possible future variants of each uncompromised *soi* are infinite. This is the meaning of his isolation. Similarly, the real object of *Emile*, as I wish to show, is the formation of a protective framework for the freedom of the potential self, no matter what its character may be. Rather than with any definition of universal man, of some classical ideal, Rousseau is preoccupied with the measures and conditions to be established if an outlet for personal individuality, aborted in the *Second discours*, is to be realized. Education means in part the formation of devices — physical, psychological, intellectual, moral, and religious — with which to hold back the crushing weight of environmental pressures. This education also consists, not in giving something to the pupil from outside, but in leaving form and subject-matter undefined and silent, in controlling through the tutor the environment around the child, in thus fostering the appearance of original traits, and finally in transferring this control, whether of passion, obsession, or environment, to the pupil, who in that sense becomes his own protector, continues to create his inner self. His unique and unknown nature can thus come through to the surface in the expression of feelings, thoughts, and deeds.

Certainly, as has been pointed out so often in the past, *Emile*, with its private education, prepares the individual for personal life, whereas the public education of the *Economie* prepares him for his place as citizen or subject in the state and makes him obedient to the laws of the nation as interpreted by government. Man must look toward both family and national responsibility. But with *Emile* there appears an emphasis new and of special value to Rousseau's political system, the relationship of uniqueness to sovereignty. No longer, as in the *Economie*, is the chief concern of education that of creating in the people a general will. The goal there is the patriotic fervor which must fill every heart if the country is to survive. But in *Emile*, the emphasis is on the preservation and liberation of the individual will, so that the notion of sovereignty in turn may itself become truly vital and dynamic. As the *Economie* offers a solution to society at the governmental level and parallels the negative descent of civil society by a positive restatement of the civil order, so now *Emile* formulates a plan of education paralleling and controlling at the individual level the passage of man through the same cycle in a way that reconciles uniqueness with legitimacy.

The setting of Emile, like that of the primitive state of nature of the *Second discours*, is carefully selected. It is a normative condition planned for the purpose of a thought experiment. It does not claim to derive from all of reality. Rousseau's awareness of the need to eliminate details of time and place is much in evidence. The education he proposes is to be "suitable for man," "well adapted to the human heart." Rousseau must neglect the "thousand circumstances it is impossible to determine except by a particular application of the method to such and such a country" (p. 3). The pupil has been screened to assure the validity of the results. He has an "ordinary mentality" because superior minds make their own original way in spite of education (p. 26). He is a product of a certain region. Men "are not everything they can be except in temperate climates" (p. 27). He is an orphan so that the tutor has complete authority over the experiment (p. 28). The investigation is not to be abandoned except by "our consent," because a sense of permanence is essential to the attitudes of both teacher and pupil (p. 28). The child must be normally healthy to assure that the relationship is genuinely that of pupil and teacher, not patient and nurse (p. 29). The body of the child must be vigorous to assure that its tie to the passions and to the soul is normal (p. 29). The subject is to be artificially isolated from most other persons. He is to be without nationality but of noble descent, of a class rich enough to have become thoroughly sophisticated, removed from nature, so that what can be controlled in him will be practicable *a fortiori* for children of other classes (p. 27).

As in the *Second discours*, too, the evolutionary process is evoked, here embryonic, preceding the clearly distinguishable human form, but is immediately set aside by the clear-cut establishment of an arbitrary begining, that is, actual birth: "Everything we do not have at our birth and which we need when adults is given to us by education" (p. 7). The same apparent bias of the *Second discours* for nature over necessity and society is expressed, but, as in that discourse, all three elements are seen as inseparably related and "the concurrence of the three educations is necessary to their perfection" (p. 7). But one cannot work on natural endowment directly. In fact the object is to leave it free, not to change it, to encourage it instead to resist harmful environmental pressures. Without education by necessity or "what is acquired from our own experience of the objects that affect us," in other words, education "of things," and without society, which is "education by men," the teacher cannot deal with nature, which "does not depend on us," which is the completely independent "inward development of our faculties and our organs" (p. 7). Necessity training amounts to regulating the pupil's contact with his physical surroundings. Social education ("of which we are really the masters," since human relationships are easier to change than physical *milieu*) controls his relations with people and institutions. These two means are directed to the goal of assisting the individual self, which is beyond our grasp: "It is toward that education over which we can do nothing that it is necessary to direct the two others" (p. 7). This means simply that for the psyche to appear in real life, necessity and society must be rearranged by the tutor to produce a sheltering condition.

Human nature in *Emile* must be left undefined, except as the tendency to continue itself, "love of self," and as pity, which is not operative at the birth of the individual any more than it is in the isolation of the state of nature. In the *Second discours,* the self is given as something predetermined, not formable, but which does not completely fulfill its potential because necessity and society are permitted to stand in its way as stronger determinants. Love of self goes underground and in reaction to environment, climate, other animals, scarcity of food, and rivalry with other men, is transformed into *amour-propre,* pride, vanity. Self in *Emile* is similarly predetermined. It is also threatened by the presence of a civilized world already developed, in which *amour de soi,* except in the tutor, is for the most part absent, replaced by *amour-propre;* in which *pitié* is largely inoperative; in which perfectibility or the problem-solving bent for greater and greater sophistication is much in evidence and is kept under control only through the tutor. At their beginnings, both the *Second discours* and *Emile* generate anticipation of crises to come through physical, emotional, moral, and intellectual evolution. The first work bears witness to the decline of mankind, degeneration of *amour de soi* and *pitié* into *amour-propre.* The second must find within the artificial civil order and within the natural organ of the family, the means for protecting in each man the full significance of *amour de soi* and *pitié.*

It is pertinent at this point to ask if this education should not be seen as a new kind of conformity, a new virtuous ego simply replacing *amour-propre* and its built-in denial of others. Yet *amour-propre,* an acquired social attitude, as we have seen, has as its object external possessions, so that in the *Second discours* man's self has been thwarted by the denial of its three educations, control of necessity and society in order to release nature. Necessity and its objects to be competed for, society and its challenge, its competitiveness, have created a man of incomplete being, a conformist in the sense that all men are seeking the same objects and differing only in the degree to which they succeed. *Amour de soi* and *pitié,* on the contrary, need have no such externally imposed limitation, for the self can yield endless variation, and pity is an instinct of forbearance which recognizes the self in others. Never, therefore, can this self be known definitively, which means that education to bring out individuality must be tailored to each person. Any use of a model of what man is supposed to be would produce leveling and conformity.

The search conducted by education is for an unknown ego different in each man and lost by him as he moves into necessity and society by the stumbling steps described in the *Second discours*. As true education proceeds and succeeds, it calls for more and more adaptability in order to meet the new challenges to unfolding originality: "But proportionately as I advance, my student, guided differently than yours, is no longer an ordinary child; he requires a regime made specifically for him" (p. 25). The method is designed to discover uniqueness of self, so that education is as much a science as an art: "Moreover, I call the master of this science governor rather than preceptor, because it is less a matter of his instructing the pupil than of conducting him. He must not lay down precepts. He must teach his pupil to discover them" (p. 26). The movement of the *Second discours* was from potential in nature to its denial. The movement of *Emile* is from potential to fulfillment as each of the inhibiting stages of the *Second discours* are simulated, reinforced, or counteracted, depending on their relationship to the release of the pupil's self: "It is therefore to his primitive inclinations that everything should be related" (p. 8).

Rousseau explicitly rejects any rigidly positive educational format: "Be distrustful of those cosmopolites who go far afield to find in their books duties which they themselves make no effort to follow in their own lives" (p. 9). The goals of class-conscious education must be discarded, too, in this age in which "ranks alone remain and men change them continually" (p. 12). The concept of universal man, with its attachment to certain virtues, certain characteristics common to all men, certain duties and obligations, can be confused perhaps with another term, "homme abstrait." Rousseau does say that we must become "general in our views" and see in our pupil abstract man. But this is man exposed to all of the "accidents of human existence" (p. 12). Clearly the call for generalization has to do not with an ideal of virtue or duty to be imposed on the pupil, but rather with the location of areas of the human condition pertinent to education: "Our true study is the study of the human condition" (p. 12). Man, in other words, requires an educational antidote to neutralize step by step the effects of civilization if he is to retain the integrity of his person.

The first area is the human body in its origins, Emile as the newly born child, a condition corresponding to the first state of nature. He must be made more fully alive, so that he can find his potential: "True education consists less of precepts than of exercises.... to live is not to breathe, it is to act, to use our organs, our senses, our faculties, all the parts of ourselves, which give us the feeling of our existence" (pp. 12, 13). In civilization, only the child can penetrate the barriers of culture and come to experience life directly through his organs. Life is measured not in number of years but in intensity of living. That man has lived the most who "has felt life the most" (p. 13). To feel life means to rub against one's surrounding environment as primitive man did in a state of complete relaxation, uncurbed by restrictions imposed by other men. Rousseau's recommendations against swaddling clothes, against head shaping, and in favor of breast-feeding have been praised as medically sound, but he stresses as much the beneficial effects to the ego of this uncurbed development. Guided freedom is essential to give future man the feeling of the vital forces within him. Satisfying the urges to stretch, to move, to nuzzle, and to enjoy the mother or to nurse allows the self to come forth uninhibitedly. Most civilized men do not have this habit of freedom because they have lived according to "servile prejudices" (p. 13).

Rousseau's argument is always oriented toward freedom of self rather than toward standardization. The tutor is not to give his charges any gratuitous mold: "The first imprints they receive from you are so many chains." Rousseau is talking in part of physical structure and force of body, but also of psychological traits which may have been introduced inadvertently from outside: "Could not such cruel constraint have an influence on their disposition as well as on their temperament?" (pp. 14-15). At the other extreme, over-indulgence encourages the child to be passive. The robust child is not only more resistant to disease but because of his strength is freer to live. Sickness, a denial of personality, is imposed on children by mothers, who "as a result of immersing their children in softness... open the way to their suffering" (p. 19). Any child who is not "robust," whose self is overshadowed by a delicateness encouraged by the mother, would not be a valid subject for experimental education. An outside influence, society's sophistication, would have already interfered to invalidate the experiment. The selves Rousseau is to be concerned with are undiminished, active, healthy.

But this assumes that nature as ego is essentially healthy and active, that all selves are to be active and healthy, which gives less latitude to uniqueness. Rousseau's response would be that environment is a challenge and threat to the child's body: "It [nature] continually exercises her children; it hardens their constitution by tests of all kinds; it teaches them very early what pain and grief are. In cutting their teeth they experience fever. Acute colics give them convulsions. Sustained coughing suffocates them. Worms torment them. Plethora corrupts their blood; various leavens ferment in it and cause dangerous eruptions" (pp. 19-20). Health, vigor, sickness and passivity have nothing to do with uniformity of self, except that the last two are the usual products of society.

All of these terms apply, however, to conditions in which the self must appear. Health and vigor are a better condition for the survival of self than are sickness and passivity. The body by its nature must know suffering. The instructor therefore hardens the body. That is nature's way and it should be followed both to overcome sophisticated patterns of existence and to permit the self to survive. Hardship is not an end but the means to an end — survival: "Experience reveals that more children die when they are delicately raised" (pp. 20-21). The child who has been plunged "into the waters of the Styx" will be strong against the challenges that face him (pp. 21-22).

Corporeal uniqueness must then amount to the difference in degree of participation and potential for participation in life. At one end of the scale is the perfectly healthy, active individual; at the other, the child so sickly as to be threatened by death. Independence from others varies in direct proportion to this vitality, the means for fending off the impact of others, for being one's own man. This same reasoning applies to man's relationship to medicine and doctors. The primitive state of nature is free of illness. In a society abounding in doctors and cures, the tutor must teach the child to endure sickness (p. 31). Temperance, work, and time are the true doctors. The child must be given confidence in his body, belief in his own resources; he must learn the independence that goes with nature, for "When the animal is sick, he suffers in silence and remains still" (p. 31). Without the crutches of medicine and doctors, man lives more for himself and others than does "the man who is for thirty years their victim" (p. 32). He is courageous, thinks more of life than of death, "dies in peace." This may be called the attitude of perseverance, of fortitude, of stoicism, but the point is that Rousseau is not emphasizing these virtues for their own sake. They may be by-products, but Rousseau is building into the child habits to permit independence from doctors, medicine, and fear of death. If one says that independence is the conformist trait that has found its way into Rousseau's system, the answer has to be that independence is meaningless alone and undefined. Its content is derived from the particular self of each man. Independence, like health, is not the quality of self but the condition to permit the appearance of self.

Rousseau's devices build into the child's being a feeling for freedom — freedom from physical constraint as he exerts himself against objects, from sickness, from thoughts of death, from passions incited by grown-ups. His nurse is to be by her stolidity almost a natural object, in her health and need close to animal unsophistication, in her behavior expressing the no-nonsense authority that animals exert over their young. Free of the characteristics of society's woman, she will be a healthy peasant, will follow as much as possible a vegetable diet, will never be overindulgent in her food, and will provide "with her milk, attentions requiring zeal, patience, kindness, cleanliness" (p. 34). This protection of the inherited form and innocence of the child extends to the very air around him. City air is bad: "I prefer to have him go breathe the good country air than to have the nurse come to breathe the bad city air" (p. 36). The breath of man is fatal to his fellowman: "That is no less true literally than figuratively" (p. 37). The human race is waning and dying in the city, is constantly being renewed in the country. The child's body must absorb through its pores, so to speak, an atmosphere not of decadence and death but of vitality: "[The air] penetrates into a delicate and soft skin through all the pores, it powerfully affects these growing bodies, it leaves them with impressions which are not effaced" (p. 36).

The tutor must therefore constantly watch over his charge, his nurse, and all the members of the family, to see that the impact of physical and social environment does not diminish the capacity of the self. He must maintain, too, a keen lookout and control over the first signs of moral and intellectual activity: "He watches over the nursling, observes it, attends it, spies with vigilance upon the first glimmering of its feeble understanding" (p. 40). Rousseau emphasizes that the purpose of this careful observation is to adjust education to the individual. The point he makes is exactly that the content of the particular self is an unknown; we have no idea what it can become. We know only the starting point common to all men, "the primitive state of ignorance and stupidity natural to man," but we do not know the other extreme, "what our nature permits us to be; none of us has measured the distance which may be found to exist between one man and another" (p. 41).

Enslavement takes the form of habit. Men abort the child's originality by their own ways. They accustom him to eat and sleep at given times, to being carried on one arm more than on the other, to offer one hand rather than the other, not to sleep alone, to be afraid of unexpected objects — bugs, spiders, ugly, strange, bizarre animals, masks: "The only habit one must allow the child to take is that of not acquiring any habits" (p. 42). Habit is the opponent of independent will. The child must be freed "by putting him in a condition to be always master of himself, to follow his will in everything, as soon as he has one" (p. 42). The habit of having no habits is liberation: "By slow and skillful steps one makes man and child unafraid of anything" (p. 44). At five years old Emile can face life as did primitive man, without needless inhibitions. The feeling of liberty is disciplined into his every fiber. He is on the way to finding a pattern of life which is his very own.

The second stage of the *Second discours*, during which human relations were on a basis of casual association, people meeting to cooperate in their hunting for short periods, was characterized principally by necessity. Environment threatened man's existence, at times forced him to migrate. Cold, other animals, and cataclysmic events goaded him, inspired his problem-solving. What occurred for the race, Rousseau finds, must occur in each individual life. As the child learns to move in his environment, he understands that not everything is himself and his own sensations, "that there are things which are not ourselves" (p. 44). This recognition must be constructive, which means that the meeting of self with necessity should permit continued development of independence in the individual self. The problem is dual. First, adults must not by overprotection prevent a realistic relationship between the individual and his environment. Second, his own struggle with necessity must not be allowed to destroy his character, but must give it unity, oneness, identity in the sense that he knows his strength.

Unaided by adults, merely guided by the tutor, the student is left to his own resources. Objects are distant from him. He reaches out to take them and fails. Gradually, he learns what distance is (p. 45). This exploration is natural and good and should be encouraged, but there is a problem, since the child is not isolated, as was man in the state of nature. If parents are present, they may strike the child, punish the self for expressing its desire (p. 47), for during his waking hours he is like a robust savage, "he feels within himself... enough life to animate everything surrounding him" (p. 49). The parents should understand that his desire in itself has no basis in morality or immorality. The child is merely active and amoral: "Whether he puts things together or takes them apart, it does not matter, it is enough for him if he changes the state of things" (p. 49). Other parents may become the child's slave, allow themselves to be turned into his instrument: "That is how they [children] become troublesome, tyrannical, domineering, ill-natured, unruly" (p. 49). If parents can be by-passed as his own power increases, the child, like primitive man, operates by another principle, "the movement necessary to our self-preservation" (p. 49). His desires are limited to his own strength to have and to hold.

In the matter of language, this means making every word he knows and uses relate to the expression of his own needs, feelings, and desires. He does not verbalize beyond his intellectual means, any more than he possesses beyond his physical strength. At this stage he is close to the capacity of the peasant, who generally, with a small vocabulary and fewer ideas than city people, nevertheless "sees the relationships" between his ideas very well (p. 58). Emile, acting and speaking in proportion to his powers, has no misconceptions about where he stands with respect to persons and things. He does not command men because he knows he is not their master; he does not command things, because he knows that "they do not hear him" (p. 48). When Emile falls and is hurt, he accepts the fact: "The harm is done, it is a necessity which he endures" (p. 59).

During his period of helplessness, the child is trained in such a way as to maintain his health and his natural inclination to activity. He resisted the dependence which comes with sickness and passivity. When he can do things for himself, he is trained to rely on his own being alone, to recognize the exact extent to which he can control the forces around him and the extent to which he must remain their victim. He has more than his health and strength. He now has conscious knowledge of his identity in terms of what he can perform for himself. This is recorded for him in his developing memory, which holds the past experiences of "all the moments of his existence" (p. 61). He has passed from the timelessness of his early helpless childhood to a period of purposeful action by pitting himself against necessity. He has "consciousness of himself.... he becomes truly one, the same person, and consequently is already capable of happiness and misery" (p. 61). Because the tutor has led him to develop from within, he is not what a boy of his age is universally said to be. He is not the negation or fulfillment of his father's ideal. He is the past experience of his relationship with necessity, an experience and a relationship which in emotion, muscle, and nerve are peculiar to him.

The third stage of the *Second discours* was a golden age. Happiness and unhappiness were consciously experienced. Passions had not become excessive. The pleasures of family life had not yet been compromised by developing arts and sciences and the competition for possessions. Men hunted and fished, benefited by mutual assistance, raised their children. As Rousseau there regretted the removal of man from this age, so now he discourages Emile's passage, between the ages of five and twelve, from a parallel childlike insouciance to "a barbarous education," an uncertain future, the adult opinion of what a child should know in order to find some "supposed happiness" he will probably never enjoy (p. 61). This change must be prevented. The child should be encouraged in his innocent joys during this "age in which laughter is always on the lips and the soul at peace" (p. 62). Traditional education sets out in this period to correct what are called "the bad inclinations of man," whereas Rousseau in his negation of the inhibiting education of his day seeks results in terms of human temperament: "And how will you prove to me that these evil penchants of which you intend to cure him do not come from your ill-advised attentions much more than from nature?" (p. 62). The simple, naive pleasures of childhood should be permitted to take firm root in man's soul. Happiness, in the relative terms Rousseau finds acceptable, is the exact balance of man's desire with his capacity to enjoy. This means liberating man from imagination, "which extends for us the limits of the possible" and makes the desires of man constantly exceed his power (p. 64). Happiness as a mode of existence is present whenever man, like a spider in its web, is content where he is, when he lives his life, not his ambitions or dreams (pp. 64-65). Imagination can be a part of happiness only if its flight does not create frustration through goals impossible of accomplishment. The child or man who reaches too far beyond his grasp, his talent, his physical, intellectual, or moral powers, has lost contact with life, is pursuing an obsession rather than knowing his own reality. We have already seen that freedom for Rousseau is partly in the completeness of Emile's exploratory activity, which is only possible in good health; that Emile's identity is the measuring of necessity and environment, by his personal powers. Now, his happiness, too, must be totally empirical, based on his own individual and unique capacity for enjoyment.

Rousseau's fourth state of man in the *Second discours* was war, with egos quantitatively trying to expand their selves into other selves by means of riches and power. Childhood has its equivalent between the ages of five and twelve: "It is a natural disposition in man to consider that everything in his power is his own. In this sense Hobbes's principle is true to a certain extent:

multiply along with our desires the means for satisfying them, and each man will make himself the master of everything" (p. 73). So long as the power of the child to attain is not frustrated by excessive desires, there is no emotional state of war within him. The words obey and command must be "banished from his vocabulary, and those of duty and obligation even more." All he must see and feel around him is the physical world. It is pointless to reason with children as if they were adults. Deliberation is "a language they do not understand" (pp. 76-77). The child must have implanted within his own nervous system the limits other men will inevitably give to his lust for power. He is made to sense that he is weak, that the tutor is strong: "Over his proud head let him feel at an early age the harsh yoke that nature imposes on man" (p. 79).

This use of environmental barriers is in no way designed to break the child's spirit. This could result if another will was obviously imposed on his. He must be made to see this necessity "in things, never in the whim of men; let the check which holds him be force and not authority" (p. 79). The distinction is vital. It is the distinction between a man's forbidding an action and his physically preventing it. Emile is not being told that another's judgment is better than or superior to his, which would destroy his will and enslave him. His action is to be stopped "without explanation, without reasoning" (p. 80). Force is to settle everything, as in the state of war. Since, however, what he wants to do and is prevented from doing is always in fact regulated by the standard of need, that is, since only the wants which actually exceed need are prevented, the child experiences the state of war or of force in a constructive way. He expects to have need satisfied; he expects to have a demand in excess of it refused: "It is in this way that you make him patient, steady, resigned, calm, even when he does not have what he wanted; for it is in man's nature to endure patiently the necessity of things, but not the bad intentions of another man" (p. 80). If one objects that the greed of man is a part of the state of war, it is to the point that "evil intent" in the *Second discours* and here has been defined as the will, arising from hate or desire, to take another man's need. Emile, knowing and acquiring his need by experience, will refuse to bow to such a will. His own desires under control, he will not inflict his lust on another.

This training by sheer necessity, unlike the usual motivation of pedagogy — "emulation, jealousy, envy, vanity, greed, base fear" — relates directly to natural instinct in man, *amour de soi*, which "does not have any necessary relationship to other men" (p. 81). The child is motivated, not by the atmosphere of the state of war, not by emotional give and take, but completely by forces within himself. His relation to other men is sound, not subject to negotiation, to debate, to being confused, because necessity has established in his nervous system his exact, proportionate place, the needs of his person. Therefore in his dealings with men he is not yet morally but only physically involved. He is "an insensitive being" fashioned like "an automaton" (p. 84).

This feeling for subsistence need is reinforced through a bloodless conflict with the human race staged by the tutor. The latter sets himself as example, reveals his own responsible role in the community. Emile observes and senses the integrity of his master in his dealings with other men (p. 85). In contrast, those who by their actions and passions reflect the state of war are presented as persons suffering from sickness. Anger, for example, with its "inflamed face" is the sign that "this poor man is ill" (p. 87). Physical pressure and observable social prestige are the real teachers. The power struggle among men cannot henceforth destroy Emile. His self has learned to refuse invasion. It refuses, also, to expand its will by conquest over other selves.

The state of war ends in moral terms with the awakening of Emile's conscience, which corresponds to the fifth state of the *Second discours*, the invention of agreement, legitimacy. Emile must learn what property is. People defend themselves; things do not. Therefore Emile must first learn respect for property (p. 89). The tutor, Emile, and Robert (the gardener), in a conflict over melons and beans, reenact "the right of the first occupant based on labor" (p. 91). The law of agreement — you respect the results of my labor, I shall respect the results of yours — enters his mind on the basis of utility and soon, evoking natural pity or altruism, is etched into his heart as "a law of conscience, as an innate principle ... an idea ... engraved in our hearts by the author of all justice" (pp. 92-93). This "primitive law of agreement and the obligation it imposes" must not only hinge on self-interest, but become an "inner feeling": "Whoever keeps his promise only out of profit is scarcely more bound than if he had promised nothing" (p. 93).

Emile has relived the steps of his race and imprisoned himself by the principle of justice, legitimacy: "The little scamp hardly thought, by making a hole in which to plant his bean, that he was digging a dungeon in which his knowledge would not be long in locking him away" (p. 93). The self is not to be the right of the strongest, Emile's right in Robert's absence. There is to be continuance of possession only on the basis of need and consent by the parties concerned. Emile is no longer completely an automaton. He has become a moral being, has accepted a code relating him on a regular basis to another person's will. His heart and mind tell him it is good to keep the contract in force, bad to break it without the consent of the other contracting party. This in no way means that the self has become subject to its property. On the contrary, the self is consent and still has its condition of independence, since it alone is judge of what is to be made the subject of contract.

Morality leads to a new stage, the sixth of the *Second discours:* "the door opened to vice. With agreements and duties are born deception and lying" (p. 93). Two kinds of lies affect Emile and destroy his feelings for justice, the lie about facts, which concerns the past, and the lie about right or agreement, which concerns the future (p. 94). He has no reason to lie about what he has already done because all pressures have been removed: "You do not reprove him, you do not punish him for anything, you ask nothing of him" (p. 95). He has no reason to break agreements, promises for the future, for a similar reason: "We do not ask them to make any promises they may be tempted not to keep" (p. 95).

Not lying is related to an even more basic principle. Man in his solitude could not hurt another. It is less important that Emile do good to others than that he refrain from doing them harm, which means that he should be as disinterested a member of society as possible, since "the good of one [man] is necessarily the evil of another" (p. 99). In other words, the self is not to become its competition with other men, its power to acquire goods at their expense.

Rousseau's goal is to build this self-denial with respect to goods into the personality, but not in any obvious way. The problem is one of making the senses themselves react responsibly to environment. If men fall from civil liberty, it is largely because their senses, intellect, and conscience have acquired a distorted scale of values not their own. Education, according to Rousseau, is again at fault. Rather than acquiring control of these organs and faculties, children have spent their time learning culture, which is and always has been an indoctrination into slavery. The education of words imposed on most children under twelve leaves them wearing a mask of sophistication, but with little knowledge of the reality of their condition. Before that age education should busy the mind with images and sensations. The child's memory can be trained only by these, not by ideas, which assume in him the ability to compare and judge (p. 103). In any subject, "without the idea of the things being represented, the signs doing the representing are nothing" (p. 106). We must speak to his personal need and grasp. He should not be treated as a peasant to be ordered about until his will has atrophied, but as a person bent on self-preservation. He is put into the position of the "savage . . . without any other law than his will," who is "forced to reason about each action of his life," who does not make a movement, a step, "without foreseeing the consequences" (p. 118). The savage does not look to others for advice or to display his knowledge.

It is not going too far to say that Rousseau expects the child to think during this sixth stage in a manner appropriate to his situation, to "judge, anticipate, reason about everything immediately related to himself" (pp. 117-19). But in fact, of course, this is guided education. The tutor must lead without the pupil knowing it, must "let him always believe he [the pupil] is the master" (p. 121). To do this, knowledge of man is not enough for the tutor. One has a right to assume that the tutor has a gift for "studying man and the individual" (p. 122). Provided with knowledge of his pupil and with the priorities established by the history of man, he lays the very basis for all later knowledge the individual is to acquire, knowledge that the natural genius transcending any master would come to learn by himself: "The first kind of reason in man is a sensorial reason; it serves as the basis for intellectual reason; our first masters of philosophy are our feet, our hands, our eyes. To substitute books for all that is not to teach us to reason, but to make use of the reason of others, to believe a lot, and never know anything" (p. 128).

From the sensualist theory of his time, Rousseau has drawn the logical consequence, the need to train the receptors of knowledge: "To learn to think, it is therefore necessary to exercise our limbs, our senses, our organs, which are the instruments of our intelligence." This notion is closely related to the previous strengthening of the pupil's health: "to draw the greatest possible advantage from these instruments, it is necessary that the body which supplies them be sturdy and healthy.... it is the good constitution of the body which makes the operations of the mind easy and sure" (p. 128). Man must be deliberately taught to use his own senses, and they must be sharpened to their highest degree. The implication to man's liberation from society's lying, its mask, its conformity, is great. Each man is to make his unique, sensorially based evaluation of the world around him.

Between the ages of one and five (Book I of *Emile*) education means the infant's bodily freedom to express himself totally in an environment safe from harm, from the restrictive child-raising methods of the past. This same freedom from pressure characterizing the primitive state of nature is to be a base for all the rest of Emile's education. In Book II, ages six through twelve, natural education takes on additional meanings. The child, gaining strength, competes against environment and finds the boundaries necessity imposes on him, and establishes his identity in terms of what he alone is able to do. This stage, corresponding to the second in the life of the race, environment set into motion, is soon accompanied by the more positive expression of vitality as happiness, the equivalent of the race's golden age, in which needs are in exact proportion to the individual's capacity to enjoy. Potentially this stage can lead to a fourth period paralleling history's state of war, if the happiness-seeking child, encouraged by indulgent adults to extend himself, is not curbed by the presence of other men, by the tutor's manipulation of force and his exemplary behavior, and by Emile's carefully coaxed entrance into a new stage, moral this time, that of agreement, the transformation of first-occupant possessions into property, the self as consent. With this fifth period, Emile enters society as a make-believe participant.

He senses duty and obligation as conscience, as solidarity with other men on the basis of respect due to work and to contract — legitimacy.

This feeling is constantly in conflict with other forces, fear, desire, vanity, the sixth stage (illegitimacy) of the *Second discours.* It becomes the task of the tutor to anticipate these pressures, to prevent them from warping Emile's psyche. He must lay within Emile the grounds for lucid judgment, must sharpen the senses to their outermost limit. Emile's self is not sickness, debility, obsession with the necessity that limits him or with pleasure, power, or vice, a feeling for inequality, the need to hold sway over others. He is not the result of the deficiency of any of his senses. He is health, freedom, identity, innocent happiness, a feeling for property to the extent of his personal need, a feeling of justice as a moral being who makes and keeps promises he wants to enter into. He is the full development of his senses, which are the source of his unique understanding of the exterior world.

All of these sentiments stem from independence, the condition with respect to persons and environment which allows him to be himself. With one necessary exception, no area of his will is subject to another person without his knowledge and consent. If his training makes him bow at times to objects, to necessity, it is in order to avoid an obsession with them, to avoid a desire to conquer environment and thus to define the self as that conquest. If he is subject to his agreements with others, it is to satisfy his personal need. The exception is that he is totally the subject of his tutor, but this is unwitting, not a conscious abandonment of his will. It is, too, subjection for the purpose of freedom, a reliance from which he is to gain autonomy later.

Education to forestall illegitimacy by lucid judgment goes by degrees beyond the senses to higher orders of abstraction. Emile's safe passage through the graveyard of materialistic science is the subject of Book III, ages twelve through fifteen, when he has, in addition to the strict balance between his needs and the power to satisfy them, the necessary "excess in faculties and powers" (p. 183). Because of his emotional and mental development, more formal study is in order. The main purpose of this philosophic tour conducted by the tutor is to find through a survey of the sciences Emile's particular bent. But essential to this task is another, that of taking the sham out of science, of reducing it to the level of the boy's intelligence: "Let him not know anything because you told him about it, but because he learned it himself; let him not learn science, let him invent it" (p. 186). Authority is to be subordinate, for if you "ever substitute authority for reason in his mind, he will reason no more; he will be nothing more than the plaything of the opinion of others."

Rousseau's concept of education, which up to now has consistently emphasized uniqueness, in direct contradiction to the classical notions of universality that critics have tried in the past to attach to his method, more and more becomes a sequence of measures improvised for bringing out Emile's individuality, for freeing him from the standardizing effects of society, a task already accomplished at the feeling and sensual levels. Necessity is again to be the real teacher. Necessity drew man into society; necessity will awaken the perfectibility, the problem-solving instinct in Emile. He is, as it happens, on the earth and sees the sun. Through local geography, he must acquire rudimentary knowledge of his surrounding habitat, this global island with its brilliant star. He is kept from any positive inculcation by his tutor. The level of comprehension is strictly his own (p. 187). He is safeguarded from verbalism; never is the sign substituted for the thing except when the thing cannot be observed (p. 189). In his lessons of cosmography and geography, he learns not what is useful to others but what is useful to him at his age (p. 191). The aim is exploratory, to arouse his interest, to show him the method of learning the sciences, so that later, if he has developed a taste for them, he will be able to pursue it (p. 192). Therefore he follows not the philosopher's "chain of general truths" but the down-to-earth interrelationship of a common man's problems, according to which "each particular object leads to another" (p. 192). Curiosity about a magician's use of the magnet ties to lessons in physics and also frees Emile from the pride that often goes with science. His curiosity is a part of him and determines his approach. Gradually, by using his hands to create and manipulate tools of science, by thinking about the results observed, he learns the basic laws of nature: "He becomes a philosopher and believes he is only a worker" (p. 199). Curiosity, which is at the basis of science, has become his private, very particular curiosity.

Necessity, too, helps him learn about the unpleasant in order to forestall an evil still more unpleasant and to learn foresight (p. 200). This utility orientation, supplementing curiosity, is implanted by the use of only one book, *Robinson Crusoe*: "I want him to become submerged in it, continually busy with its castle, goats, plantings... he should come to believe he is Robinson himself" (p. 211). Utility restricts the unfathomable depths into which his curiosity alone might lead. But utility must be circumscribed, too. Rousseau's point would seem to be that everything serves some good in the framework of society, especially in a society which gives prestige "to the different arts in inverse ratio to their real utility" (p. 213). Emile's judgments are not to be controlled by this sophistication. He is to understand his world in terms "of the chains of necessity" which have made of him up to this point essentially a "physical being" (pp. 214-15). Useful is to mean the "perceptible relationships" which sciences and arts have with Emile, with his "utility, his security, his self-preservation, his well-being" (p. 215). Iron will be more valuable than gold, glass than diamonds, a baker than the entire academy of sciences. Another restriction on utility is the "relationship which binds them [sciences and arts] in necessity," or attribution of value on the basis of which sciences and arts are the prerequisites of others, the more generally used, or the most indispensable to the race. By this measure, agriculture takes precedent over any other art (p. 216).

This clear indoctrination, which is to persist, is not in Rousseau's judgment a contradiction with the principle of uniqueness. The tutor's control counterbalances society and draws its emphases from history, never from the personal will or whim of another individual. It is significant that at this point Rousseau, intent on the goal of Emile's personal development, warns the tutor against the impact of his own interests, "a mistake difficult to avoid for the occupations with which the master himself is fascinated." The child must remain "central, everything in the matter" (p. 217).

From the sciences dealing with the physical laws of the universe — physics, chemistry, cosmography — the tutor has led Emile to the sciences related to production of consumable goods

— metallurgy, agriculture, building. He now directs him into a consideration of the political arts and sciences. In Book II, Emile developed feelings about property, agreement, justice. He now extends his knowledge to money, standards of weight and length, all the means useful to permit him to become an active member of society. Exchange of any kind, whether between persons or of things, requires standards of measurement. This somewhat subtle insight permits a transition to the study of politics ("All society has some conventional equality for its first law") and again the subject is to be examined strictly in Emile's terms (p. 217). He is led by his own senses to make comparisons between the meal set for the wealthy and the wholesome frugality prevailing in the home of a peasant. His criterion for measurement is not society's taste but his own pleasure: "Emile's choice is not in any doubt; for he is neither talkative nor vain; he cannot stand ceremony, and all our fine dishes do not please him; but he is always ready for a run in the country-side, and he very much likes good vegetables, good cream, and good people" (p. 221).

Emile has been escorted through the entire range of the sciences in a way meaningful to him. Those built on the race's curiosity have been made to relate to his private curiosity. Those close to the race's concept of utility, the practical arts and sciences, have been made to bear on his own self-preservation. The social sciences, dealing with communication and agreement among men, have been presented in terms of his own needs to buy, to measure, to satisfy hunger, to choose between opulence with inequality and rustic simplicity with equality. Rousseau repeatedly underlines his concern for individuality. If the tutor has been clever and a good observer, the secrets of Emile's interests and inclinations have become an open book: "By thus passing before him all the things it is important for him to know, we put him in a position to develop his taste, his talent, to make the first steps toward the goal appropriate to his character, to indicate to us the road which must be opened to him in order that nature may be assisted" (p. 221). Because of the general nature of this tour, he will have avoided the prejudices of others for their own particular art or science. His choice will be strictly in terms of his own abilities and interests.

This passage from private curiosity to private utility to sense of social place must be carried one step further. Knowledge cannot just be related to curiosity, utility, and the interdependence of men in an intellectual way. It is not enough to find one's taste and capacity. Emile must become an active member of society. He must give to society in order to deserve its protection. He cannot live in isolation, always sheltered by his tutor. He would be departing from what is natural if he tried to live the life of a solitary person in society, "for the first law of nature is the need for self-preservation" (p. 223). Rousseau's reason for having Emile learn a trade is not, however, simply the one usually emphasized, that he cannot be assured always of being rich and that the time of revolution is approaching (p. xiii). Certainly his trade means that he will never go hungry (p. 229), but it means much more. He is to become an artisan because the artisan is independent of favor, of fortune, "depends only on his work; he is free" (p. 226-27). Freedom means he does not have to play the game of society, the pantomiming of Diderot's *Neveu de Rameau*. The emphasis again is on being oneself, speaking one's mind freely, like Rousseau finding his freedom in Book VIII of the *Confessions*. Emile will not have to be "cowardly and mendacious in the presence of nobles, compliant and fawning with scoundrels, base and complacent with everybody, a borrower or thief" (p. 228). Rousseau stresses, too, that Emile has found this kind of work on the basis of his own gifts: "It takes finer observations than one might think to be certain about the true genius and taste of a child, who reveals much more of his desires than of his inclinations" (p. 231).

A trade, it should be added, is not to be his whole life. Emile is to work "as a peasant" and think "as a philosopher," to be given "the taste for reflection and meditation" (p. 236). He is not a savage but must live in society. To do that he must be "a savage made for living in cities ... finding what he needs, benefiting from their inhabitants, and living, if not like them, at least with them." He will learn not so much truths as "how one must go about discovering the truth" (p. 240). He will make use of "his own reason and not that of others" (p. 242). He "considers himself without regard to others" and "counts only on himself" (p. 244). Surrounded by people, he is through his training to be as independent as the primitive man isolated in the state of nature. We shall see later that his very independence is perhaps his greatest contribution in any just society, which depends on the absolute, uncompromised separation of the wills which form the general will.

In Book I through Book III, ages one through fifteen, the emphasis is on discipline. Around the child has been created a shelter from damaging aspects of sophisticated society as they were detected and described in Rousseau's first two discourses. Emile has passed through the stages of man's history, but always with positive results. Built into his being are a feeling for his own nature, the ability to express his own temperament, an awareness of the power of necessity, the urge to happiness, a sense of balance between need, desire, and capacity, a feeling for legitimacy, and a sensory and intellectual awareness of the surrounding environment: "He has a healthy body, agile limbs, a sound mind free of prejudices, a heart free and without passions. Vanity, the first and most natural of all [passions] is still scarcely aroused. Without troubling anyone's tranquility, he has lived content, happy and free, as much as nature has permitted" (p. 244). These feelings and thoughts have been made possible by an education designed to screen out extraneous influence and encourage native abilities, traits, and tastes. The task of Book IV is to lure all of Emile's still largely unconscious drives out of the zone of automatic self-expression into an area requiring a clear choice for order or chaos. The question is to be that of how the individual metaphysically sees the universe and his place in it, as either the product of will or of blind necessity. The tutor must force Emile to opt for either freedom of will or determinism, for belief in a self under control or belief in a self submerged by the flux of events.

Emile is threatened at the age of fifteen by violent drives awakening within him: "This stormy revolution is announced by the murmur of nascent passions" (p. 246). As instruments of self-preservation, they need not be feared unless aggravated by contamination from people around him. He must learn to utilize them properly, to bring them under the control of his will, and this has been and is to continue to be the tutor's goal. The latter has advantages already derived from the task of training Emile. Emile's imagination has not been corrupted. His senses alone create his urges, and "nature's instructions are sluggish and slow"

(p. 251). The boy has lived among "coarse and simple people," so that "a blessed ignorance" has prolonged his innocence (p. 252). He has been kept from "a dangerous curiosity" (p. 254). The tutor's knowledge of man and of Emile must now produce devices first to "order the affections" and later to shift responsibility to Emile (p. 250-57).

Rousseau's principle is to counteract passion with passion. Education becomes the science of forces and counterforces. Love is only one of the passions. The tutor finds the best sequence for their appearance and gives precedence to pity, commiseration, mercy, and generosity. Emile is made to feel deeply the suffering of others (pp. 259-60). Love, "this fire of the adolescent," can be diverted toward pity and also toward friendship, a new form of control the tutor now has over him. Rousseau aims at this stage to keep Emile from being overpowered by his selfish passions, the atavistic urges of social man. Notions of justice are to be deliberately aroused in his heart, for "by reason alone, independently of conscience, one cannot establish any natural law" (p. 278). Emile has *amour de soi* and *pitié*, but love of self can become vanity and ambition. It is necessary that he meet the poor, see the inequality that exists among men, be taught to pity even his supposed inferiors. History is to be not an end in itself but a means of showing him the trials and sufferings of even the greatest of heroes and kings (pp. 281-90). He can learn, too, about the passions of men from the fables of La Fontaine. As a result of this guidance, *amour de soi* develops into a concern with mankind: "It matters very little to him who receives as his share the greatest happiness, provided he contributes to the greatest happiness of all: that is the first interest of the wise man after his private interest; for each one of us is a part of his species and not part of another individual" (p. 303). Rousseau has made the microcosm embrace the macrocosm. Emile, deeply aware of suffering and injustice, embraces suffering humanity, not through reason alone but through his very individual, personal tenderness.

After compassion and justice, another affection, religion, must become an object of Emile's curiosity at the appropriate time: "When he begins to worry about these great questions, it is not because he has heard them proposed, but it is when the natural progress of his understanding carries his investigation in that direction" (p. 313). The *Profession de foi du Vicaire Savoyard* indicates the religious instruction one man's empirical knowledge can offer, a natural religion which serves as the bridge in Rousseau's thinking between Emile as automaton and Emile's first deliberate option for freedom of will.

The Vicar's reasoning makes each individual the measure of belief: "Let us consult the interior light, it will lead me astray less than they [philosophers], or at least my error will be my own, and I shall become less corrupted following my own illusions than giving myself up to their lies" (p. 324). One of the Vicar's findings is that in animal bodies, as opposed to inanimate and vegetable matter, there are two kinds of movement, "communicated movement" and "spontaneous or voluntary movement" (p. 328). The Vicar understands this "because I feel it." By personal observation, too, he knows the world is in a different kind of movement than "the spontaneous movements of man and animals." By analogy he concludes that its "regular, uniform movements, subjected to constant laws," since it is not "a great animal which moves by itself," must be subject to "some cause foreign to itself" (p. 329). This force may be called God: "A will moves the universe and animates nature" (p. 330). This will is "powerful and wise; I see it, or rather I feel it" (p. 334). He observes, too, that the universe, its matter, its animals, except for man, are in harmony, but "men are in chaos" (p. 337). Man must therefore be free: "I am not free not to want my own good, I am not free to want my pain, but my liberty consists in that very fact that I am free only to want what is right for me, or what I consider such, without letting anything alien to myself determine me" (p. 340). Man is thus responsible for his acts; he cannot blame God for the mistakes which have caused him to err (p. 340). Each man must defend his freedom against himself and other men by following his conscience (pp. 342, 352).

These ideas and others the Vicar and Emile acquire "by study of the universe" (p. 364). To go further than such study is to leave nature, to "have recourse to extraordinary means." Emile must decide for himself what additional beliefs he may accept on the authority of one of the "three great religions" (pp. 364, 373, 387-88). The point for the tutor is that Emile has been lifted in his thinking above mere knowledge of the senses, above necessity.

"We have removed him from the sway of the senses" (pp. 324, 327, 388). The profession has not been offered as "a rule of the sentiments one must follow in religious matters," and it is important to emphasize this warning by Rousseau. There is no doubt about its being his own belief, but he wants to indicate his deeper purpose and intent, the need to train Emile's independence, to leave his nature the sole criterion even in the matter of faith. Rousseau says this teaching is "an example of the manner in which one may reason with his pupil" (p. 387).

As a result of these new ideas the tutor has tightened his control over Emile (p. 389). When the passions of sex erupt in their full force ("You will sense the critical moment"), the tutor is ready with the means now at his disposal — compassion, friendship, justice, goodness, the distinction between good and evil, aspirations for God's way — to change completely his role with regard to Emile. He resigns his authority over him, makes him totally responsible, an autonomous being: "He is still your disciple, but he is not your pupil. He is your friend" (p. 392). No more is Emile to be led by "ruse and by force." He must be made to choose between necessity alone and necessity plus God, between passion alone and passion plus reason and God, between Emile lost in error and Emile free. The anxiety created by unknown urges rises in him and frightens him. The tutor tells him of the dangers they create: "Let one show him the sanction of these same laws [of nature] in the physical and moral evils which their infraction brings down upon the guilty" (p. 403). Information about marriage and chastity is given. Emile in his trouble asks the tutor to continue his role: "Take back the authority you want to lay down at the very moment when it is the most important for you to keep it" (p. 404). Reluctantly, it is made to seem, the tutor takes up again his burden on the condition that Emile will promise to follow him out of the present crisis (p. 405). His authority restored, the tutor continues to guide Emile's affections. He distracts him from sex in many ways. The image of an ideal love is evoked (p. 409). To protect him from self-abuse, he is never left alone. Tutor and pupil go to Paris to perfect Emile's taste in literature (pp. 424-31).

Through the tutor Rousseau has made Emile take several important steps. The pupil has chosen freedom of will, that is, has decided that a belief in order is better for him than a belief in necessity alone. In making this choice, he has recognized his ignorance and has assumed the value of the tutor's science. Behavior is known to him in terms of a hierarchy of categories. Action in ignorance is better than action according to erroneous science, but true science is better than ignorance in some instances: "The same man who must remain stupid in the forests must become reasonable and sensible in the cities." He must be drawn "neither by passions nor by the opinions of men." No authority must guide him "except that of his own reason" (p. 306). Yet in fact he has not been guided by his reason alone. If Emile has consciously for the first time accepted the value of the teaching presented by his tutor, he is still being led by him, but less blindly. His eyes are opened to the alternatives, but without his friend it is clear that performance may not follow intention. Emile is free at the level of intention only, not at the level of behavior. Without continued guidance, "the furies of an ardent temperament" might still be invincible (p. 416). Emile has not proved the fact of his freedom but has accepted the idea that he can resist the current of the *Second discours,* can opt in his actions for nature, legitimacy, and divine order, for the educator's creation. No more than the possibility of a new man has appeared, but this is an advance, and the tutor can answer the doubters who say that "young men are not made that way" with his arguments against a skepticism which would even deny that "a pear-tree ever was a big tree, because there are only dwarfs in our gardens" (p. 305). Freedom means at this level avoidance of any partial existence, any habit or vice already contracted and become a pattern for the race. Emile is not a universal model for all men but a unique creation. The tutor tells him, "You are my good, my child, my work; it is from your happiness that I await mine; if you frustrate my hopes, you steal from me twenty years of my life" (p. 402). Following this regime of avoiding extraneous influences and encouraging feelings, ideas, and beliefs which enhance the self's particular inclination, other men, too, may cease to be dwarfs and reach full stature, but it will be in terms of their own unique capacities.

It can be argued that Emile is still the tutor's man in too full a sense, that his option for freedom of will is not enough, that he must break that control and learn to stand alone in action. Rousseau does not think so. In Book V, Emile, now a man, is guided even more carefully than before. Rousseau stresses the need for such control, refuses to "imitate Locke," who abandoned his "young gentleman" at the moment he was ready to marry. He then proceeds to outline in detail the woman Emile needs to complement himself. Obedience, fidelity, tenderness, and the care given to her children are the natural consequence of her condition: "The true mother of the family, far from being a society woman, is scarcely less of a recluse in her house than the nun in her cloister" (p. 489). She must know the obligations of her difficult life, the pleasures to be given up before she enters into the contract. Great attention is given to compatibility. The courtship is carefully planned. The tutor maintains his authority over Emile in spite of the attraction exerted by Sophie: "If he comes at his ease, slowly, and dreaming of his love, Emile is nothing more than the lover of Sophie; if he arrives in a hurry, heated, although in a somewhat scolding mood, Emile is the friend of his Mentor" (p. 554). He still reflects his training. He is to be a mate consistent with his freedom, capable of distinguishing between the needs of suffering humanity and the needs of his personal happiness: "Sophie, you are the arbiter of my fate, you know that very well. You can make me die of sorrow; but do not expect to make me forget the rights of humanity: they are more sacred than yours, I shall never renounce them for you" (pp. 562-63). His will must follow his own conscience, not another's. [2] On the authority won from Emile in Book IV, the tutor imposes a two-year wait on the lovers, time for Emile to know the world and its governments, to find his place, to test the durability of his and Sophie's love (p. 571).

The voyage undertaken educates Emile in all of Rousseau's political theory: "To travel just to travel is to wander... to travel to instruct oneself is a still more vague object... it remains for him to consider himself in his civil relationships with his fellow-

---

[2] When in the *Amours de Sophie et Emile*, sequel to *Emile*, Sophie has fallen, Emile's decision to start anew reflects again his freedom to resist the contaminating decadence around him, to seek a way compatible with his own conscience.

citizens" (p. 581). After two years of studying abroad, Emile chooses to settle in his homeland and to marry Sophie. Again the outcome has been prepared. The sexual relationship of the lovers, the delay in its consummation, the consent of Sophie are all carefully arranged by the tutor (pp. 610-14). When after this union the tutor says, "Here ends my long task," it is clear that Emile is still in every sense the captive of his teaching. He will be the mentor to his own children, since he has inherited the will and the capacity to do so. The tutor is to remain his guide: "But remain the master of young masters. Advise us, govern us, we will be docile; so long as I live, I shall need you... guide me in imitating you" (p. 614).

This continuing control by the tutor seems perfectly consistent with part of Rousseau's definition of freedom of will: "My liberty consists in the very fact that I can want only what is right for me or what I consider to be right" (p. 340). Primitive man of the *Second discours*, according to this definition, was free. He entered society unwittingly and to his own harm, which he nevertheless believed to be his good. He constantly reacted to necessity, invented legitimacy for his advantage under the force of circumstances, but then followed illegitimacy under continuing pressures. The tutor with a transcendent view of history's cycle knows man's good and conditions Emile to want that good. Emile is therefore free, too.

But there is more to Rousseau's definition. If authority is surrendered by the tutor, it is always returned, as in the last page of Book V, and there is no question but that the tutor's teaching has permeated Emile's being and become his own, so that the tutor's absence or presence is really no longer relevant. This seemingly total submission poses a difficulty for the last part of the definition of freedom, that a person who is free cannot want anything except what is right for him, "or what I consider to be right, without anything alien to me determining me" (p. 340). By this fuller definition primitive man, compelled by the necessity exterior to him, is not free. Emile, determined by the tutor's training based on the standards of nature and legitimacy described in the *Second discours*, is not free. This beneficial enslavement can be explained away in several ways. The prevalent course of history has been harmful enslavement and the weight of history would seem to favor this subversion of man's natural state. The tutor and his training represent nature, but passion is a part of man and society constantly incites passion, so that at every moment society's attraction represents a real option and makes the choice against history and for the tutor in every moment of trial a genuinely free choice, a matter of will.

But the problem is again not that easy. If Emile, knowing his good, choses the way of necessity, he is not free. If knowing his good he chooses his good he is free but how can he know what is his good. He can say he knows because the tutor says so. The tutor is not God, but he has a complete view of history and of Emile and can know Emile's good. Since the tutor, this good, and Emile's self, guaranteed by that good, are all synonymous, no element of his training is foreign to Emile, so that in choosing, he is free, at least according to Rousseau's definition. In other words, there is a return to the idea that freedom of will consists essentially of scientific knowledge of history, of the standards of liberty and legitimacy, and of the art needed to inculcate into the individual the habits required to overcome the forces which limit the self, which prevent it from becoming unique as a private person and also from becoming legitimate, that is, a good citizen free of the vices that lead to tyranny. Freedom, then, means being determined by an art or education based on a transcendent view of nature and history. A choice in which freedom is absent is the choice to follow the course of history outlined in the *Second discours*. Rousseau would seem not to be interested in the old notion of freedom of will as a real choice. Inescapably, freedom of will remains successful conditioning for uniqueness and legitimacy. The alternative is necessity, materialistic determination.

These two concepts, uniqueness and legitimacy, complement one another in an essential way. The unique individual is free because he has been conditioned to reject the influence of his untutored elders, their enslavement to sickness and to obsessions outside the self, whether these obsessions be conquest of nature as physical environment or pursuit of pleasure, power, riches, rank, artistic achievement, sex, and war. These negations can in no way make a universal type, unless independence to be one's personal self is a universal model. The independent self, protected by its habits of negation, is encouraged to appear by a matrix of conditions carefully staged by the tutor at numerous levels as the boy's life unfolds. As the self appears, each new condition bestows a habit never to be lost again, a habit freeing the self to perform. A feeling of freedom, the child's uninhibited state of nature, encourages expressiveness. The second stage's contact with necessity gives him an awareness of identity, the sense of animate oneness, of the struggle to preserve self. By the third stage the self is introduced to happiness as excitation over innocent pleasures, innocent because need is matched to capacity; in other words, enjoyment occupies the self but the self does not lose its identity to pleasure. From stages corresponding to the states of war and legitimacy, the self acquires notions of moral identity, basically the awareness that the self, in order to retain its own intimate being, must forego enslaving other selves by force. Rather the individual's goal must be to sharpen his own senses, to find his own taste, talent, work, and religion, to understand what his personal contribution within the family and the nation can be.

Emile in fact has not been raised "uniquely... for himself" (p. 11). Rousseau has in an important sense combined domestic education and public education, for the integrity of the individual self, of the individual will, the uniqueness Rousseau wants to foster by education, will be seen to be at the heart of the idea of legitimate contract. Illegitimacy and usurpation are essentially the destruction of the collectivity by a breakdown in the independence of each will, a breakdown which permits one will to impose its private will and good as the general will and good. The definition of legitimacy in terms of the sacredness of the self enlarges substantially on the concept given in the *Economie*, by which the prince-legislator, with selfless knowledge of the general good, whether law or projected law, forms the minds of each member of the sovereign to want that good. Within his family, whenever he is not part of the sovereign, Emile's uniqueness is expressed in his work, his taste, his personal attitudes, his efforts to form his own children. As subject he would obey the law because of his sense of place, history, and man's predicament. As a part of the sovereign, he would guard his independence of voice in spite of possible inequality of fortune. As a member of the sovereign, too, he would be ruthless in detecting interference by private interest, whether his own or that of others; he would be capable, if his uniqueness consisted of penetrating vision, to be the legislator or to verify the good the legislator and prince seek. If a nation were to be made up of Emiles, each unique in his own way, the notion of sovereign would become living and dynamic. Rousseau expresses this idea at the close of Emile's travels: "Liberty is not in any form of government, it is in the heart of the free man; he carries it with him everywhere... go live in the midst of them [men], cultivate their friendship... be their benefactor, their model: your example will serve them more than all our books" (pp. 605-06).

CHAPTER VIII

SUSTAINING THE INDIVIDUAL WILLS

AMONG THE PROJECTS ROUSSEAU was considering after 1756 was a study of political institutions. The idea for it, he says in Book IX of the *Confessions*, in fact went back thirteen of fourteen years to when he was in Venice (1743-1744) serving as secretary of the French ambassador. But not until 1751 was the vast plan given serious attention and reduced to practical proportions. The actual writing of the *Du Contrat social ou principes du droit politique* [1] was probably delayed even more until 1756 or as late as 1758. By August of 1761 he told his publisher, Marc-Michel Rey of Amsterdam, that the work was ready, and the treatise appeared in April of 1762, several weeks before *Emile*. The success of the *Nouvelle Héloïse* and *Emile* at first eclipsed the *Contrat social*, which became popular reading only after 1788 or 1789, the beginning of the French Revolution. At the time of its publication, the *Contrat social* was denied entry into France and circulated there only clandestinely. The book was at first available in Geneva, but there too in June of 1762 the magistrates condemned it along with *Emile:* these books were to be burned as "reckless, scandalous, impious, tending to destroy the Christian religion and all governments" (Pléiade, 3: cxi).

Some writers of the twentieth century, because of their own concerns, two world wars, and other limited wars, have been

---

[1] All citations for this work, unless otherwise indicated, are to the 1762 version of the text as it appears in the Pléiade edition of the *Œuvres complètes*, vol. 3.

tempted to approach Rousseau's political thought in terms of the ideological conflict between liberalism and totalitarianism.[2] The debate, at times unscrupulous, often anachronistic, seems destined to continue.

Those who play up the totalitarian side insist heavily on two aspects of Rousseau's thought: the weight he gives to state religion and the extent to which the general will and good are to bind the individual consciences. According to such criticism, these two concepts leave no area in which the citizen can think in private, personal terms, for he must always subordinate his particular interest to the general good, even within the *for intérieur*, the inner recesses of the soul. They claim that not only do Rousseau's theories of the citizen, of the partial existence within the whole, and of the subordination to a national collectivity encourage this point of view, but his praise of the great heroes of antiquity, the superpatriots of Sparta and early Rome, makes it clear that for him there is no authority higher than the state.

The other side can be convincing, too. Those who defend Rousseau as a liberal emphasize that for the eighteenth century the great conflict was not the individual versus the state (the people as whole), but rather the individual against the divine-right monarch, a private person who, in the name of superior intelligence or of his mission to represent God on earth, imposed on the people goals of conquest or dynastic right, which meant exploitation of the nation's work force and public treasury for the sake of personal ambition. The concept of the people as a whole was, therefore, not the real enemy. And even if it was, Rousseau, according to this way of thinking, took ample precaution within

---

[2] For the totalitarian interpretation, see Jacob Leib Talmon, *The Rise of Totalitarian Democracy* (Boston: Beacon Press, 1952). R. A. Leigh's "Liberté et autorité dans le *Contrat social*," in *Jean-Jacques Rousseau et son œuvre: problèmes et recherches* (Paris: Klincksieck, 1964), pp. 249-62, is an effort to refute Talmon's position. The same year, in his introduction to the Pléiade edition of the *Contrat social* (3: cviii), Robert Derathé seems to move toward the totalitarian viewpoint: "No one insisted more than Rousseau on the protection the state owes its members, and preoccupation with the safety of the citizens was as intense with him as with Montesquieu. But it is clear that one finds in Rousseau a conception of liberty which has nothing in common with liberalism. The latter fears the extension of the state's powers."

his formula for union, since each individual who gives himself to the collectivity, the national will, gives to an association of which he is a part and whose will, including his own voice, is the legislative organ of the state, the true sovereign for which the executive, whether monarch or democratic or aristocratic assembly, is the mere agent.

This two-way orientation has been useful. It has brought out many facets of Rousseau's thought and has led to questions about the structure of modern democracy, both totalitarian and liberal versions of it. Unfortunately, it has a drawback. This perspective, if relevant to our own times, conceals other aspects of Rousseau's system which tie more closely to his own personality as revealed in the *Confessions* and other autobiographical sources. It discounts to the point of distortion the theme of uniqueness of the individual, which is deeply embedded in all of the works so far examined, from the *Discours sur les sciences et les arts* to the *Lettre à d'Alembert;* and it reaches a high point in the *Nouvelle Héloïse* and *Emile*. It is my conviction that for Rousseau this one absolute right — the right to be a free, unique self — is the only basic right in the last analysis which can be drawn from the state of nature. The self in absolute isolation is all-important to Rousseau. Only this right, freedom for the potential endowment in each individual, may determine the national condition, not a multitude of apparent rights which relate more to *amour-propre*, vanity and pride, than to the ultimate standard of "love of self." The rights of passion, such as happiness, property, and exploitation of environment, are justifiable only to the extent that they are a means to the free self. The validity of this approach will become clear, I hope, from my discussion of the one side of the *Contrat social* to be treated in this chapter, the relation of each member of the nation to the collectivity, a relation which for Rousseau constitutes national domestic liberty.

In the *Second discours* the earliest state of nature existed in timelessness. Environment had not started to move; it was held in suspension to coincide with the purpose of Rousseau's thought experiment. Later, under the hypothesized effect of cataclysmic events, man was chased from his state of isolated repose and led deep into society by his problem-solving reaction to necessity. The eventual establishment of civil society, bringing a momentary slowing of stylistic tempo, contrasts with the frenetic activity of the state of war but soon gives way again to turbulence, expressed as fear of the present and future, time as legalized attrition. Selfish action characterized the decline of the race into inequality, and the *Economie politique,* recognizing the predominant role of government in that action, sought to solve the problem of the individual's disfranchisement solely within the area of the executive by replacing corrupt government with enlightened government.

The *Contrat social* changes the emphasis. Time has become total perspective. Writer and reader are placed above history and asked to find a solution in terms of the relationships of the parts to the whole, of the individual, including the prince, to the nation. Rousseau has become the theorist of form who deals with the constitution of the state, the assemblage of its parts before it begins to function: "I make it live and not act. I describe its sources of energy and its pieces. I arrange them in place" (3: 281). Liberty is to consist in joining right with self-interest and law with men as they are. The solution proposed is not to be utopian but to rest on the behavior of down-to-earth men. Liberty is dependent on structure, the relationship between men established by laws regulating their condition. Emphasis is not placed on any list of natural rights around which the structure is to be built, such as security of life and limb, right to property, freedom of speech, of thought, of religion — rights which Voltaire, for example, listed repeatedly in his writings. Liberty for Rousseau is not usually viewed from outside in that way. Liberty for the most part is expressed inherently in the form of association: "'a form of association which will defend and protect with the whole common force the person and goods of each associate, and through which each by uniting himself to all, may however obey only himself and remain as free as before'" (3: 360). Rather than the ideal of liberty, the precise relation of each individual self to the congregation is paramount.

Several interpretations have been given to the phrase "aussi libre qu'auparavant." Some writers have said that it indicates only the vague intention that man should be "as free as before," or that Rousseau was merely speaking hyperbolically, not logically, for in fact the liberty of the precivil period has been compromised, since it no longer includes the right to continue personal expansion in goods and power over others, to satisfy the right of the strongest. My point of view, in contrast, is that Rousseau means literally what he says, that for him freedom does not include in any absolute sense the claim of passion to pleasure, possessions, and power. In the context of history this claim is not a right. Rousseau deplores it in the *Second discours* (3: 176-77) and accepts it only to the extent that it is in conformity with the right of free survival, that is, with the "love of self" which reduces the extent of one's holdings to the subsistence need of the first occupant and his ability to work the soil to satisfy that need, an idea repeated in the *Contrat* (3: 366). It is even possible to go further, to eliminate private property from the social contract on the basis of Rousseau's supposition that the national association might occur before individuals have taken private possession of land: "It may also happen that men begin to unite with one another before they possess anything and that, later taking possession of land which is enough for all, they enjoy it in common, or share it among themselves, whether equally or in a proportion established by the sovereign" (3: 367). It follows from this that property is a claim that does not have to be guaranteed by society, is not an essential part of liberty, that what constitutes the claim of man in precivil society is freedom of the self — its separation from other selves and from usurpation by them, the freedom of the isolated man in the earliest state of nature. Rousseau's concern is the union of wills to form a collectivity or sovereign without diminishing the uniqueness of each will. The wills are no longer alone, they become parts of a whole, but they are not to be standardized by this process. They keep their own individualities.

Thus Rousseau's works up to now have shown that within each citizen is a free-willing individual who because of his uniqueness can help change the shape of the whole rather than allow the whole to reduce him to conformity. The *Contrat social* bears out this hypothesis; it refuses any value system which would downgrade some individuals to the benefit of others. In Rousseau's analysis of the various theories of sovereignty, the support of authority came erroneously to reside in the prince rather than in the people for one reason — the defeat of *amour de soi*. This simple instinct of free survival inherent in each man was deformed into *amour-propre,* vanity and pride, which succeeded in turning inferior passion into superficially reasonable and acceptable arguments justifying the ruler's absorption of the wills of the others. A number of convincing arguments were used to reduce the selves to a conformist pattern.

One argument is based on the value assigned to intelligence. Theorists make only that faculty the standard of measurement, place everyone on its gradation line, and indicate with or without proof that the prince is at the top of the scale. This device Rousseau summarily rejects: "As a shepherd is of a nature superior to that of his flock, the shepherds of men, who are their rulers, are also of a nature superior to that of their peoples.... Aristotle before any of them [Caligula, Grotius] had also said that men are not naturally equal, but that some are born for slavery, and some for the domination of men" (3: 353). Rousseau attributes this reasoning also, unjustly, to Hobbes. But his own point is clear, that any gradation in intelligence among men is insufficient to make one naturally king, another naturally slave.

Another argument for leveling man is drawn from the parallel that can be made between the father of the family and the king. This basis, already rejected in the *Economie,* is also contrary to observable behavior. The children are not bound by any enduring paternal right to rule. In nature, their defense is their own responsibility as soon as their powers permit; this responsibility is attached to their *amour de soi:* "His [man's] first law is to take precautions for his own preservation, his first cares are those he owes himself, and as soon as he reaches the age of reason, he alone being the judge of the proper means to preserve himself becomes by that fact his own master" (3: 352). Any continuance of this relationship after that age is voluntary and conventional. Kingship is similarly based only on the will and consent of the subjects. The only possible, although insufficient, natural support for authority would then have to reside in the love of a father for his children, a love based in the *pitié* of the state of nature. But in kings this is pretext, no ground for authority at all, merely self-flattery or sentimentality, because the "pleasure of commanding takes the place of the love the chief cannot have for his people" (3: 352).

The theory of dynastic right Rousseau similarly reduces to absurdity. Ridicule is part of his attack: "I have said nothing of King Adam, nor of Emperor Noah, father of the three great monarchs who divide the universe." Such a distant source of right would allow any man, Rousseau jokes, even himself, to establish a right to rule. But again, as with the argument of intelligence and that of paternity, his underlying argument is based on the isolated, uncompromising ego. Only on that basis could a right traced to Adam have validity, but on that basis the individual will has right only over its own self in exclusion of all others: "In any event, it cannot be disagreed that Adam was sovereign of the world, like Robinson of his island, as long as he was the sole inhabitant of it; and the advantage of such authority was that the monarch, secure on his throne, had no fear of rebellion, wars, or conspirators" (3: 353-54).

Finally, there is Rousseau's argument against the right of the strongest. He relates all facets of his reasoning to the isolated will and its refusal by nature to be compromised. The gradation of men on the basis of power is as unconvincing as the Platonic and Aristotelian gradation on the basis of intelligence. Man is not just his power any more than he is just his intelligence. This quantitative measure cannot bind: "The strongest is never strong enough to be always the master." Quantity has nothing to do with right because it does not relate to the whole man, which is the unanalyzed, undiminished being expressed through his will, not through his fist: "To yield to force is an act of necessity, not of will; at the very most it is an act of prudence. In what sense can it be a duty?" (3: 354).

But the right of the strongest is insidious from another point of view, too. According to the traditional vicious circle, force gives to the man of muscle the power of life and death over his fellowmen. Instead of death, he offers his victims slavery, that is, the life that is left after will has been stripped away, so that consent to slavery must presuppose a slavish submissiveness in the first place: "By taking an equivalent for his life, the victor has not done him a favor; instead of killing him unproductively, he has killed him usefully," for life without freedom is no life at all (3: 358).

The circle becomes even more nonsensical and confused because this particular relationship of the individual wills to one another — the effort of one to destroy the others by reasoning supported on nonreason, force alone — has been tied to the right of conquest in war. War is a state applicable only between nations, a condition in which individuals are no longer complete but have become servants to a function, defense of the state. As soon as the war is over the victor can claim no right over the entire individual but only over his soldiering function. With the loss of a nations's will to fight, that function no longer exists: "War is not therefore a relationship between man and man, but between state and state, in which individuals are enemies only accidentally... as soldiers; not as members of their homeland, but as its defenders." With the defeat of the nation, the conqueror cannot raise the stakes from conquest over the mere soldier to conquest over the entire man.

As we have seen, Rousseau has refused to level the entire self on any basis, whether that basis be the intelligence of kings, or their pleasure in commanding (which hides behind an analogy with paternal love), or the belief in blood traceable back to Adam, or their love of being the strongest, or the right of conquest: "The goal of war being the destruction of the enemy state, one has a right to kill its defenders so long as they are bearing arms; but as soon as they lay them down and surrender, ceasing to be enemies or instruments of the enemy, they become again simply men, and one no longer has a right over their life" (3: 357).

Rousseau's reasons for refusing to compromise the individual self are not the ones that are successful in history. The reasons for enslaving man used by the prince, all of them variants of arguments from *amour-propre* or necessity, have usually guided mankind's evolution, according to Rousseau, and in one way or another have subverted the legitimacy which existed for a moment of history, at the time of civil association. All of these arguments contain the Machiavellian principle of success — thinking and doing whatever is required to manipulate man into following the prince's own vision, into reducing man to a part of himself, while the prince retains his whole being and even embraces legitimacy at times when it serves his purpose.

To say that Rousseau's argument is the argument of liberty against slavery is not to oversimplify the issue. History's liberty, as defined by kings, depends on the enslavement of the many, the right of each strong man to expand to the limit of his abilities, to coordinate under his individual will as many wills as possible. In this system of the right to total independence, everyone takes his chances and anyone may become the strongest in the course of time. The key is to find one's strongest asset and make that the standard for reducing all other men to subservience. The only answer to this way of arguing is Rousseau's refusal to have the will reduced to any one element shared by all men. Each man, on the contrary, has his own unique combination with its own intrinsic value, not to be reduced, not to be made second to any other combination. Quality is in the whole individual, as if the individual still lived in the state of nature, uncompromised by comparison with anyone.

Even the most transcendent genius, the legislator, is not to be placed in a position of superiority to other men. His vision is to be utilized but not to be made a basis of authority for subjecting and reducing other wills, for placing himself above the law. Just as the least endowed of men has the right to neither more nor less than his self, so the seer must live up to his individual capacity and promise but must not overrun his personal will and control other wills. Unlike the princely figures representing leadership in the past who have been according to Rousseau deniers of the selves of others, the legislator embodies personal containment; when he thinks in terms of laws for the nation he does not project his ego over the universe. He wills to be selfless in his thinking. Just as a man in becoming a soldier temporarily abandons the whole self to become a part but must not permit this part to pass for his whole being, so the legislator must not confuse his function with his full self and expect because of his particular talent to embody legislative authority.

Particular talent is not the man. With this understood, with moral value assigned to the whole individual rather than to the talent, the greatest legislative genius need not be a threat. Rousseau offers historical arguments for this selflessness of the legislator. In contrast to the founding father conceived by Machiavelli — a person of insight, of persuasive force, but also a man with legislative power who imposes his will on the people — Rousseau's concept of the legislator emphasizes selfless vision alone: "I look at modern nations: I see many makers of laws and not one legislator. Among the Ancients, I see three principal [legislators] who deserve particular attention: Moses, Lycurgus, and Numa" (3: 956, 1461). Moses had one goal, to make a "free people." Lycurgus was equally selfless in his vision "to institute a people already degraded by servitude and the vices which are the effect of it.... from this continual constraint, made noble by its goal, was born that ardent love of the homeland" (3: 957). Numa "by mild institutions" managed to unite the Romans, to attach them to their soil.

Other allusions define the characteristics the modern legislator must have if he is to rival his ancient predecessors and succeed in a task much more difficult and complex than theirs. The legislator is extreme in all of the qualities needed to make him a creator, but has the behavior of a God in his creation: "It would take a superior intelligence which might see all the passions of men without experiencing any of them, which would have no relation with our nature and would know it to the depths, whose happiness might be independent of us, an intelligence which however would want to occupy itself with our happiness; finally, an intelligence which would with the unfolding of time prepare for itself a distant glory, be able to work in one century and enjoy in another. It would take Gods to give laws to men" (3: 381). This function relates the legislator to law only, not to men. His self remains uncompromised by his function. The selves of other men in turn remain uncompromised by his particular and superior mission. Just because he is a legislating type, is the best among his peers, the power of his personal self is not to be expanded, allowed to touch men as well as law: "it is a special and superior function which has nothing in common with human rule; for if he [government] who commands men must not have power over the laws, neither must he who has command over the laws have command over men" (3: 382). The legislator is not to become government any more than he is to replace the sovereign will of the people. After the legislator has done a creative act, his function disappears until it is needed again; it is unrelated to his ordinary action as citizen. This separation of function from self is necessary to keep private interest out of the laws: if he violated it "he would never be able to avoid letting his private views mar the sanctity of his work" (3: 382).

Five elements have been involved so far in this discussion of the legislator (Book II, Chapter 7): selfless legislative vision; the isolated, unique self living for its own sake *(amour de soi);* the self as passion and private interest; the collectivity or sovereign; and the government or executive. Again, to keep a single faculty, power, or talent from becoming the basis for usurpation of power, as in the earlier discussions of the bases of authority, the concept of the unique, isolated self is vital. In its absence, the legislator's vision can be seen by his *amour-propre* as the justification for uniting under himself, rather than separating, the executive (government), legislative (will of the sovereign people), and lawgiving (legislator) functions. Only if the legislator's vision is not a supreme value, only if it is dominated by the concept of the isolated self as supreme value, can the lawgiving vision be used, then harmlessly dissipated, and the legislator return to his normal self.

If this curbing of the legislator attests to the presence in Rousseau's argument of the irreducible self, then the legislator's goals, too, are guided by this principle. They are best treated in two steps: his creation of the collectivity and his protection of its will from the prince and from environment.

The principle of the isolated self appears in Rousseau's presentation of the state of nature, in his rejection of traditional reasoning about the sources of princely authority, and in his statement about the unfitness of the legislator for power. It is evident also in his description of history in the *Second discours*. The individual wills refused to accept any other authority than that based on unanimity of the individual wills in congregation. This principle of legitimacy could have been preserved if each concrete instance of the resistance to pressure from any one individual will, resistance which for Rousseau is a matter of psychological fact, a pattern of human behavior, had been supported in real life by a legislator's genius, by leaders of the caliber of Moses, Lycurgus, and Numa. But most beginning nations were not so blessed. "The political state remained still imperfect, because it was almost the work of chance" (3: 180, *Second discours*). As a result, legitimacy in history prevalently fell by the wayside and was lost to *amour-propre*'s justification of other principles, which placed one individual self, the prince, above all other selves and thus sapped the strength of the collectivity. The legislator's task, then, is to make men withstand the onslaught against the collectivity. This amounts to replacing liberty as unrestricted passion with liberty as general will, an artificial equivalent of nature. But the legislator faces a hopeless task. Ignorance, stupidity, ruse, and passion have characterized the race, are on the side of ambition: "For a nascent people to be able to value sound political maxims and follow the fundamental rules of civil reason or reason of state, the effect would have to become the cause, the social spirit, which should be the product of institution, should preside at the very moment of institution, and men should be before law what they must become by means of laws" (3: 383).

The legislator must therefore have recourse to the supernatural. His laws concerning union, form of government, and utilization of natural resources, and a thousand other rulings which control necessity and maintain the association must appear to emanate from the mouth of God. Awe more than force and reasoning binds the minds of men and makes them accept their own good. The establishment of society by agreement is artificial, then, not just in the sense that society by convention is not present in the state of nature, but also in the sense that the very sanction of law by the group is arranged by the legislator, produced through him. When the time is right a prophet must be made to appear. Accompanying the constitution proposed by the legislator and its sanction by the legislating general will of the people is the frame of mind of the signers, which itself must be created by the legislator. It is not enough that they unite and by unanimity agree to a constitution for the nation if they are led by a shrewd and self-interested man who is intent on guaranteeing by law his own possessions. The spirit of the nation under such circumstances is derived more from necessity than from true statecraft and the extravagant production of such an impostor "will soon perish with him" (3: 384). The constitution must be solidly grounded, free of self-interest, and the sanction granted it by a people must be associated with the sacred aura of divinity if the formula for union is to be lasting. Religion is consciously used by the legislator; it becomes the instrument of politics: "In the origins of nations one [religion] serves as instrument of the other [politics]" (3: 384).

Statecraft, rather than passion and necessity, must make men opt for order. Just as Emile in Book IV chooses God, the tutor's order, and his own education by a conditioned act of his conscious will, so the people, instead of being duped as in history, follow the legislator's order, which has been based on nature's *amour de soi* and a history refined to include only elements which are consistent with natural order — useful problem-solving, innocent family comforts, property as subsistence, and agreement as unanimity. Prior to the education of the unique individual is a tutor embodying a God-given concept of nature operating within society. Anterior to truly legitimate civil society there must be an image of unity, the legislator seeming to represent a God-given concept of a planned social equivalent of nature, that is, of the individual self sheltered within a protective equilibrium, so that the people believe they recognize in these works the real God, "the same power in the formation of man and in the formation of the city" (3: 383). Faith in man's ability and need to pass from nature to art without the errors of necessity is inspired by the legislator's very appearance, his words, his science: "It is not just anybody who can make the Gods speak.... The great soul of the legislator is the true miracle which must be the proof of his mission" (3: 384).

The result of his mission is to change substantially the condition of man. In the primitive state, man was one, solitary, totally independent, with potential for perfectibility, for *pitié* or expansiveness, for *amour de soi*, the struggle for survival, including the continuance of a unique self at peace with environment. In the natural state of war which eventually followed, he was one and independent but no longer solitary, threatened with the compromise of his self by an enslavement imposed by the strongest. Uniqueness had been replaced by the worst kind of conformity, since each was at war with his neighbor for riches and power, each at war with environment, trying to tear from physical nature its secrets. Legitimate civil society, prepared by the legislator, makes man part of a greater whole, a legislated, artificial whole, the nation. Thus it restores peace with liberty and prevents any compromise of self by another individual.

Yet this new order, designed by the legislator to denature man, that is, to make him think in certain areas always through the general good, even though it saves the individual from enslavement by other individuals, seems in the general will's name to have gone too far, to have become totalitarian: "So that if each citizen is nothing, can do nothing except through all of the others, and if the force acquired by the whole is equal to or superior to the sum of the natural forces of all the individuals, one can say that the legislation is at the highest point of perfection it can attain" (3: 382). Critics in the past have emphasized the apparently repressive aspects of this and other statements in the *Contrat social,* but Rousseau is concerned at this point with holding back passion and illegitimacy, man's Hobbesian pursuit of endless goods and power, what the defenders of liberalism associate with the independence of the individual, his freedom, but what for Rousseau is the part of history taking place in the *Second discours* just before civil society's initial legitimacy, a period of individualistic greed, a state of war which made civil society necessary and subsequently destroyed society.

The threat from this force to the integrity of the individual, to the legitimacy designed to prevent individuals from overstepping the bounds of self, is repeatedly expressed in the *Contrat social.* Legitimacy is in effect up against an iron law which spells its own doom in advance: "In a perfect legislation, the particular or individual will must be at zero, the corporate will belonging to the government very subordinate, and, consequently, the general or sovereign will always dominant and the unique rule of all the rest.... According to the natural order, on the other hand, these different wills become more active in proportion as they are concentrated. Thus, the general will is always the weakest, the corporate will holds the second place, and the private will comes first of all; so that in the government each member is first of all himself, and then a magistrate, and then a citizen, a gradation directly opposed to the one required by the social order" (3: 401). In other words history has shown that the collectivity designed to protect the individuality of the wills is weak. The true enemy is passion, the centrifugal force which resists legitimacy, which tries to capture the collectivity in the name of one or several egos and then to deprive the rest of the wills of their freedom.

Another pressure threatening to destroy legitimacy is physical environment. If the legislator fails to find the laws appropriate to any given geographical location, any given moment in the history of a people, appropriate in the sense of Montesquieu's *rapports* but with emphasis on liberty, then the nation will be destroyed (3: 393). The purpose of the collectivity is not to inhibit uniqueness but to neutralize the forces which threaten its will; its structure is designed to shelter the selves from the battering forces of human vanity and physical environment.

The legislator's political science, utilizing religion, may remove man from the role of tyrant to himself and other selves which necessity, as *amour-propre* and environmental pressure, had forced upon him during history's course. *Amour de soi* and *pitié* may therefore be active again. But man within the nation's structure is still made up of his natural endowment plus the passions of history. The difference is that now he has become a conscious player of roles. The legislator has freed him in the sense that man is no longer dominated exclusively by necessity, but also by science and art. Opposing forces are struggling for his soul. He may follow the conditioning of environment, let *amour-propre* lead, or he may follow the program set for him by the spontaneously transcendent natural genius, the legislator. He may in time, like the legislator, replace the support of religion with his own transcendence, that is, equate God with order rather than with mystery. If he plays the role of legitimacy, he has learned not to capture the selves of others by expanding beyond his own self and thus losing his own natural identity. The new man who follows the guidelines of legitimacy has little to do with the isolated creature of the first primitive condition. In his ignorance, that man was deeply solipsistic. Artificial man is at the threshold of enlightenment, first through awe, then by consciously playing the role of solipsist in order to avoid a repetition of history's war among the selves.

Few men are qualified to be either legislator or prince. The insights these roles require and the temptations each must overcome are too great. Most men play the complementary roles of subject and citizen. The subject obeys laws already established; the citizen, as part of the sovereign, actively sanctions laws coming into being: "*Citizens* as participants in the sovereign authority, and *Subjects* as men submitted to the laws of the state" (3: 362). It has been argued that Hobbes's political doctrine leaves more freedom to the individual than does Rousseau's, because for Hobbes the individual is free wherever the law does not prescribe, whereas for Rousseau, since the citizen is part of the sovereign and therefore a lawmaker, the general will binds every section of the individual's conscience, even those areas in which the law does not yet prescribe. This view is in error because it fails to distinguish between Rousseau's definition of subject and that of citizen, between the person submitting to present law and the person participating in the creation of law.

There is no question but that the subject is obliged to obey only the law prescribed, for if he were bound also by what his conscience tells him should be or may be the law in the future, he would in the name of that higher law, his conscience, be free not to follow the existing law already established by the sovereign will of the people. This is clearly not at all Rousseau's intention. No man is free on his own either to expand or to contract the area in which the law applies.

It is also clear, however, that the concept of law is dynamic. The laws may be changed by the group to meet the needs of the group and its individual members within or in spite of the context of the moment. Even with the guidance of the legislator, the voice of passion may win out and the law be degraded to fit the desires of a part of the whole. If a law were passed that through some system of representation less than the entire group in assembly would be empowered to revise the fundamental laws, then private and corporate interests in the nation would have won and the independence of the state of war would have been partially restored under the guise of legitimacy. Subsequent legislation could alter the limitation on property holdings, could change it from the status quo at the time of association to unlimited holdings. The gap between rich and poor could thus be widened. The rich would be in a position to buy favored treatment under the law.

On the other hand, the structure of the law might be improved to enhance the position of the poor. The meaning of unanimity could be redefined. The serfs, in Rousseau's plans for a reconstitution of Poland, were not initially to have a voice because their previous position had been one of servitude. Although they were not to be part of the original unanimity required for acceptance of a social contract, it was anticipated that after a period of education they might, as freemen, become part of the future unanimity needed in constitutional matters: "Consider that your serfs are men like you, that they have in them the qualities to become everything that you are: work first to prepare the means for it [liberty], and do not free their bodies until you have freed their minds. Without that preliminary step, you can be sure your operation will succeed only poorly" (3: 974, *Gouvernement de Pologne*). A law reducing the holdings that the rich had at the moment of entrance into civil society would be another example of an extension of freedom in the sense of *amour de soi*, since the subjects would be closer to equality and therefore less open to pressure from holders of wealth and power. The point is that the laws have a future; they may move in a way to benefit passion, to destroy the rights of some members of the group, or they may change to benefit the integrity of each individual self.

The threat to liberty, then, is not in subordination of all members as subjects to the national will and its legislation, but in unequal subordination. Rousseau's intent is always toward equality. For that reason he insists that each member in forming the collectivity must give himself and his goods without reservation to the community: "Each giving himself absolutely, the condition is the same for all, and the condition being equal for all, no one has any interest in making it burdensome to the others" (3: 360-61). Rousseau does compromise with passion and necessity in this giving, since he indicates that in order to gain unanimous consent the collectivity will usually restore to each individual an amount of property equal to what he gave, but that at other times the group might decide on a strictly egalitarian redistribution of property among the members, or might provide that property be held by all in common. But even within the framework of status-quo giving and receiving, the principle of even-handedness guards the integrity of the individual wills. If one individual has ten acres to give and gives only five but receives protection for the ten, whereas each of the other members has five and contributes five, then the one member would have expanded at the expense of all the others. The integrity of each of the individuals would have been violated, the many made subservient to that extent to the one. In another, very different matter the reasoning is the same. Atheists are not to be allowed membership in the community. An atheist is unable to give himself totally. He is less than a complete self, since the state of nature shows in man the instincts of both *amour de soi* and *pitié*. *Pitié* is expansiveness of affection which can extend to other men and to God. An atheist, by not giving his total self to the state, weakens the state's cohesive force, its ability to protect legitimacy. Rousseau softens this principle by not excluding the atheist who, like Wolmar, performs the rites required for the security of the group.

The death penalty is tied to this same principle of total and even-handed alienation. If a man commits murder, he must according to Rousseau will to give his own life, will his own death: "It is in order not to become the victim of an assassin that one consents to die if one becomes an assassin" (3: 376). This is reasoning partly from utility, but Rousseau goes deeper. Hobbes argues on the basis of nature's law of self-preservation that no man can will his own death. Rousseau's argument would appear to be in violation of nature, but this is not so. Man's condition in nature is one of isolation, of the self free and uncompromised. It is not enough just to survive; man must survive in freedom. By taking another's life, a man has violated the instrument designed to preserve freedom and therefore has become a "public enemy," has in fact willed his own death before the murder. He wills it by any violation of the law, since life without freedom is no life at all. Free life depends on the instrument, law. Life is law. Rousseau supports this interpretation when he indicates not only that murder is to be punished by death, but that "every criminal, attacking the social order, becomes by his crimes a rebel and traitor to the homeland, ceases to be a member of it by violating its laws, and even makes war upon it. Then the preservation of the state is inconsistent with his own, and it is necessary that one of the two should perish. When the guilty person is put to death, he is less a citizen than an enemy" (3: 376).

This hard reasoning does not place the state above the individual. The end, complete integrity of each individual life, requires that no citizen hold anything back in his giving, that he not will to impinge upon or reduce the freedom of another, that no weakening of the moral and legislative structure of the state occur. If while enjoying the rights of a citizen the individual has taken back his own contribution, has returned in essence to the state of war and is still bearing arms against his fellow citizens in any substantial way, he has ceased in effect to be "a moral person" and is simply "a man." He is operating only according to the right of the strongest who denies, in Hobbesian fashion, any self but his own: "It is in that situation that the right of war is to kill the vanquished" (3: 377). This is not the same "right of war" that exists between states, which never permits killing the vanquished (3: 357). This is warfare of another order, of the state against a "traitor to the homeland." Killing the soldier of an enemy state has no justification, because once he has laid down arms he is only a man, not a threat to the conqueror, whose only goal is to defeat the other state. But a traitor must be removed from the state by any means, "cut off by exile" or "by death." He is a man playing two roles at once. Masquerading as a moral being, as a subject, he has returned in fact to necessity, *amour-propre*; therefore he jeopardizes the integrity of each self with which he comes into contact.

The principle of even-handed giving also saves man from enslavement to any part of the congregation: "Each in giving himself to everyone does not give himself to anyone" (3: 361). As in the system of Hobbes, the group in unanimity could agree to give themselves to one person designated as the sovereign. Each member of the group would have given himself equally to a person representing the will of the assembly. Sovereign and government would be united in the same figure. Such giving for Rousseau would not be, however, even-handed in a true sense; it would be logically and by structure dedicated to survival alone, or to happiness, or to reasons of necessity, because the naming of one over another would have to be merely on the basis of some utility to the consenting group, not in the name of nature. Hobbes's state of nature, as violence, makes the utilitarian motive everything. Rousseau's flight from the state of war is likewise in the name of utility. But there is also the nonutilitarian reason, unrelated to passion and fear of death, that is, freedom as uncompromised self. This requires the expedient not simply of a sovereign but of a particular kind of sovereign, an artificial one whose sovereignty does not deny the integrity of the individual self. Hobbes's sovereign denies that integrity in two senses. A man, to be sovereign, to represent the collectivity, either loses his own personal self by reflecting all of the selves in his one self and will, by becoming Leviathan, or he may, as history usually indicates, revert to his *amour-propre* and enslave the other selves.

It can be argued that Rousseau's total giving to the collectivity in order to gain individual freedom, a guarantee against "all personal dependence," is at the same time the utmost enslavement to the whole, since "whoever refuses to obey the general will shall be constrained to do so by the whole body: which means nothing else but that he will be forced to be free" (3: 364). But this servitude exists only if the powers of the state, its force, are made the only source of liberty. Derathé seems to imply this in his citation of Rousseau's words, "It is only the force of the state which assures the liberty of the members" (3: cviii). But a distinction must be made between Hobbes's position and Rousseau's. Hobbes's sovereign prince would have the same power derived from the unanimous consent of the congregation, but in an extreme case that sovereign would be bound, as we have seen, to guarantee the people, by the political structure formulated, no more than utility, survival, and enslavement of some or all if that were necessary to survival, for the natural freedom of the selves has become secondary, that which remains after survival and some degree of felicity have been assured. Life for Hobbesian man is more important than liberty. In Rousseau's system, on the contrary, civil order rests not on the protection of life alone but on a more basic principle, on natural liberty of self as the highest good, as more important than life itself. Civil liberty does rely on collective will and force, but that collectivity is defined not simply by any means to survival but by the means that can guarantee the social equivalent of the primitive natural state, an equivalent in which the preservation of the self in freedom is the supreme value and the justification of law and force.

Apart from this basic difference in structure, Rousseau's liberty often seems very close to Hobbesian peace. Both would cut the state of warring passion back to a point where the individual can survive and prosper in the company of other men. But for Hobbes this felicity is no more than a byproduct of prudence. For Rousseau it is a return to nature. *Amour de soi* had potential for more positive fulfillment in history than the conversion to *amour-propre;* its fulfillment could be expressed as family happiness, as the occupancy of land and the work required for subsistence. The laws, which may seem burdensome to the individual because of the need to still the passions and establish liberty, yield positive joys and the opportunity for personal expression. Within the shelter of the state, the subjects can live again in terms of *amour de soi* and *pitié*, their own gifts and expansiveness. They can seek their way and their happiness innocently: "the most certain sign that they are preserved and prospering.... is their number and their population" (3: 420). They can develop uniquely, in the manner of an Emile, without being leveled by any one behavioral characteristic, whether lust for power, wealth, display of talent, or problem-solving. Restored to his true nature, man finds new energy. The species seems enriched by a new vitality. This may have nothing to do with "letters and arts," with "the vulgar self-interest which makes authors speak," with "the brilliance" of a country, with the fact that a poet may receive "a hundred thousand *livres* in income." But it does have a relationship to deep inner qualities of a nation's subjects, "the virtues of its citizens, their morals, their independence," the flight of their souls when they are out from under "the yoke" which crushes their spirit if control has been tyrannical: "A little agitation gives energy to [men's] souls, and what truly makes the species prosper is less peace than liberty" (3: 420). Liberty, in the context of this note of the *Contrat social*, is the agitation of civil dissent and rivalry, which keeps the leaders occupied defending their interests against other factions and thus allows the private subject to go his own way, but the result is the same atmosphere of independence promised by civil liberty or legitimacy, an atmosphere in which each man may follow his own taste and inclination, may prosper, marry, have children (3: 420).

The implication of this return to nature is that there are, for Rousseau as for Hobbes, definite areas in which the law does not prescribe. This is supported by Rousseau's own words. For the individual as subject, conscience is bound only to obey the existing law. In areas outside the law, his natural right prevails. He is a man before being a citizen and subject. He plays these two roles only in certain areas and at certain times: "But, apart from the public person, we have to consider the private persons who compose it [the public person or collectivity] and whose lives and liberty are naturally independent of it. It is therefore a matter of clearly distinguishing between the respective rights of the citizens and [those of] the sovereign, and between the duties which the first [the citizens] have to fill as subjects and the natural right they should enjoy as men" (3: 373). This natural right amounts to being bound not by laws but only by one's own faculties: "It is necessary carefully to distinguish natural liberty, which is bound only by the powers of the individual, from civil liberty, which is limited by the general will" (3: 365). Limitations on this natural liberty can be made only by the standard of community need: "We agree that what each alienates by the social compact is only that part of his power, goods, and liberty which it is important for the community to control, but it must be agreed also that the sovereign [people] alone is the judge of what is important" (3: 373). The group, for example, decides that the subject must defend his country if it is in danger, and makes this a law. When the government decides that a condition of peril for the nation has arisen, the subject must then die for his country if necessary (3: 376). But before passage of such a law in the first place, before there can be any such limitation of natural right, justification has to be certain and clear: "The sovereign ... cannot burden its subjects with chains which are useless to the community ... under the law of reason [agreement] nothing is done without cause, any more than under the law of nature" (3: 373).

Where the laws do not prescribe, the subject is free absolutely to go his own way: "Every man can dispose fully of what has been left to him of his goods and of his liberty by these conventions" (3: 375). The *Lettre à d'Alembert,* the *Nouvelle Héloïse,* and *Emile* have described the richness of life in those areas

Rousseau would leave outside the law. The subject, too, is to have the last judgment as to whether the regime is legitimate, whether the public good and the voice of the people are being followed: "There are some circumstances in which a man may be more useful to his fellow citizens outside his homeland than if he were living within its embrace. In such a situation he must listen only to his zeal and bear his exile without a murmur; this very exile becomes one of his duties" (*Emile*, p. 606). This argument is not exactly to the point, since Rousseau has in mind here a personal protest against a situation in which there has been subversion of the collectivity by a part of the citizens rather than against the appearance of laws which are too restrictive, laws passed legitimately and in the name of liberty but which bind the individual too much. Yet the comment has its bearing. The individual, an Emile returning home from his voyage, is judge of the quality of liberty provided by his nation. His own lucid vision, his independent self, judging legislator, sovereign, and government, decides whether or not to return.

Liberty for the individual as subject thus has three meanings: a legislated code of behavior designed to keep the selves making up the nation from engulfing one another; obedience to only the established laws, not the unlegislated good or will of the collectivity; and areas in which the selves are totally free of prescription by the law. Rousseau drastically reduces the concept of self as *amour-propre*, as the passions of necessity developed in history, but this reduction is never to jeopardize freedom of self for the sake of mere survival. The law, Rousseau insists, is never to tell the self what it is, to pick and choose among its endowments, to say one natural gift is more important than another, to grade the selves on the basis of the quality or amount of their endowment. No comparison is to be the basis for setting one self morally above the other in the legislated order. This is not simply equality before the law, any law so long as all subjects are equal before it. The content of law must preserve the freedom of the individual, must guarantee him his vote, his right to feed into the collectivity his own will, the expression of his own combination of natural gifts. Moreover, the areas in which *amour de soi* can develop into *amour-propre* are not eliminated completely. Any reduction of *amour-propre*'s claims has to be justified in terms of fact, evidence that without such reduction the integrity of the selves will be substantially threatened. Rousseau makes it clear that leeway is to exist, that varying from society to society, depending on the exigencies of time and place, population density, maturity of a people's character, and wealth or poverty of a country, there are for men as subjects areas in which the law need not prescribe. Curiosity, pleasures, belief, and acquisition of possessions need be controlled only to the point of mutual protection. Furthermore, even the curb by these liberty-oriented restrictions of *amour-propre* applies exclusively to the public actions of the self. It does not apply to private feeling, conscience, moral or religious attitudes. The institution of marriage is to protect the rights of Julie and Wolmar only in terms of action. Her expansive feelings for Saint-Preux are not to be curbed or blamed, except by her own moral, religious, or philosophic standards. The soldier may be sent to die in defense of his country, but he can feel and think that war is unjust. The state requires him to accept articles of religious belief, but he can, like Wolmar, be an atheist in his heart or hold beliefs in addition to the state religion, provided he does not by propagating his position divide the nation and thereby weaken the safeguards of liberty.

As he plays the role of subject, the individual's integrity or *amour de soi*, its endowments, and a large part of *amour-propre*'s acquisitiveness have been left untouched. In the role of citizen, each person's uniqueness is even more vital. There the general good must enter man's soul to the exclusion of any conformist attitudes of *amour-propre*. One might even argue that the patriot's preoccupation with civil order or legitimacy should be an obsession parallel in enthusiasm, if not in seerlike brilliance, to the dedication of the legislator. This emptying out of selfish goals has been made to seem a cold business, an absolute denial of self for the common good. Yet this crossing over from the state of nature to the civil state, from the individual as instinctive physical endowment, man as a species of animal, to this creature made artificially moral, the species turned into legislating citizen, this transformation, if for Rousseau also a denaturalization, is change in an expansive sense. It is the fulfillment through science and art of the potential already present in the origins of self, to be viewed with enthusiasm as an increase in the powers of each man, giving him virtue, justice, and conscience: "This passage from the state of nature to the civil state produces a very remarkable change in man by substituting justice for instinct in his conduct and giving to his actions the morality they had lacked before.... He ought to bless continually the happy moment which tore him from it forever and made out of a stupid and limited animal an intelligent being and a man" (3: 364).

The self, far from being dispossessed by this new object, the common good, is involved, while pursuing it, in the discovery and support of conditions necessary to its own personal survival and integrity. All the usual materialistic interests — pursuit of pleasure, power, possessions, prestige, idle curiosity — must now be subordinated to the essential private interest of each member. This requires defining the common good: "Only the general will can direct the forces of the state according to the end of its institution, which is the common good: for if the conflict between private interests made the establishment of societies necessary, it is the agreement of these same interests which made societies possible. It is the common element in these different interests which forms the social bond, and if there were not some point about which all of the interests are in agreement, no society could exist. Now, it is solely on the basis of this common interest that society must be governed" (3: 368).

These bonds are not abstractions in the mind of the legislator or in the minds of the citizens who have to examine his proposals for law. Agreements reflect the very palpable predicament of a group of men in a given time and place who feel the pressures of environment and of one another, pressures arising from scarcity of food, surrounding enemy groups, climatic conditions, and conflicts between family groups and between individuals. The survival of a people and of the liberty it can maintain for each individual is at stake. The citizens, lacking the brilliance of the legislator, may not understand his solutions: "There are a thousand kinds of ideas which it is impossible to translate into the language of the people" (3: 383). His science involves elements of history, psychology, economics, jurisprudence, mathematics. He must determine if his people can be free, for liberty is not "a product of every climate" and is not "within the grasp of all peoples"

(3: 414). In some areas liberty is possible only if a very delicate adjustment is made between environment, people, government, customs, and religious belief. Largely out of awe the citizens at first sanction his proposals for institution, but it is not intended that they remain in a state of blindness. The legislation they have accepted changes them by slow stages into moral beings. The law is a developing, unfolding phenomenon. The needs of men in the future must be answered by future legislative acts: "The sovereign may indeed say, I now will what a certain man wills or at least what he says he wills; but the sovereign cannot say: what that man shall will tomorrow, I also shall will; since it is absurd for the will to give itself chains for the future, and since it is not the responsibility of any will to consent to anything contrary to the good of the being which wills" (3: 368-69). Rousseau has provided thus for the evolving needs of the subjects. At the same time he has given the citizens participating in the sovereign will an opportunity to grow, to follow better the arguments of the legislator, to debate his proposals in assembly.

In these deliberations, Rousseau insists, the integrity of each will must be maintained, uncoerced and unintimidated by any other private or corporate will. The separateness of the wills must be absolute: "If, when sufficiently informed, the people in its deliberations had no communication one with another, the general will would be the result of the great number of small differences, and the deliberation would always be good" (3: 371). This is why pressure groups, "factions, partial associations," must be eliminated. Such independence of viewpoint requires, too, that serious differences in wealth should not exist within the state, that there should not be heavily rich and desperately poor groups: "These two states, naturally inseparable, are equally fatal to the common good; from one of them come the friends of tyranny and from the other the tyrants themselves; it is always between them that dealings at the expense of public liberty take place; one group buys it, the other sells it" (3: 392).

Other potential sources of pressure, the legislator and members of the government, must have no part in the deliberations except as private citizens, must have no hold whatsoever over the members of the sovereign: "The supreme authority can no more be modified than it can be alienated; to limit it is to destroy it"

(3: 432). The legislator is to have no "legislative right" (3: 383). Monarchy is a bad form of government, since it tends to usurp the legislative power: "There is no [government] in which the private will... more easily dominates the other wills" (3: 409). Democracy is a bad form of government, because the people, forced to legislate in general terms as sovereign and to execute in specific terms as prince, loses the gift of "general views," no longer has legislative detachment. Pressure groups, as many as there are private interests, make any focus on the general good impossible (3: 404), make each individual seek out only his future private executive advantage in each legislative decision.

A completely sincere man could, according to this theory of the absolute independence of the wills, exclude himself from the social contract: "There is only one law which by its nature requires unanimous consent. It is the social contract: for civil association is the most voluntary act in the world; every man being born free and master of himself, no one can under any pretext whatsoever make him subject without his consent.... If, therefore, there are dissenters at the time of the social pact, their opposition does not invalidate the contract, it only prevents them from being included; they are foreigners among the citizens" (3: 440). The independence of each man's vote is sacred because within the social framework the vote is man's contribution to civil liberty, represents his abandonment of his own defense, "the strength and the liberty of each man being the first instruments of his self-preservation" (3: 360). The new collectivity is thus valid only if it has each member's separate, totally voluntary consent on the substantial issues.

The object of the search, the general good, has so far been discussed in broad terms — the liberty of each man and of the state. The interest of the whole has been made the vital interest of each part. There is, then, no real sacrifice for the citizen if he is dedicated to the safeguarding of self more than to private gain by the use of passion. The means for discovering the good, deliberation, has similarly been related to the separateness of the legislating wills. Finally, the integrity of each subject's self is to determine the perspective used in the legislative process: "I mean that the law considers subjects as a group and actions as abstract, never a man as individual or an action as private" (3: 379). When thinking legislatively each member has no intention of touching another individual and no fear of himself being touched as an individual. Abstract thinking is essential if individuals are not to be bound unequally by the law. Equality of condition must underlie equal binding, because, to the extent that one individual is subordinated to another, his vitality or liberty is sapped by the atrophying effect of slavery: "Liberty, because any private dependence is so much force taken from the body of the state; equality, because liberty cannot exist without it" (3: 391). In addition, it is essential that the binding be total; that is, there is to be no questioning of the collectivity, its laws, or its power to change the laws. To adulterate the laws, either as citizen legislating or as subject obeying, is to opt for dependence on persons rather than on a general selfless will: "Each citizen is in a perfect independence of all the others and in an excessive dependence on the city . . . . for it is only the force of the state which assures the liberty of its members" (3: 394).

This view is in no way oppressive. Rousseau's point is that each citizen in his independent search for the general good ("it is important . . . that each citizen deliberate only according to his own conscience" [3: 372]) has paralleled the state of nature, the isolated, primitive man's unconscious, instinctive search for survival in complete independence. The difference is that civilized man must work through an instrument, a legislative structure embodying liberty. Both man and the state have a "constitution that is more or less robust and suited to the task of self-preservation for a longer or shorter time." Man's constitution is natural, the state's is a work of art: "It is not in men's power to prolong their lives; it is their responsibility to prolong the life of the state as long as possible by giving it the best constitution possible" (3: 424). The life of the state depends ultimately on the citizen's determination to be the ultimate source of authority, to fulfill his high mission of envisioning himself and others in the abstract according to his own inner conviction. The independent wills may never rest but must constantly work to improve the laws if the life of the state is to be prolonged: "There is not, nor can there be, any kind of fundamental law which obligates the people as a body, not even the social contract" (3: 362). Inner conviction, too, excludes the use of representatives, except when the size of the nation makes that necessary, and Rousseau's words indicate his reliance on the notion of the privacy of each voting citizen: "The person of the lowliest citizen is as sacred and inviolable as that of the first magistrate, because when the person represented is present, there is no longer any representative" (3: 427-28). For Rousseau, the ability to will generally, abstractly depends on each individual's rediscovery of the meaning and value of his private self. The very idea of representation is a denial of the importance he gives to the private source of legislative vision.

Rousseau's major preoccupation is that the collectivity should not be subordinate to government. But by his approach to the operation of that collectivity's will it is evident also that the separateness of the individual wills ties directly to nature, thus making the decision of the collectivity valid. The relation of the parts to the whole is not, for the citizen, one of quantity; that is, the part does not have to adjust to a preconceived whole. The relation is rather one of quality, and it is the quality of the parts, their integrity, their vision of liberty derived from instinct and lasting through all subsequent stages of history, that gives birth and authority to the dynamic whole that becomes the general will. To the extent that quality leaves the individual will, the sovereign withers: "When the prince no longer administers the state according to the laws and usurps the sovereign power, then a remarkable change takes place; not the government but the nation is diminished; I mean that the great state is dissolved and that another is formed within the former, a state composed of the members of the government" (3: 422).

Thus the problem of the individual's enslavement by the prince and the issue of the individual's subordination to the collectivity are essentially the same question. The self is compromised by the collectivity only when a private will — any prince, any corporate interest — has succeeded in merging the independent wills: "So that at the very moment the government usurps the sovereign power the social pact is broken and all the private citizens, returned then by right to their natural liberty, are forced, but not morally bound, to obey" (3: 423). The collectivity in health does not enslave the selves. Its processes provide for fierce debate, eventual agreement, and conclusions voiced into laws transcendent of any one human will. Liberty, emanating from the independent wills and operating through their full integrity, is the force charging the general will with energy. Such an authority is nothing without the individual wills. The more free each will is to express its unique vision, the more thoughtful and complete the debate, the stronger the collectivity is.

The force of a nation which has been brought under subservience to one individual will lies in the ruler's ambition and faculties, in the cowardice or conformity of the people. In Rousseau's system, in contrast, the will of each man inspires the state with its own particular powers, whether in debate or in battle. In war each man pays with his person, not with money. He must give his person to public affairs enthusiastically: "In a well directed city each man flies to the assemblies" (3: 429). The will of each man must participate because it is forced not from outside but from within. If the general will has entered the will of the individual, it is in the name of nature, of survival in freedom: "As soon as any man says of the affairs of the state, *what difference does it make to me?*, you can be sure the state is lost" (3: 429). Rousseau believed that most modern nations were enslaved because their citizens had not learned that the nation belonged to each of them, was the responsibility of each of them, must take its form from the nature of each of their varied beings. Through the artificial complex making up the state the spirit of mankind reigns. This instrument of science and art provides a return to what is essential to human nature, liberty providing for the integrity of each unique self. To this end, *amour-propre* must abandon a large part of its urge to power and wealth, the principles of nations which are dying, because those goals enslave and dwarf the individual spirit.

For Rousseau there is wealth in the infinitely varied content of the independent self. This richness, potential in the state of nature, was sidetracked by *amour-propre*'s conforming search for environmental or object-oriented identity in terms of pleasure, power, and possessions. The legislator, guided by science and art, must revisit nature in spirit; he must then fashion out of legislation formative yet flexible and expansive molds capable of restoring man's self to independence. Uncompromising uniqueness is to fill the nation, give life to its structure, push and shape it, and thus constantly renew the nation to match the evolving needs of the individual selves, so that the artificial state may live permanently.

This is neither liberalism nor totalitarianism in any modern sense. Not liberalism because the nation is seen as an essential support of the individual, who can find his true freedom only through the ever-increasing defense the state offers him against other individuals, environment, enemy nations. Not totalitarianism because the self, the part, allows no leveling, denies any concept of sovereign which would destroy the individual wills. A better term for this kind of regime would seem to be legitimacy or solipsistic structuralism. The unique self, the evolving equivalent of *amour de soi*, is both end (intrinsic value) and means (source of national energy). Structure is no more than the means or instrument of release.

My interpretation of Rousseau's kind of liberty rests on visible evidence. First, Rousseau, after distinguishing between *amour de soi* as survival of the free individual and *amour-propre* as the passions of necessity, calls for a return to a civil equivalent of the former. Survival of the self can mean a matter of life-and-death resistance to other animals, including men, or the defense of the integrity of each man's *génie*, of his own unique character against encroachment or possession by the passions of others. It is in this sense that civil society's man is as free as, if not freer than, the lustful man of necessity. This concept of wholeness is used by Rousseau to reject vanity's inclination to level man, to grade him on the basis of some one characteristic — intelligence, physical strength, lineage, talent, divine gift. All of these characteristics have provided traditional arguments for placing authority in a sovereign ruler rather than in a sovereign collectivity which provides for the natural goodness or absolute value of each man's unique combination of faculties.

Second, structure is seen by the legislator as a means to hold back two kinds of pressure, physical environment and the passions of man, both of which take man outside himself, destroy or inhibit the individuality Rousseau prizes: "The savage lives within himself; sociable man, always outside himself, knows how to live only in the opinions of others" (3: 193, *Second discours*).

Legislative devices are designed to make the subjects equal in condition and equal before the law, whether in matters of ownership, punishment, military service, religion, or right to participate in the sovereign, so that in areas where there is need for obedience to law, no one self can be compromised by another. There are positive areas in which the life of the subject is governed totally by natural law alone, by the law of compassion for one's fellow man, *pitié*, areas in which he is not influenced at all by legislative prescription. In addition, laws must not be legislated arbitrarily, without due cause, that is, without a reason relating them to liberty itself as the sacred wholeness of the individual. Never is the integrity of the individual as subject to be violated by the law. If it is, the citizen has a duty to strive at home or in exile for the return to legitimacy.

As citizen, the individual's will is part of the collectivity. His will is partial, not in the sense that it is absorbed by another personal will, but in the sense that it contributes to a new whole into which many independent wholes (call them parts if you like) pour meaning without diminishing their own selves. Many independent private wills contribute to one general, artificial will. This general will is less a rigid, quantitative area into which pieces fit and by which they are limited, than a potential spirit continually reforming under the evolving collective expression of many wills. Every legislative measure Rousseau favors bears out this concern for separate, uncompromised legislating wills.

Rousseau's goal cannot be explained simply as freedom of the wills from dependence on other wills. He insists on the positive results of their independence and diversity. Each man finds his natural endowment. Permanence and continued growth of the nation depend on this variety and vitality of the wills. Free voices expressing themselves in public assembly inspire the sovereign, make it alive, prevent its ever being irreversibly bound by law established at a given moment. The constitution itself expands and grows in meaning as the free wills of the citizens push outward, make form yield to content, and assure their continuing freedom as subjects.

CHAPTER IX

HISTORY AND INTERNATIONAL RELATIONS

My ANALYSIS OF THE *Contrat social* has attempted to make clear that, in Rousseau's view, freeing the energy within the individual self is the goal of the prospering nation. All domestic structures are designed to encourage and protect private capacity. The tutor forms education to that end. The family provides the atmosphere conducive to a training which, if private, is at the same time public in the sense that it develops the independence essential to legitimacy. The contract further guarantees the integrity of the individual self as subject and the legislating freedom of the self as citizen. Since the individuality of man is an intrinsic good and institutions at all levels are no more than instruments, it follows that nations must be as varied and changing as the evolving combinations of men they are intended to shelter. Foreign policy, in turn, is for Rousseau a dynamic yet subordinate notion which must adjust to the concept of educational, familial, and national matrices fashioned to receive persons and socialities in evolution. Just as there can be no positive, classical model for defining the nature of man or of the nation in their becoming, so there can be no one fixed pattern for conduct among nations. Foreign policy must derive from knowledge of a nation's particular past and immediate circumstances and from earlier grim records of nations which have destroyed their particular geniuses through international encounter. The present chapter, after giving a brief account of Rousseau's statements about history pertinent to internal and foreign politics, shows these insights at work in the opinions he held concerning numerous ancient and modern nations. In the next chapter, Rousseau's views about the attrition operating among nations, thwarting their potential for growth and permanence, are related at the international level to the formulation and meaning of some of his fundamental ideas about liberty, contract, sovereignty, the legislator, government, and religion.[1]

Rousseau is often severely critical of historians. He complains that they speak as if they were omniscient gods. They say with overbearing certitude just what went wrong for one side in a battle and how the other side maneuvered to victory, whereas an element of chance, an unobserved natural phenomenon, may have had much more to do with the outcome: "A tree more or less, a rock to the right or left, a whirlwind of dust raised by the wind, how many times have such factors determined success or defeat in combat without anyone having noticed." The much-vaunted modern criticism is only an "art of conjecturing, the art of choosing among several lies the one which seems closest to the truth" (*Emile*, p. 283). In describing a battle, a revolution, or an election, historical writers give in detail their own short-sighted explanation. If they have a theory, it usually involves the strength or weakness of leaders, the soundness of their schemes, the size of their forces. Regardless of the facts, historians are repeatedly saying in effect that one army was victorious because it had a better grasp of the military art than the other. Rousseau's point is that history is not merely knowledge, skill, and deed. In large part, physical circumstance, the environment in which man lives, determines the course of events.

Abrupt and frightening illustrations of this type of causation are volcanoes, earthquakes, floods — so-called accidents of nature. Rousseau is fascinated by their impact. The groupings of men into societies are in large part the result of overflowing seas, shattering eruptions and earthquakes, fires started by lightning. Everything capable of terrifying and dispersing men "must have later brought them back together to repair the common losses."[2] Other causes,

---

[1] For a description of Rousseau's views on the nations of ancient and modern history, see M. L. Perkins, "Rousseau on History, Liberty, and National Survival," *Studies on Voltaire and the Eighteenth Century* 53 (1967): 79-169.

[2] *Œuvres complètes*, ed. Charles Lahure (Paris: Hachette, 1865) (hereafter cited as Lahure) 1: 389, *Essai sur l'origine des langues*.

less violent, "more general and permanent," are climate and the march of the seasons (Lahure, 1: 390). People born in hot areas migrated to cold areas and multiplied. Then because of overcrowding, they returned to their point of origin. This action and reaction helps explain "the revolutions which occur on earth and the continual agitation of its inhabitants" (Lahure, 1: 384). In hot regions, the situation of springs and lakes determined the location of settlements (Lahure, 1: 390). Fertility of soil hurried the advance of society in some parts of the globe, as aridity delayed it in others (Lahure, 1: 392). Toward the tropics, too, "needs are born of passions," whereas in cold areas "passions are born of needs." As a result, languages, "sad daughters of necessity," varied sharply in characteristics between the two regions, reflecting their origins (Lahure, 1: 391). In the north, the language of gesture was first replaced by the language of words because it was necessary to explain complicated mutual needs arising from the rigors of environment (Lahure, 1: 394). Northern peoples, too, were strong and robust because only the toughest could survive and children kept the "healthy constitution of their fathers" (p. 393). Even liberty is partially dependent on climate, as Montesquieu had already pointed out. New evidence shows that it cannot survive among all peoples (Pléiade, 3: 414, *Contrat social*). The very fate of a nation depends to some degree on size, as determined by natural boundaries, richness of soil, the extent of mountains, plains, and rivers.

Physical causation must be supplemented by the quality of national spirit, another sin of omission Rousseau finds most historians making. They usually fail to see the moral background of events: "They often find in a battle won or lost the explanation of a revolution which, even before this battle, had already become inevitable. War hardly does more than bring to a point of crisis events already determined long before by moral causes which historians rarely detect" (*Emile*, p. 285). The influence of Montesquieu is strong here, but Rousseau stresses more the means of detection. Facts which reveal the moral condition of a nation are often to be found in the personalities and deeds of its great men. These men must be brought to life by the intimate details which modern portraitists, because of a false sense of propriety, dare not introduce: "Physiognomy is not revealed in broad outlines, nor character in important actions." When a leader is on display, he is seen as he pretends to be. Men are as dressed up by our authors in their private lives as they are on the stage of the world." We know only "the public man," an image arranged to be seen by the crowd. He is never shown in "his office, with his family, in the midst of friends." We know his uniform rather than his person. This kind of reporting has far-reaching consequences. Rousseau boldly claims that individual character is the key to national spirit. The genius of a people may be very different from the character of an individual, and attempting to know the human heart without studying it "in the crowd" would lead to very imperfect knowledge. But he insists that the evaluation of men must begin with the study of the individual, that a person who "knew perfectly the inclinations of each individual [of a nation] could foresee all the effects [of these inclinations] when they were combined in the body of a people" (*Emile*, p. 286). Numerous samplings of individual character permit an estimate of national fiber and a prediction of national intent.

It is because of a breakdown in empirical method, then, that modern historians fall short in most of their undertakings. Rousseau states flatly that voyager-historians, hopelessly unprepared, have not learned much during the three or four hundred years they have travelled to all parts of the globe. Bound by their own preoccupations and conceptions, they repeat only what Europeans already recognize or imagine they understand: "I am convinced that the only men we know are Europeans; because of the ridiculous prejudices which have not yet died out even among writers, it seems that each does little more, when he pompously claims to be making a study of man, than to give an account of the men of his own country" (Pléiade, 3: 212, *Second discours*). This blindness in the presence of the distinguishing features of another civilization, especially a distant one, can be blamed on the types of visitors who do the reporting: sailors, merchants, soldiers, and missionaries. The first three groups lack most of the qualifications Rousseau in *Emile* made essential for accurately observing men: interest in knowing them, impartiality in judging them, a sensitive heart capable of understanding all the human passions, and enough equanimity not to be personally involved (*Emile*, p. 291). Members of the fourth group are too preoccupied with their sublime calling to indulge in investigations "out of pure curiosity."

Lacking the special talent it takes for seeing differences, writers always miss "those authentic traits which distinguish people from one another" (Pléiade, 3: 212, *Second discours*). Rousseau senses keenly the need for experienced scholars, of the caliber of Montesquieu, Buffon, Diderot, Duclos, to fill these serious gaps with detailed analyses of the institutions, customs, and manners of many regions. From such voyages would come the expert knowledge required to replace the opinion of amateurs, "of crude travellers" engrossed only in what is familiar to them. Rousseau's ambitions are high. The physical, moral, and political history of distant areas would uncover the distinguishing features of exotic lands, of a rich new world of nations. Recognizing the contrasts with their own customs and institutions, Europeans would be more aware of the shared and varied characteristics of the peoples of the earth. For the first time "we would thus learn to know" our own civilization (3: 213-14).

Such theory is far removed from the practice of Rousseau's time. No country prints more histories and accounts of voyages than France, yet there is no nation in which the genius, beliefs, and customs of other peoples are better concealed. Rousseau is deliberately attacking the French as the source of European prejudice and notes three blind spots which affect the writers' vision. First, most writers have a preference for what is highly civilized. Interpreting reactions to his *Premier discours*, Rousseau says he has had little success in convincing his listeners that "barbarous" and "criminal" are two very different ideas, that having bad laws is less indicative of corruption than having contempt for the laws of one's country. Regardless of his explanations, his point of view is considered scandalous. He has dared to defend and praise creatures who do not know how to read and write. His opponents deny that there can be decency among people who go bare and virtue among those who eat raw flesh (3: 61, *Lettre à Grimm*).

The second blind spot is the preference for political upheaval, violence, and catastrophe over prosperity and calm. No nation attracts attention until it has ceased to be self-sufficient, until it has become inseparably linked to its neighbors, dependent on them for its needs: "All our histories begin where they ought to end. We have in detail the histories of peoples who are destroying one another; what we lack is the history of peoples whose populations are multiplying." This kind of bias is essentially a preoccupation with the corrupt and the dying, with the nation "already in decline." Governments which have the most merit in their conduct are talked of the least or ridiculed by history's approach (*Emile*, p. 282).

Partiality for civilization and its corollary, concentration on sick and declining nations, are accompanied by the modern fondness for grandiose systems which invent a framework to explain the status quo in one neat package: "The madness for systems having taken possession of all of them [writers of this century], none try to see things as they are, but as things agree with their system" (*Emile*, p. 285).

From this brief survey comes some indication of Rousseau's thinking about the purpose, content, and value of recorded history. Properly written, it gives the reader informative insights into the character of individuals and the spirit or genius of each nation, its liberty, its sophistication, its institutions and laws. The rise and decline of each state may be understood in terms of long-range factors, physical circumstances, and the moral atmosphere emerging from reason's adaptation to them. An understanding of the evolution of a nation in those terms should be the historian's chief concern. To deepen his insight, he must be aware of the characteristics of many peoples, whether barbarous or sophisticated, rising or declining. He must avoid as much as possible controlling the facts by the straitjacket of a philosophic system. History, as Rousseau conceives it, makes each people a value unto itself. The object is to know the mechanics of a nation's prosperity or ruin within its own framework. In its response to the pressure operating upon it, the smallest state may have discovered a clue useful to the theorist.

Under the influence of this idea, which makes each nation an experiment, Rousseau draws upon the customs, laws, and institutions of many countries in formulating and testing his moral and political doctrine. His comments permit, after sifting and analysis, a clear impression of his knowledge of four continents and many nations. The order in which they are presented here is my own and moves from Africa to south America, to Asia, and finally to Europe. This scheme provides observations about ancient societies and modern nations, about pawns, such as Geneva, Corsica, Poland, and Venice, and about major agents in the struggle for hegemony — Spain, the German Empire, Prussia, Russia, France, Holland, and England. I have incorporated Rousseau's two principal criteria for evaluation: the influence of physical causation, such as climate, natural resources, and surrounding nations, and the role of moral causation in each society, including the level of sophistication, the condition of national character, the status of individual liberty, the attention to the people's will, and the goals of foreign policy. Consistent with my main theme, I shall stress, whenever his statements permit, the attention he gives to the attitudes, customs, and political structures which have assured individual liberty and, through that force, the power of the nation, or those which by thwarting aspirations for freedom have led to national decline.

Africa for Rousseau means Egypt and the little-known tribes of remote wildernesses. Egypt, "first school of the universe," was benefited by a fertile climate and thus became one of the first powerful states. Under Sesostris she aspired to world domination, a goal and policy which strained her resources to the point of exhaustion. The admiration of her people for learning also introduced weakness. While bearing the title of mother of philosophy and fine arts, Egypt became in quick succession the conquest of the Persians, Greeks, Romans, Arabs, and Turks (3: 10, *Premier discours*). The rest of the continent discloses scenes of ignorance and European inhumanity. The "vast and unfortunate regions" of Africa are apparently "destined only to cover the earth with herds of slaves" to the shame of mankind. Saint-Preux is filled with horror and pity when he sees members of the human race brutally "changed into beasts for the service of others" (2: 414, *Nouvelle Héloïse*).

South America, its subjugation the result of physical circumstance, is for Saint-Preux that "vast continent which lack of iron submitted to the Europeans." Depravity of every kind accompanied the event. Cruel, marauding armies, supported by cavalry with superior weapons and armor, laid waste a rich and fertile land in order to guarantee possession of it. For profit, perhaps for the sake of destruction, which they seemed to regard as profit in itself, the invaders invoked the "right of war" and set fire to entire cities, defenseless before the onslaught of the "learned, humane, and polished peoples of Europe." Greed and the right of the strongest allowed no restraint in the exploitation that followed. While Lisbon and London drained off the treasures of Brazil, the natives of the country dared not touch the gold and diamonds which righfully belonged to them. In Mexico and Peru, the situation of the Aztecs and Incas was similarly pitiful. Sad remnants of two once powerful peoples, they were "burdened with chains, shame, and misery amidst their rich metals" and lamented the day the heavens saw fit to lavish upon them so many treasures, to make them the coveted prize of the conquistadors. The enormity of the imperialistic claims of the Habsburgs in the new world appalls Rousseau. Saint-Preux "is struck with wonder" by the idea that a coast fifteen hundred leagues in extent and the largest ocean in the world could be "under the sway" of a single power, that Spain in effect "holds the keys to one hemisphere of the globe" (2: 413).

Africa and South America are for Rousseau exploited continents, the first for its Negroes, the second for its gold, silver, and land. Such goals are indications of the degenerate values of declining European nations, which place their faith in technology, riches, and force, as did to some extent the Egyptians, Aztecs, and Incas before them. Asia, including the Middle East, offers lessons more positive in nature.

The Jews are remarkable in Rousseau's eyes for the lasting ties which make them endure as a people. Their leaders deliberately isolated them from the more cultured and idolatrous peoples on their confines. After the dispersals, in spite of frequent contact with Egypt and Greece, they failed to make significant headway in the sciences. The evidence is in the inferior quality of their scholars and philosophers, for Flavius Josephus and Philo Judaeus, two very average men in Rousseau's opinion, were considered prodigies of erudition by the Jews. Legislation was oriented toward religion, the nation's principal object (3: 393, *Contrat social*). If man "is made for society, the truest religion" might be supposed to be "the most social and humane" religion. Facts, however, disprove the assumption. The Jews, with their revealed religion, were "the born enemies of all other peoples."

They founded their nation by "destroying seven nations, according to the positive, precise order they had received to do so" (Lahure, 3: 88-89, *Lettre à M. de Beaumont*). Religion, contributing more than anything else to their isolation and spirit of cohesiveness, guaranteed the longevity of their nation. "To prevent his people from becoming merged with foreign peoples" Moses purposely formed within them a distinct mentality and character. Religious customs and practices were fraternal bonds separating the Jews from other clans, turning them as one man against hostile neighbors. The frequent subjugation and ruin of his people has always been more apparent than real: "Its customs, laws, and rites remain and will last as long as the world, in spite of hate and persecution from the rest of mankind" (Pléiade, 3: 956-57, *Gouvernement de Pologne*). By thus molding the Jews, Moses performed a miracle in lawgiving which "five thousand years have not succeeded in destroying or even altering." Resisting the disintegrating influence of curiosity's search for materialistic knowledge, more inclined to creeds, sacraments, and solemnities, the Jews by the power of Mosaic insight received a religious institution so sound and vigorous that they outlasted their civil structure.

Glimpses of the national character of the Arabs may be obtained, Rousseau believes, from aspects of their justice and religion. They are less harsh with captives than are Europeans. Without pity or kindness, their justice is still superior because it is free of economic taint. Arabs expect a man to perform and accomplish to the limits of his capacity and then they demand no more. In determining guilt, they do not, like the Europeans, penalize a person for being weak, therefore a poor investment. They accuse bad intentions alone. Negro slaves would rarely suffer under the Arabian system. Under European justice they sicken, die, are in fact often murdered, because for their masters they are but "instruments of work" whose chief crime is their inability to labor hard enough and long enough to satisfy their owner's lust for gain (Lahure, 3: 27, *Emile et Sophie*).

As for religion, Rousseau indicates that the theocratic concepts and claims of the Mohammedans, unlike those of certain Christians, have historical justification. The destiny of the Arabs has always centered about religion, a fact reflected in their laws and institutions (Pléiade, 3: 393, *Contrat social*). With this background, faith is not for them a source of division, as it often is within Christian states. Firmly embedded in the hearts and minds of the people, an integral part of state policy and interest, Islam is the nation, an inspiring, cohesive force which explains Arabia's civic solidarity, its one-time ascendency in west Asia and in parts of Africa and Europe.

Farther to the east, Persia offers Rousseau the spectacle of a great empire ignominiously defeated in spite of an originally healthy community life. Though scorned by the *philosophes* as superstitious, the Persian religious beliefs were valuable for their effect on both rulers and populace. The bridge called Poul-Serrho is the way "over the eternal fire" and "the true final judgment." There the good are separated from the evil, a belief which accomplishes two purposes: it helps deter people from committing crimes and it comforts those without redress against injustice to know that death brings a final settling of accounts. Tyrants unrestrained by such a teaching have little concern for the welfare of their subjects. The inclination of the *philosophes* to ridicule this and other credos is socially harmful. Their newly invented moral systems often seem impressive, but none of them can replace the Poul-Serrho (*Emile*, p. 389). Religious beliefs lie deep in the national soul and inspire and sustain it better than any artificial doctrine borrowed from abroad. Rousseau thus sides with Montesquieu and Voltaire against Bayle and the materialists, particularly D'Holbach, who were upholding Bayle's view for their own purposes.

China had several governmental procedures of interest to Rousseau. With respect to public revolt, he notes the emperor's refreshing maxim that in all troubles which arise between him and his people the blame must fall upon his officials. Oriental despotism maintains itself in the final analysis because it is "more severe on the nobles than on the people." In this regard, statistics support the Chinese way. There is "no abatement" in the population of China, whereas in European states the "population diminishes everywhere by one tenth every thirty years" (3: 285, *Economie politique*; 843, *Lettres écrites de la montagne*). Nevertheless, China has a people wallowing in vice and crime and dangerously lacking in patriotism (3: 11, *Premier discours*). Her vast population is for the most part submitted in slavish fashion to a handful of brigands. Soft from luxury, she is conquered whenever attacked and will always be the prey of less civilized nations (2: 413-14, *Nouvelle Héloïse;* 3: 431, *Contrat social*). Her ability to continue as a nation rests on two means: the attention each ruler pays to the animal wants of the populace; and the fascination Chinese culture holds for each new conqueror, a victor in the military sense but a victim in turn of the refinement which made conquest easy.

Rousseau, it is clear, felt intensely the need for freeing his thinking from the European values stressed by contemporary historians. Partially removed from the eighteenth-century ambient, he can condemn many customs and institutions of Europe while admiring their healthier moral counterparts in the Near and Far East: the cohesive force of the Jewish people; justice as practiced by the Arabs, their total union of religion and state; certain beliefs of the Persians; the methods used by the emperors of China to know the grievances of the people and to protect them from excessive tax burdens. From the information he has about Africa and South America, he can find intellectual and emotional reinforcement for convictions basic to his understanding of international relations. These provide support at most for the following conclusions: the usual inefficacy of international law; the prevalence of the use of force in affairs between states; the frequent predominance of the profit motive in European justice and foreign policy; and the importance of religion to national unity and survival. He is made very aware of the violence and weight of seapower in conflicts between states. The rivalries of navies, undiminished by the vast expanses in which they maneuver, make each nation's seamen, in the words of Saint-Preux, the implacable enemies of the crews of foreign vessels: "In the vast ocean, in which it ought to be so pleasant for men to meet other human beings, I have seen two great ships seek, find, attack, fight one another in fury, as if that immense space was too small for both of them. I have seen them vomit iron and flame against each other. In a rather short combat I saw the image of Hell. I heard the shouts of joy given by the victors cover the cries of the wounded and the groans of the dying" (2: 414, *Nouvelle Héloïse*).

Information about countries in Africa, South America, and Asia helped to free Rousseau from the framework of his contemporary Europe. A similar liberation can be felt in the passages he devotes to ancient Athens, Sparta, and Rome. Their citizens are for him like giants when placed in imagination next to a Frenchman, an Englishman, or a Spaniard.

The early moral strength of the Greeks rested on simplicity. They had only primitive needs, were dedicated to the state, and took pride in their military prowess. Bowing to no obstacle, they were able to conquer Asia twice, first at Troy, later in its heartland. Their feeling of isolation, which made them see all other peoples as barbarians, their use of slaves, and their theater contributed to the formation of a strongly patriotic character. In Rousseau's account, the ability to defend one's borders, then to drive back and defeat surrounding nations, is the measure of national health,

The prevalence of slavery among the Greeks, if not condoned, is at least accepted by Rousseau. It was not a vicious, profit-making device, but rather, because of difficulties in gaining a living from the soil, an essential ingredient of liberty. The use of slaves gave the Greeks time to assemble in the public square and decide issues related to the common good: "Everything that is not a part of nature has its inconveniences, and civil society more than anything else. There are unfortunate situations in which one's own liberty cannot be preserved except at the expense of another's, and in which the citizen cannot be perfectly free unless the slave is extremely enslaved" (3: 431, *Contrat social*).

Athens, city of philosophy, rhetoric, and taste, was for Rousseau essentially the object-oriented culture expressed in its great buildings fashioned from marble, a culture admired and imitated all over the world, the symbol of artistic, literary, commercial, and industrial value. Such an orientation meant placing arts and letters above national survival. The far different reputation of Sparta rested on heroic deeds, more fitting monuments, Rousseau believes, than statues and edifices in marble (3: 12-13). Each citizen was trained to incorporate the nation into his own being. But the Spartans had two flaws. Their love of conquest eventually resulted in a softness as harmful as that caused by the Athenian love of luxury: "The fatigues of war were the softness of Sparta."

Pursuing this inclination, they were fated to become ordinary men. Partly out of weariness, they were pushed back from their former dominions to their own territorial limits. But fatigue was not the only cause of their decline. The homeland was too dear to them. In order to save it, they would sacrifice all else. Love of country, for which they were "always ready to die," had become their highest good. Patriotism, attachment to rock, hill, and soil, was even stronger in them than love of liberty itself, a far superior inspiration in Rousseau's opinion, alone capable of making a people staunch in the face of the enemy, unbending to the end even at the cost of the nation itself (3: 541-43, *Parallèle entre Sparte et Rome*).

The superiority Rousseau grants Rome over Sparta is for the most part based on this distinction between patriotism and liberty. Jewish religious unity was unexcelled. Sparta stood for individual character growth to the extent that patriotic interest silenced selfish interest. With Rome, as Rousseau interprets its history, the collective spirit of a people reached new heights. The phenomenon included elements of both the Jewish and the Spartan kinds of cohesiveness, but surpassed them through the people's greater dedication to liberty and to the means of preserving it. A highly respected legal structure expressed the needs of the people, safeguarded their rights, and perpetuated Roman love of order long after the soul of the nation had died.

The first two kings who "gave form to the republic and instituted its customs and manners" were crude and unsophisticated. Romulus was a warrior and spent his life waging war. Numa was completely dedicated to "religious rites" (2: 971, *Préface de Narcisse*). Religion and military courage help to account for Rome's early spirit of solidarity. Numa, the "true founder of Rome," welded into a united citizenry the brigands Romulus had merely assembled. He succeeded "less by laws" than by common institutions which "attached them to one another and all of them to their land." The sacred rites he introduced may have appeared "frivolous and superstitious," but they had a powerful and effective hold over the people. Romulus, too, in spite of his fierceness, his reputation for founding the military institutions of Rome, also helped establish common religious beliefs and practices (3: 957-58, *Gouvernement de Pologne*).

Accompanying this rustic foundation of shared religious rites and military courage was Roman love of order. Of all peoples, the Romans "transgressed their laws the least" and had the "finest laws" (3: 357, 1441, *Contrat social*). This attitude strengthened assemblies, courts, and police, made Roman jurisprudence almost indestructible, a force felt long after the old physical form of the empire had disappeared. Respect for Rome so effectively "survived her power" that many jurisconsults later raised the question "whether the Emperor of Germany was not the natural sovereign of the world; and Bartoldus went so far as to treat as heretic anyone who dared to question it" (3: 567-68, 1544, *Projet de paix perpétuelle*).

Part of the true worth of Roman law lay in the continuing protection it was able to give to institutions and values important to both leaders and people: respect for family, for father and mother, for liberty. The law had simply to encourage the prevalent integrity of family life. Each home was a school for citizens. Authority there was precisely designated and effectively exercised. The control of the father over his children was limitless, his private policing of manners severe. "More feared than the magistrates," he was a censor of morals and the enforcer of laws (3: 261-62, *Economie*). Rome also prized its women. Their influence, Rousseau suggests, permeated all the affairs of the state in an acceptably ornamental and inspirational manner. They were closely associated with moments of glory and victory, with sorrow, with the need for courage in times of trouble. The presence of women on festive occasions "honored the exploits of great generals." Women publicly wept when the fathers of the homeland died. Their marriage vows and periods of mourning were regarded with solemnity. As for liberty, the Romans in their best years were superior to other peoples "by the consideration the government had for individuals and by its scrupulous attention in respecting the inviolable rights of all the members of the state." Nothing was so sacred as the life of the ordinary citizen. "To condemn him" it was necessary to hold an "assembly of the entire people" (3: 257-58, *Economie;* p. 377, *Contrat social*).

But Roman liberty was more than respect for the life and rights of each citizen. Liberty was also self-government. "The Roman people itself, that model of all free peoples," was not in the beginning capable of governing itself. It was necessary to raise men up gradually, to accustom them to "breathe the salutary air of liberty" until they had reached "that severity of manners and that pride in courage which made of them finally the most respectable of all peoples" (3: 113, *Second discours*). Rousseau's aim in Chapter 4 of the *Contrat social* is to determine "how the most free and powerful people of the earth exercised its supreme power" or sovereignty (3: 444).

Overlooked or at least much neglected in the past is this highly significant relationship between "most free" and "most powerful," a linking which occurs frequently in Rousseau's writings. Pressure on each state from international rivalries was always implicit, usually explicit, in his treatment of the countries of Africa, South America, Asia. Sparta was presented in a warring context. Rome, too, surrounded by enemies, a fact of its physical environment, had as its primary concern the need to survive. Her moral condition — liberty as self-government, made possible by a character derived from early religious and military institutions, from respect for law, family, and the individual — regularly appears as the source of national power in Rousseau's account of Rome. The liberty-power-survival nexus occurs both in his analysis of Rome in health, that is, during her period of democratic rule, and in his study of Rome in decline, when usurpation had worn away liberty's substance.

Rousseau's discussion of Rome's ascendent democratic institutions which served to express the people's will and to channel it into action is not so much in terms of the individual's right to participate in community decisions, or of the protection of this and other rights as ends in themselves. It is rather in terms of the entire people's involvement, its sense of belonging to a movement greater than any person or faction, of having confidence in aims relating to the national past and to goals capable of transforming by force and law the ancient Mediterranean and European world through the combination of personal integrity and collective power. In his interpretation of this very active, living communal association, I perceive five principal characteristics by which Rousseau measures the nation.

In the first place, tradition perpetuated an early preference for drawing the nation's leaders from the rural population.

Because of the "taste of the first Romans for country life," the nation consistently held the country tribes to be superior and relegated to the cities "the arts, the trades, intrigue, wealth, and enslavement." Rousseau's authority is Pliny, who "says positively that the country tribes were honored because of the men who composed them, whereas the cowards, whom one wanted to disgrace, were transferred in ignominy to the city tribes." The small village was the "nursery of those robust and valiant men" who defended Rome in time of war and nourished her in time of peace. According to Rousseau, this unprecedented distinction between "tribes of the country" and "tribes of the city" aided Rome in "the preservation of her manners and customs and the growth of her empire" (3: 445-46, *Contrat social*). Rural leadership is seen as essential both to Rome's liberty and to her might.

Second, for a long time the people through its assemblies was "truly sovereign both *de jure* and *de facto*." The Romans were divided into tribes, centuries, and curiae. When the assemblies or *comitia* were called together, they met either as *comitia curiata, comitia centuriata,* or *comitia tributa.* Since every citizen was "enrolled" in one of these groups, and "no law received its sanction and no official was elected except in one of the *comitia*," it can be said that "no citizen was excluded from the right to vote" (3: 449, *Contrat social*). Even after corruption had sapped the strength of the republic, the collective will continued to be expressed, though distortedly: "In the midst of all these abuses, the vast people, thanks to its ancient regulations, never stopped electing magistrates, passing laws, judging cases, and carrying through business both public and private almost as easily as the senate itself could have done" (3: 453). In addition to expressing the sovereign will, the assemblies in fact "usurped" the most important functions of government, so that it is true in a sense that they determined "the fate of Europe" (3: 449-50). The liberty which Rousseau admires in this passage had a long reach. It was capable of extending the will of the Roman people to the ends of the ancient European world.

Third, the Roman people was steadfast in its determination to express its will directly rather than through intermediaries. The size of the population hampered discussion, debate, and voting. Rousseau reports that the last census showed in Rome "four hundred thousand citizens bearing arms" and for the empire more than four million citizens, "not counting [non-voting] subjects, foreigners, women, children, slaves" (3: 425). In the time of the Gracchi, the crowd was so numerous some citizens had to "cast their votes from the roofs of buildings" (3: 430). In spite of difficulties "in frequently bringing together the population of the capital and its suburbs," there were "few weeks that the Roman people was not assembled, and even several times" (3: 425). The obstacles were aggravated by those magistrates inclined to oppose the people's control of the legislative and executive bodies. Any yielding of the people in this arduous fight for direct sovereignty, Rousseau leaves no doubt, would have meant more than a loss to the individual. The death of the nation would have ensued. When citizens are "greedy, cowardly, faint-hearted, more in love with repose than with liberty, they no longer hold out for long against the redoubled efforts of government." As a result, sovereignty of the people vanishes; thus the "majority of states fall and perish before their time" (3: 428).

Fourth, the vitality and health of the people's will could be measured not only by its capacity for remaining inalienable, for resisting representation, but also by its indivisibility. Devices were repeatedly found to prevent one class of the population from imposing its own will to the detriment of the common will, to assure, in other words, that the will of the people remained truly collective. From this point of view the *comitia centuriata* were superior to the *comitia curiata* and the *comitia tributa*. Since the populace formed the majority in the assemblies of *curiae*, they were "suited only to tyranny and evil schemes." The rural tribes were also absent. The *comitia tributa* were "the most favorable to popular government" but excluded the senators. Thus forced to obey laws on which they could not vote, the senators were on this point "less free than the meanest citizens" (3: 451-52). The *comitia centuriata*, which were the most favorable to aristocracy, were at the same time the best of the assemblies, since they alone included all classes of citizens. Rousseau's praise of these assemblies stresses the collective ideal and the significance of its fulfillment for the glory of the nation: "It is clear that the whole majesty of the Roman people lay solely in the *comitia centuriata*" (3: 452).

Religion, through the traditions of Rome's earliest beginnings, was the fifth essential force contributing to the cohesiveness of the community, to the preservation of liberty, to the predominance of her power. Rousseau believed the Romans made better use of religion than do modern nations. Civil in function, religion was subordinate to the state. When Caesar pleaded for Catiline, he tried to show that the soul is mortal. In refuting him, Cato and Cicero did not indulge in speculations about the truth or falsity of the dogma or its relation to conscience. They simply pointed out that Caesar's arguments made him a bad citizen, since his doctrine of mortality would harm the nation (3: 468). Religion, conceived as an instrument of the state and its freedom, helped give the Roman soldier his dedication to victory. Instead of soldiers fighting for God, as in the Christian tradition, the gods fought for the legions. The Romans asked their gods for victory and assumed them to be superior to those of the peoples they attacked (3: 466-67). Christians, afraid of tempting their God, would not dare take an oath to victory, as did the soldiers of Fabius. The Romans, Rousseau concludes, could have beaten and crushed most modern Christian nations.

Religion in this context is an instrument of free men. It is designed to increase their courage and strength but to leave their minds and hearts untouched by any authority higher than the collective sovereign of which they are a part. Allegiance to an authority higher than the general will would have divided the state and thus diminished Roman vitality and imperial influence. One of Rousseau's main arguments in Chapter 8 of the *Contrat social* is that civil religion, which is compatible with liberty as personal integrity since it does not bind the private soul, and with liberty as community will, generates national power, whereas Christianity dissipates it.

These positive principles of Roman political structure do more than illustrate the theory of social contract. Rousseau has made it clear through his vocabulary that they are instruments of a liberty which yields tremendous power. He refers repeatedly to the "preservation" of Rome, the "growth of its empire," the impact of its assembled people on the "fate of Europe," to the "majesty of the Roman people," to the courage of the Roman soldier inspired yet left united in his allegiance by state religion, to Rome, "mistress of the world."

Rousseau's emphasis on the threefold relationship — liberty, power, and survival — may be seen again in his willingness to give value to additional devices of Roman democracy that are incompatible with liberty as personal integrity and as popular sovereignty, but are compatible with liberty as the necessary means to power and survival, as an instrument to be protected at all times, even temporarily removed in moments of crisis until circumstances permit its restoration and the return to normal function. The Roman political machine had its safety controls (censors, tribunes) and emergency alternate system (dictatorship) which supplemented personal liberty in a goal essential to liberty itself, that of maintaining the state in vigorous health under extreme conditions. Censorship, with its edicts describing the moral laws, exerted a preventive rather than a reformative influence on conduct. Men love good, Rousseau says, but it is "in determining the good that they make their mistakes." Rome's two censors, if they curbed freedom's natural course, were still "useful" in guiding judgment, "in preserving morality, but not in restoring it" (3: 458-59). The tribunes, closer to the spirit of liberty but still in violation of its principle of self-sufficient integrity, served as legal defenders who protected the people against unfair treatment by the magistrates. Without any positive right to originate legislation or to execute laws, they could stop all action in the senate and assemblies, "keep anything from being done" (3: 454). In their presence, "those proud patricians, who always held the entire people in contempt, were forced to bend" (3: 454). The third device, dictatorship, overcame the ponderousness of freedom's laws in times of crisis, when circumstances required their suspension. During the first period of the republic, Rome often resorted to this expedient because "the state had not yet a firm enough basis to be able to maintain itself by the strength of its constitution alone" (3: 456-57). Rousseau thinks there was little danger of its abuse in those early times and finds the Romans of the late republic too sparing in its use.

Rousseau leaves no doubt that liberty, far from being just an ideal end, is operational, the life-blood of the state, the essential ingredient permitting the vigorous function of all the organs of the nation. He returns to this point repeatedly. The force of Rome increased or diminished in direct proportion to the rise or decline of liberty. The relationship of liberty to the nation's total energy, to the swing from growth to decline, from life to death, is never subordinate in Rousseau's analysis of Rome (3: 385, 421-22). Liberty is the principle shared by Sparta and Rome but enjoyed by the Romans to a higher degree, since they placed liberty above Rome itself. They never believed, according to Rousseau, that "their homeland could outlive liberty." It was through this vitalizing, power-yielding belief that Rome in the years of ascendency was triumphant over all of her enemies (3: 543, *Parallèle entre Sparte et Rome*).

The Romans excelled in matching their laws to growing corruption in the populace, but the downfall could not be postponed indefinitely (3: 452-53, *Contrat social*). At the end, the same environment of hostility which built Roman liberty and power brought Rome to her knees. New conquests accentuated a degenerative luxury, and generals, long absent from Rome and wanting tyrannical rule, brought spiritless citizens to heel with mercenary armies. Her liberty lost, Rome was overrun by the barbarians always on her frontiers.

By returning to Rousseau's statements about nations in Africa, South America, and Asia, I have tried to show that in his view they were largely molded by international pressures and conflicts, and by their responses to these stimuli in terms of national character, customs, beliefs, and institutions. Ancient Sparta and Rome elicited from him even greater respect. Both nations illustrated convincingly the effects of physical and moral causation. Spartan love of country, which transcended every other principle, and her love of conquest were in part products of hostile environment — powerful, encircling enemies. Rome owed her periods of liberty, glory, and decadence to her need to conquer in order to survive. Both nations by means of integrity and discipline succeeded for a long time in resisting attack and turning events to their own advantage, Sparta mainly by force of patriotism, Rome more successfully by the sounder principle of her free collective will. Roman liberty was for Rousseau an active intellectual and emotional sharing of responsibility, the participation of each citizen in the community's voice, a vigorous, purposeful phenomenon which, living in and through the people, relating to its past traditions, customs, beliefs, and history, explains for him Rome's success in imposing her goals, policies, and law throughout Europe. In the past, writers have stressed Rousseau's attention to the features of Rome's constitution which permitted popular sovereignty to endure. My object has been rather to observe Rome in the international context, to show that Rousseau conceived her liberty, not in a vacuum and only as an end in itself, but rather very often as the instrument to survival and overwhelming power.

Doubt and pessimism are reflected in Rousseau's earliest remarks about modern Europe and persist in the statements he made late in life. Unlike Rome, the nations of Europe, founded in confusion, did not have simple, rustic beginnings. They were also more immediately vulnerable to foreign cultural influence. Rousseau points out the difficulty in a note from the *Second discours:* "Today, now that commerce, travel, and conquest bring the various nations closer together and their ways of living are continually made more and more similar by frequent communication, it can be seen that certain national differences have diminished" (3: 208). The fact that nations absorb one another's weaknesses has serious implications, since the predominant nations, Spain, France, and England, are far down the road to decadence. Because of the inevitable cross-fertilization of national traits, little promise exists for most of the nations of Europe. If there is any hope for a healthy national life under these conditions, it lies with three small states, Geneva, Corsica, and Poland.

History was to give a severe twist to even this limited optimism. For our purpose nothing more needs to be added here about most of the works so far discussed in which references are made to Geneva. But in view of Rousseau's praise of that republic a word must be said about the *Lettres écrites de la montagne.* No doubt the idea for the meditations to be found in this work had been present in Rousseau's mind in 1762 at the time of Geneva's condemnation of *Emile* and the *Contrat social,* but composition of the work probably did not begin until 1763, when the plan to defend his philosophic position was broadened to include a respectful, but uncompromising judgment of certain aspects of the Genevan government, particularly and ironically its resistance to current demands for a more popular basis of representation. The work appeared in late 1764.

As for the *Projet de constitution pour la Corse*, Rousseau no doubt prepared his notes on Corsican institutions and did a part of the writing between January and October of 1765, first while at Neuchâtel and later on the Ile Saint-Pierre. The Treaty of Versailles (May 15, 1768) attached Corsica to France and caused Rousseau to abandon the project while it was still in an unfinished state (3: ccviii).

Poland, the other European state which Rousseau respected for its tradition of freedom, was in the throes of conflict and betrayal from within and abroad when Rousseau took up its cause. Back in Paris in 1770, he was enthusiastic for the rights of the Polish patriots or Confederates of Bar and their resistance to the schemes of Catherine II of Russia. Using documents supplied by Wielhorski and Rulhière, heroes and representatives of the Confederates, he worked on his *Considérations sur le gouvernement de Pologne* at top speed during the winter of 1770-1771 and probably finished it by June 1771 (3: ccxxxvii). But Poland's fate was soon to be sealed. The first treaty partitioning Poland was signed between Prussia and Russia in February 1772. Rousseau's neglected manuscript was not printed until 1782.

So much for disillusionment and lost causes. Rousseau's evaluation of these three nations gives insight into his views on liberty. He believes that in many respects Geneva is to be envied. Her boundaries, rights, and security are guaranteed by honorable treaties. Wars and conquerors no longer threaten the state's tranquillity. Because of a protected location, the price of liberty is not high. Her constitution is basically sound, although threatened from within. Laws, made for the most part by a sovereign people, are usually well administered by worthy magistrates elected by the people. The character of the citizens is not yet seriously endangered. Although they profit by selling manufactures throughout Europe, the great wealth which induces softness is largely absent. Nor is the country so poor as to be dependent on foreign nations (3: 113, 115, *Second discours*). Integrity is evidenced in the people's willingness to serve the state. They do not pay others to take their place, whether as soldiers, officers, magistrates, or workers. They are "always ready to pay with their person" (3: 1010-11, *Gouvernement de Pologne*).

Rousseau may take comfort in these conditions and qualities which favor Geneva, but he also sees cause for uneasiness and fear. A serious danger lies in actions taken to limit the general council and increase the powers of the Council of Twenty-five, or Little Council, through the *Règlement de l'illustre médiation* (3: 1675). The General Council is not just an organ established by law. It is not the deputy of anyone. It is "sovereign" and the "living and fundamental law which gives life and force to all the rest and knows no other rights than its own." It is not "an order in the state" but the state itself. Yet Article III of the *Règlement* limits the power of the General Council (3: 826, *Lettres écrites de la montagne*), and Article II provides for the syndics to be chosen exclusively from the Council of Twenty-five. The latter limitation is contrary to the very purpose of the syndics, who are elected for two reasons, to judge the people and to protect them. Serving for one year, the syndics are supposed to guard against, not sympathize with, the possible encroachments proposed by the life members of the Council of Twenty-five, a council the people does not choose (3: 824-25). Rousseau seems to see more clearly than the Genevan bourgeois themselves that their sovereignty is being subverted. The Council of Twenty-five is "minister and police, prosecutor and judge at the same time: it gives orders and executes; it issues summonses, it seizes, imprisons, judges, punishes all by itself; it has the power at hand to do everything" (3: 875-76). Because of the Council's predominance, any paid official of the state is not really a citizen. He is from the date of his appointment "the slave and satellite of the twenty-five and ready to trample under foot the homeland and the laws as soon as they [the twenty-five] order it to be done.... As individuals" the bourgeois of Geneva are slaves of "an arbitrary power," slaves of twenty-five depots (3: 835, 879).

The Corsicans, with similar problems but in an even more beleaguered position, Rousseau believes may learn from Genevan attitudes and policies and may prove fertile ground for new legislation. In spite of Genoa's opposition, which includes insidious efforts to establish an academy to corrupt them, the Corsicans have a remarkable ability to "recover and defend liberty." They must be studied and taught to preserve freedom by positive law. Rousseau believes that someday "this small island will astonish Europe" (2: 967, *Préface de Narcisse*; 3: 391, *Contrat social*). He gathers information concerning its geography and resources: a map with districts named and delineated; a description of the entire island, its natural history, products, cultivated lands, divisions into districts; the number, size, and location of its cities, towns, and parishes; as close an estimate of the population as possible; the status of the fortresses and ports; its industry and arts, navy, trade, and potential for commerce. He asks questions related to social structure: the size and influence of the clergy, its teachings, its attitude toward the homeland; the number of old families, of privileged groups, the existence of a nobility. His study requires data about municipal rights and the will of the cities to safeguard them; national behavior, including the customs of the people, their tastes, occupations, amusements; the features of the military establishment, chain of command, divisions, discipline, manner of warfare. Finally, he wants to learn more about the history of the nation to the present, its laws, statutes, current government, difficulties of administration, practice of justice, sources of public income, methods of levying and collecting taxes, and the amount of the people's annual contribution. His aim in collecting data about the physical, social, behavioral, and institutional aspects of the nation is to find the "national genius." [3]

This interest in background does not mean that he proposes simply to adjust government to the people's weaknesses and strengths. A wise method may be to "form the government for the nation." There is, however, "a much better way, forming the nation for the government" (3: 901, *Constitution pour la Corse*). Vigorous and healthy, Corsica can "give itself to the government which will maintain its vigor and health" (3: 902). The existing effects of climate, geography, and previous history are not to be passively accepted. Rousseau introduces the more creative idea of calculating cause-and-effect relationships between land, people,

---

[3] *Correspondance générale*, ed. Théophile Dufour and Pierre-Paul Plan (Paris: Colin, 1924-1934) (hereafter cited as Dufour-Plan), 11: 351-54, *Lettre à M. Butta-Foco*, 1764.

and government. The basic principles which determine his proposals are three: take advantage of the natural characteristics of the people and country; develop and coordinate the strengths peculiar to Corsica; be independent and think no more about foreign nations than "if there were none" (3: 904). The third idea should not be misinterpreted. Rousseau's intention is to make the Corsicans "independent" of external corruption. Every measure he proposes recognizes the existence of the European community and the need to give the Corsicans the character and discipline to resist its influence (3: 916). The version of the social pact he proposes for them is an instrument both of domestic solidarity and of resistance to the corrosive effect on national spirit of the foreign policies of Genoa and France. His recommendations, adapted to environment, at the same time read like antitheses to European sophistication: preference for democracy and agriculture; opposition to nobility, cities, capitals, commerce, finance, great fortunes, academies; somewhat futile reliance on the principle of liberty to oppose a conscienceless invasion by Choiseul's troops, a conquest by French gold after iron had failed (Dufour-Plan, 19: 256-57, à M. de Saint-Germain, 1770).

In his counsels to Poland, as in those to Geneva and Corsica, Rousseau emphasizes liberty and patriotism. Building on the soundness of her character, he hopes to give to the nation the "soul of the confederates" of Bar, to fill the hearts of the Poles with their republic, to create the moral fiber to resist any attempt to impose Russian ways and manners. Keenly aware of the dangers of Polish anarchy, he still fears overcentralization under hereditary monarchy more than instability. He therefore stresses counterweights to the executive and only modification, not abolishment, of the *liberum veto* and of the federative principle, both of which he sees as part of the spirit of liberty and equality he wants to preserve and strengthen in Poland. Cohesiveness and security are to come from common traditions, from a civil system stressing merit and economic reform. If dismemberment through partition should occur, this sad reduction in size might nevertheless prepare the way for more efficient administration (Pléiade, 3: 954-1016, *Gouvernement de Pologne*). Avoiding the balance-of-power politics which has drained her resources in the past, Poland must look to her own defenses, perfect the hit-and-run tactics of the cavalry. Poland's unfortunate physical reality is that she is "a large state surrounded by still more powerful states, which by despotism and military discipline have a great offensive force. Feeble in contrast by her anarchy, she is, in spite of Polish valor, subject to every kind of outrage" (3: 959).

Rousseau's very specific comments on Geneva, Corsica, and Poland have often been studied for the contribution they make to an understanding of his theories on civil liberty. My own purpose, has been to underscore the fact that his recommendations reveal an almost obsessive preoccupation with the external pressures operating on the state. Usurpations by Geneva's Council of Twenty-five, by the Corsican nobility, by a possible hereditary king of Poland are feared by Rousseau certainly as blows to individual right, but even more for their weakening effect on each nation's collective will, therefore on the state's capacity for survival.

If Corsica has already fallen, if the existences of Geneva and Poland are jeopardized by their increasing sophistication as well as by the designs of France, Russia, England, and their allies, the source of these dangers, Rousseau knows, lies ultimately in the causes behind the European power situation. Competing in Africa, America, and Asia, the great countries of the European system of equilibrium have extended that continent's values and antagonisms to the entire world. Rousseau's references to Venice, Spain, the Empire, Prussia, Russia, France, Holland, and England usually stress the determinants of their domestic and foreign policies.

Venice illustrates for Rousseau the passage of sovereignty first from a people to their government and then from government by many to government by a few (3: 421, 441-42, *Contrat social*). Numerous ill-conceived and unsuccessful wars with other European powers and the Turks marked the rise of minority interests and the state's decline.

Spain was equally vulnerable to decay because of the misguided policies of a government grown heedless to the interests of the people. With vast domains and riches, with great personal talents, Charles V believed the goal of universal monarchy to be within his grasp. Rousseau makes this inferior motivation the source of disaster. Philip II had the same desire for preponderance in Europe, but maneuvered less skillfully. Richer than his father, he was less influential, although his efforts to hold together and expand his empire kept Europe in a state of tension: "No prince reigned in security, if he did not get along well with Spain." After Philip II's death, the decline of the nation's fortunes became more evident. Philip III, as ambitious as his father, was less shrewd. If other nations still by habit believed Spain supreme in Europe, her power had in fact continued to weaken. The Netherlands were soon in revolt. Struggles with England used up Spanish reserves. Participation in the civil wars of France was a drain on treasures reaped in the New World. The division of the house of Austria into two branches led to disunity in objectives. Insistent upon consolidating his authority in Germany, the emperor soon alienated most German princes, who formed leagues and "almost dethroned him." These events are evidence, for Rousseau, that "the decadence of the House of Austria" had been prepared far in advance. Spain's ambitions, now thwarted, now renewed, met with diminishing success because of growing opposition from other rising powers — France, Holland, and England. Only time and opportunity were needed for them to break the yoke of her hegemony (3: 596-97, *Jugement sur le projet de paix perpétuelle*).

The impulse for freedom from Spain was mounted in part by the princes of Germany, whom Rousseau is inclined to see as pivotal in the system of Europe. More solid than negotiations is the fact that the Empire, "almost in the center of Europe," holds "all the other parts in respect" and thus exerts a stabilizing influence. Although very large, it has a great number of separate peoples, each with fine qualities, each with a diversity of loyalties which keeps them from joining together to invade others. They are a treacherous "reef" for would-be conquerors and vital to maintaining the peace of Westphalia and the balance of power (3: 572, *Extrait du projet de paix perpétuelle*).

For one of the princes of the empire, however, Rousseau has little admiration. "Innate love of justice" and a "secret affection for France" inspire Rousseau's aversion for Frederick II, a man who "thinks as a philosopher" and "behaves as a king." He has abandoned France and reveals by his Machiavellian maxims and conduct that he despises natural law and "all of the human obligations" (1: 591-94, *Confessions*). Like Adraste, king of the Dauniens, he scorns the gods and seeks to deceive men. In spite of Prussian successes, Rousseau believes Frederick doomed in the long run. Caught up in the rivalries and wars of Europe, he has spurned the opportunities peace has given to build his nation (1: 599-600).

Rousseau believes that one of Prussia's rivals is also suffering from opportunism, although in a different way. He is contemptuous of Russia's facile acceptance of foreign influence, a fault which prevents her people from having an authentic national character. Having inherited a nation of barbarians, Peter the Great immediately set about civilizing them, transforming them into Frenchmen, Germans, and Englishmen; thus he aborted their true genius and growth, their future. Playing the European game of rivalry and conquest, the Russians want to subjugate Europe and will no doubt be subjugated themselves. The Tartars and their neighbors are destined eventually to become the masters of Russia and of all Europe, the inevitable result of the wars of attrition waged by European powers among themselves (3: 386, *Contrat social*).

Rousseau's frequent expression of love for France makes his testimony concerning her moral and political degradation seem all the more damaging. The French have become "enemies of virtue and common sense." The crowd "grovels in misery; all men are the slaves of vice." Crimes still not committed are "already deep in their hearts" and await only the "assurance of impunity" (2: 969, *Préface de Narcisse*). In England, men of commerce and business command respect because of their wealth, influence, and contribution to the national economy. There a "merchant who proposes to raise troops" is listened to carefully (Lahure, 3: 96, *Lettre à M. de Beaumont*). If merchants and peasants attempted to lead a rebellion in France, it would be a laughing matter. The country favors only valets and masters. Deep moral decay explains her complacency, intolerance, distrust of liberty, and humiliating defeats. Through his detailed account of the traits of her upper classes, Rousseau makes France the brilliant symbol and source of corruption in Europe, yet for Rousseau the most disturbing aspect of France is the isolation and ignorance of its people. French books, art, and science have spread over Europe, but a countermovement has not occurred. The French, dedicated to sophistication, are largely unaware of the ideas and institutions of other countries. The politics permitted by irresponsible and slavish subjects has therefore become one of domestic intrigue and unsuccessful foreign wars. The effects of favoritism and laxity are evident in the military operations that drain the nation's resources. In Rousseau's opinion, the French soldier is competent; when he believes in his captains, he is "invincible." Unfortunately, he must often depend for guidance on court favorites whom he detests. Informed of the latest intrigues, the officers of enemy armies need only make their attacks coincide with the arrival of a weak leader (Pléiade, 2: 586-87, Nouvelle Héloïse).

For Voltaire, Diderot, and other *philosophes*, Prussia, Russia, and England are usually vigorous, rising nations, the sometimes enlightened heirs to the earlier predominance of Spain and France in the European system. Holland is often seen as the guardian of liberty. Rousseau, on the contrary, discounts the potential greatness of Prussia and Russia. In a reference to Holland's activities in Cape Colony, he stresses what he considers to be the character of the Dutch, "miserly, patient, hardworking," capable through "perseverance" of overcoming difficulties which have defeated the heroic efforts of other nations (2: 414, *Nouvelle Héloïse*). He objects to their mercenary attitudes (1: 1097, *Rêveries*) and speaks very briefly of their successful use of the confederative principle to resist Austria (3: 427, *Contrat social*). He mentions Dutch freedom only in passing (3: 1038, *Gouvernement de Pologne*). Within his frame of values, even the liberty and emerging power of England are to be downgraded.

In preparing his version of Saint-Pierre's *Projet de paix perpétuelle*, Rousseau first wrote that the "English will have lost their liberty in twenty years," then later in 1760 sarcastically added to his publisher, Bastide, that he should have said "the rest of their liberty, since they are foolish enough to believe they still have it" (Dufour-Plan, 5: 299-300). By that time, too, England will be ruined and its agriculture near exhaustion. Since London is growing, the countryside with its farms must be perishing and the whole kingdom gradually becoming depopulated. The English, who wish to be conquerors, will soon be slaves (Pléiade, 3: 573,

Extrait du projet de paix perpétuelle). Their superiority over the French is more apparent than real. While admitting England's merits, Rousseau stresses nevertheless the people's unwitting surrender of the legislative function.

This generally negative attitude does not substantially change in Rousseau's later works. His view is amplified, however, at times by measured praise for the English nobility. The English, in Milord Edouard Bomston's words, have the "most enlightened, the best informed, the wisest and bravest" nobility in Europe. They are "friends of the prince" rather than his slaves, and "leaders" of the people. Between people and king they establish "an invincible balance." In dealing with a ruler they seek to know not his will but rather his right. Their first duty "is to the nation," their second "to the one who governs" (2: 171, 263, *Nouvelle Héloïse*).

Nevertheless, the quality of England's liberty is inferior. Her citizens are hardly more than slaves. Rousseau says this is so because the people, the true sovereign, has delegated its powers to representatives, the members of Parliament, which has become sovereign by law. The operation of this system, a regrettable expedient made necessary in part by the size of the nation, offers valuable insights. When the king presides over Parliament, that body becomes everything. Its function is then distinct from the role of each of its chambers considered separately. Including king, lower chamber, and upper chamber, it represents the entire nation. It is the "unique and supreme power from which each of these three parts draws its existence and its rights." Vested with the legislative authority, Parliament "can change even the fundamental law by which each of the orders composing it exists: it can do this, and, moreover, it has done so" (3: 824, *Lettres écrites de la montagne*). The people is truly sovereign, therefore, only when electing the members of Parliament. After the election, they return to subservience (3: 430, *Contrat social*). This subjection by due process is all the worse because representatives, if hard to deceive, are easy to corrupt. The Court has only to buy the Parliament once every seven years to have its way (3: 975, *Gouvernement de Pologne*).

Within the framework of his strictures, two virtues Rousseau sees in the English system are its ability to get things done and its support of law. In spite of the confusion to be expected in a "body of seven hundred members, everything is anticipated" and this "great monarchy moves along at a good rate," a fact remarkable for several reasons: the importance of the matters under discussion, the great number of varying interests in conflict, the cabals competing with one another, and the right and opportunity of each member to stand and speak his mind before the assembly (3: 831-32, *Lettres écrites de la montagne*). When justice prevails in this country, it is largely, Rousseau believes, because of this great body. Through it the law has such force that the rights of each subject cannot easily be violated. If the king tried by the smallest infraction to violate the provisions of the law, he would be without right and power: "No one would want to obey him." Even the ministers themselves would "fear for their heads" in going against parliamentary opinion in such a matter (3: 875). Rousseau finds in England's checks and balances some guarantees to liberty that the Genevan constitution does not provide.

In Rousseau's presentation of the nations of Europe, adversity and destruction in one form or another are the great physical facts overshadowing free, tyrannical, and despotic states alike. Venice, Spain, and France are like shells, their substance of character, liberty, and equality drained from them by domestic misrule and by a foreign policy given to aggression. Geneva, Corsica, and Poland do not live in security from the false values prevalent in the cities and capitals of Europe. If they succeed in resisting corrupting influences, they are still subject to the storms of balance-of-power politics. Though relatively sheltered from both refinement and embroilment by her mountainous environment, Geneva is already showing signs of deterioration in her national character and in the sovereignty of her people. Corsica and Poland are being bargained for, bartered, or dismembered by the right of the strongest as if they were merely real estate. The public law of the Empire and the uncompromising independence of many German principalities are stabilizing factors in Europe, but one member of the Empire, Prussia, is involved on the battlefield for high stakes and is a major contributor to the general agitation and violence. Russia, deliberately infected by Peter II with the customs of more sophisticated nations and therefore without authentic national character, finds her people the submissive instrument of an aggressive foreign policy. England, so often praised for respecting and protecting individual life, property, freedom of conscience and religion, does not have liberty in the sense of popular sovereignty. Her people, enslaved like those of Spain and France, in a few years will by a policy of conquest have advanced far along the road to moral and physical decline. Suffering like the Spartans from the fatigues of war, they will be outdone by new nations in which the public force is still relatively vigorous.

Rousseau's hopes for Switzerland, Corsica, and Poland were based largely on his faith in the individual's investment in the nation, the total giving of self and goods which as in early Rome was the source of power. His explanation of the decline of Venice, Spain, and France rests on their abandonment of the principle. They more than England have destroyed within themselves society's motive force. In his prediction of England's ruin, the most serious consideration is moral degradation, basically the loss of liberty as the active participation of citizens in the community or sovereign. For Rousseau this means that the foundations of her liberty are unsound, that the outreaching might of her foreign policy is near collapse.

CHAPTER X

LEGITIMACY AND NATIONAL POWER

BRIEF DESCRIPTIVE REMARKS HAVE already been made about most of the works to be discussed in this chapter. Only a few words need be said about Rousseau's *Extrait du projet de paix perpétuelle* and his *Etat de guerre*. The first, a shortened version of the Abbé de Saint-Pierre's *Projet de paix perpétuelle* (1712), an ambitious plan for a peace-keeping union of European nations, was prepared by Rousseau after 1756. In the *Confessions* Rousseau says he performed this task at the suggestion of Mme Dupin, who out of respect for the good Abbé wanted to revive the "stillborn" works of her friend (Pléiade, 1: 407). The *Extrait* appeared in 1761. The *Jugement* [1] designed to accompany it was not published until 1782. The *Etat de guerre* was probably written during the period 1756-1758. It was never completed, although the fragments of the manuscript have been edited and printed in twentieth-century editions of Rousseau's political writings (3: 601-16). All three studies, often neglected in the past, contribute to an understanding of Rousseau's political system, especially of the relationship he sees between the internal structure of the nation and the pressures bearing upon it from abroad.

From Rousseau's views on history and the descriptions of nations which have been assembled from his statements, the

---

[1] Hereafter the *Extrait du projet de paix perpétuelle* and the *Jugement sur le projet de paix perpétuelle* are referred to respectively as *Paix perpétuelle* and *Jugement*. All citations in this chapter, unless otherwise indicated, are to the Pléiade edition of the *Œuvres complètes*.

evidence is convincing that he deliberately sought through study a liberating displacement in time and space. This was not, however, an abdication of his own century. In a sense his attitude is analogous to that of Saint-Preux, who, during his voyage and after a storm has stranded the crew on the Island of Tinian, expresses his love of solitude, his regret at being separated from Julie, and his wonder at the fatal desperation with which men seek again the bonds of civilization: "I came upon a second abandoned island more unknown, still more charming than the first [Juan Fernández] and on which the cruelest kind of accident almost confined us forever. I was the only one perhaps whom so sweet an exile did not frighten; am I not from now on an exile wherever I am? I saw in this delightful and fearsome place what human industry can attempt in order to remove civilized man from a solitude in which he lacks nothing and to immerse him again in an abyss of new needs" (2: 414, 1584, *Nouvelle Héloïse*). Rousseau's unfettering, time-transcending concern with non-European cultures, with more vigorous societies, ends always in a similar reluctant return and application of new insights to the problems of eighteenth-century Europe.

In his opinion many of his contemporary writers, because of their confining obsession with one kind of civilization, overlook the concept of change as it applies to nations; therefore they neglect the principles that determine the course of empire. For Rousseau, material circumstance is a prime mover both in his theory of the origin, rise, and fall of states, and in his account of the internal and external evolution of many nations of Africa, America, Asia, and Europe. Iron and wheat, the arts of metallurgy and agriculture, have been the big factors in advancing society. Europe, since it had soil fertile in wheat and rich in ore, was civilized more continually and systematically, if not sooner, than the other continents (3: 172, *Second discours*). In Europe, the chance arrangement of mountains, seas, and rivers determines the boundaries and therefore the number and size of nations. In a way, the "political order" of this part of the world is the "work of nature" (3: 570, *Paix perpétuelle*). Topography, climate, and material resources predestine each of these nations to unending rivalry. The so-called balance of power, which statesmen so shrewdly attempt to manipulate, is in fact another circumstance of nature, one which goes its own way in spite of the plans of men: "This balance subsists, it needs only itself to be preserved without anyone meddling with it; and even if it were broken for a moment on one side, it would reestablish itself soon on the other; so that if princes, whom one has accused of aspiring to universal monarchy, have really had that aspiration, they showed thereby more ambition than genius." The fact is that no king in Europe is superior enough in strength to become master. This balance is beyond human control. It is a natural force. It "was never established by anyone," and "no one has ever done anything intentionally which preserved it" (3: 570).

Most historians, too, Rousseau complains, neglect the national character which follows from the state's problem-solving efforts to adjust to the accidents of nature. Rome perhaps represents for Rousseau the most complete progression of moral causes contributing to decline. Physical necessity leads the way as man by reacting perfects his reasoning and by his solutions contributes to the moral advance or decline of the nation. Circumstances force the community to see alternatives and make decisions, but circumstances offer no guideposts. The processes of history lead to liberty or enslavement without preference for one or the other. In fact, by Rousseau's own account the odds favor enslavement. Yet there is not the least doubt about the value of liberty in Rousseau's mind. Repeatedly in his evaluations that standard is the ultimate measure. The Kafirs in their ignorance are at present incapable of it. In Poland, measures must be taken to raise the civic awareness of the peasants. The Spartans were at fault when they valued liberty less than their homeland. Rome's strength resided in her great collective will freely expressed through her assemblies. Venice, Spain, Prussia, Russia, and France have already lost their liberty. England erroneously believes she retains hers. Geneva is in danger because of encroachments by the Council of Twenty-five.

Liberty thus used as a standard is independent of history in one sense. Physical circumstance left unassisted yields liberty only by chance. The view of history as adjustment to necessity can offer no distinct criterion in itself. Rousseau ultimately derives his norm not from history but from the state of nature, from the hypothesized original condition of man. This natural liberty, remote from reason as duty or obligation, is essentially the rule of blind instinct. This claim inherent in man, the sentiment, natural to him, to fulfill his own self, to reach the limits of his natural capacity, permits the lawgiver to recognize in history activities compatible with nature — occasional cooperation with other men in the search for food and shelter, the simple joys of family existence, resistance to the will of the strongest, the right of the first occupant to land and goods to satisfy subsistence need, association between men on the basis of legitimacy, the right to revolution when legitimacy has failed. Derived from both nature and history, the concept of civil liberty or legitimacy was found gropingly as Rousseau studied the modifications given to natural liberty in hypothesized societies existing prior to civil society and in specific nations of history. If Rousseau is inclined to insist that natural freedom and civil freedom are equivalent in liberty, since each person seeks a convention by which he "obeys only himself and remains as free as he was before," civil freedom is unquestionably natural freedom artificially restored and maintained within the structures needed to counterbalance the enslaving forces of existing society (3: 360, *Contrat social*). There is, however, still another condition imposed both on natural freedom and on civil freedom, one overlooked in the past. Adjustment of liberty to the internal situation of particular communities is not Rousseau's sole concern. The concept of liberty is modified further by his understanding of the external conditions under which nations must survive.

First, communications threaten the integrity of a nation's character. The crusades, commerce, navigation, long sea voyages, the discovery of the Indies, all of these events caused an exchange among the nations of their vices but not their virtues and undermined for each the "customs which are appropriate to their climate and to the constitution of their government" (2: 964, *Préface de Narcisse*). Second, each nation must compete relentlessly in the world arena of rivaling states. The Abbé de Saint-Pierre by mistake used as precedent for his peace project the so-called grand design of Henry IV to organize Europe on a permanent basis, but this project was in fact a French scheme to gain hegemony at the expense of Austria: "all he [Henry] needed to do to become the most powerful himself was to divide the patrimony of the only ruler more powerful than he." While promoting his plan Henry made preparations to have the force to win at the proper moment by filling his treasury and his arsenals. Usurpation, revolt, invasion, and "mutual animosity" rather than "fraternity," describe the relationship of the European nations: "Let us therefore admit that the state existing among the powers of Europe is in fact a state of war, and that all the specific and limited treaties between some of these powers are more like fleeting truces than true peace" (3: 565-69, 598-99, *Paix perpétuelle*).

Conflict is an inherent part of national existence. Men make up the state. Land nourishes men; it must be sufficient therefore to provide for them: "There should be as many inhabitants as the land can support." Such an optimal proportion determines the "maximum strength of a given number of people." This ratio in turn fosters or discourages certain types of war. If a nation has too much land, the tilling of it by its people will be inadequate, and yet its yield will still be abundant. That nation to keep its excess land will have to fight defensive wars. If a nation does not have enough land, it is dependent on its neighbors for what its agriculture cannot provide. The cause of offensive wars is then present. It must subjugate and thus change its position or become nothing (3: 389, *Contrat social*). Under these basic pressures the forces for stability, including the Peace of Westphalia, the public law of Germany, and the defense of freedom by the princes of the Empire, are far from sufficient to assure peace. The state of war exists, not only because of physical forces — proximity of the nations of Europe and differences in their size, wealth, and force — but because of acquisitive foreign policies, the reflection of the nations' moral conditions.

Rousseau's solution to the problem of survival under these grim conditions is new. He repeatedly discusses the state's means of resistance. Materialistic science and art, so often seen as sources of power in the eighteenth century, are for him destructive of character and incapable of building the economic health and moral defenses of the nation. The swarms of barbarians who inundated Europe and Asia were united in their goals; therefore they dared attack and succeeded in defeating nations noted for their wealth, industry, commerce, and military discipline. Conquest, however, is not a sound basis for survival, either, since the victors are always corrupted by the conquered. Rather than technology or conquest, the science of freedom is for Rousseau the most solid foundation of national power. Defense of freedom is the driving force which explains, for example, the successes of Rome against powerful enemies.

The term liberty has two senses in Rousseau's account of nations. When he talks of the freedom of the Spartans, the Romans, the Genevans, the Corsicans, the Poles, and the English, he means by liberty, first, the individual's association with the state either as part of the sovereign or as subject under the sovereign; and second, the sentiment of belonging to one nation, a meaning less reasoned, more instinctive and emotional than the first. Liberty as association has many facets and relationships, including the contractual formula, the sovereign, the legislator, the government. Liberty as emotional attachment relates to customs, religious beliefs, and rites. It is my conviction that each of these fundamental aspects of Rousseau's doctrine bears the mark of the external pressures which figured extensively in his references to most areas of the globe.

In Rousseau's account of the event, the formation of society by contract presupposes the state of war. Otherwise, the strongest members of the community could not be induced to invent the compact. An objection to the theory of mutual giving of themselves by all parties to the agreement is that the strongest by this procedure seems at first glance to be more favored than the weak, since he has by contract converted more possessions into property. But the advantage is not real. The justification for the poor, much clearer, is to be found in the civil protection they receive. They are no longer subject to oppression by men stronger than they. From the moment the compact goes into effect they depend no longer, or at least in smaller degree, upon force and are sustained in their rights by laws of the community of which they are a part. The logic by which the strongest can accept the contract is much more difficult, since no such advantage obtains for him. He is in effect asked to give up the "right" of the strongest, the right to exploit the weak, the natural claim that goes with his power. The pact hampers his efforts to acquire new wealth. He must forego the individual sway he previously held over weaker neighbors. The argument of self-preservation by which Rousseau explains the willingness of each person to accept the compact — "I suppose men to have reached that moment when the obstacles which stand in the way of their preservation in the state of nature effectively resist the resources which each individual may use to maintain himself in that state" — can in fact be meaningful to the strongest only if there is a threat from a community rather than an individual, whether that community is already formed or is about to be formed (3: 360, *Contrat social*). Rousseau leaves no doubt about the situation. Anyone outside the first society would have to join it or form another to resist it: "It is necessary to imitate it or be swallowed up by it" (3: 603, *Etat de guerre*). Additional communities are formed in an atmosphere of threat from established communities: "One can easily see how the formation of a single society makes the establishment of all the others indispensable, and how to resist united forces, it was necessary for other men to unite in turn" (3: 178, *Second discours*). The strongest accepted society because its invention had become part of the inevitable chain of events. With the appearance of the first pact there could be no holding or turning back.

The atmosphere of war is present in the contract's generation of the power needed for survival. By the oath of the Corsicans, the citizens swear to "live and die" for the homeland. Citizenship is automatically awarded those patriots who have already struggled to deliver "their nation at the price of blood." Their union in defense of the nation must create, Rousseau says, the public force present in Sparta but even more characteristic of Rome: "Sparta did not even have over Rome the advantage inherent in small states of firmly withstanding attacks from the greatest nations, reversals in fortune, and the approach of complete ruin.... Always ready to die for his country, a Spartan loved the homeland so tenderly that to save it he would have sacrificed liberty itself. But the Romans never supposed that the homeland could outlive liberty or even glory" (3: 542-43, *Parallèle entre Sparte et Rome*). If one purpose of the pact is to establish freedom and equality by removing any one individual or private group from control, the power generated by this kind of union is in the Roman context of survival an equally important consideration.

A third characteristic of the pact is the artificiality of the creature it forms. The force of the nation is not absolute but relative, an attribute which helps explain the state of war itself. The view that the nation is a product of artifice rather than of nature, and thus is beyond what is human in its capacities, a view developed also by Hobbes, is supported by evidence Rousseau draws from experience. He asks how states so solidly established can collide with one another: "Shouldn't their own constitution maintain them in eternal peace?" His answer stresses down-to-earth observations about international relations. The state, faced with the necessity of constantly gauging its strength, must look to its borders for an indication of its status. The power situation abroad is the measure of each nation's domestic power: "The state... being an artificial body has no fixed measure, the size which is appropriate to it is indefinite, it can always increase, it feels weak so long as there are others stronger. Its security, its preservation require that it become more powerful than all of its neighbors.... Thus the size of the political body being purely relative, it is forced to compare itself continually with others in order to know itself; it depends on everything which surrounds it and must be interested in everything that takes place there... it becomes small or great, weak or strong, accordingly as its neighbor expands or contracts, grows strong or becomes weak" (3: 604-05, *Etat de guerre*). All nations, but especially a new nation like Corsica or a nation being reformed like Poland, must recognize and withstand the destructive currents of this competitive maelstrom.

The logic of the first convention, its generation of power, and its artificiality relate to the state of war. The general will formed by this association is in part defined by the same hostile atmosphere. A people is free for Rousseau to the extent that its will is the sovereign, the legislative source of the nation. In replying to the question of what national survival ultimately means in the ever-present conflict between states, Rousseau discounts the importance of the prince's role or of the position of any other private person or corporation. The essence of the state is the agreement which joins together "land, money, men, all that is comprised within the confines of the state." The enduring strength of Rome lay in its successfully resisting efforts to represent and divide this will to union. Voices of all the classes were heard directly through the various assemblies. The warnings Rousseau issues to Geneva, Corsica, and England concern safeguards for the legislative. He advises the Poles that a hereditary crown could never be sufficiently subordinate, that the health of Poland depends on the nation's "entering again [upon the death of the king] into all of its rights, thus recapturing a new vigor." On the integrity of the sovereign people depends the life or death of any nation, but particularly of Poland because of her embattled position. War is for Rousseau the extreme case which probes to the roots the validity of the nation's constitution. This is so because the function of war is to destroy the collective will formed by compact. It is in this sense that the state may be "killed" without a single member of the state dying (3: 357, *Contrat social;* p. 608, *Etat de guerre*). If adulterated by private interests, the bonds of union may prove insufficient and collapse under the stress of actual conflict. If pure in its expression of the national genius, the union will be more likely to hold.

The moral worth of the sovereign and its will to survive are tested by the might of other nations. The limits of the nation's legislative arm are likewise set by the state of war, by the moral vacuum existing just outside each country's frontier. In international affairs, no state can see justice except from the point of view of its own interest. In matters of foreign policy, if public deliberations were to take place, the decision by a state's collective will would doubtless be in error if judged by any transcendent standard. The will is general only for one community, valid therefore only in that framework and not in the context of other societies which have their own wills. This solipsism of each nation with regard to others explains the short duration of treaties, the clauses of which are violated before their ink has dried. It explains the little effect produced by the rules of international law, "chimeras even more weak than the law of nature," which "speaks at least to the hearts of individuals, whereas the decisions of international law, having no other guarantee than the utility of the party which submits to it, are respected only so long as self-interest confirms them" (3: 610, *Etat de guerre*). Even a well-governed nation could therefore conduct an unjust war (3: 246, *Economie politique*).

The concepts of compact and sovereignty have been seen to be closely related to the state's exposed condition; the first by its logic, its generation of power, its artificiality; the second by its vulnerability and its limited view of justice. The concept of the legislator shows a similar influence. He must neglect none of the aspects of the nation's situation, for each may affect its survival. If Rousseau imitates the great lawgivers of antiquity, Moses, Lycurgus, Numa, he very clearly goes beyond them in his attention to the complexity of national problems under hostile conditions. He stresses particularly the pressures on the nation that a legislator must anticipate: "The state must give itself a certain basis for solidity, in order to withstand the shocks it must certainly experience and the efforts it will be forced to make in sustaining itself: for all peoples have a sort of centrifugal force by which they act continually against one another and tend to grow at the expense of their neighbors, like the vortices of Descartes. Thus the feeble risk being swallowed up, and scarcely any can preserve itself except by entering along with all the others into a sort of balance of power which makes the pressure almost equal on all sides" (3: 388, *Contrat social*). Within this atmosphere of survival, the legislator considers the size of the nation, its location, topography, soil, resources, and genius, and fits to them laws determining government, economy, military force, and foreign policy. If he errs, if he "assumes a principle different from the one which arises from the nature of things... one will see the laws gradually grow weak, the constitution change, and the state will be continually agitated until it is destroyed or changed and invincible nature again reigns" (3: 393). In this context the ultimate standard is survival. Liberty for most states, not all of them, can be the best means to that end.

The power generated by the association of free individuals is neutral, a potential for good or evil. The nation's legislative force, if not alienated or divided, expresses the nation's good in laws recommended by the legislator. The government, as presented by Rousseau in the *Contrat social*, usually appears as a corrupting force which, unaware of its mission as outlined in the *Economie*, instead uses the nation's power without reference to the collective will. Although he does not approve of the sovereign's interference in the executive function, the control of the early Roman people over government as well as over legislation helps explain for him that people's preservation of their freedom. The leaders of Venice, after usurping sovereign authority, succeeded next in reducing the participation of the aristocracy in government. In Spain, Prussia, Russia, and France, sovereignty as well as government soon passed into the hands of a few. Geneva, Corsica, and Poland by a system of checks and balances must prevent such subversion. Rather than eliminate the *liberum veto* and confederation in Poland, Rousseau seeks ony to modify them. They help guard against encroachments by the executive. All governments have the inclination to undermine gradually the general will; thus they reduce public unity until mercenaries are needed as much to control citizens as to guard the nation's borders. In their declarations of war and peace, princes rarely have the public interest in mind. Most of them follow in international affairs short-range rather than real interests: "A prince who submits his cause to the hazards of war is aware that he is running risks, but he is less impressed by them than by the advantages he hopes to gain... if he is powerful he counts on his strength, if weak, he counts on his alliances; sometimes it is useful for him to purge ill tempers within the state, to weaken unmanageable subjects... and the clever politician knows how to draw advantage from his own defeats.... The ministers need war to make themselves necessary, to give the prince troubles from which he cannot extricate himself without them, to bring about the ruin of the state if necessary rather than the loss of their position" (3: 594-95, *Jugement*. The sophist of any royal court prefers "a large territory and a few impoverished subjects" to a "happy and flourishing people." Under the regime proposed in theory by Rousseau, the prince would be responsible to the people if his foreign policy (the domain of the executive since it consists of specific acts) should jeopardize individual liberty and national survival, the ultimate concerns of the general will.

If the legislator has been successful, the laws he has created tie each individual to the general will and make of union a potent force. The very perfection of his laws, however, may cause divisive rather than cohesive attitudes among the people, since respect for wisdom, an appeal to reason, gradually changes to curiosity, questioning, and doubt about the bases of law. The true legislator, therefore, uses a principle stronger than reason. He binds the emotions with national customs, public games, spectacles associated with the national past, and exclusive religious rites, ceremonies, and beliefs. By such means Moses succeeded in giving to his nation a will which outlived the body of the nation for five thousand years and which still lives. His aim was to make of a wandering, servile multitude "a free people." The Arabs and Persians, too, owed much of their solidarity to shared religious beliefs. Liberty means for Rousseau in this context the sense of being separate, distinct, and unified as a people, the fostering of "manners and customs incompatible with those of other nations" (3: 957, *Gouvernement de Pologne*).

The mutual surrendering of men with all of their goods and forces to the community produces spiritual and material strength for resisting or conquering an enemy. The will formed in this creative act must continue to express the national genius discovered by the legislator and voiced by the people. If the legislative process peculiar to liberty is hindered or aborted by government, the continuing sense of collective creativity which generates survival power is lost and the prior and persisting pressure from outside brings dissolution of the nation. Each aspect of liberty as defined by Rousseau — contract, sovereign, legislator, prince, and national tradition — reflects this state of war.

When assembled, Rousseau's comments about various aspects of ancient and modern societies provide a general and often clear view of his understanding of the continents. His analyses of regions of Africa and America — their cultures, resources, or policies — show why they are exploited lands. In terms of the physical and moral evolution of their countries, the Middle East and Asia appear as either the stronghold of despots or the domain of religiously oriented peoples. Rousseau takes little interest in the potential of any of these territories except as areas of conflict for European states. Some of the nations of Europe's past, particularly Sparta and Rome, are made to stand through the brilliance of their civil liberty in sharp contrast with European societies of his time. The latter either have already totally sacrificed their freedom or are tempted like the Genevans to forsake liberty while uncritically embracing the dubious advantage of commercial and industrial prosperity. Predicting England's immediate financial ruin and loss of liberty, Rousseau seems seriously to question the continuance of the rising might which was already giving her preponderance in Europe. Similarly, because of their leaders' policies of conquest and usurpation, he is led to discount the lasting importance of Prussia and Russia in the European balance of power. He somewhat astutely evaluates the roles of the Peace of Westphalia and of the German Empire as stabilizing forces in Europe. At the same time, because of the colonial goals and the schemes for hegemony pursued by the dynasties of Spain, France, Austria, and England, his realism forces him to see Europe as a jungle of conflicting interests. The world, through seapower, is the theater of war among powerful but declining nations, nations spiritually decadent and moribund in their leviathan thirst for territory and power.

Given this view and his requirements for a cohesive national spirit and sound civil structure, Rousseau, more out of conviction than for belittlement of the nations of his day, must find Corsica (and later Poland) the only country in Europe still "capable of legislation" (3: 391, *Contrat social*). But his principles, if incompatible with more prosaic projects for superficial reform, are not conceived and formulated in a vacuum. Although he rather traditionally originates his standards in a hypothetical state of nature, they are later closely allied with the framework of history and international politics he has built from his own observations and from accounts and reports by ancient and contemporary writers.

Man in his most primitive condition lives in isolation. He depends on the elements and animals. He has natural liberty. Later, men assemble informally without adopting any system of authority. Through rivalry the life of each person is threatened. For preservation of themselves, men then form civil society by means of an initial agreement acceptable to all members of the community. The equivalent of natural liberty is in this way reestablished by political instruments guaranteeing to each participant rights which are nearly uniform and therefore limited but which permit natural capacities to speak. This is not the only modification of natural liberty. At this stage it is not just a matter of safeguarding the individual and his rights to cooperation, happiness, and goods on the domestic level. One society gives rise to many more, and the life of each nation is constantly threatened either physically or morally. Rousseau's information about the evolutions and relationships of numerous nations of history provides him with the perspectives and insights he needs to understand this predicament and to discover some of the causes for the rise and fall of nations, some of the reasons for their success or failure in the struggle for survival.

Certain nations offer evidence of physical influence: Rome's encirclement by powerful enemies, which underlay the integrity of her collective will, her inevitable policy of conquest, the subsequent decline of her free assemblies; the fall of the Mexican empire, determined in part by lack of iron; the healthy influence of the central position of the German empire on the European equilibrium; the advantageous location of Switzerland, which has slowed her loss of liberty; the hindrance of size to any projects to establish free institutions for Corsica and Poland.

Other nations indicate the passage by moral stages from national integrity and liberty to an object-oriented, materialistic, enslaved society, especially Egypt, Persia, Athens, and imperial Rome. Sparta and republican Rome, early citadels of liberty, hold lessons and warnings for liberty's more doubtful, modern champions, Geneva and England. The cohesive force of custom, ceremony, and religion is best felt in his treatment of the Hebrew nation, Persia, Sparta, Rome, Arabia, and Venice. In many of the lands he discusses, liberty has been threatened from within by instruments which have undermined the people's participation in the legislative process: dictatorship, originally used by Rome as an emergency measure, and excessive use of the representative principle by Venice, Geneva, Poland, and England. The difficulties that free institutions encounter in competing within the hostile environment of the balance of power are illustrated in his descriptions of Corsica, Poland, and England.

The basic principles of Rousseau's concept of civil liberty are worked out within the context of the state of war that his knowledge of history has imposed on his thinking. The liberty-power-survival nexus, characterizing beleaguered Rome, permeates the logic by which the strongest accepts the contract, explains the union's capacity for generating power, and underlies the danger to all countries implicit in the nation's artificial and therefore limitlessly expanding will and structure. The object of war, destruction of a state's ability to survive, helps identify the sovereign, for rather than any partial will, like that of king or representative assembly, only the people's collective will may be so totally vulnerable. The infallibility of that sovereign's justice, moreover, is terminated without equivocation by the chaos of conflicting interests lying beyond each nation's boundaries. It is also partly in the name of survival, as well as for individual and collective freedom, that government is made subordinate to the sovereign and that the wisdom of the law is buttressed by the stronger cohesive force arising from common customs and beliefs. The legislator's task is all the more complex because of the demands the state of war places on his understanding and skill. If he fails to match principle with environment, the death of the state necessarily follows. Even his choice of moment to bring the nation into being must be carefully gauged, for the country capable of free institutions must from its inception have the force to resist "a sudden invasion," to defend itself alone against each of its neighbors, or "to use the help of one to repulse the other" (3: 390, *Contrat social*).

Desiring to escape the values of the declining nations of Europe and to find modern bases for society in which homeland, freedom, and glory, as in Rome, are inseparably bound together, Rousseau produces concepts of contract, sovereignty, legislator, government, and religion which make personal liberty through collective will an end in itself, but which simultaneously turn this private liberty, through the spiritual and physical power it holds, into an instrument of survival to defend the nation against opinion from abroad and against foreign political and military pressure.

Chapter XI

THE UNIQUELY EVOLVING SELF

IT IS A HUMBLING EXPERIENCE to try to trace the patterns of Rousseau's feelings and thoughts, to weigh the images he uses to express them, to find the shifting and multiple meanings which underlie his words and give them their power of renewal. The clues to interpretation he forces upon us in the autobiographical works do not relieve the frustration that troubles him and all men in their efforts at intimate communication. The barriers to communication are at times of his own creation, for the more he tries to be his own analyst, the more we are compelled by his own request and style to find deeper answers, to see him as the object to be observed, the botanist become plant. Faced with the task of evaluating each nuance of expression, each variation in the returning themes, their new temporal perspective, and the wealth of accumulated feeling stored within them, the writer must often be satisfied with limited conclusions, with hypotheses gathered from the prevailing drift and direction of Rousseau's attitudes and tenets. I can do little more than hope that my particular approach may have brought to view in a way clearer than before a number of the facets of a most complex and controversial figure and doctrine.

In the *Confessions* Rousseau denies the importance of so-called universal patterns of behavior. Each man's store of feelings can never be duplicated, and the autobiographer must try to present himself in such abundant detail and in so individually expressive a style that the reader is forced to contrast his own life with that of the informant, to see differences, to become aware of what is peculiar, private, and often unfathomable in motivation. Most shared experiences (the several ages of man, for example) under close scrutiny reveal rich variation. In a sense each of us is struggling against other persons, institutions, all the elements of environment which in their inflexibility inhibit the complete unfolding and self-realization of our psyches. Nature, our endowment, and history, the social past and present in which we are submerged, wage constant warfare and become compromise — the everyday lives we bear, to which we conform out of pleasure, comfort, ambition, or fear. Aspirations for love and friendship remain pure only in feeling, in the secret affinities between two or three persons which become timeless in memory: Jean-Jacques on his knees before an Italian housewife, the day at Tournes, Madame de Warens and Rousseau at Les Charmettes in the early mother-son relationship, certain moments of the Madame d'Houdetot affair, moments which are called dreamlike only because of the coarser, intruding life of matter-of-fact to which we must make sacrifices. This kind of affective betrayal, known to the sensitive self, is always present in Rousseau, a new form of interior castle he has opened, more fully to modern readers perhaps with their interest in the psychologically complex, than to many readers of his own day, used to a more aphoristic account of motivation.

The belief that a man may attain moral justification on private grounds is in turn also crushed, according to Rousseau, by the refusal of most men to enter another person's world of values. Similarly, the most idealistic and loyal citizen is soon intimidated by the hypocrisy, the greed, and the struggle for power which destroy or sully the inner vision of what a patriot should be. Only truthseeking remains, the penetration of mankind which permits the sincere individual to see how society gradually lost its soul. Curiosity, intellect, which unfortunately gave man materialistic ends and a problem-solving view of the physical world, can nevertheless become the servant and ally of the natural genius. Unlike most men, who are locked in the present, the genius alone is both in and above time, can see man's moral abdication and death. Utilizing his art to reveal his personal struggle, the visionary frees other men to see their predicament — the destruction of uniqueness which is latent in their endless discontent, their craving for amusement, work, and travel, their repeated flight to find meaning outside themselves.

The perspective which best affords relief from such suffering is one of looking back. The real Geneva of Rousseau's youth, the real Les Charmettes were for the experiencing Rousseau filled with trouble and the desire to escape. Pressures from everyday reality (the ill-tempered master, the sexual appetites of Madame de Warens) disturbed those periods, eventually brought them to a close. Only in retrospect, with the distance provided by long absence, did they become idealizations. The impotence of man, then, is his inability to bring his ideals into the present, to transform through action the matter-of-fact. Felicity should not be simply a past recreated with omissions and distortions, a flight from reality. The man who is partly free through his reveries must through the flame of emotionality reach and stir the layers of feeling held within each self, if its expansiveness, buried deeply in the past life of the individual and in the history of the race, is to be released.

The total effect of the *Confessions* is in the last analysis largely defeat, because what Rousseau has become is not his basic self but a compromise. He is what society, law, and government have by leveling produced. He has escaped perhaps more than other men, but his plea for understanding presupposes a vision of self and of mankind which is perhaps impossible of fulfillment even in the future. His desperate effort at communication stems from more than the need for personal victory, which his acceptance by the reader might give him over Grimm and others. He is asking for the rebirth of each human being. His memoirs are not silent as to this unique self, the Rousseau that might have been. Through references to his earlier works, the *Confessions* point to the philosophy and statecraft which by new institutions could have made him a complete individual, unique not as oddity, as stranger to his surrounding culture, but an Emile of the future who knows self-realization in the company of other men living their own very personal selves.

Each of the works I have studied has its own organizing principle which contributes to this plan for recapturing the full potential of each human life. Already at mid-century the *Discours sur les sciences et les arts* calls for a new science and a new art, a statecraft to guide the rechanneling of knowledge toward one predominant goal, the freedom of man. This goal is placed in opposition to civilization as money, power, talent, or the climb to success according to exterior, superficial standards. These standards, for example, force even a Voltaire to please existing taste rather than to express his deepest insights. They gradually turn healthy, vigorous nations, conscious of the solidarity of their peoples, into characterless quantities of men without unifying spirit. Domestic and foreign policy is flailed in Rousseau's attack on the economists of national wealth, the Pettys and Melons who measure a man's worth by his simple beast-of-burden price rather than by his value as a subject and a citizen. No detail of human life and its environment can be left unnoticed by the natural genius, the counselor to princes, if necessity — human passion and the force of events — is not to destroy the nation by relentless, non-humanly-oriented pressures. A sheltering providence for each individual is not a given part of man's political universe. Man must provide for himself by placing moral and political art and science at the summit of the arts and sciences.

This first principle, a new statecraft grounded in human need and circumstance, permeates Rousseau's thinking because he believes that man cannot depend on nature to survive. Man is in history, and history's currents and direction, described in the *Discours sur l'origine et les fondements de l'inégalité*, must be plotted and counterbalanced if each individual is to attain virtue in the deepest sense, that is, to join his private person to society without diminishing his natural gifts. The downward spiral of blind necessity, ending in revolution, must be redirected to permit future reconciliation between nature and society. As the *Second discours* unfolds, we are made aware of the accumulation of forces operating on man's evolution. Progressively, from each of its stages is abstracted a form of positive behavior consistent with the notion of the original, isolated, potent, primitive being. Man's first problem-solving encounter with necessity, with cataclysmic environment, must be limited. Curiosity uncurbed takes man too far outside himself, makes him become his knowledge. Utility fends off necessity and humanizes curiosity, leaving man whole but without the security of the first timeless state. Although man is no longer alone, he has a possible guidepost. His social goal has been defined with respect to all future man-to-man relationships: a utilitarian participation with other men, but never at the expense of the individual self. The golden age later supplements this criterion. Man's active search for pleasure is not all bad, only its tendency to comparison, to judgment on the basis of superficial traits — goods, beauty, talents. A family designed to shelter and encourage growth in each individual is a form of happiness consistent with *amour de soi*, love of self. Similarly, the state of war, the urge to dominate other selves by aggressivity and the wealth and power it has accumulated, can be reduced to proportions consistent with basic nature. The need to possess does not have to become the Hobbesian right to everything but can exert itself through labor as the valid right to subsistence of the first occupant. Later, the reconciliation of nature and social history is expressed through a civil order based on unanimous agreement: the safeguard to individual liberty is the promise of a totally selfless (that is, artificial) instrument, legitimate collectivity. As legitimacy falters, becomes despotism, history offers a final recourse, revolution. This reassertion of passionate liberty or nature offers the possibility of a new reconciliation of society with the private self, whether through chance or through the vision of the political genius and his statecraft.

The *Discours sur les sciences et les arts* shows the need for a new science. The *Second discours* stresses the definition of its object, virtue, and the problem of joining nature to society in a way that controls necessity and prevents the unwinding of society into decadence. The *Economie politique* underlines just as heavily the weight of history in Rousseau's thinking. History involves men in action, in competing with one another and with environment. As a result of this striving, the deeds of one man, the prince, have always prevailed. With realism, then, Rousseau must turn partly to him for the *Economie*'s solution to the problem of legitimacy, since only the prince can effect the change. He alone has the strength required and sufficient motivation in his love and capacity for leadership. Rousseau assumes that no prince who has suffered the influence of the *philosophes* can believe in divine right or in Platonic higher reason as sanctions of authority. These doctrines have been associated repeatedly in public opinion with arbitrariness, private ambition, myopic policies which destroy the nation.

But the ruler's thirst for control of a nation's fate remains. He can therefore be led to see the great potential for power lying within the concept of popular sovereignty, to understand that stronger than his personal will is the will of a collectivity sanctioning laws its members know in terms of the public good. His execution of law, whether in matters of domestic or foreign policy, can then be truly in the name of a group which is united by the prince's most powerful weapon, his own and the legislator's moral and political science and art, a group made one by common customs, inspired lawgiving, education, and civil religion. Every will is then consolidated behind the prince. Rather than to dazzle the people by the brilliance of his court or his conquests, his task is to win confidence, the surest way to power: "Respect liberty, and your power will increase every day; do not ever go beyond your rights, and soon they will be without limits" (3: 258, *Economie*).

The ruler no longer has to prod a reluctant, senseless rabble for his narrowly personal gain. He may experience the total executive power that can come from dedication and responsibility, may guide an enduring, coordinated, and therefore endlessly potent, lifelike machine. Selfless agent of the national will and interest, with the whole might of the nation at his fingertips, he nevertheless knows that the secret of such sheer power is in his own virtue. His power resides in his very ability to wield awesome might by touching the other wills never quantitatively, as in the natural state of war, but only legitimately through application of laws already agreed upon by the civil collectivity, itself an almost sacred mystery combining nature and society.

The *Economie* sees the nation from the point of view of the executive matter-of-fact, of domestic measures to be followed and attitudes to be induced in order to permit a carefully legislated structure to win out against necessity. In this context of survival a major concern of the prince is foreign policy. The *Lettre à d'Alembert* makes international relations a central theme, in this instance the effect of foreign cultures on a native culture. Through the mechanics of influence, carefully defined by Rousseau, a nation may be gutted from within by the impact of institutions borrowed from abroad. Rousseau insists that there is no one standard for measuring the value of a people's national spirit. Genevan character is something lived, a past of flesh and blood, not to be enhanced from outside. Relativism must be maintained in our judgments about a people. Just as no one person can, when viewed in his totality, be ranked below another, so no one nation can be said to be inferior. Its culture is an intrinsic value, for it unifies a people, guarantees its liberty, expresses its soul.

The *Nouvelle Héloïse* opens up the question of a new source of atrophy within the national organism. Family life must move in two directions, outward in support of society, the artificial unit, and inward in support of each of its members, its natural units. The family under d'Etange and also under Wolmar is a failure when its structure is considered with reference to the individuals depending on it. The final Julie / Claire / Saint-Preux union overrides the novel's artistically negative close, its implicit protest, and provides in terms of strong emotional attachment and civic and religious leadership the shelter required to bring into full expression the individual potentials of the remaining members of the family.

Emile, resisting the notion of universal man, intensifies the Wolmar theme of education destined to release natural capacity. The individual, led through the steps of man's evolution, acquires at the feeling level the race's experience of isolation, necessity, pleasure, power, agreement, and injustice. The object is to make him aware of the force of each of these elements of his environment, while preventing through habit his falling slave to any of them. Later he becomes a consciously moral being. He is introduced to the traditional fields of knowledge and to religious sentiment and thought, and he learns the habits and attitudes which will save him from necessity's course in each of these domains. He is not free in the sense that he can choose passion over the way prescribed by his tutor. He has been conditioned to choose liberty. If he follows the corrupt way of the society into which he was born, that will not be by a so-called act of free will either. It will be through a flaw in his training, a defect in the tutor's science and art. To the extent that he follows his conditioning against usual environmental influences, his unique nature may be fulfilled. This refusal to be leveled by enslaving corruption imposed from outside automatically gives him the essential qualification of citizenship — independence of will with respect to and in the company of other men, particularly in congregation at the time for making legislative decisions. A member of society, he has become at the same time his own man, able to make a private evaluation of the direction in which the general good lies.

In the *Contrat social* man experiences freedom which is partly natural, partly social. First, the nation is a shelter formed of laws to be obeyed, but where the law does not prescribe, the subject is unrestricted in his *amour de soi*, the preservation of his private endowment, and is unrestrained in his *amour-propre*, his pride, the claims of passion coming from society. Second, as a member of the sovereign actively participating in the formation of law, the citizen is the more effective the more unbound he is by other wills. The character of the nation is continually modified by the evolving demands voiced in assembly by each individual self. With discussion, legitimate insights gained through ego's urge to survive may prevail so long as the source of motivation is in the separated selves. Each legislating self has integrity, diversity of viewpoint, of capacity, and is therefore perfectly consistent with nature although it has become part of a collectivity.

If this doctrine is a form of rationalism, that term does not mean the reason of antiquity, the Platonic absolute, a fixed concept of the whole into which the parts must be made to fit. Rather it represents organistic or mechanistic statecraft. The second term seems preferable to the first, since it avoids any implication that civil society is natural or preformed and suggests very appropiately the adaptiveness of this lifelike machine to a wealth of needs rising out of continuing debate among a multiplicity of natures or selves. Preference is to be given to justice over law. Laws are to change, to be reformed with greater and greater attention to the sentiment of liberty as the individual selves become more informed. Supporting neither liberalism's distrust of the collectivity nor totalitarianism's worship of the will and force of the nation, Rousseau's form of solipsistic structuralism favors individual freedom and sees the inevitability of variants according to time, place, and circumstance and also according to the indwelling potential of the human spirit itself. This approach helps reveal Rousseau's somewhat sociological view of national character, but there is also a deep emphasis on personal uniqueness, its operation in harmony with other individualities, and the infinite richness implied in the diversity of the personal units. Rather than with modern statism's iron-framed whole limiting the parts, or with liberalism's effort to diminish any formative hold of the central authority over the individual, Rousseau seems to speak to a need, perhaps still more modern, for a society which can nurture, adopt, and express the goals of individuals across time as the human psyche itself becomes gradually more conscious of its still hidden recesses of sentiment.

The ultimate source of power for Rousseau is in legislative foundations designed to release this natural capacity, its energy, its ideas and feelings. States based on false principles which warp and diminish the diversity of man, which reduce him to the military function alone or to the status of beast of burden, or which standardize him for any other exterior motive are already declining nations. The true homeland, reconciling nature and society, may find the force to resist history's cycle of necessity, including despotism, revolution, and the threat of enemies practicing an offensive foreign policy. More than any other principle, uniqueness, the freedom to be one's personal self within society, explains Rousseau's moral and political system.

Any loss in integrity of the separate self, any surrender to another self, means also the corruption of the general will. Without the constantly renewed vitality derived from many independently willing selves, the sovereign legislative power, guided by the legislator and the prince, cannot maintain its dynamic vision, must cease to perfect law in the spirit of justice or the evolving national good, must grow irresponsive, static, and must die, a casualty to the conditions of war which surround the nation and accentuate its slightest flaw. All the works I have discussed help us to understand this new dimension, the international orientation of Rousseau's thought. Statecraft, if it dehumanizes man in the sense of controlling his excessively self-limiting passions, is dedicated principally to the restoration of the individual self, first, for its intrinsic worth, the value of the fresh, not-to-be-duplicated pattern for growth in each man, and, second, for the power true individuality produces within the collectivity.

I have been concerned throughout this book with three fundamental levels of Rousseau's thought. First, nature is the primitive origin described in his thought experiment. In the state of nature each man is only potentially whole. He is his own uncompromised self, *amour de soi*, his *pitié* or compassion for others, his perfectibility — all of them undeveloped. In the second stage, perfectibility takes possession of man, warps him by problem-solving, pleasure, wealth, power, and illegitimacy. This is nature as necessity, *amour-propre*, selfish interest reacting to environment. Individual man's potential has been denied by conformism; he has lost his self, the freedom of his uniqueness, his separateness, the liberty that is more basic than life. In despair, he may then in theory exercise his last freedom, regain command of life by suicide (2: 383-84, *Nouvelle Héloïse*). But there is a better way. At a third level, nature or freedom is equated with statecraft. The natural genius, who has escaped necessity, may through this new science and art of statecraft make society a formative but flexible framework capable of sustaining the individual selves. The persisting sense of Rousseau's works is that freedom as science and art, as future action to discover and protect the self, must replace freedom as death or self-destruction in any form, whether fear, hedonism, ambition, quietism, despair, or suicide. This struggle can never end, for virtue means the reconciliation of nature with society in a new sense. In the future the object will not be to compromise nature, to produce the leveled selves of a Julie, a Saint-Preux, a Rousseau, but to transform society, its private and public education, its familial and civil structures, so that it may receive unknown selves, each one unique and therefore indefinable before it appears.

Rousseau's new man is subject, citizen, and natural man. As subject, he obeys religiously the laws that have been prescribed, conscious because of public education that disrespect for law opens the door to rule without law, to the impact of another private will directly on his own, a private will eager to reduce all life to the competition for wealth and power. Dwelling in a small state, he is patriotically responsive to laws which are designed to defend his country from military and cultural aggression. But this is not an excessive patriotism. In spite of his admiration for Rome, ambition for new territory is not a part of Rousseau's doctrine. He has shown effectively that history is strewn with the hulks of nations that have followed that course.

As for culture, the informed subject would not believe in the superiority of his country's spirit over that of another and would not be reluctant to appreciate the artistic production of another nation. He would, however, believe that originality is more favored by national mores and taste than by any rigid, universal standard based on the supposed preeminence of certain preferred cultures. He would believe, too, that to borrow uncritically the art forms of a highly sophisticated nation, without first adapting those forms to the native culture, would represent a serious threat to the nation's collective spirit. For the subject to accept cultural inferiority, to say in effect that a foreign culture is superior to his own, not only is to accept an untruth, but also indicates political decadence, since the soul of a people, from which art must spring, is the life, the mainstay of the nation.

As citizen, the new man is active in prescribing the law. His purpose is never to increase, as an end in itself, the control of the community's law over the individual. The emphasis has always been for Rousseau on the justification of each new law in terms of the protection it affords the individual self. New laws are to replace old ones if the latter have been found unjust — if they increase rather than diminish inequality in possessions, an inequality which can become the means of buying votes and gaining special privilege. The only inequality in power and prestige to be tolerated is that based on individual gifts. The prince, the agent of the sovereign and its law, for example, is to be a prince of merit in the eyes of those who elect him. He must have executive talent and also the will to reign by law alone, leaving the other wills untouched by his private will. The citizen with his zeal for liberty would constantly resist usurpation, any effort by the prince, legislator, or any corporate body, to make the sovereign legislate in behalf of a private interest. But, one might object, this individual zeal for liberty is to be joined with other wills to become collective, the general will, and that general will's dedication to the science and art of freedom means discipline, a restriction on the individual self, an imposed sense of responsibility. Rousseau's answer would have to be that such freedom is consistent with nature, not an imposition. After consultation with legislator and prince, the general will, by the structures it establishes and the disciplines it requires, has returned man to his most natural sentiment and inclination, the thirst for freedom, to be expressed now in a disciplined way — within a legal structure which does not jeopardize the rights of others.

As subject the new man obeys the law and defends the nation, which is essentially its spirit expressed in law. As citizen, the new man, to the extent of his capacity, participates in making laws (and reforming old ones) in the name of a higher standard, justice equated to the guarantee of liberty to each subject. But the sense of Rousseau's reasoning and vocabulary returns repeatedly to the notion that laws are to be held to a minimum. In many areas the law will not prescribe at all, and there the new man may become again natural man. Outside the functions of subject and citizen and as the result of having performed them, he may indulge his own desires with abandon, live only for himself, be (if such is his inclination) like Rousseau of the *Rêveries*. He may choose to enter into association with his fellowmen on an informal basis, as in the second stage of the *Second discours*, but remains free also to neglect that commitment whenever his personal feeling or need dictates. He may assume the burden of father of the family, essentially the burden of designing a particular and protective education to lure forth the personal gifts of his children, to guide those gifts to full development, and to foster in his children only one absolute — the love and habit of liberty. That liberty, natural to primitive man in his isolation, must include, since man lives in an evolving and potentially hostile social environment, an important choice — the child's commitment, once he has reached the age of reason, to respect his own freedom and the freedom of others. The self to be freed is not any one talent or strength susceptible to gradation but the unique combination of gifts held by the individual, the combination which, as a value unto itself, renders absurd any comparison out of pride or envy.

SELECTED BIBLIOGRAPHY

IN THE PREPARATION of this study, the Pléiade and Lahure editions of Rousseau's works, the Vaughan edition of the political writings, and the Dufour-Plan and Leigh editions of his correspondence have been essential sources of information. The opportunity to spend the year 1967-1968 in France permitted me to return to editions of his writings which circulated during his own century. Another advantage was the opportunity to use materials on a subject broader than this book, the concept of international order in eighteenth-century France. I have made no direct effort to relate Rousseau's theories on this question to those of other thinkers of the time, except as Rousseau himself discussed their writings. Indirectly, however, it is certain that my point of view has been influenced by the wider topic, certainly by knowledge of the complexity of its problems, for I had time to use in some of the libraries of Paris, especially the Bibliothèque Nationale and the Bibliothèque de l'Arsenal, materials by pacifists of the era, by major authors, including Montesquieu, Diderot, and Voltaire, by economists and international law theorists such as Quesnay, Turgot, and Necker, and by princes and ministers of the period, including the Marquis de Torcy, Fleury, Malesherbes, Choiseul, and Frederick II.

Among the other institutions whose texts have been used are the Widener and Houghton Libraries at Harvard University, the William Rainey Harper Library of the University of Chicago, the John Hay Library of Brown University, the libraries of the University of California at Berkeley, Davis, and Los Angeles, and the Memorial Library of the University of Wisconsin. Microfilm copies of many important eighteenth-century editions, including most of those related to Rousseau in the Pierpont Morgan collection, were available.

For the person who has a beginning or renewed interest in Rousseau, the collective efforts directed by D. C. Cabeen, *A Critical Bibliography of French Literature*, Vol. 4, *The Eighteenth Century* (1951), and by R. A. Brooks, its *Supplement* (1968), are a useful point of departure. They will introduce him to necessary tools: more extensive bibliographies, periodicals which list or review each year's output on Rousseau; editions of his complete works, of particular works, of his correspondence; biographies; books, monographs, and articles dealing with many aspects of his personality and writings.

It is impossible in the space allowed here to give a full list of the studies which have influenced my own approach. I have limited myself under the first section to listing the editions which have been often cited in the text or frequently consulted, and under the second section to giving those authors whose studies have been particularly helpful because of the evidence they offer about the topics under investigation or because they provide support for or disagreement with my own position.

WORKS OF JEAN-JACQUES ROUSSEAU

Correspondance complète. Edited by R. A. Leigh. Geneva: Institut et Musée Voltaire, 1965—.

Correspondance générale. Edited by Théophile Dufour and Pierre-Paul Plan. Paris: Colin, 1924-1934. 20 vols.

Du contrat social, Discours, Lettre à M. d'Alembert. Paris: Garnier, 1962.

Discours sur les sciences et les arts. Edited by George R. Havens. New York: Modern Language Association of America; and London: Oxford University Press, 1946.

Emile: ou de l'éducation. Edited by François and Pierre Richard. Paris: Garnier, 1964.

La Nouvelle Héloïse. Edited by René Pomeau. Paris: Garnier, 1966.

Œuvres complètes. Edited by Bernard Gagnebin et al. Paris: Gallimard, 1959—. [Cited in the text as Pléiade.]

The Political Writings of Jean-Jacques Rousseau. Edited by C. E. Vaughan. Cambridge, England: Cambridge University Press, 1915. 2 vols.

La profession de foi du vicaire savoyard. Edited by Pierre-Maurice Masson. Paris: Hachette, 1914.

Secondary Sources

Bloom, Allan. "Jean-Jacques Rousseau." In *History of Political Philosophy*, edited by Leo Strauss and Joseph Cropsey, pp. 514-35. Chicago: Rand McNally, 1963.

Burgelin, Pierre. *La philosophie de l'existence de Jean-Jacques Rousseau*. Paris: Presses Universitaires de France, 1952.

Cassirer, Ernst. *The Question of Jean-Jacques Rousseau*. Translated and edited by Peter Gay. New York: Columbia University Press, 1954.

Chapman, John W. *Rousseau—Totalitarian or Liberal?* New York: Columbia University Press, 1956.

Château, Jean. *Jean-Jacques Rousseau: sa philosophie de l'éducation*. Paris: Vrin, 1962.

Cobban, Alfred. "New Light on the Political Thought of Rousseau." *Political Science Quarterly* 66 (1951): 272-84.

Crocker, Lester G. "The Priority of Justice or Law." *Yale French Studies* 28 (1961-1962): 34-42.

———. "The Relation of Rousseau's *Second discours* and the *Contrat social*." *Romanic Review* 51 (1960): 33-44.

———. "Rousseau et la voie du totalitarisme." *Annales de philosophie politique* 5 (1965): 99-136.

Davy, Georges. *Thomas Hobbes et Jean-Jacques Rousseau*. Oxford: Clarendon Press, 1953.

Derathé, Robert. *Jean-Jacques Rousseau et la science politique de son temps*. Paris: Presses Universitaires de France, 1950.

———. *Le rationalisme de Jean-Jacques Rousseau*. Paris: Presses Universitaires de France, 1948.

Dodge, Guy. *Jean-Jacques Rousseau: Authoritarian Libertarian*. Lexington, Mass., 1971.

Ferrero, Guglielmo. "Genève et le *Contrat social*." *Annales de la Société Jean-Jacques Rousseau* 23 (1934): 137-52.

Gay, Peter. *The Science of Freedom*. Vol. 2 of *The Enlightenment: An Interpretation*. New York: Knopf, 1969.

Green, Frederick Charles. *Jean-Jacques Rousseau*. Cambridge, England: Cambridge University Press, 1955.

Grimsley, Ronald. *Jean-Jacques Rousseau: A Study in Self-Awareness*. Cardiff: University of Wales Press, 1961.

Havens, George R. "Rousseau's Doctrine of Goodness According to Nature." *Publications of the Modern Language Association of America* 44 (1929): 1239-45.

Hayman, Franz. "La loi naturelle dans la philosophie politique de Jean-Jacques Rousseau." *Annales de la Société Jean-Jacques Rousseau* 30 (1943-1945): 65-109.

Hendel, Charles W. *Jean-Jacques Rousseau, Moralist*. London: Oxford University Press, 1934. 2 vols.

Hubert, René. *Rousseau et l'Encyclopédie*. Paris: Gamber, [1928].

Jost, François. *Jean-Jacques Rousseau Suisse.* Fribourg: Editions Universitaires, 1961.
Lanson, Gustave. "L'unité de la pensée de Jean-Jacques Rousseau." *Annales de la Société Jean-Jacques Rousseau* 8 (1912): 1-31.
Leigh, R. A. "Liberté et autorité dans le *Contrat social.*" In *Jean-Jacques Rousseau et son œuvre: problèmes et recherches,* pp. 249-62. Commémoration et Colloque de Paris. Paris: Klincksieck, 1964.
Masson, Pierre-Maurice. *La religion de Jean-Jacques Rousseau.* Paris: Hachette, 1916.
Masters, Roger D. *The Political Philosophy of Rousseau.* Princeton: Princeton University Press, 1968.
Plamenatz, John. *Man and Society: Political and Social Theory, Machiavelli through Rousseau.* New York: McGraw-Hill, 1963.
Roddier, Henri. "Education et politique chez Jean-Jacques Rousseau." In *Jean-Jacques Rousseau et son œuvre,* pp. 183-93. Paris: Klincksieck, 1964.
Sabine, George H. *A History of Political Theory.* New York: Holt, 1937.
Schinz, Albert. *La pensée de Jean-Jacques Rousseau.* Northampton, Mass.: Smith College, 1929.
Shklar, Judith N. "Rousseau's Images of Authority." *American Political Science Review* 58 (1964): 919-31.
Spink, John S. "Les premières expériences pédagogiques de Rousseau." *Annales de la Société Jean-Jacques Rousseau* 35 (1959-1962): 93-103.
Starobinski, Jean. *Jean-Jacques Rousseau: la transparence et l'obstacle.* Paris: Plon, 1957.
―――. "La pensée politique de Rousseau." In *Jean-Jacques Rousseau,* pp. 81-99. Neuchâtel: La Baconnière, 1962.
Strauss, Leo. *Natural Right and History.* Chicago: University of Chicago Press, 1959.
Talmon, Jacob Leib. *The Rise of Totalitarian Democracy.* Boston: Beacon Press, 1952.
Wright, Ernest H. *The Meaning of Rousseau.* London: Oxford University Press, 1929.

INDEX

Abélard, Pierre, 204
Académie de Dijon, 49, 54, 64, 73
Adaptation, 91-92. See also Environment
Affection, 20, 37-39, 41, 44, 46, 176, 190-91, 200
Africa, 276, 278, 281, 282, 285, 290, 296, 304, 314
Agreement, 220, 229. See also Collective will; Legitimacy
Agriculture, 95. See also Science
Alceste, 149, 152, 156
Alembert, Jean le Rond d', 43, 148, 150, 158, 159, 161, 166
Alexander the Great, 59
America, 296, 304, 314
Amour de soi, 76, 84, 87, 88, 93, 98, 111, 135, 145, 191-95, 197, 200, 202, 207, 210-11, 220, 230, 241, 243-44, 249, 251, 253, 255-56, 259, 261-62, 269, 322, 325, 327
Amour-propre, 135, 210, 241, 244, 246, 250, 253, 257-59, 261-62, 268-69, 325, 327
Anet, Claude, 42
Animality, 77, 80, 86-90, 93, 102. See also Nature, state of
Aquinas, Thomas, 74
Arabs, 279, 281, 314, 316
Arcesilas, 56, 66
Aristotle, 74, 79, 244
Art, 15, 17, 28, 31-32, 44-48, 53-54, 61, 64, 66, 71-72, 80, 84, 87-88, 98, 100-01, 108-09, 111, 114, 117, 120, 123, 125, 129-30, 132, 142, 146, 150, 153-54, 156, 158-67, 178, 182, 218, 226-27, 229, 251, 253, 263, 268, 282, 309, 320-21, 323, 327
Asia, 58, 276, 278, 282, 285, 290, 296, 304, 314
Atheism, 256
Athens, 114, 118, 144, 150, 282, 316
Austria, 144, 297, 315
Aztecs, 278

Bacon, Francis, 66-67, 69, 111
Balance of power, 16, 301, 304-05, 306-07, 313, 315
Bartoldus, 284
Bayle, Pierre, 280
Berkeley, George, 57
Berne, 43
Bible, 79, 85, 91
Bodin, Jean, 139
Bonté naturelle, 15, 71, 74, 76-77, 87-88, 98-102, 105, 130
Bordes, Charles, 49, 65
Bossey, 36
Bossuet, Jacques-Bénigne, Politique tirée de l'Ecriture Sainte, 74-75
Bouchardy, François, 56
Brazil, 278
Buffon, George Louis Leclerc, 80-83, 275

Career, theme of, 37, 44, 46-48
Catherine II (Russia), 292
Cato, Marcus Porcius, the Elder, 55-56, 61, 109
Catullus, Gaius Valerius, 66
Chance, 91-92. See also Destiny; Necessity
Character, 37, 40-42, 46, 53, 55-61, 65-70, 161, 211-12, 259, 263, 322

China, 57-58, 133, 280-81
Choiseul, Etienne-François, Duke of, 43, 295
Cicero, Marcus Tullius, 66
Citizen, theme of, 102, 104, 110, 137, 327-28
Citizenship, 27-28, 37, 42-43, 46, 52, 60-62, 67, 121-22, 137, 237, 246, 254, 261, 270, 309, 325-26
Civil society, 84-85, 97-99, 105, 108, 112, 114, 116, 122-23, 126, 138, 145, 165, 243, 250, 252, 262, 316
Clarens, 16, 120, 171-73, 176
Collective will, 13, 76, 97-98, 100-102, 104, 106-07, 113-14, 116-18, 122-23, 125-26, 129-30, 133-34, 137, 139-40, 142-44, 160, 165-67, 178, 202, 208, 237, 240-41, 249-52, 254-55, 258, 261-62, 264, 267-68, 270, 285, 287, 305, 310-14, 316-17, 327-28
Collectivity, 162-63, 165, 167, 237, 242, 248-50, 252, 255, 259, 265-68, 270, 322
Comparative anatomy, 77, 85, 91
Confederates of Bar, 292, 295
Confederation, 14
Confessions (Rousseau), 15, 19-20, 43, 46-47, 49, 83, 92, 144, 149, 174, 228, 239, 241, 303, 318-20
Conflict, 20, 27
Conscience, 230, 232-38, 254, 259, 263, 266
Considérations sur le gouvernement de Pologne (Rousseau), 16, 255, 292-93
Constitution pour la Corse (Rousseau), 16, 292, 294
Contract, 16, 75, 99, 103-04, 122, 162, 255, 308-09, 312, 317
Contrat social (Rousseau), 16, 43, 45, 51, 53, 68, 71, 101, 115-17, 122, 133, 136-38, 143, 168-69, 239-70, 272-73, 278, 291, 309, 317, 325-26
Corneille, Pierre, 153-54
Corporate will, 252, 328
Corsica, 43, 167, 291-93, 295-96, 301-02, 308-09, 311, 313, 315-16
Crébillon (Prosper Jolyot de) (père), 153

Custom, 308. *See also* Collective will
De Arte Poetica (Horace), 54
Death, theme of, 176, 185, 186, 187
Death penalty, 256
Defoe, Daniel, *Robinson Crusoe*, 226, 245
Democracy, 241, 265
Descartes, René, 67, 69, 111, 312
Despotism, 322, 326
Destiny, 15, 28-32, 34, 39, 44, 46-48, 51, 58-61
Determinism, 108. *See also* Necessity
Devin du village (Rousseau), 44-45
Dialogues (Rousseau), 144
Diderot, Denis, 19, 38, 49, 115, 149, 150, 154, 275, 299; *Neveu de Rameau*, 228
Dijon Academy, 49, 54, 64, 73
Discipline, 230. *See also* Character; Citizen; Virtue
Discours sur l'économie politique (Rousseau), 16, 68, 70, 115-18, 122, 125-34, 136-39, 142-43, 145-46, 148, 169, 205-06, 208, 237, 242, 244, 311, 322-24
Discours sur les sciences et les arts (Premier discours) (Rousseau), 15, 44, 49-51, 54, 57, 59, 61, 64, 68-73, 109, 111, 117, 144, 150, 154, 168, 205-06, 241, 320-22
Discours sur l'origine et les fondements de l'inégalité parmi les hommes (Second discours) (Rousseau), 15, 26, 44, 68, 70, 73, 76-78, 87, 91, 96, 105, 108-09, 112, 115-22, 124, 127-31, 133-38, 140, 142-46, 148, 169, 202, 205-11, 215, 217-18, 220-21, 224, 233, 235-36, 243, 249, 275, 309, 321-22, 329
Divine right, 75, 240, 269, 322
Domaine public, 139
Droit des gens. *See* International law
Droit naturel, 79
Duclos, Charles Pinot, 275
Dupin, Louise-Marie-Madeleine de Fontaine, 303
Dutch, 59
Duty, doctrine of, 74. *See also* Legitimacy

Dynastic right, 245, 269

Economie politique. See *Discours sur l'économie politique*
Education, 63, 64, 88, 132, 135-36, 142-44, 154, 174, 203, 205-38, 272, 329
Egypt, 277-78, 316
Emile (Rousseau), 16, 39, 41, 68, 70, 88, 120, 169, 205-39, 261, 272, 274, 276, 324-25
England, 144, 291, 296-97, 299-302, 305, 308, 311, 315-16
Enlightened despot, 130-32, 134-36, 139-41, 144, 146, 169
Ennius, 66
Environment, 77, 82-83, 87, 91-92, 214-15, 253, 269, 272, 277, 304-06
Epictetus, 207
Epicurus, 56, 66
Epinay, Louise-Florence-Petronille Lalive d', 43, 49
Equality, 84, 86
Etange, Julie d', 39, 169-204
Etat de guerre (Rousseau), 303, 309, 310. See also War, state of
Europe, 277, 291, 304
Evil, 92. See also Vice
Exposure, theme of, 42-43
Extrait du projet de paix perpétuelle (Rousseau), 303, 304, 306-07

Fabricius, 56, 61
Fact, matter of, 100, 144-47, 323
Fall, the, 74, 77, 88, 96, 105
Family, 16, 94-95, 168-204, 206, 272, 324
Far East, 281
Fate. See Destiny
Fear, 93
Feeling, 79-80, 84, 102
Fénelon, François de Salignac, *Télémaque*, 69
Flight, theme of, 42-43
Fontenelle, Bernard le Bovier de, 67
Foreign policy, 16, 129, 272-302, 323, 326
France, 144, 159, 169, 291-92, 295-99, 301-02, 305, 313, 315
Franks, 59
Frederick II (Prussia), 297-98
Freedom. See Liberty

Freedom of will, 74, 76, 87, 89, 90, 95, 108-09, 231, 232, 233-38

Gauls, 59
Gautier, Joseph, 49
General good, 116-17, 133, 137-38, 178, 237, 240, 262, 266
General will. See Collective will
Geneva, 28-30, 35, 38-39, 42-43, 45, 92, 114, 120, 148, 150, 157-59, 161-64, 166-67, 169, 291-92, 295-96, 301, 305, 308, 311, 313-14, 316, 320
Genoa, 293, 295
German Empire, 284, 296-97, 301, 307, 315-16
Germans, 58
Glaucus, statue of, 82
God, 87, 93, 230-32, 240, 250-51, 253
Golden Age, 94, 113, 134, 138, 217-18, 223, 322
Goths, 59
Gouvernement de Pologne. See *Considérations sur le gouvernement de Pologne*
Government, 16, 68-69, 98, 101-07, 115-19, 125, 129-31, 134, 142-43, 148, 205, 241, 244, 248-50, 253, 258, 308, 312-13, 317, 320, 322-23
Greece, 278, 282
Greeks, 162
Grimm, Baron Friedrick Melchior, 19, 29, 37, 41, 149, 320
Grotius, Hugo, 75, 79, 244

Happiness, 76, 94, 98, 106
Héloïse, 204
Henry IV (France), 306-07
Hermitage, 169, 205
Higher reason, 74. See also Rationality; Reason
History, 78-79, 82-83, 105-06, 109, 112, 114, 18, 230, 235-38, 241-42, 244, 250-51, 272-302, 306
Hobbes, Thomas, 67, 75, 79, 85, 88, 218-19, 244, 252, 254, 257-60, 310
Holbach, Paul Thiry, Baron d', 67, 280

Holland, 144, 296-97, 299. *See also* Dutch
Horace, *De Arte Poetica*, 54
Houdetot, Elisabeth-Sophie-Françoise, Comtesse d', 27, 38-41, 46, 149, 169, 319

Ignorance, 51. *See also* Nature, state of
Incas, 278
Incas, Les (Marmontel), 206
Indies, 306
Individual self, 216, 225, 228, 236, 238, 240-41, 246, 249, 272-74, 277, 321-22. *See also* Self
Individual will, 129-30, 208, 216, 229-30, 244-45, 247, 252, 268, 270. *See also* Will
Inequality, 80, 83-84, 86, 96, 100, 104, 106, 110-11, 114, 120-21, 135, 242, 255, 261, 266, 269-70, 328. See also *Discours sur l'origine et les fondements de l'inegalité parmi les hommes*
Innocence, 78, 89-90, 93
Instinct, 80
Instrumental reason, 123. *See also* Art; Perfectibility; Science
Intellect, 89-92, 244, 246, 269
International law, 14, 16, 311-12
International organization, 14
International relations, 122, 127-29, 272-302, 304-17, 323-24. *See also* Foreign policy
Islam, 280
Isle Saint-Pierre, 23, 30, 36, 43, 47
Italy, 38

Jean-Jacques Rousseau et le droit des gens (Lassûdrie-Duchêne), 14
Jews, 278, 281, 316
Josephus, Flavius, 278
Jugement sur la paix perpétuelle (Rousseau), 16, 303
Julie, 39, 169-204
Justice, 96, 114, 126, 129, 133, 135, 137, 205, 224, 228, 230, 263, 311, 329

Kafirs, 305

Lacedaemon, 150

La Chaussée, Nivelle de, 154
La Fontaine, Jean de, 230
LaMettrie, Julien Offroy de, 67
Lassûdrie - Duchêne, Georges, *Jean-Jacques Rousseau et le droit des gens*, 14.
Lausanne, 40
Law, 100-03, 114-17, 122, 125, 127, 132-35, 137, 242-43, 247, 254, 256-57, 320; international, 14, 16, 311-12; positive, 88, 129
Lawgiver. *See* Legislator
Law of nature, 129-30. *See also* Natural law; Nature, state of
Law of the strongest, 107. *See also* International relations; Necessity; Right of the strongest
Lecat, Claude-Nicolas, 49, 65
Légataire Universel (Regnard), 152
Legislator, 67-69, 101, 105, 114, 133-34, 143, 178-79, 237, 247-53, 263-65, 269, 308, 312, 314, 317, 327-28
Legitimacy, 15, 76, 99-101, 103-05, 107-08, 111-14, 119-22, 124-25, 130, 132, 136, 145-46, 162, 169, 206, 220-21, 224, 235-38, 246, 249, 252-54, 256, 259, 261, 269, 272, 303-17, 322
Leibnitz, Gottfried Wilhelm von, 67
Les Charmettes, 35, 38, 42, 45
Les Délices, 148
Lettre à d'Alembert sur les spectacles (Rousseau), 15, 41, 45-46, 148-67, 169, 205-06, 241, 260, 270, 323-24
Lettres écrites de la montagne (Rousseau), 291, 293
Lévite d'Ephraïm, Le (Rousseau), 42, 46
Liberalism, 17, 239-70, 325-26
Liberty, 14-17, 43-44, 52, 76, 87-88, 93-94, 96-102, 104-10, 113-15, 119-21, 128, 130, 134-37, 145-46, 163, 169, 206-07, 211, 213, 215, 218, 225, 228, 232-34, 240-43, 247, 250, 252-53, 255, 257-59, 261-63, 266-69, 279, 282, 285-86, 288-92, 295-96, 299, 305-06, 308, 312, 314, 316, 317, 321-22, 324-25, 328-29

INDEX 339

Locke, John, 234
London, 299
Lucidity, 76
Luxembourg, Charles-François-Frédéric de Montmorency-Luxembourg, maréchal-duc de, 29, 38, 39, 43, 205
Luxury, 140-41
Lycurgus, 58, 61, 101, 108, 121, 143, 146, 248-49, 312

Machiavelli, Niccolo, 128, 246, 248
Mahomet (Voltaire), 154
Malebranche, Nicolas de, 67
Man, nature of, 17. See also Individual self; Nature, state of
Mandeville, Bernard, 67
Marcus Aurelius Antoninus, 207
Marmontel, Jean-François, *Les Incas*, 206
Marriage, 173, 204. See also Family
Martial, Marcus Valerius, 66
Maupertuis, Pierre-Louis Moreau de, 81
Medicine, 213
Melon, Jean-François, 63, 321
Mercure de France, 49
Metallurgy, 95
Method, 79-80
Mexican Empire, 278, 316
Middle Ages, 51
Middle East, 278, 314
Misanthrope, Le (Molière), 149, 152
Mohammedans, 279
Molière, Jean Baptiste Poquelin, 152, 154, 156; *Le Misanthrope*, 149, 152
Monarchy, 265
Montesquieu, Charles Louis de Secondat, baron de la Brède et de, 141, 150, 159, 253, 273, 275, 280
Montlouis, 40, 42, 47, 149, 205
Montmorency, 43, 205
Morality, 45, 71-72
Mores, 154, 158-59, 161-62, 164, 166
Moses, 248-49, 278-79, 312, 314

Nation, concept of, 116-17, 124-30, 132, 135-36, 139, 141, 150, 166-67, 202-03, 239-70, 273-74, 277, 305, 309-10, 312, 314

National good, 116-17, 122-23, 125-26, 137, 146, 162
National power, 172, 303-17
Natural goodness. See *Bonté naturelle*
Natural law, 16, 74, 79, 84, 86, 145, 270
Natural rights. See Rights, human
Nature, 48, 78-79, 81-86, 93, 100-01, 105, 108, 111-12, 114, 116, 166, 211-12, 251, 321-22
Nature, state of, 77-78, 80, 84-85, 87-91, 93-94, 97-98, 105, 107, 109, 111, 116, 134, 138, 223, 241-43, 247-49, 256-57, 263, 266, 268, 306, 326
Near East, 281
Necessity, 15, 83, 91, 95, 100-01, 105-06, 109, 113-14, 119-24, 127, 134, 136, 146, 148, 165-66, 178, 182, 202, 209-10, 214-16, 218-20, 223-27, 232-38, 243, 246, 251, 253, 257, 269, 272, 277, 305-06, 312, 322-24, 326-27
Netherlands, 297
Neuchâtel, 43
Neveu de Rameau (Diderot), 228
Newton, Isaac, 67, 69, 111
Nouvelle Héloïse (Rousseau), 16, 39, 45, 120, 164, 168-204, 205-06, 239, 241, 260, 324
Numa, 248-49, 283, 312

Origins, concept of, 81-83, 85-87
Ovid, 66; *Tristia*, 54
Ownership. See property

Paix perpétuelle. See *Extrait du projet de paix perpétuelle*
Parallèle entre Sparte et Rome (Rousseau), 309
Paris, 29, 38, 42, 45, 49, 73, 156-57, 161, 169
Passion, 232, 241, 244, 253, 255, 269
Paternal authority, 244
Patrie, 64. See also Citizen; Nation, concept of
Patriotism, 134-35, 160, 162, 164-65, 282, 295, 327
Peace of Westphalia, 307, 315
Perfectibility, 15, 76-78, 87-94, 101, 109, 207, 210, 251, 277, 327

Persia, 58, 63, 280-81, 314, 316
Personality. See Uniqueness of personality
Peru, 278
Peter the Great, 298
Petty, Sir William, 63, 321
Philinte, 152
Philo Judaeus, 278
Philosopher king, 130-32, 134-36, 139-41, 144, 146, 169
Philosophes, 42, 47, 109, 150, 158-59, 236, 280, 299, 322
Pitié, 76, 84, 88, 145, 191-92, 194, 202, 207, 210, 230, 244, 251, 253, 256, 259, 270, 327
Plato, 69, 74-75, 79, 85, 141
Pliny the Elder, 286
Poetics, 148-67
Poland, 291-92, 295-96, 301-02, 305, 308, 311, 313, 315-16
Political power. See Nation, concept of; National power
Politics, 45, 228, 251
Politique tirée de l'Ecriture Sainte (Bossuet), 74-75
Pompadour, Jeanne-Antoinette Le Normand d'Etiolles, marquise de, 43
Positive law, 88, 129
Power, 53, 76, 93. See also Nation, concept of; National power
Préface de Narcisse (Rousseau), 49-51, 72
Premier discours. See *Discours sur les sciences et les arts*
Pride. See *Amour-propre;* Passion
Prince, 68-69, 74, 114, 126, 133, 142-44, 148
Private interest, 249, 267. See also *Amour-propre*
Problem-solving, 94-96, 98, 101, 109, 112. See also Perfectibility
Profession de foi du Vicaire Savoyard (Rousseau), 231-32
Progress, 89-92, 94. See also History
Projet de paix perpétuelle (Saint-Pierre), 303, 306-07
Property, 75, 83, 95-96, 100, 106, 111, 123, 137-40, 220-21, 223-24, 229, 243, 255-56
Providence, 178. See also Religion; Theodicy

Prudence, 76
Prussia, 296, 299, 305, 313, 315
Public finance, 115-47
Pufendorf, Samuel, 75, 79

Racine, Jean, 153-54
Rationality, 93. See also Reason
Raynal, Guillaume-Thomas, 49
Reason, 75, 78, 233, 322. See also Higher reason; Instrumental reason
Réaumur, René-Antoine de, 67
Regnard, Jean-François, *Légataire Universel*, 152
Religion, 76, 78-79, 88-89, 188-89, 201, 230, 240, 251, 253, 278, 288, 308, 314, 316. See also Atheism; God; Theodicy; Theology
République confédérative des petits états (Windenberger), 13
Responsibility. See Legitimacy
Rêveries (Rousseau), 144, 329
Revery, 78. See also Feeling
Revolution, 108-09, 114, 119, 121, 125, 128, 145, 228, 306, 322, 326
Rey, Marc-Michel, 239
Right, 99-100, 102, 108, 111, 113, 241
Right of the first occupant, 96-97
Right of the strongest, 76, 96, 100, 105, 106-07, 113-14, 120, 145, 220-21, 242, 245-46, 257, 269, 278, 301, 306, 308
Right of war, 257, 278
Rights, human, 17, 80, 130
Robinson Crusoe (Defoe), 226, 245
Romanticism, 185, 188. See also Death, theme of
Rome, 43, 47, 56-59, 118, 124, 135, 139, 144, 160, 172, 240, 248, 283-87, 289-91, 302, 305, 308-10, 314, 316, 327
Romulus, 139, 283
Rousseau, Jean-Jacques. See individual works by title
Russia, 295-96, 298-99, 301, 305, 313, 315

Saint-Germain-en-Laye, 73
Saint-Pierre, Charles Castel, Abbé de, 14, 169; *Projet de paix perpétuelle*, 303, 306-07

INDEX 341

Saint-Pierre, Isle, 23, 30, 36, 43, 47
Saint-Preux, 170-204
San Spirito, 36, 42
Saxons, 59
Science, 15, 17, 50-51, 53-54, 58, 60-72, 81, 92, 101, 108-09, 111, 126, 129-30, 132, 136, 142-43, 146, 178, 182, 218, 224-27, 229-30, 233, 251, 253, 263-64, 268, 309, 320-22, 324, 328
Scythians, 58
Second discours. See *Discours sur l'origine et les fondements de l'inégalité parmi les hommes*
Self, 44, 112, 114, 206, 213-14, 221, 224, 237, 242, 257, 262, 267, 268. See also *Amour de soi;* Individual self
Self-preservation, 84, 98. See also *Amour de soi; Amour-propre*
Seneca, Lucius Annaeus, 207
Senses, 222, 224
Sensitivity, 80, 84
Sentiment, 31-37. See also Feeling
Sex, 232-33. See also Affection
Shelter, theme of, 42-43
Slavery, 282. See also Liberty
Sociability, 75, 86, 116
Social contract. See *Contrat social*
Society, 86, 112, 115-16, 210, 228, 233-38, 243, 250, 322
Socrates, 55-56, 61
Sophistication, 166, 168, 211-12, 222, 226-27, 230, 277, 295-96, 299
South America, 276-78, 281-82, 285, 290
Sovereign, 104, 118, 125, 127-29, 205, 208, 237-38, 241, 244, 248-49, 254, 257-58, 261, 264, 270, 277, 286, 308, 311-12, 325-26
Sovereignty, 16, 75, 116-17, 120, 122, 126, 130, 138
Space. See Environment
Spain, 59, 144, 277-78, 291, 296-97, 299, 301-02, 305, 313, 315
Sparta, 43, 47, 57-58, 61, 63, 101, 108, 118, 121, 144, 160, 164, 172, 240, 282-83, 285, 290, 302, 305, 308-09, 314, 316
Spinoza, Benedict, 67
Spirituality, 89-90. See also Freedom of will

Stanislas Leszczynski (king of Poland), 49, 65
State. See Nation, concept of; National power
Statecraft, 60-61, 63, 65-69, 71-72, 74, 93, 106, 108, 114, 122-24, 169, 251, 320-21, 325-28
Stoics, 127
Switzerland, 43, 58, 144, 205, 302, 316

Talent, 269. See also Individual self; Uniformity, mask of
Tartars, 298
Taste, 52, 150, 153-54, 156-59, 161-65, 228
Taxation, 137-41
Télémaque (Fénelon), 69
Tell, William, 163
Terence, 66
Theater, 148-67
Theodicy, 88, 90-91
Theology, 77-79
Thone, 36, 38
Time, 32-39, 43-44, 46-48, 91-92, 95-96, 112, 217, 241-42
Totalitarianism, 17, 239-70, 325-26
Tristia (Ovid), 54
Troy, 282
Turks, 296

Unanimity, 100, 104, 255-58
Uniformity, mask of, 52, 211, 213, 223, 243, 251
Uniqueness of personality, 15, 20-32, 37, 44, 46-48, 69, 71, 88, 112-14, 173-74, 203, 206-08, 211-13, 215, 218, 223, 225-26, 229, 234, 236-38, 241-43, 247-49, 251-53, 258, 268-69, 318-20, 324-29
Universal man, 206, 211, 225, 236, 324
Utilitarianism, 93, 257-58

Venice, 42, 239, 296, 301-02, 305, 313, 316
Verisimilitude, 20-25, 31, 46-48
Vevey, 16, 173
Vice, 45, 92, 221, 224, 234
Vincennes, 49
Virtue, 40, 44-46, 50, 52, 101, 108,

133-36, 140, 150, 154, 159, 174, 176, 196-97, 327
Volonte générale. See Collective will
Voltaire, François Marie Arouet, 148, 150, 153, 206, 242, 280, 299, 321; *Mahomet*, 154

War, 13, 14, 98, 129. See also International relations; Right of war
War, state of, 75, 96-98, 100-101, 105, 119, 125, 127-29, 134, 136, 138, 145, 218-20, 223, 243, 251-53, 256, 258, 306-11, 314, 317, 322. See also *Etat de guerre*
Warens, Françoise-Louise de La Tour, Madame de, 27, 29-30, 38, 319-20
Will, 15, 31, 48, 99-102, 104, 113-14, 136, 225, 228. See also Collective will; Freedom of will; Individual will
Windenberger, J. L., *République confédérative des petits états*, 13
Wolmar, 170

Zeno, 56, 66

www.ingramcontent.com/pod-product-compliance
Lightning Source LLC
Chambersburg PA
CBHW021831220426
43663CB00005B/210